The New Extremism in 21st Century Britain

Since the early 1990s, ther................
and the public about t'...............
Western world. This bo............
'new' extremism in twer.................
it by both the state and ....

Although a variet.............alle .ge.s to the liberal political mainstream have emerged, the main focus of attention recently has been on new ethnic and religious movements, including both the growing support for the extreme-right and militant Islamist groups. Both pose critical questions for those concerned with the development of a more cohesive and stable society. Unlike many studies, this volume adopts a holistic approach, bringing together experts from a variety of disciplines to examine the factors that cause support and the potential policy responses, including key issues such as:

- examination of the current level of support for Islamism and right-wing extremism;
- evaluation of current responses to Islamism and the extreme right, such as Preventing Violent Extremism (PVE), wider public policy and the role of policing and civil society;
- analysis of the limited success of the BNP, despite recent reports that many voters apparently share its policy concerns.

Challenging broad assumptions and bringing together leading scholars in this rapidly developing field, this work is essential reading for all those with an interest in terrorism, fascism, political extremism, social cohesion and the future of race relations.

Roger Eatwell is Professor of Comparative European Politics at the University of Bath. His research has focused on a variety of issues relating to extremism, especially historic fascism and the contemporary extreme right.

Matthew J. Goodwin is ESRC Postdoctoral Research Fellow. U.... ty of Manchester. His research focuses on contemporary extr............
cohesion and political behaviour.

Routledge studies in extremism and democracy

Series editors
Roger Eatwell, *University of Bath* and
Matthew Goodwin, *University of Manchester*
Founding series editors
Roger Eatwell, *University of Bath* and
Cas Mudde, *University of Antwerp-UFSIA*

This new series encompasses academic studies within the broad fields of 'extremism' and 'democracy'. These topics have traditionally been considered largely in isolation by academics. A key focus of the series, therefore, is the (inter-)*relation* between extremism and democracy. Works will seek to answer questions such as to what extent 'extremist' groups pose a major threat to democratic parties, or how democracy can respond to extremism without undermining its own democratic credentials.

The books encompass two strands:

Routledge Studies in Extremism and Democracy includes books with an introductory and broad focus that are aimed at students and teachers. These books will be available in hardback and paperback. Titles include:

Understanding Terrorism in America
From the Klan to al Qaeda
Christopher Hewitt

Fascism and the Extreme Right
Roger Eatwell

Racist Extremism in Central and Eastern Europe
Edited by Cas Mudde

Political Parties and Terrorist Groups (2nd edition)
Leonard Weinberg, Ami Pedahzur and Arie Perliger

The New Extremism in 21st Century Britain
Edited by Roger Eatwell and Matthew Goodwin

Routledge Research in Extremism and Democracy offers a forum for innovative new research intended for a more specialist readership. These books will be in hardback only. Titles include:

1. **Uncivil Society?**
   Contentious politics in post-communist Europe
   Edited by Petr Kopecky and Cas Mudde

This work is an ambitious attempt to examine in detail the causes and impacts of far right extremism alongside Islamist inspired extremism. Many may be uneasy about such comparisons but this volume lays to rest such concerns. Above all, it contains choice articles by a strong team of experienced researchers and commentators. There are superb contributions on state–group relations, policing issues and public attitudes. It should be consulted by all those interested in extremism in modern Britain.

Shamit Saggar, Professor of Political Science, University of Sussex, UK

This book provides some real academic rigour to support the growing development and practice of community cohesion. It will help academics, policy makers and practitioners to understand how this agenda fits together and how national and local interventions in this complex but crucial area can be underpinned by empirical research.

Ted Cantle CBE, Executive Chair, Institute of Community Cohesion (iCoCo), UK

The New Extremism in 21st Century Britain is by far the most important consideration yet of the two principal extremist challenges to the existing political order, namely militant Islamism and far right politics. Eatwell and Goodwin have assembled an expert range of contributors to explore the causes, challenges and coping strategies associated with the rise of extremism in a hitherto largely benign polity. Chapters draw upon a range of attitudinal and electoral evidence to assess the levels of potential and actual support for the British National Party amongst the white working class and for Islamic militancy among British Muslims. Measured, informed and well researched throughout, *The New Extremism* needs to be read by any student interested in the ongoing challenges to consensus in British politics.

Jon Tonge, President, Political Studies Association of the UK, University of Liverpool, UK

This book sheds considerable light on the causes and consequences of extremism in society. The evidence and argument presented by an expert set of authors is convincing and compelling. This book deserves a wide readership in academia and also among practitioners and policy-makers.

Gerry Stoker, Centre for Citizenship, Globalization and Governance, University of Southampton, UK

For too long politicians have failed to understand, or chosen to ignore, the reasons for the rise of the BNP. It might make uncomfortable reading but Britain, and Britain's politicians, need to wake up to the realities of the rise of Nick Griffin's racist party. This book provides one of the most challenging and in-depth studies of the BNP. The authors lifted up the stone and peered beneath. It may be an unpleasant picture, but it must not be ignored.

Eric Pickles, Chairman of the Conservative Party, UK

The New Extremism in 21st Century Britain

Edited by
Roger Eatwell and
Matthew J. Goodwin

Routledge
Taylor & Francis Group

LONDON AND NEW YORK

1006417503

First published 2010
by Routledge
2 Park Square, Milton Park, Abingdon, Oxon, OX14 4RN

Simultaneously published in the USA and Canada
by Routledge
270 Madison Ave, New York NY 10016

Routledge is an imprint of the Taylor & Francis Group, an informa business

Transferred to Digital Printing 2011

Typeset in Times New Roman by Glyph International Ltd.

British Library Cataloguing in Publication Data
A catalogue record for this book is available from the British Library

Library of Congress Cataloguing-in-Publication Data
The new extremism in 21st century Britain / edited by Roger Eatwell and Matthew Goodwin.
    p. cm.
Includes index.
1. Radicalism – Great Britain – History – 21st century. 2. Muslims – Great Britain. 3. Social isolation – Great Britain. 4. Great Britain – Politics and government – 21st century. I. Eatwell, Roger. II. Goodwin, Matthew.
HN400.R3N48 2010
303.48'409410905 – dc22   2009031343

ISBN 13: 978-0-415-49434-2 (hbk)
ISBN 13: 978-0-415-49435-9 (pbk)
ISBN 13: 978-0-203-85961-2 (ebk)

ISBN 10: 0-415-49434-6 (hbk)
ISBN 10: 0-415-49435-4 (pbk)
ISBN 10: 0-203-85961-8 (ebk)

Contents

Illustrations

Figures

Tables

Contributors

Erik Bleich is Associate Professor of Political Science at Middlebury College. His research focuses on ethnic diversity, integration, violence and policymaking in Western Europe. He has published in journals such as *Comparative Politics* and the *American Behavioral Scientist*. He is the author of *Race Politics in Britain and France: Ideas and Policymaking since the 1960s* (2003) and editor of the special issue of the *Journal of Ethnic and Migration Studies* on 'Muslims and the State in the Post-9/11 West' (2009). His next book examines how democracies have balanced freedom against a desire to oppose racism.

Bobby Duffy is Managing Director of the Ipsos MORI Social Research Institute, overseeing their work for all public sector and political bodies. He has a particular focus on large-scale evaluations of policy, work in deprived areas and issues of civic renewal. He has written and presented widely on these, often focusing on reanalysing existing survey datasets, including during his time as User Fellow at the Centre for Analysis of Social Exclusion (CASE) at the London School of Economics (LSE).

Roger Eatwell is Professor of Comparative European Politics and Dean of the Faculty of Humanities and Social Sciences at the University of Bath. His research has focused on a variety of issues relating to extremism, especially historic fascism and the contemporary extreme right. Recent publications include (joint editor) *Western Democracies and the New Extreme Right Challenge* (2004) and (joint editor) *Charisma and Fascism in interwar Europe* (2007). His current main research focuses on support for and opposition to migration in Europe and is sponsored by an EU FP7 grant.

Robert Ford is Hallsworth Research Fellow at the Institute for Social Change in the University of Manchester. He holds a DPhil in Sociology from the University of Oxford, and has published in journals such as the British Journal of Sociology and Political Studies. His current research focuses on public attitudes towards immigrant minorities and the political impact of immigration in Europe.

Jonathan Githens-Mazer is a senior lecturer in Politics at the University of Exeter and is Co-Director of the Exeter Centre for Ethno-Political Studies. He is currently conducting research on radicalization as principal investigator on an Economic and Social Research Council grant entitled 'Cultures of Repression', which examines the resonance of myths, memories and symbols of past injustices in contemporary acts of political violence. Dr Githens-Mazer's first book, *Myths and Memories of the Easter Rising* (Irish Academic Press, 2006) examined popular Irish radicalization in the wake of the 1916 Easter Rising.

Matthew J. Goodwin is ESRC Postdoctoral Fellow in the Institute for Political and Economic Governance (IPEG) at the University of Manchester. Previously, Matthew completed his PhD at the University of Bath where he was also Temporary Lecturer in Politics. His research focuses on political behaviour (with a particular emphasis on extreme right-wing movements and activists) and the politics of ethnic diversity and its effects. He is the author of various publications on these topics and is currently working on a book which examines the rise of the British National Party (BNP).

Frank Gregory is Professor of European Security and Jean Monnet Chair in European Political Integration in the Division of Politics and International Relations in the School of Social Sciences at Southampton University. His research interests are linked to the terrorism, crime and policing aspects of the EU's internal security policy area with special reference to UK related matters. He was co-opted as a member of a specialist ACPO-TAM sub-committee (Explosives Detection), he was a member of a UK government advisory panel on emergency responses (SAPER) and is a Visiting Professor at Cranfield University.

Robert Lambert is co-director of the European Muslim Research Centre (EMRC) at the University of Exeter. In January 2010 he submits his PhD his PhD (entitled 'The London Partnerships: An Insider's Analysis of Legitimacy and Effectiveness) in the Department of Politics at the University of Exeter. He is a part-time lecturer at the Centre for Studies in Terrorism and Political Violence (CSTPV) at the University of St Andrews and a member of an EC Expert Panel on radicalisation.

Vivien Lowndes is Pro Vice Chancellor (Research) at De Montfort University, Leicester, and an expert on local governance and citizen participation. She has designed and led action research on the Preventing Violent Extremism Pathfinder Programme. She has also undertaken research on faith engagement in local governance and is the co-editor of *Faith in the Public Realm: Controversies, Policies and Practices* (Policy Press, 2009). She has also served on the management group of the Institute of Community Cohesion (ICoCo), of which De Montfort University is a founding partner.

Maria Sobolewska is Post-doctoral Prize Research Fellow at Nuffield College, University of Oxford. She specializes in political behaviour and attitudes of British ethnic minorities, especially of postcolonial origin. Her research is mostly based on secondary analysis of large-scale survey data. In 2006, she completed her doctoral thesis on electoral participation and party choice of ethnic minority groups. Since then she has started work on British Muslims' political values and integration. She is also a member of the team designing the next Ethnic Minority British Election Survey, funded by the ESRC, to be carried out at the next general election.

Basia Spalek is Reader in Communities & Justice in the Institute of Applied Social Studies at the University of Birmingham. Her research focuses on crime, victimization and social justice, diversity and difference and community-based approaches to counter-terrorism. She is the author of *Communities, Identities and Crime* (2008) and *Ethnicity and Crime: A Reader* (2008). She also recently led a research project entitled 'An Examination of Partnership Approaches to Challenging Religiously Endorsed Violence involving Muslim Groups and Police'.

Leila Thorp is Research Fellow at De Montfort University, Leicester where she works primarily on community cohesion. She recently completed an action research project on the Preventing Violent Extremism pathfinder programme. Her broader research agenda concerns interests include: changes to political interest representation, group recognition and identification within the context of globalizing trends. Her PhD assessed the changes to Polish civil society within this context and, in other work, she has explored citizenship for Polish new migrants in the UK.

Abbreviations

AFA	Anti-Fascist Action
APACS	Assessments of Policing and Community Safety
ARNI	Animal Rights National Index
BCU	Basic or Borough Command Unit
BNP	British National Party
BPP	British People's Party
BSA	British Social Attitudes Survey
CAA	Comprehensive Area Assessment
CS	Citizenship Survey
CT	Counter-terrorism
CTIOs	Counter-terrorism intelligence officers
CTSAs	Counter-terrorism security advisors
CTUs	Counter Terrorism Units
DFP	Danish People's Party
EDL	English Defence League
EFP	England First Party
EHRC	Equality and Human Rights Commission
ETA	*Euskadi Ta Askatasuna* (Basque Homeland and Freedom)
DCLG	Department for Communities and Local Government
FA	Football Association
FN	*Front national* (National Front [France])
FPÖ	*Freiheitliche Partei Österreichs* (Freedom Party of Austria)
GIA	*Groupe Islamique Armé* (Armed Islamic Group of Algeria)
GMP	Greater Manchester Police
HT	*Hizb-ut-Tahrir* (Party of Liberation)
IRA	Irish Republican Army
JTAC	Joint Terrorism Analysis Centre
KKK	Ku Klux Klan
KPD	*Kommunistische Partei Deutschlands* (Communist Party of Germany)
LAAs	Local area agreements
MPACUK	Muslim Public Affairs Committee UK

MPS	Metropolitan Police Service
NCDE	National Coordinator for Domestic Extremism
NETCU	National Extremism Tactical Coordination Unit
NF	National Front (Britain)
NPOIU	National Public Order Intelligence Unit
NPP	National Policing Plan
OSCT	Office for Security and Counter Terrorism
PFLP	Popular Front for the Liberation of Palestine
PIRA	Provisional Irish Republican Army
PLO	Palestinian Liberation Organization
PTA	Prevention of Terrorism Act
PVE	Preventing Violent Extremism
RAF	Red Army Faction
RICs	Regional Intelligence Centres
RVF	Racial Volunteer Force
RVTJ	Radical violent takfiri jihadism
SB	Special branches
SRP	*Sozialistische Reichspartei Deutschlands* (Socialist Reich Party)
UKIP	UK Independence Party
VB	*Vlaams Belang* (Flemish Interest)
WMP	West Midlands Police
WNP	White Nationalist Party

Preface

The academic origins of this book lie in a series of conversations that took place mainly in Bath during 2004–6, while Matthew Goodwin was writing his PhD under the supervision of Roger Eatwell. Although the main emphasis of this thesis was on the question of why some citizens choose to join and become active in the British National Party (BNP), a separate research project undertaken by the two authors for the Home Office on the causes of, and responses to, extremism highlighted the importance of a more holistic approach to issues of extremism.

These conversations revolved around two observations. First, typically those who work on extreme-right groups and parties take little or no serious academic interest in other forms of extremism, such as Islamism – and vice versa. While there are good reasons to be cautious about comparing different types of social movements or political parties, surprisingly little attention has focused on the interplay between different forms of extremism, such as the question of whether one extremist movement mobilizes support against another, possibly leading to a spiral of 'cumulative extremism' (Eatwell 2006). Second, there is a tendency among academics studying these issues to either downplay or ignore outright questions that are concerned more with public policy, such as how best to respond to different forms of extremism and what implications research findings hold for those who are involved in the implementation of policy and practice at both the national and local level. While the growing electoral importance of extreme-right parties since 2001, most notably the BNP, and the challenge posed from Islamic extremism, has encouraged a sea change in terms of the latter, we argue that there is still a yawning gap between, on one side, theory and research and, on the other, policy and practice.

We decided, therefore, that the time had come to conceive a book that would bring together experts on both Islamism and right-wing extremism and which would set explanations of support alongside a focus on policy responses. Although the task of examining the interplay between different forms of extremism and the implications for public policymakers lies beyond the scope of a single edited volume, we believe that the following chapters and the questions and empirical research they introduce make a timely start. Building on earlier work (Eatwell 2003), we have also been careful to adopt a multi-level approach and address both the 'demand' and 'supply' of extremist mobilization. In terms of the demand-side, attitudes and perceptions in wider British society will broadly determine the extent to which extreme-right parties, such as the BNP, or Islamist groups, enjoy fertile terrain. Yet examining the demand-side is not enough. It is also important to look at the specific mechanisms of activist recruitment, as well as the changing ideological appeals that different movements (and their recruiters) supply in an attempt to meet wider demand. Similarly, in terms of policy we include chapters that adopt a broad (and at times comparative) perspective but also case study research that examines local variations in policy response, for example in respect to the Preventing Violent Extremism (PVE) agenda.

To these ends the main focus in Part I is on Islamism, in particular responses to terrorism, an area of growing concern among both academics and policymakers following events such as those on 11 September 2001. The evidence presented in this section indicates that the Muslim community is far less alienated from British society than is commonly assumed, and that while there have been some problems important progress is being made in countering the threat from Islamic extremism. Part II on right-wing extremism includes less emphasis on the question of response as this issue has been of much lower concern both to public policy and academics. The new evidence presented in this case shows that there are good grounds to fear the threat posed by the BNP to democratic stability and values, not least as there appears to be more support for policies and positions associated with parties on the extreme right than is commonly assumed. Aside from the question of *potential* support, Part II also addresses *actual* support, presenting new research on the growing number of people who have voted for the BNP since 2001, a trend underlined most dramatically by the election of two BNP MEPs in 2009. Reflecting the discussion in Part I, it also considers responses to the extreme right, including changing 'anti-fascist' strategies, media and mainstream party responses. These central chapters are premised by an Introduction, which explains what is 'new' about these two forms of extremism, seeks to elucidate on the elusive term 'extremism', stresses the importance of studying both causes and policy responses and provides brief highlights of the chapters that follow, partly to illustrate the importance of adopting a more holistic approach. In the Conclusion, we ask whether the broad implications of Parts I and II do not swing the pendulum too far away from the conventional wisdoms about the primacy of the Islamist over the extreme-right threat to British democracy and society, and set out an agenda for further research to help refine the answers.

Roger Eatwell and Matthew Goodwin

Bath and Manchester

July 2009

References

Eatwell, R. (2003) 'Ten theories of the extreme right', in Merkl, P.H. and Weinberg, L. (eds) *Right-wing Extremism in the Twenty-first Century*, London: Frank Cass, pp. 47–73.
—— (2006) 'Community cohesion and cumulative extremism in contemporary Britain', *Political Quarterly*, 77(2): 204–16.

Acknowledgements

Although the book originated in discussions between the editors, an important stage in its development was a pre-submission writing colloquium, held at the University of Manchester in November 2008. The colloquium was followed by a wider conference that was organized by Matthew Goodwin and hosted by the Institute for Political and Economic Governance (IPEG). This event invited contributors and other speakers to discuss their research and its implications among an audience of policymakers, practitioners and members of the security services. The aim of the event, much like this book, was to encourage a lively and evidence-based discussion between 'communities' that too often talk past each other. We are grateful to all the participants at this conference and also IPEG for providing administrative and financial support. The editors were also helped by a team of contributors who responded quickly to comments, and who supplied their final chapters on time (a unique experience for Roger Eatwell, for whom this is his sixth edited book). We are especially grateful to the contributors for providing chapters that are valuable contributions in their own right, but which we hope collectively cast a little more light on the challenge posed by extremism in twenty-first-century Britain. Matthew Goodwin is also particularly grateful to Alan Harding, Peter John and Charlotte Jackson at the University of Manchester for their support during the completion of the book, his parents for support during his doctoral research and Bobby Duffy from Ipsos MORI. Matthew Goodwin's contribution to this project was also supported by a Small Research Grant from the British Academy (SG 47717) and the Economic and Social Research Council (PTA-026-27-2117). Roger Eatwell would like to thank his father for (once again) helping with the proof reading. Finally, both editors greatly benefited from the anonymous reviewers' comments on the first draft of the manuscript, and from wider discussions about the book with Routledge's Senior Publisher, Craig Fowlie, both during its inception and later stages.

Introduction

The 'new' extremism in twenty-first-century Britain

Roger Eatwell and Matthew J. Goodwin

In the twenty-first century, academics, policymakers and practitioners face several interrelated challenges. At a broad level, immigration and changing migration patterns have raised concerns over the impact of increased ethno-cultural diversity on social cohesion. In established Western democracies, recent years have seen intense debates over the integration of minority ethnic groups (though in particular Muslims) and the more general effects of increased diversity on the fabric of local community 'life'. Seen from one perspective, at least in the short term, immigration and increased diversity have a negative effect on levels of social trust and social capital, and citizens who reside in more ethnically diverse communities are more distrusting of their neighbours and tend to withdraw from community life (Putnam 2007). Faced with higher levels of immigration and changing neighbourhoods, there is now a large body of research to suggest that citizens in contemporary Europe feel threatened by and hostile toward ethnic 'out-groups' and, as a consequence, have become more supportive of stricter immigration controls (e.g. Gorodzeisky and Semyonov 2009). Confronted with the perceived threat from immigration and diversity: 'Like a turtle in the presence of some feared threat, we pull in' (see Putnam 2007).[1]

Similar arguments have been voiced in Britain. Following the urban disturbances that occurred in three northern towns in the summer of 2001 several commentators suggested that some communities had become highly segregated, and that citizens are leading 'parallel lives' (Cantle 2001). Closer examination of the evidence base, however, suggests that the 'moral panic' and claims over segregation has been seriously exaggerated (Finney and Simpson 2009: 166). Others have produced evidence that overall levels of racial prejudice in Britain are in decline (e.g. Ford 2008), and that rather than focus on cultural differences greater attention should be directed toward underlying and stubborn socio-economic inequalities that remain in twenty-first-century Britain and which are only likely to sharpen in the midst of severe economic recession (e.g. Letki 2008).

Against these broader debates is the more specific challenge that is posed by organized ethno- and religious-based extremism. Whether in the guise of a 'modernized' and more electorally successful extreme right wing or more radical and violent Islamism, the 'extremist challenge' is of growing concern to those who are involved in the development of socially cohesive local communities. In this book we shed light on both the causes and consequences of this challenge, presenting new empirical research that speaks directly to questions such as what is driving support for the extreme-right British National Party (BNP) and violent Islamism, and how best can local and national government respond to this challenge. In terms of *causes* we examine underlying support for these different forms of extremism, whether in respect to the more diffuse latent support for extremism or more 'concrete' acts of support such as casting a vote for the BNP or joining an Islamist movement. In terms of *consequences* we depart from much of the existing literature by considering policy responses to extremism both at the national and local level.

In particular, the chapters that follow critically examine two pieces of conventional wisdom in debates over the challenge posed by extremism. First, Part I examines arguments relating to the view that there are high levels of alienation within the Muslim community spawning a major 'home-grown' threat. Second, the first three chapters of Part II provide new evidence that there exists a serious threat from the extreme right, especially in the electoral arena – a threat which has been downplayed by most commentators.[2]

In the first section of this Introduction we discuss what we mean by the 'new' extremism, in the process underlining why Britain is an important case study for examining this trend. In the second section, we probe the notably elusive term 'extremism', a particularly important task given that the book focuses on *both* terrorist extremism and also a form of electoral politics that, though essentially non-violent, still poses a major threat to liberal democracy. Third, we stress the importance of studying forms of extremism that are normally considered separately, and relating these forms to important policy issues. In the final section we offer brief highlights from the chapters that follow, not least to underline the importance of studying these phenomena holistically.

The nature of the 'new'

At various points in postwar Europe governments and others have faced the challenge posed by different forms of extremism, whether nationalist-separatist groups such as the Irish Republican Army (IRA), the Basque *Euskadi Ta Askatasuna* (ETA) or groups on the extreme left-wing such as the German Marxist-Leninist Red Army Faction (RAF) and Italian Red Brigades. In more recent years violent animal rights, ecological and anti-globalization groups have added to this challenge. However, while these forms of extremism have posed varying threats to life, property and public order they have not threatened a radical de-stabilization of Western democratic politics and society.[3]

In this book we use the term 'new' to point, first, towards the threat from violent Islamism and, second, to highlight signs of a major electoral breakthrough by the 'modernized' extreme-right BNP, which, in June 2009, built on gains at the local level by sending its first (two) representatives into the European Parliament. These involve forms of identity politics that, while not new, have sprung to prominence in recent years. Clearly, there are other forms of ethnic and religious politics in Britain that might be considered 'extreme', some of which have manifested themselves outside of the realm of electoral politics and organized extremist mobilization. Examples include the violent Sikh protests against the allegedly blasphemous play *Behzti* in Birmingham in 2004, street clashes between members of Turkish and Kurdish communities, a demonstration by residents in Luton in 2009 in response to a protest by Muslims against returning British troops from Iraq and racially motivated attacks that forced Romanian immigrants to leave Northern Ireland in June of the same year. It is possible that such developments could lead to major street violence and even isolated acts of terrorism. Meanwhile, the conviction of four animal rights activists in December 2008 following a blackmail campaign against suppliers of animal testing research centres underlines the additional challenge posed by alternative forms of organized extremism. Yet these alternative forms do not currently pose anything like the same level of threat to social and political stability as the two forms of extremism which are the focus of this book. While al-Qa'ida and associated groups currently represent the most significant terrorist threat to national security, in the electoral arena organized right-wing extremism and its underlying ideas constitutes a significant threat to the liberal democratic polity.

In terms of the first of our points of focus, concerns about 'Islamic Fundamentalism', and partly linked fears about the integration of Muslims into British society, can be traced at least as far back as the Salman Rushdie affair in 1988 (Ruthven 1990). This ongoing saga began with Iran's Ayatollah Khomenei pronouncing a *fatwa* on the apostate Indian-British author. This led demonstrators around the world to call for the banning of his book *The Satanic Verses*, with many clearly supporting the carrying out of the Ayatollah's death sentence on the apostate for blasphemy (events that also led to splits in Britain between some Muslims and left and liberal 'anti-racists', who saw the affair as revealing an authoritarian and recidivist face to Islam, and that encouraged local government in some areas to promote links with specifically Muslim groups to help promote 'multicultural' harmony and integration).

More recently, concerns about Muslim integration into British society have been further heightened. The disturbances that occurred in northern towns during the spring and summer 2001, and subsequent official reports that noted the 'parallel lives' lived by many residents in these communities, sparked a new wave of fears. This social apartheid owed much to the fact that Muslims constituted the poorest, large, ethnic minority group in Britain, and discriminatory housing policies of some local authorities and estate agents. However, radical Muslim groups have heightened fears of self-imposed isolation, and Conservative leader David Cameron has specifically warned about the dangers of communal separation, arguing that: 'those who seek a sharia state or special treatment and a separate law for British Muslims are, in many ways, the mirror image of the BNP'.[4] Such concerns were similarly evident in a Civitas report which, based on analysis of Muslim school websites, suggests that some Muslim schools are threatening social cohesion by promoting a fundamentalist version of Islam and encouraging a ghetto mentality among children that will make it difficult for them to function in wider British society (Civitas 2009).

The events of 9/11 and 7/7 and failed subsequent plots, plus the revelation that many of those involved in Britain were 'home grown' terrorists, have been an even greater cause for concern. They have been widely seen as highlighting the danger of an extended campaign of violence from 'Islamists' (a term that increasingly came to replace 'Islamic Fundamentalism' in academic discourse as a means to distinguish violent readings of the *Koran* from fundamentalist ones, which do not involve such conclusions).[5] Unlike earlier IRA campaigns, the threat from suicide bombers specifically targeting large civilian groups has aroused widespread fears.

These dramatic events were accompanied by a growth in polling of Muslim opinion, which further heightened fears over (1) whether sympathy with Islamic terrorism extends beyond a small fringe; and (2) the extent to which Muslims feel fully British. A Pew Global Values study indicated that only 7 per cent of British Muslims considered themselves first to be British rather than Muslim, whereas 81 per cent answered in the reverse. This is a remarkable figure given that in France, a country with many poor Muslims, some of whom rioted extensively in 2005, the figures were 42 and 46 per cent, respectively (Pew Global Attitudes Project 2006: 2). Following the 7/7 terrorist attacks, a poll by YouGov indicated that 13 per cent of British Muslims felt a 'lot' of sympathy with the bombers and 11 per cent felt a 'little'.

It is important not to read too much into such polling data, a point that is taken up by Maria Sobolewska in Chapter 1. Nonetheless, these figures underscore why there is serious concern over the threat posed by Islamic extremism and the question of whether a wider reservoir of sympathy for such movements exists in contemporary Britain. In 2008, British intelligence sources stated that as many as 2,000 Muslims in Britain were linked to terrorism, while Home Office figures showed that since 2001 1,200 terrorist suspects had been arrested, 140 charged and 45 convicted (*Daily Telegraph*, 9 November 2008). Such findings are reflective of a broader European trend, with some research pointing toward the growing lethal threat posed, for example, by militant Sunni Islamists across West European states (Nesser 2008).

Against this backdrop, the structure and followers of grassroots jihadist networks and the interrelated questions of *how* and *why* some individuals become radicalized into radical violent Islamism have received increased attention (Githens-Mazer in Chapter 2; Jordan *et al.* 2008; Sageman 2004). The closely linked question of how and why some participants *leave* terrorist movements has also been the focus of recent research (e.g. Bjørgo and Horgan 2009). There is a clear need for more research to be undertaken into terrorist recruitment within Britain, but it appears that there is no single pathway to participation. Personnel, whether in the form of family networks or some form of charismatic recruiter, appear to play a crucial role in turning more diffuse sentiments into action. One major external factor is the belief that the Muslim community around the world is under threat, often vividly illustrated by extremist Internet sites, which portray 'atrocities' committed by Americans, Britons and Israelis in places such as Iraq and Palestine. Within Britain, various factors such as a criminal past, low prospects, social marginalization, the experience of white 'racism' and Islamophobia, also appear to play a part.

Whilst the underlying causes will continue to be scrutinized, growing attention has also focused on the question of how best to respond effectively to this challenge. After the 2001 riots and 9/11, the main focus of government policy was on promoting 'community cohesion', implicitly a critique of earlier 'multiculturalism', which was seen as permitting people to live 'parallel lives' and helping to create *de facto* forms of apartheid in parts of Britain (though see Finney and Simpson 2009). After 7/7 the focus turned more to combating directly home-grown terrorism. In April 2007, the Department for Communities and Local Government launched the action plan, *Preventing Violent Extremism: Winning Hearts and Minds* (DCLG 2007a), which set out proposals designed to support a response across society to the threat posed by terrorism. An integral component of the national framework has been the Preventing Violent Extremism (PVE) Pathfinder Fund, a £6 million scheme that was launched in October 2006 and which aimed to support around 70 local authorities to develop community-led responses to the challenge posed by violent extremism (see Lowndes and Thorpe, Chapter 6).[6] This was followed in June 2008 by the publication of 'Preventing Violent Extremism: a Strategy for Delivery' (Home Office 2003a) and 'The Prevent Strategy: a Guide for Local Partners in England' (Home Office 2003b). In the same year, it was announced that £80 million would be made available over the next three years for community-led work to tackle violent extremism (DCLG 2008b), and in December 2008 an additional £13.8 million was allocated to the government's Prevent programme to help tackle violent extremism.

Our second point of focus is the challenge that is posed by organized right-wing extremism, in particular the BNP. At times during the 1970s there were similar concerns about an electoral breakthrough by the National Front (NF), but these faded rapidly during the 1980s. Of more concern after the 1970s was harassment and violence targeted especially at 'immigrants' and 'anti-racists' – though the more violent groups, like Anti-Fascist Action (AFA), arguably gave as good as they took. The number of extreme-right activists by the 1990s was at most 1,000–2,000, but there seems little doubt that they helped create a culture that reinforced racism in others through contacts in pubs, football gangs and print propaganda. Much of this propaganda was put out by the BNP, which was formed in 1982 and quickly became the main group on the extreme right as the NF broke up into miniscule warring factions. However, while the BNP won a much-publicized local election seat in 1993, this was quickly lost and the party never appeared likely to make a major electoral impact before the onset of the new millennium.

As discussed by Goodwin in Chapter 8, a crucial prelude to electoral advance came in 1999 when Cambridge university graduate Nick Griffin took over as leader. Although previously active in more hard-core extreme right circles, Griffin has steered the party toward a more moderate public face, adopting a more populist-style approach (Copsey 2008; Goodwin 2010). By 2003, the BNP was the second largest party on Burnley borough council, helped by the 2001 riots and shrewd local campaigning. The party has since made further notable gains at the local level, such as in Barking and Dagenham, and Stoke, where at one point during the late 1990s the Labour Party held every seat on the city council.

The BNP's rise helped it to register in national opinion polls. In April 2006, 7 per cent of respondents told YouGov pollsters they would vote for the party while another 13 per cent of respondents said they would seriously consider doing so. The main reason given for supporting the BNP was the feeling that Britain had become a 'foreign country'; second was the desire for tougher action against Muslims 'who want to destroy this country'. While the BNP currently remains confined to a small number of areas, there is evidence to suggest that there exists a sizeable reservoir of untapped extreme-right support (see Ford's Chapter 7 and Goodwin *et al.*'s Chapter 9), which echoes earlier arguments made in the 1970s in respect to the NF (e.g. Studlar and Welch 1981), when disillusionment with the mainstream parties was lower than it has been in recent years thus providing more of a shield against party-system change. Although the United Kingdom Independence Party (UKIP) mainly benefited from the latter sentiments in the 2009 European elections, the fact that the two BNP MEPs were returned underlines the party's progress in the new millennium and will provide both a source of funds and publicity that should help further growth.

The focus in this book on both the extreme right and Islamism further highlights a potential for interactive violence that is not present between animal rights, ecological or anti-globalization movements, whose supporters sometimes straddle these groups (though it has been central to Irish Republican and Loyalist conflict). For example, some of the radical anarchists who travelled to Genoa in 2001 were also active in violent ecological campaigns. However, while a handful of extreme right-wingers, such as Horst Mahler in Germany, have looked to Islamist anti-Americanism and terror as a source of inspiration, there is no comparable communion of interests and membership between the vast majority of Islamists and members of the extreme right.

Indeed, especially since 2001, the BNP has increasingly sought to demonize Islam in its propaganda, claiming that Muslims have sympathies with terrorism, engage in criminal behaviour and that the religion of Islam more generally is incompatible with 'British' and European values (a theme echoed by extreme-right parties elsewhere in Europe). This one-dimensional propaganda makes no reference to Islam's positive contributions to Western development, including its preservation of classical Athenian and Roman learning, which was lost in the European Dark Ages, and major new developments in fields such as medicine and mathematics. The party's portrayal of Muslims as alien and backward has unquestionably heightened fears among Muslims. For example, in July 2005 Shahid Malik MP warned about 'gangs of BNP members in pubs' preparing to invade Muslim areas, a claim which was used by the BNP to argue that Muslims were seeking to polarize Britain.[7]

The point is not simply one about propaganda, it is also about physical threat. Although the statistics concerning attacks on ethnic and religious minorities must be treated with caution, there is evidence that physical and especially verbal attacks on Muslims rose after 7/7, as white racism turned to focus more on 'Paki bashing' than blacks. Certainly an ICM poll for the television programme *Dispatches* on the third anniversary of 7/7 showed that 36 per cent of Muslim respondents said that they or members of their family had suffered 'hostility or abuse' on account of their religion since the bombings. While most such attacks were carried out by people not directly connected with the BNP, this party figures prominently in Muslim campaigns that stress the problems of 'racist' attacks (Muslim sources tend to mirror the British tendency to use 'racist' to refer to prejudice based on both colour and religion). Conversely, the BNP portrays whites as the main victims of racist attacks, though its focus is not entirely on alleged Muslim attackers. This was the specific theme of a 12-page pamphlet entitled *Racism Cuts Both Ways*, issued in November 2008 in greater hardcopy numbers than any previous BNP publication. Earlier, the Young BNP had run a competition for under 18-year-olds (including an aged five–nine group) with Game Boy Advances as prizes – the accompanying leaflet claimed that 'Every year there are 150,000 racist attacks, but although 111,000 of these are against white victims the media almost always ignore them.'

This interaction points to the potential danger of 'cumulative extremism', namely the way in which one form of extremist could spark off a spiral (Eatwell 2006). This could involve rioting of the type seen in 2001, which began when white racist provocation in Oldham encouraged a response from increasingly assertive and 'macho' Muslim youth who sought to defend 'their turf' from incursion (though interethnic tensions in these cases were also linked to control of drugs and criminal activity). More recently, the potential danger of cumulative extremism is highlighted by the activity of the English Defence League (EDL), an organization with links to the football 'casuals' movement and which organizes street-based demonstrations against violent Islamism in areas such as Luton, Birmingham and Manchester. In contrast to 'traditional' extreme right groups in Britain, the EDL leadership presents the single-issue movement as a multi-faith and multi-ethnic organization. Whilst it is difficult to assess the future direction of EDL, it is important not to overlook the potential of cumulative extremism. Even more seriously, if a further Islamist bombing were to be followed shortly afterwards by an extreme-right attack on a major Muslim target, Britain might witness a spiral of violence and communal polarization.

The call to violence is widely distributed on the Internet and in propaganda such as *The Turner Diaries*, which appears to have inspired the 1995 Oklahoma bombing, which caused the largest terrorist loss of life on US soil before the terrorist acts committed on 9/11. A study of American right-wing extremist websites indicates the belief that events such as the 2005 Paris Muslim riots demonstrate impending racial Armageddon (Michael and Mulloy 2008). Also revealing of growing paranoia is the fact that after Barack Obama's presidential victory, the Stormfront extremist website crashed following heavy traffic. BNP associates have also been linked to white supremacist racial violence in South Africa.[8] The Redwatch website has listed details of anti-fascist and left-wing activists in an attempt to incite violence[9] and various small groups, such as the Racial Volunteer Force (RVF), seek to promote the cause of violent politics. In Britain, during 2007 10 extreme-right alleged terrorists were arrested by the police, many of whom had propaganda distributed by hard core extremist groups, and one former BNP candidate was jailed after stockpiling explosives in the belief that uncontrolled immigration would soon lead to civil war.[10]

However, it is important not to be unduly alarmist, as fringe elements in the British extreme right have plotted 'war' against racial and other enemies since at least the 1960s without succeeding in mass killing, though a former BNP-member in 1999 planted three bombs aimed at blacks, Bangladeshis and gays, which resulted in three deaths. As highlighted in what follows, there is a general need for research that looks more closely both at the potential for white terrorism and for cumulative extremism. As a result, these issues do not figure as a central concern in Parts I and II of this book, though the issue of right-wing extremist groups outside the BNP is discussed briefly in Matthew Goodwin's Chapter 8 and is picked up again in the Conclusion.

Elusive 'extremism'

This discussion of recent terrorism, together with the emergence of a 'modernized' BNP, which claims to reject any form of violence, points to a need to explain how we employ the term 'extremism' in this book. It is especially important to note that linking the two does not involve any view of necessary equivalence: a person voting for the BNP because a daughter has lost out in a housing queue to a new immigrant is not the same as an Islamist deciding to plant a bomb with the intention of mass killing (nor of a white racist planning the same)! However, both Islamism and the extreme right pose notable threats to the liberal democratic political order, and share other concerns including a tradition of anti-Semitism and homophobia.

In a political or social context, 'extremism' is typically related to actions and value systems that lie beyond the moral and political centre of society. However, 'extremism' is a notably elusive word to define more precisely. It is also clearly not a value-neutral academic term in a way that terms such as 'centrist' or 'mainstream' would normally be. Although American Presidential contender Barry Goldwater famously opined in 1964, at the height of the Cold War, that 'Extremism in the defense of liberty is no vice [and] moderation in the pursuit of justice is no virtue', 'extremist' is almost invariably used as a term of damnation. Certainly, few individuals or parties, which seek widespread electoral support, would be willing to define themselves as 'extremist'.

The concept of 'extremism' in political thought can be traced back to Ancient Greece. Here it was used to refer to *both* democracy (rule by the easily swayed and often ill informed and prejudiced masses) and oligarchy/tyranny (rule by the few or one man with no checks and balances). These were contrasted with the advantages of a mixed constitution. However, the term 'extremism' in a political context did not become common until after the First World War, when it was most typically applied to communism and fascism. After 1945, it was often linked to the concept of 'totalitarianism', a dictatorial form of pseudo-political mass-mobilization in which alternative viewpoints were suppressed.

Predictably, most parties that academics today term 'extreme right' totally reject this label (and similarly pejorative terms like 'neo-fascist' or 'Nazi'). Their preferred term of self-reference is 'nationalist' and increasingly 'populist', which in the BNP's case is linked to the claim that the party speaks for ordinary British people who are allegedly neglected by politically correct and self-serving elites. This has led some academics to prefer the term 'radical', which etymologically refers to getting to the roots of the problem, as a more appropriate generic term. American scholars in particular tend to write about the 'radical' rather than 'extreme' right (e.g. Hale Williams 2006). A similar distinction can be found in references to recent Islamist terrorism, with US government statements talking of Islamic 'radicals'. Conversely, the British government has tended more to talk of violent 'extremism', though at other times it has sought to delete the word 'extremism' in this context from public discourse, clearly in an attempt to encourage accommodation with 'mainstream' Muslims, and the term 'radicalization' is also common in Britain in the context of conversion to Islamism. However, a major problem with this approach is that it loses the ability to distinguish between radical and extreme. For example, Thatcherism was a radical challenge to the Buskellite big-state postwar consensus, but was it really extreme? Similarly, there are many Muslims who seek a wider recognition of *sharia* law within Britain in fields such as marriage and the family, a proposal supported by the Archbishop of Canterbury and the Lord Chief Justice in 2008. While this would involve a radical change concerning how to accommodate difference, it would not involve 'extreme' change. Or rather it would not unless *sharia* law is misconstrued as necessarily involving brutal punishments, such as stoning to death for adultery – a fate which befell a 13-year-old girl who had been raped in Somalia in 2008, a horror that attracted notable attention within the British media, parts of which have been accused of recurring Islamophobia (Moore *et al.* 2008).

One possible way of distinguishing between the two is to argue that extremism involves either the implicit or overt acceptance of violence as legitimate. Certainly political 'extremism' historically has most typically been associated with violent movements and regimes, especially fascism and communism. However, this line of approach has many problems. One crucial issue is the way in which few in the contemporary world would admit to supporting 'violence' (compare Honderich 1989). For example, many Islamists would reject that they advocate 'violence', preferring to use terms such as 'acts of resistance' against Israeli occupiers in Palestine, and seeing themselves as 'freedom fighters' against an over-powering West. Moreover, it could be argued that Thatcherism was perfectly happy to use the 'force' of the state not only in the war against Argentina over the Falkland (Malvinas) Isles, but also against internal opponents such as the coal miners during 1984–5, when the power of the state to enforce compliance and conformity by other means had failed.

A more fruitful way of approaching the conundrum is to consider the German case, where since the 1970s constitutional law distinguishes between radical groups, which are *verfassungsfeindlich* (in opposition to some of the principles of the 1949 Basic Law, which delineates the German liberal democratic system) and extreme ones, which are *verfassungwidrig* (unconstitutional in a more fundamental sense of the word). The latter are officially monitored by the Office for the Protection of the Constitution in Germany's *wehrhafte Demokratie*, or defensive democratic model, and extremists are banned from work in the public sector. This is often contrasted with the American First Amendment model. While this right to free speech is typically seen to be curtailed by considerations of time, place and manner (TPM), it has been used, inter alia, to (in)famously defend the right of the Ku Klux Klan (KKK) to march in the Jewish area of Skokie during the 1970s. The German model, in contrast, allows for the banning of political parties if they threaten democracy. A crucial test here is not just whether parties openly or implicitly accept violence, but whether they accept the legitimacy of a broad variety of views and of the institutions necessary to represent such views (Eatwell and Mudde 2004). Thus in the 1950s both the neo-Nazi Socialist Reich Party (SRP) and Communist Party (KPD) were banned in West Germany on the grounds that they clearly sought to overthrow liberal democracy.

Although these countries' constitutional systems are different, the core German approach has strong similarities with that of a classic American academic work written in the 1970s (Lipset and Raab 1971: 5–31). This argues that at the heart of the democratic political process is 'pluralism', namely a willingness not just to tolerate diversity but to accept different points of view as legitimate and allow the 'open market place of ideas'. Put another way, 'pluralism describes a society which tends to protect and nurture the independent coexistence of different political entities, ethnic groups [and] ideas' (Lipset and Raab 1971: 5). Standing opposite to this embrace of diversity and change is extremism, or 'monism'. Monism involves the belief that there is only one true way for society, one correct interpretation. Thus Marxism is the only guide for communists, and a narrow and slanted reading of the Koran is the only true way of Allah for Islamists. As Lipset and Raab explained, 'the application of any "fundamental" ... truth to the political scene, being undebatable, makes impossible the open market place of ideas and powers. If every political issue is a doctrinal struggle between good and evil ... and there is only one revealed path to salvation, the market place must be closed down' (1971: 12). This monistic impulse was aptly demonstrated in the BNP's television broadcast in the run up the 2004 European elections, in which Nick Griffin stated; 'You can have Muslim fundamentalism *or* democracy. You can have Muslim fundamentalism *or* women's rights. You can have Muslim fundamentalism *or* peace. But you can't have both.'[11] This monist mentality is accompanied by a commitment to authoritarianism, in particular a desire to impose the 'correct' line on others. If there is only one truth, then those who disagree with this truth must at best be fools, and at worst, evil people who are involved in some kind of conspiracy or plot to subvert the true way. The clear implication is that those who stand in the way deserve to be expelled from society, punished or even killed!

This discussion of the relationship between extremism and values involves a different emphasis from current usage by part of the British police in relation to some other types of terrorism. The National Extremism Tactical Coordination Unit (NETCU) website on such terrorism refers to unlawful action that is part of a protest or campaign, and includes actions such as 'disrupting lawful business or intimidation'. Here the focus is clearly on groups such as animal rights campaigners, or those who oppose genetically modified (GM) food, which encourage direct action. 'Extremism' in these cases is understood in terms of a spectrum of behaviour that implicitly distinguishes between legitimate democratic rights such as peaceful protest, and extreme behaviour such as intimidation of the owners of animal testing laboratories or violent street protest aimed at the police and/or property. While it could be argued that such 'extremists' have a monist view of the 'truth' about animal rights or ecological deprivation, most such activists would undoubtedly see themselves as 'democratic' and/or 'liberal' in a wider context – for example, accepting a multi-cultural society in Britain.

Extremism is, therefore, best seen as having two dimensions – an *action*-based one and a *values*-based one. As Goldwater has noted, it is possible to conceive of using extreme actions in defence of liberal democratic values. For example, violent street protest could be used against a state that abused civil liberties, such as the right to freedom of speech. Conversely, it is possible to use democratic means to advocate anti-democratic values, both implicitly and explicitly. For instance, after the failure of the violent 1923 Munich *putsch*, the Nazis increasingly saw the electoral road as the means to power: when Adolf Hitler became chancellor, the Nazi Party was supported by almost twice as many voters as the second largest party. Although the British first-past-the-post electoral system does not favour very small parties, it is possible to win both local seats and even a parliamentary majority on well under 50 per cent of the vote. Moreover, Britain now uses a variety of more proportional systems, for example in the 2009 European elections where under 10 per cent of the vote produced two regional seats. Indeed, the BNP actively targets less costly and more proportional elections as part of its 'ladder strategy', through which the party aims to achieve a national breakthrough via success in secondary elections.

These last points are important in terms of the decision to include the 'new' BNP in this study. This party claims to be democratic and represent the true will of the people, which is not being represented by an increasingly corrupt political establishment. Indeed in 2009 it claimed that it was 'Britain's Most Democratic Party' – in contrast 'with the other parties' increasing totalitarianism'.[12] While the BNP under its founder John Tyndall called for a complete overhaul of the parliamentary system, clearly seeking a more authoritarian order, in the post-2000 period the BNP's programme includes 'democratic' commitments such as implementing a bill of rights 'guaranteeing fundamental freedoms to the British people', citizen-initiated referendums, and an English parliament. Its locally based 'community politics' is also contrasted to the way in which the major parties now rarely campaign on the doorstep (a reflection of factors such as declining memberships and the mediatization of politics). Its new stress on peaceful activity is also contrasted with the way in which some anti-fascist groups continue to operate a policy of street confrontation. For example, after Unite Against Fascism demonstrators pelted Griffin and fellow new MEP Andrew Brons with eggs outside the House of Commons in 2009, *BNP News* claimed its leaders had been prevented from speaking to the media by a 'gang of thugs' and claimed it was launching a 'Petition to Support Democracy'.[13]

However, these new freedoms would clearly include the right to say things prohibited by 'totalitarian' post-1960s race legislation, while potential referendum topics would include immigration and capital punishment, issues over which the BNP believes that 'will of the people' is at odds with a politically correct establishment. It seems clear that if a BNP government was ever elected it would be likely to expel some 'immigrants' and repress the radical left, which it frequently equates with 'anti-fascist' street opposition. Indeed, until recently the core policy of the BNP was the compulsory repatriation of non-white groups (a policy that has been retained by some smaller extreme-right groupings). Although the BNP now states that it accepts the presence in Britain of good, hard-working ethnic minorities who can be assimilated, it is clear that Muslims especially would be likely targets for deportation.

Moreover, as well as banning almost all non-white economic migration, the BNP would be likely to use referendums to seek to repress rights, especially the right to asylum. 'Populists' are hostile to such human rights, which they associate with liberal elites, and hold that true rights belong to the majority. The slogan 'Rights for Whites' has been a common one in BNP campaigns. The populism of parties such as the BNP tends to dichotomize issues into good and evil. This makes a politics of bargaining and compromise difficult, a form of politics that lies at the very heart of liberal democracy. The 'modernized' BNP may not be extreme in the same way that an Islamist terrorist is, but the party poses an arguably greater threat to British society and values in the foreseeable future.

This leads back to the question touched upon when discussing German constitutional law: namely, whether extremists should be banned. Although the British capital has sometimes been referred to as 'Londonistan' on account of the variety of Islamic militants who made it their home before 9/11 (Phillips 2006), especially since 7/7 the government has been willing to use exclusion orders against Islamists such as Omar Bakri Muhammad, who led *Al-Muhajiroun* until it was disbanded in 2004. Nevertheless, the government clearly realizes that banning free speech is a delicate issue. A discussion paper issued to further education institutions advises that 'if a right under the European Convention of Human Rights is to be restricted or limited in any way', it is necessary to demonstrate that the decision is careful consideration of the evidence in relation to issues such as the need to prevent crime or disorder, the need to protect the rights of others, and that the response is proportionate (DIUS 2008).

It is also important to note that extremists may seek to recruit converts to violence by indirect propaganda. For example, Abu Hamza, a radical cleric who preached at Finsbury Park mosque and who was found guilty in 2006 on a variety of charges relating to terrorism, sought to use contemporary and localized experiences rather than grand ideology to groom terrorists. Much of what he said was related to issues such as perceptions of discrimination and racism in Britain, or to external events such as the lack of support for Muslims in the Bosnian wars of the 1990s. In a sense, therefore, it could be considered a legitimate discourse that was shared even by some non-Muslims, though Hamza's intention was to create a sense of anger and victimhood which would lead to violence.

Turning to the extreme right, the Dutch MP and producer of the anti-Islamic film *Fitna*, Geert Wilders, was banned from entering Britain in 2009 apparently because of fears of both causing offence to Muslims and provoking public disorder. But there is little chance of the government acceding to demands to ban the BNP. As noted above, the BNP does not openly advocate violence, and its leadership argues that it is a democratic party because it seeks to win power through elections. This claim can be countered by arguing that what it seeks is more an 'ethnocracy', which seriously risks what J.S. Mill classically termed the 'tyranny of the majority' (or perhaps 'minority' would be more appropriate here, as recent general elections have been won on 40 per cent or less of the vote). Nevertheless, there are a variety of further reasons why a ban in unlikely, though there are other legal measures that could be used against the BNP, such as race relations legislation (for more on this see Chapter 10).

The British nexus

It should be clear from the preceding sections why we see Britain as an important case study of these issues. The BNP has not yet achieved the extensive, albeit volatile, national support of parties such as the Austrian Freedom Party (FPÖ) or Jean-Marie Le Pen and his French National Front (FN), which in recent years have won as much as 27 and 19 per cent of the vote, respectively. But the BNP appears to have the potential to attract support approaching at least the lower figure (see Chapter 7). As well as the socio-economic factors that are helping the BNP, it is important to note the growing alienation towards mainstream parties, especially among Labour supporters. Following the 2009 MPs' expenses scandals, an IPSOS-MORI poll showed that 50 per cent believed that at least half of MPs were corrupt, with 80 per cent blaming not just the MPs but the 'parliamentary system' more generally. This alienation came on top of a long-term trend of both parties and civil society groups, especially trade unions, becoming more divorced from the working class. The trend is an ominous one as historically, electoral extremism has tended to grow when mainstream leadership is distant and weak (sometimes even aiding extremism directly or indirectly) and civil society fails as a prophylactic.

Moreover, although Britain does not have as large a Muslim population as France, this growing group is relatively poor and is characterized by other problems such as low educational achievement and a sense of rejection by an Islamophobic majority. As well as a common perception that much of the media has been Islamophobic for some time, there is a widespread perception that the government's anti-terrorist PVE campaign unfairly targets Muslims in general (Thomas 2009). The new CONTEST strategy unveiled in 2009, which targets those who are considered to have 'extreme' views such as hostility to democracy even if they do not endorse violence, appears if anything to have worsened relations. The Muslim community also suffers from a problem of leadership, including the new moderate leadership, which many appear to see as co-opted by the 'system'. Poll evidence seems to show that within this community there resides a significant minority who are 'tacit' supporters of extremism, including some who express sympathy with terrorists, as well as a small number of potential terrorists (Saggar [2009], though see Chapter 1 on the reliability of such poll evidence and Modood [2005] on the potential for multicultural rapprochement in Britain).

Against these threats, this book seeks to address two noticeable gaps in the current knowledge of organized extremism – bringing together the study of different forms of extremism, and relating this to the developing policy agenda on related matters. First, there has been a tendency to examine different forms of extremism in isolation from one another. Studies of the contemporary extreme right rarely engage with the literature on Islamic extremism and vice versa. There have been few attempts to integrate insights from both of these literatures and to look more closely at the question of whether similar processes underpin different movements and their adherents.

In contrast to much of the wider literature, a core guiding assumption underpinning this book is that we need to look more holistically at the challenge posed by different forms of extremism. As noted earlier, it is vital not to lose sight of the possibility of cumulative extremism. Major terrorist attacks, such as 9/11 and 7/7, have led to the loss of many lives, in the process causing much grief and anguish. However, they have not posed a serious threat either to social or political stability in Britain or the USA. A spiral of violence could be a different matter. Given forecasts that Britain is likely be one of the Western countries most affected by the onset of new recession, there is no cause for complacency – although it is important to reiterate the point that there is no simple link between extremism and socio-economic factors.

A second gap concerns the way in which few studies bridge theoretical and empirical research on extremism with policy and practice. Social scientists tend not to translate their data and research into forms that can impact on policies and public practice (Vertovec 2007: 1047). One example is the academic literature on right-wing extremism that has tended to focus on the social characteristics of voters and the impact of macro socio-structural change, rather than investigating what implications this holds for policy and practice (exceptions include Bale [2003] and Schain [2006]). Another is the ivory-tower, policy-less discussion of concepts and theories. For example, there has been a major discussion about whether the BNP is best termed (neo-)'fascist', 'extreme right', 'populist', etc. This debate is often linked to wider discussions of generic fascism though is devoid of any clear policy recommendations, such as whether a party's 'right' to provocative free speech and assembly should be curbed (e.g. Copsey 2007). Or take the discussion about whether Islam is compatible with secular liberal democracy, especially given the absence in the *Koran* of any equivalent of the *New Testament*'s 'Render unto Caesar the things which are Caesar's, and unto God the things that are God's' (Philpott 2007: 515ff.). The latter has not prevented Christians supporting countless non-democratic regimes, while the former in no way precludes Muslim engagement and participation that is already growing in countries like Britain.

Meanwhile, debates amongst policymakers and practitioners are often disconnected from the wider evidence base and/or unaware of academic approaches. For example, there have been notable efforts since 2001 to develop multi-agency approaches, which link police, social workers, schools and others. This is an important development. However, at times it can involve a naïve 'public interest' assumption about actors' behaviour – namely, that men and women working in these fields are working for the common good. Public choice theory posits a different form of behaviour – one in which the competition for scarce resources means that honourable collaboration rather than budget and status maximizing behaviour is far from guaranteed. 'Myth-busting' campaigns, which seek to supply facts about the economic importance of immigrants, relative spending on different communities and so forth, also assume liberal rationalism, whereas cognitive dissonance theory would predict that those who are prejudiced do not take on such facts. Indeed, a study of anti-racist print advertising has even argued that it can make readers more unfavourable to immigrants (Maio *et al.* 2007). Put bluntly, there has been a tendency to develop theory-less policy – and policy-less theory.[14]

Outline of the book

Against this backdrop, this book aims to stimulate discussion about how we move toward a more effective and holistic approach to the extremist challenge. To this end, the chapters brings together: (1) studies of broader attitudinal change in contemporary Britain; (2) empirically grounded research on the demand and supply of extremist group support; and (3) studies that examine the issue of policy response from a variety of perspectives.

In this book we seek to adopt a Macro-Meso-Micro (MMM) approach, which encompasses: broad national and international trends; localized perspectives and trends; and a consideration of individual actors. All too often studies of extremism focus on just one of these, especially neglecting the meso dimension which is especially important given how, for example, support for the extreme right can differ notably in similar socio-economic localities (Eatwell 2003).

As a result of their differing focus, the following chapters draw upon diverse theoretical and methodological traditions. For instance, while survey data enable us to paint a broad picture of changing attitudes it is less suited to the study of recruitment to terrorist groups where targeted qualitative interviews and ethnographic research is more appropriate. Meanwhile, action research is particularly well suited to providing unique insight into the complexities of implementing public policy in local arenas. While employing different methodological approaches, the contributors also arrive from different disciplinary backgrounds, bringing with them particular and novel insights into those issues above.

The book is divided into two parts. Part I focuses on the challenge posed by Islamic extremism, examining both the cause (i.e. support for) and consequence (i.e. response to). Based on analysis of polling and survey data, in Chapter 1 Maria Sobolewska adopts a broad perspective and examines the attitudes and views of Muslims in contemporary Britain. In particular, the chapter investigates the issue of potential support for Islamic extremism, testing and questioning the assumption that there are large numbers of alienated and disenchanted Muslims who are 'on the brink' and who may be pulled toward extremist activism by an alternative Islamic identity.

In Chapter 2, attention shifts from potential to actual support, in the form of recruitment to radical violent *takfiri* jihadism (RVTJ). Drawing on qualitative interviews with individuals who previously experienced recruitment into terrorist activities, and who were associated with the Islamist scene around Finsbury Park Mosque, Jonathan Githens-Mazer adopts a 'bottom-up' approach to examine the mechanisms that underpin radicalization and the expression of extremist violent behaviour. In doing so, Githens-Mazer highlights the dynamic nature of the recruitment process, drawing attention in particular to the way in which the messages of recruiters resonate with the lived experiences of potential terrorists.

The remaining chapters in Part I turn to the question of how best to effectively 'tackle' extremism through policy and practice. In Chapter 3, Erik Bleich adopts a broad perspective, examining the response of the British state to Islamic extremism since 2001 and setting the 'three-pronged strategy' in wider comparative European context. The following two chapters focus specifically on the crucial role of policing in counter-terrorism strategy. As Frank Gregory notes at the outset of Chapter 4, recent years have seen a heavier emphasis on community-policing and partnership with Muslim groups. However, challenges remain. While examining the broader context for the policing of extremism and four case studies of the 'Prevent' strategy Gregory also draws attention to three potential problem areas. In Chapter 5, Basia Spalek and Robert Lambert draw on the results of qualitative research on police engagement with Muslim communities for the purposes of counter-terrorism, including an insider's analysis of the London-based Muslim Contact Unit (MCU). By adopting this micro-level approach, the chapter highlights the way in which engagement is often complex and, in the process, highlight important implications for community policing policy and practice.

In the final chapter in Part I, Vivien Lowndes and Leila Thorpe offer a case study analysis of a regional PVE Pathfinder. Employing action research methods, the chapter examines the crucial (though often neglected) role of local policymakers and Muslim communities in interacting with the wider national agenda. In particular, Chapter 6 highlights the importance of local context in influencing and shaping policy outcomes while also revealing the inadequacies of drawing crude distinctions in this area.

In Part II attention turns towards the challenge posed by organized right-wing extremism, in particular the BNP. In contrast to much of the wider European literature we adopt an integrated approach, examining (1) the issue of wider electoral potential for extreme-right parties, (2) the internal development of organized right-wing extremism and (3) actual 'self-identified' supporters of the contemporary extreme right. Based on analysis of opinion and survey data, Chapter 7 focuses on the first aspect, the question of whether there exists in contemporary Britain evidence of wider public demand for policies and positions associated with parties such as the BNP (therefore closely mirroring Chapter 1). This chapter by Robert Ford reveals that key components of extreme-right ideology enjoy considerable public support in Britain and that there appears a sizeable reservoir of potential support for a party on the extreme right.

Yet the translation of wider demand into actual support will depend much upon supply-side factors such as party ideology, internal organization and membership, and the ability to cultivate an image of electoral credibility and respectability which distances the BNP from various small but potentially highly dangerous extreme right violent groups and individuals. Such factors are investigated in Chapter 8 which looks at the changing strategy of the extreme right in twenty-first-century Britain. Drawing on qualitative interviews with activists and analysis of party literature, the chapter examines the BNP's strategy of 'modernization' and the party's attempt to reposition itself in the wider political arena. These issues are then brought together in Chapter 9 which examines actual supporters of the contemporary extreme right in Britain. Drawing on new data, the chapter investigates the characteristics of extreme right party supporters and compares this support base to that which buttressed the earlier NF during its heyday in the 1970s.

The chapters on the BNP note in passing some of the reasons why the extreme right has failed to reach its potential, including factors such as the way in which the Conservatives have at crucial times owned the immigration issue and how UKIP mainly benefited from disillusion and nationalist sentiment in the 2009 European elections. However, this issue is also picked up in Chapter 10, which more generally looks at the issue of the relatively neglected range of responses to the extreme right, including from other actors such as the media – responses which have both helped and hindered its progress.

In the Conclusion we set out an agenda for further research, which in some ways asks whether the broad drift of the arguments in Parts I and II swing the pendulum too far away from the conventional wisdoms on the new extremist threat in Britain, which places primacy on the Islamist over the extreme-right threat to British democracy and society?

Notes

1 Robert Putnam on Immigration and Social Cohesion, 20 March 2008. Available online: http://www.Hks.harvard.edu/news-events/publications/insight/democratic/robert-putnam (accessed June 10 2009).

2 For example, D. Aaronovitch, 'The BNP can never make itself respectable', *The Times*, 20 November 2008.
3 An exception perhaps was in Italy during moments in the 1960s and 1970s, a period characterized by both violent extreme left and neo-fascist groups, and tensions that were at times manipulated by renegade members of the forces of 'law and order'.
4 David Cameron, 'Bringing down the barriers to cohesion'. Available online: http://conservativehome.blogs.com (accessed 30 November 2008).
5 A hundred years earlier, the term 'fundamentalism' had been used to describe radical but not violent sects within the American Christian community.
6 For examples of local case study work see DCLG (2007b).
7 www.bnp.org.uk/news_detail.php?newsId=425 (accessed 12 September 2005).
8 'BNP activist took part in terror campaign', *The Guardian*, Saturday 31 2007. Available online: http://www.guardian.co.uk (accessed 2 March 2009).
9 http://www.redwatchonline.org/ (accessed 1 March 2009).
10 'Ex-BNP man jailed over chemicals', BBC, 31 July 2007. Available online: http://news.bbc.co.uk (accessed 30 November 2008).
11 British National Party European Election Broadcast 2004.
12 BNP News, 15 April 2009. Available online: http://bnp.org.uk/index.php?s=bill+of+rights (accessed 24 April 2009); http://bnp.org.uk/2009/04/the-bnp-is-britain%e2%80%99s-most-democratic-party/ (accessed 21 May 2009).
13 http://bnp.org.uk/2009/06/oppose-liblabconuaf-violence-sign-the-petition-to-support-democracy/ (accessed 10 June 2009).
14 R. Eatwell, '"Theorists", "Policy Makers" and the Return of European Racism' (2001), conference proceedings. Available online: http://www.manskligarattigheter.se/stockholmforum/2001/page1316.html

References

Bale, T. (2003) 'Cinderella and her ugly sisters: the mainstream and extreme right in Europe's bipolarising party systems', *West European Politics*, 26(3): 67–90.
Bjørgo, T. and Horgan, J. (eds.) (2009) *Leaving Terrorism Behind: Individual and Collective Disengagement*, Abingdon: Routledge.
Cantle, T. (2001) *Community Cohesion: A Report of the Independent Review Team*, London: Home Office.
Civitas (2009) *Music, Chess and Other Sins: Segregation, Integration, and Muslim Schools in Britain*, London: Civitas – Institute for the Study of Civil Society.
Copsey, N. (2007) 'Changing course or changing clothes? Reflections on the ideological evolution of the British National Party 1999–2006', *Patterns of Prejudice*, 41(1): 61–82.
—— (2008) *Contemporary British fascism: The British National Party and the Quest for Legitimacy*, 2nd edn, Basingstoke: Palgrave.
DCLG (2007a) *Preventing Violent Extremism: Winning Hearts and Minds*, London: Department for Communities and Local Government.
—— (2007b) *Preventing Violent Extremism Pathfinder Fund 2007/08, Case Studies*, London: Department for Communities and Local Government.
—— (2008a) *Guidance on Meaningful Interaction: How Encouraging Positive Relationships between People Can Help Build Community Cohesion*, London: Department for Communities and Local Government.
—— (2008b) *Preventing Violent Extremism: Next Steps for Communities*, London: Department for Communities and Local Government.

—— (2009) *Sources of Resentment, and Perceptions of Ethnic Minorities among Poor White People in England*, London: Department for Communities and Local Government.

DIUS (2008) *Promoting Good Campus Relations, Fostering Shared Values and Preventing Violent Extremism in Universities and Higher Education Colleges*, London: Department for Innovation, Universities and Skills.

Eatwell, R. (2003) 'Ten theories of the extreme right', in P. Merkl and L. Weinberg (eds) *The Revival of the Extreme Right*, London: Frank Cass.

Eatwell, R. (2006) 'Community cohesion and cumulative extremism in contemporary Britain', *Political Quarterly*, 77(2): 204–16.

Eatwell, R. and Mudde, C. (eds) (2004) *Western Democracies and the New Extreme Right Challenge*, London: Routledge

Finney, N. and Simpson, L. (2009) *Sleepwalking to Segregation? Challenging Myths about Race and Migration*, Bristol: Policy Press.

Ford, R. (2008) 'Is racial prejudice declining in Britain?', *British Journal of Sociology*, 59(4): 609–36.

Goodwin, M.J. (2010) *The New British Fascism: Rise of the British National Party*, London: Routledge.

Gorodzeisky, A. and Semyonov, M. (2009) 'Terms of exclusion: public views towards admission and allocation of rights to immigrants in European countries', *Ethnic and Racial Studies*, 32(3), 401–23.

Hale Williams, M. (2006) *The Impact of Radical Right-wing Parties in West European Democracies*, New York: Palgrave Macmillan.

HM Government (2003a) *Preventing Violent Extremism: A Strategy for Delivery*, London: Home Office.

—— (2003b) *Prevent Strategy: A Guide for Local Partners (Part 1)*, London: Home Office.

Honderich, T. (1989) *Violence for Equality: Inquiries in Political Philosophy*, London: Routledge.

Jordan, J., Manas, F.M. and Horsburgh, N. (2008) 'Strengths and weaknesses of grassroots jihadist networks: the Madrid bombings', *Studies in Conflict and Terrorism*, 31(1): 17–39.

Letki, N. (2008) 'Does diversity erode social cohesion? Social capital and race in British neighbourhoods', *Political Studies*, 56(1): 99–126.

Lipset, S.M. and Raab, E. (1971) *The Politics of Unreason: Right-wing Extremism in America, 1790–1970*, London: Heinemann.

Maio, G., Petty, R.E. and Haddock, G. (2007) *Effects of Cognitive, Affective, and Behavioural Anti-racism Advertisements*, Full Research Report. Economic and Social Research Council, RES-000-23-0598, Swindon: ESRC.

McLaren, L. and Johnson, M. (2007) 'Resources, group conflict and symbols: explaining anti-immigration hostility in Britain', *Political Studies*, 55(4):709–32.

Michael, G. and Mulloy, D.J. (2008) 'Riots, disasters and racism: Impending racial cataclysm and the extreme right in the United States', *Patterns of Prejudice*, 42(4–5): 465–87.

Moore, K., Mason, P. and Lewis, J. (2008) *Images of Islam in the UK. The Representation of British Muslims in the National Print News Media 2000–2008*, Cardiff: Cardiff School of Journalism, Media and Cultural Studies. Available at: http://www.cardiff.ac.uk/jomec/resources/08channel4-dispatches.pdf (accessed 25 November 2008).

Modood, T. (2005) *Multicultural Politics: Racism, Ethnicity and Muslims in Britain*, Edinburgh: Edinburgh University Press.

Nesser, P. (2008) 'Chronology of *Jihadism* in Western Europe 1994–2007: planned, prepared, and executed terrorist networks', *Studies in Conflict and Terrorism*, 31(10): 924–46.

Pew Global Attitudes Project (2006) *Muslims in Europe*. Available online: http://pewglobal.org (accessed 25 September 2008).

Phillips, M. (2006) *Londonistan: How Britain is Creating a Terror State Within*, London: Gibson Square.

Philpott, D. (2007) 'Explaining the political ambivalence of religion', *American Political Science Review*, 101(3): 501–25.

Putnam, R. (2007) 'E pluribus unum: diversity and community in the twenty-first century. The 2006 Johan Skytte Prize Lecture', *Scandinavian Political Studies*, 30(2): 137–74.

Ruthven, M. (1990) *A Satanic Affair: Salman Rushdie and the Rage of Islam*, London: Chatto & Windus.

Sageman, M. (2004) *Understanding Terror Networks*, Philadelphia, PA: University of Pennsylvania Press.

Saggar, S. (2009) *Pariah Politics. Understanding Western Radical Islamism and What Should Be Done*, Oxford: Oxford University Press.

Schain, M.A. (2006) 'The extreme-right and immigration policy-making: Measuring direct and indirect effects', *West European Politics*, 29(2): 270–89.

Studlar, D.T. (1985) 'Waiting for the catastrophe? Race and the political agenda in Britain', *Patterns of Prejudice*, 19: 3–15.

Thomas, P. (2009) 'Between two stools? The government's "Preventing Violent Extremism" agenda', *Political Quarterly*, 80: 282–91.

Vertovec, S. (2007) 'Super-diversity and its implications', *Ethnic and Racial Studies*, 30(6): 1024–54.

Part I

1 Religious extremism in Britain and British Muslims

Threatened citizenship and the role of religion

Maria Sobolewska

Introduction[1]

After 11 September 2001 (9/11) a largely ignorant British public was thrown into the complex world of Islamic extremism and its animosity towards Western values and societies. Through many subsequent attacks on Western societies, culminating in the bombing of London's transport system on 7 July 2005 (7/7), the Islamic threat was, in the eyes of the British public and the government, growing and coming closer to home. In the process, many myths and confusions were raised to the status of accepted wisdom. One of the most powerful of those is the question of the role of Islam as a religion and a value system in the actual and potential support of Muslims for political extremism. The growing fear of Islamic religious radicalization feeds fears of Muslim religiosity per se, and its perception as a first stepping stone towards hostile anti-Western attitudes. In Britain, but also in most of the Western world today, the public debate is hindered by such confusion about the link between the religious and the political and the assumed connection between religiosity with potential for political extremism.

It has been argued before that Islamic extremism, especially in its violent form, has been historically a political rather than a religious phenomenon (Giuriato and Molinario 2002; Pargeter 2008). Today, in the British context, this political character of extremism is being largely ignored both in the media and in most of the academic literature, and instead the role of religiosity and religious extremism is unduly emphasized. Some authors claim that the refusal of both Muslim communities and the British government to acknowledge the role of Islam as a fundamentally anti-Western religion in the 7/7 terrorist attacks on London contributes to the threat of similar attacks taking place in the future (Bawer 2006; Phillips 2006). Such focus on the cultural and religious roots of extremism, rather than their political aspects, can also be found in studies generally very sympathetic to Muslims in Britain (McRoy 2006). All these accounts share the more or less explicit assumption that something fundamentally Islamic is responsible for the threat of terrorism coming out of this community. The concept of *ummah*, Muslim community, is particularly held responsible for tacit support for terrorism among European Muslim communities (Bawer 2006; McRoy 2006; Phillips 2006).

This tendency to place the blame for terrorism on Islam as a religion, rather than as a political movement in a particular historical and geographical context, promotes a general fear of Muslims, and in particular religious Muslims, as potential or tacit supporters of extremism and terrorism.[2]

Another piece of accepted wisdom surrounding British Muslims' potential support for terrorism is the link between the radicalization of young male British Muslims and the supposed alienation and self-segregation of Muslim communities from mainstream society. On both sides of the debate, those blaming the government for being too lenient towards undemocratic and intolerant Muslim communities (Bower 2006) and those aiming to coax the government into addressing the problems of Muslims' socio-economic disadvantage (Saggar 2008),[3] the failure of Muslims to integrate into Western society is thought to be a key factor behind the attractiveness of Islamic extremism.

The causal relationship between various social and political grievances and ideologically right-wing convictions is translated into a parallel link between exclusion and disadvantaged Muslims, and their support for fundamental religious values and increasing religiosity. This, in turn, is assumed to make them more vulnerable to the attractions of political extremism, both explicitly and in terms of 'soft' or 'tacit' support, which is usually assumed to be more widespread than the fringe who openly support terrorist acts (Shore 2006; Saggar 2008). Thus both religious Muslims and those who experience poverty, discrimination, social isolation and political alienation are branded as potential sources of recruits for organizations proposing and exercising violence in the name of Islam. This picture implies that most Muslims who thus far have not been radicalized or engaged in Islamic politics they either secretly condone them thus providing it with 'moral oxygen' (Saggar 2008), or may do so in the future. Muslim religious identity emerges in the eyes of public opinion as an alternative, rather than co-existing, identity for British Muslims, fuelled by the argument that Muslims turn to religion following their failure to integrate with mainstream British society, or their dissatisfaction with their place within this society.

These two logical steps: (1) from religious affinity to Islamic political extremism and (2) from alienation from the mainstream society to increased affinity to religion have, to date, too little empirical support to justify their status as conventional wisdom in both the media and a large proportion of academic literature. This chapter will aim to redress this problem. First, it will take stock of the polling evidence often used in support of the notion that Islamic identity is an un-British and anti-democratic alternative to the loyal and upstanding approach expected of British citizens. Second, it will challenge the picture of British Muslims as an alienated community on the verge of seeking alternatives to their British identity. It will concentrate on religious and young Muslim Britons to show that these two groups often thought to be most vulnerable to the attractions of extremism may not be as susceptible as is usually assumed. I will argue that religion has little to do with British Muslims' sense of alienation and their ambivalence towards the British state or society.

Sources of evidence: data and its quality

I will look at a mixture of evidence. First, I will look at a selection[4] of public opinion polls conducted among British Muslims in the aftermath of 7/7 bombings. These can potentially tell us two things: first, they can give us an idea about public and media concerns at the time, i.e. the reasons why these questions were asked in the first place; second, they can give us an answer to what respondents, who were asked these questions, thought. This second issue is a more tricky matter as it is affected by the frequently poor quality of opinion polls, which prevent us from drawing any strong conclusions from this source alone. Studies using these surveys at face value, as well as more popular publications, usually draw the well known picture of alienated Muslim community (Phillips 2006; Field 2007) – a picture belied by analysis of large-scale probability surveys (Maxwell 2005).

First of all, the sampling frames of these polls are usually very poor. They are small samples not drawn probabilistically, and hence over-representing specific types of people: those easier to find and more likely to respond to the pollster. On the one hand, those with the strongest views are more likely to want to express their opinion and hence answer a survey; on the other hand, those who subscribe to extreme views may give socially desirable, rather than truthful answers to the survey questions. Most often the samples are quota samples or Internet-based samples that are largely unrepresentative. Additionally, polling houses often weight the responses of their respondents to achieve a sample that represents the demographics of a certain group (and rarely report it) and so, if they do not have enough young people in the sample, they will simply multiply their responses to achieve 'more' young people. This makes the proportions quoted by these polls doubtful at best. The largest problem is the lack of transparency about these problems and how they affect the data. The large-scale national surveys often struggle with these problems as well, but they are much more transparent about their methodology with regards probability sampling, non-response, probabilities of being selected are made fully public, rather than the oblique descriptions of quota samples used in polling of Muslims.

Another problem is the lack of comparability with the white population in general, or with similar situations faced by other groups. For example, many polls asked Muslims about their attitudes towards freedom of speech following the affair with Danish cartoons, which depicted the Prophet in a manner offensive to Islamic doctrine, and compared them to the general population, a spurious comparison group. A more appropriate comparison would be with the attitudes of devout Christians after the scandals surrounding such films as *The Life of Brian* or *The Last Temptation of Christ*, or more recently the show *Jerry Springer the Opera* in London's West End. Last, but by no means least, these polls often suffer from many problems of question wording, as discussed in greater detail below. Responses to questions on sensitive issues such as support for terrorism are subject to serious reliability concerns, and as a result more sophisticated academic surveys have not generally asked such problematic questions. Sadly, this means there is no reliable data source available for comparison in assessing potential quality issues with the media polls.

Keeping these limitations in mind, this chapter will mainly rely on public opinion data as a gauge of changing public concerns about Muslims and Islam rather than as an accurate guide to mainstream British Muslim public opinion. For this purpose the chapter will use a nationally representative survey with high quality sampling and good measurement: the 2007 Citizenship Survey (CS).[5] This survey contains an over sample of Muslims and other minorities, and employs more established and consistent measures of attitudes of interest than the temporal and often vague measures in public opinion polls. This dataset contains 14,095 respondents, among whom 1,784 identify themselves as Muslims. The sample reflects the ethnic diversity of Muslims in Britain: 44 per cent are Pakistani, 16 per cent are from Bangladesh, 13 per cent have Indian background, 10 per cent are of African origin, and a small minority of 4 per cent are either of mixed origin or identify themselves as white (this most probably includes some Arabic Muslims). The CS sample includes people aged 16 and over, which ensures a good proportion of young Muslims as ethnic minorities tend to have a lower average age. Overall, 26 per cent of Muslims in the sample are born in the UK.

Where do their loyalties lie? Support for terrorism and Islamic religious identity as an alternative to British identity

British public's fear of Islamic extremism and Muslims' support for terrorism

Why is the loyalty of British Muslims questioned and their religious identity regarded as suspect after a mere handful of British Muslims were engaged in the horrific attack of 7/7? This is a strong worded question, but it is clear when one looks at recent polls that after the 7/7 attacks there existed in Britain widespread concern over support for terrorism and violence among Muslims. The aftermath of 7/7 saw a large number of public opinion polls conducted among British Muslims. In our sample of polls six were interested in Muslims' Islamic and British identity between July 2005 and December 2006, eight asked about Muslims' attitudes towards terrorist attacks in general and in a variety of specific contexts. As we can gather little direct information about the small number of Muslims actively supporting terrorism from these polls, due to methodological constraints of measuring extreme attitudes,[6] the focus of these polls has been upon concern over 'tacit' support for terrorism and on estimating the proportion of Muslims who proffer it and thus provide 'moral oxygen' for extremism (Saggar 2008). A look at Table 1.1, where recent polling questions are summarized, shows clearly the concern with Muslims' tacit support for terrorism.

Generally there are two ways in which British Muslims were asked about their support for terrorism; one in absolute, unqualified terms, and the other in ways that allowed for various circumstances and considerations, clearly designed to get at the 'tacit', weak and subtle support that supposedly provides 'moral oxygen'

Table 1.1 Support for terrorism? Public opinion polls, 2005–2006

	Terror justified: unconditional (%)	Terror justified: conditional (%)	Justification in Koran (%)	Sympathy/ understanding (%)
ICM/*Guardian*[a]	4 (any violence) 5 (in the UK)			
Communicate Research/Sky News[b]	2 (7/7)		4	
MORI/*Sun*[c]			2	
Populus[d]	7 (in the UK) 7 (against civilians)	21 (against military) 15 (in Iraq)		
ICM/*Sunday Telegraph*[e]	4 (al-Qa'eda) 1 (in the UK)	13 (against those who insult Islam)		
Populus/*Times*-ITN[f]				20
NOP/C4 *Dispatches*[g]	7 (against civilians) 9 (any violence)	16 (against military)		13
Populus/Policy Exchange[h]	7			

Notes

a Interviewed 500 Muslim respondents 15–20 July 2005.
b Interviewed 462 Muslim respondents 20–21 July 2005.
c Interviewed 282 Muslim respondents 21–22 July 2005
d Interviewed 500 Muslim respondents 9–19 December 2005.
e Interviewed 500 Muslim respondents 14–16 February 2006.
f Interviewed 1,131 Muslim respondents by telephone (750) and online (381) 1–16 June 2006. The national sample comprised 1,005 respondents interviewed 9–11 June 2006.
g Interviewed 1,000 Muslims 14 March–9 April 2006.
h Interviewed 1,003 Muslim respondents 4–13 December 2006.

to terrorists. The answers to these two types of questions are strikingly different. On the one hand, very few Muslims (between 2 and 5 per cent) support political violence and terrorism in general, the specific attacks of 7/7 or agree that terrorism is justified in the Koran (ICM/*Guardian* July 2005; Communicate Research/Sky News July 2005; MORI/*Sun* July 2005). On the other, when asked whether they find any personal sympathy with the motives behind the 7/7 bombings (Populus/*Times*-ITN June 2006), asked if terrorist attacks against military targets (Populus December, 2005; NOP/C4 *Dispatches* April 2006) or against those who offend Islam (Populus/*Times*-ITN June 2006) can be justified; or simply asked whether they 'understand' the terrorists (NOP/C4 *Dispatches* April 2006), between 13 and 21 per cent of Muslims respond positively. Similar contrasts are seen even within the same survey: the Populus/*Times*-ITN poll in June 2006 shows simultaneously that 20 per cent of Muslim respondents have personal sympathy with terrorists, 1 per cent agreed that the 7/7 attacks were 'right' and 13 per cent thought violence against those who offend Islam was 'right'. It seems unsurprising that fewer people condone violence and terrorism outright and more are ready to concede that some situations may justify them. It is equally to be expected that even more people concede that they 'understand' or 'sympathize' with terrorists' way of thinking. It would be hardly striking if non-Muslim people showed similar patterns of response. The question however is whether these Muslims who 'understand' and 'sympathize', or who justify violence under some circumstances represent the 'tacit' or potential supporters of terror that the polls are trying to get at.

An examination of how questions are asked by these polls gives the impression that they are 'fishing' for the desired answer. The polls conducted soon after Muslim terrorism became a public concern in the wake of the 7/7 bombings simply asked whether terrorist attacks were justified and violence was acceptable. These were simple questions and were normally answered simply and consistently 'no'. However, results like those make no headlines and sell no newspapers, and as we move away from the time of the attacks the questioning grew more complex, adding various qualifications and circumstances under which attacks may take place and asking about various other attitudes towards them such as sympathy and understanding. These later polls then showed much higher levels of apparent Muslim support for terrorism, clearly reflecting the public preoccupation with the potential for tacit and weak forms of support.

Sadly, the questions being asked to gauge this clandestine or potential support are not very well designed. One problem is the employment of certain words, such as 'right' or 'wrong', 'sympathy' and 'understanding', which respondents and pollsters may interpret differently. To give one example, it is not clear what we may conclude from the fact that 20 per cent of Muslims said they have personal sympathy with terrorists' motives (Populus/*Times*-ITN June 2006). Is this a sign of 'soft' support for terrorism? Is this the group that provide moral support? Or does this simply mean they can understand the terrorists' thinking, while disagreeing with it themselves? Many left-wing white Britons, one could imagine, would express personal sympathy with the motives of Palestinian terror groups, but this does not make them condone violent attacks. In this respect, the lack of comparison with the white population's attitudes is a serious problem.

Muslim identity as an alternative to British identity

Behind the debate over Muslim support for terrorism lies a preoccupation with the idea that the Islamic doctrine and religious identity is the root cause of Muslim extremism and terrorism. The debate over whether Islam is inherently illiberal and undemocratic that takes place in the academic world is very much mirrored by public concern that loyalty to Islam is inherently 'un-British'. Unfortunately, the messy and ambiguous results of empirical academic research rarely reach the public and even more rarely persuade them. Meanwhile, 'flashy' and sweeping theories that present a clear Manichean narrative, such as Samuel Huntington's vision of a 'clash of civilizations' gain widespread attention and tend to frame debates even when they are refuted (Norris and Inglehart 2004). Evidence for this may be reflected in the results of public opinion polls presented and discussed in greater detail below.

In Table 1.2 we see that 27 per cent of respondents asked by the BBC poll in 2005 say they consider Islam to be incompatible with Western democratic values. In the same poll, 19 per cent of Muslims agree, despite the earlier mentioned evidence to the contrary and the agreement among Islamic scholars is that this is not the case. From this premise, it is unsurprising that loyalty to Islam causes concern among some about Muslims' loyalty to Western democracy and corresponding values.

In our sample of polls from July 2005 to December 2006 seven public opinion polls asked Muslim Britons about their religiosity and commitment to Islam and their sense of belonging and loyalty to Britain. Any student of ethnic minorities will know that this is a lot of polls conducted in a very short space of time on an issue, which before July 2005 was a minority interest. Although some of these polls were more subtle than others, they were all interested in the question of whether British Muslims are primarily British or primarily Muslim, imposing an assumption of incompatibility between these two identities. The reason for this formulation was of course the tragic terrorist attack on London's transport system, conducted by a handful of British-born Muslims. Yet the fact that this small group of individuals made a choice between being British and Muslim (in an extreme way) does not mean that most Muslims in this country feel the need to do so. Despite the widely reported findings that 46 per cent Muslims feel they are Muslims first and British second while only 12 per cent feel the other way round (CommunicateResearch/Sky News July 2005), and 31 per cent of Muslims say that they have more in common with Muslims from other countries than with the British people (Populus/Policy Exchange December 2006), most Muslims polled quite happily agree that Islam is the most important thing in their life *and* that their primary loyalty rests with the British state, and that they belong to Islam *and* Britain. Table 1.2 shows the summary of the relevant question about religious and British identity asked in the seven polls interested in this topic. The evidence clearly shows that, for the majority of Muslims, belonging

Table 1.2 Belonging to Britain and belonging to Islam in public opinion polls, 2005–2006

	Belong to Islam (%)	Belong to Britain (%)	Islam important (%)	Islam incompatible (%)
Communicate Research/Sky News	46 (Muslim first)	12 (British first) 42 (no difference)		
MORI/*Sun*	95 (very/fairly strongly)	86 (very/fairly strongly) 2 (not strongly at all)		
MORI/BBC[a]		76 (Muslim) 73 (all)		18 (Muslim) 27 (all)
ICM/*Sunday Telegraph*		91 (very/quite loyal)		
ICM/*Guardian*[b]		10 (less loyal to UK after 7/7)		
NOP/C4 *Dispatches*	93	82	93	
Populus/Policy Exchange	31 (more in common with Muslims)	66 (no difference)	86	

Notes
a Interviewed 1,004 plus 204 Muslims 8–9 August 2005.
b Interviewed 501 Muslims 16–21 June 2006.

to Islam and Britain is not a mutually exclusive choice (MORI/*Sun* July 2005). A large majority of Muslims say that Islam is very important for them (93 per cent and 86 per cent NOP/C4 *Dispatches* April 2006 and Populus/Policy Exchange December 2006, respectively) and in comparable numbers declare their loyalty to Britain (76 per cent and 91 per cent MORI/BBC August 2005 and ICM/*Sunday Telegraph* February 2006, respectively).

Religious Muslims in the secular society

To add to the worries of Islamic identity being inherently 'un-British' and the question of whether Muslims choose religion over and above their loyalty to Britain and sense of attachment to the nation, Muslims in Britain are, in contrast with the majority, quite religious. This has led to speculation that such a strongly religious population provides a fertile recruiting ground for Islamist extremism. Yet, as has been pointed out elsewhere, this is quite untrue; evidence suggests that terrorists are more likely to recruit newly converted Muslims than people raised in the religion (e.g. Awan 2007).

The fall of religiosity in Britain per se makes the religiously fundamentalist, or even religiously devout, a minority positioned at an extreme of the general society. Thus Muslims' religiosity and their religious identity is automatically perceived as an unorthodox form of behaviour. In the Muslim world, an opposing trend of rising religiosity may even be noted since the 1980s (Pargeter 2008), thus widening the cultural gap between western and Muslim societies and further feeding into the 'clash of civilizations' myth. This cultural gap, even though it is confined to non-political values such as family, sexuality and the treatment of women both in the Muslim world and among Western Muslim communities (Norris and Inglehart 2004), is considered as a reason for concern from the point of view of political integration (Shore 2006). Some authors even go as far as stating openly that the gap between secular Europeans and religious Muslims is a 'troubling divide' (Shore 2006: 47). The general trend in religiosity and the importance of religion in one's worldview in Britain and the religiosity among Muslims are at odds, but not as much as is usually assumed.

First, Christian faith is being replaced in Britain by often non-religious spiritual beliefs that may form a similar value-laden outlook to a religion, such as humanist beliefs or popular Oriental religious concepts such as Karma. But even without these rather incidental and anecdotal trends, some authors argue that believing in God has not fallen as fast as the practice of religion (Davie 1994), although the former may simply lag the latter rather than being entirely a separate issue (Voas and Crockett 2005). The widely spread assumption that immigrants, especially from the less developed parts of the world, are more religious is a matter of generational decline as well. Voas and Crockett have demonstrated that children of immigrants also show signs of secularization in comparison to their parents. The 2005 and 2007 CS confirm this finding; young Muslims born in Britain are *less* rather than (as is frequently claimed) more religious than their immigrant parents. In the dataset used here, 75.4 per cent of Muslims declare themselves to be practicing while only 31.1 per cent of Christians and 56.4 per cent of those adhering to other 'minority' religions do, but there is evidence of shallow generational decline: 73.5 per cent Muslims born in Britain say they practise Islam, while the figure is 76.2 per cent among their parents. Data from 2005 tell a similar story. Hence the notion that religion is forming an alternative source of identity for alienated British Muslim youth (Awan 2007; Spalek 2007) already looks like an exceptional phenomenon rather than a general social trend, before we even examine the empirical evidence about actual Muslim alienation and the role that religion plays in filling this gap.

Alienation, exclusion and the attractions of Islam as an alternative

We have so far discussed public concern with Muslim support for terrorism, including conditional and potential support and worries that Islamic religious identity is at odds with British identity and loyalty and may therefore facilitate support for extremism. However, the gaping hole in both discussions is the following question: who are these Muslims who support, or may potentially start to support, terrorism and choose Islam over and above 'Britishness'? As signalled above, this question is mostly answered by conjecture and the assumed link between social, political grievances and exclusion, on the one hand, and religion, on the other. Almost all literature concerning Islamist extremism in Britain refers to a smaller or larger extent to this link (e.g. Abbas 2007b; Eatwell 2006; Introduction to this volume). A similar link between dissatisfaction and alienation among the white population and potential support for extremist ideology is discussed in Chapter 7. However, unlike for the white population, the question of potential Muslim support for extremist attitudes is directly linked with an explicitly oppositional, alternative identity. The image of alienated Muslims seeking to replace a British identity unavailable to them with a Muslim identity is often understood in terms of the adoption of a religious identity. The operation of Islam as an oppositional and a religious identity is rarely called into question (Meer 2008). However, the point that Muslim identity can operate among young people as a replacement for their parents' identification with their country of origin, rather than for their British identity, and that it may have very little to do with religion has been made before (Samad 1998; Jacobson 1998). As Saggar (2008: 164) points out, there is little hard evidence to show that Muslim identity is in any way a collective identity transcending ethnic and social divisions and most of the evidence presented for this claim is at best anecdotal.

However, the argument above had hardly any impact on current public (and also much of the academic) debate over Muslim alienation and vulnerability to extremism. It is often an accepted premise that Muslims' alienation is growing and, as a result, there is an increase in their religious affiliation and hence their vulnerability to the attractions of extremism. Thus the circle of tacit or weak support for terrorism is feared to be growing as well. For reasons explained beforehand, the actual size of this growing Muslim support is difficult to estimate with survey or polling data. Yet it is possible to question and explore, first, the image of Muslims as an alienated minority and, second, the link between Muslim alienation and their allegiance to Islam.

Before we can address the worries that Muslim Britons who are alienated from British state and society will turn instead towards religion, and then potentially towards terrorism, we first need to assess whether Muslim Britons are in fact as alienated as the government and various spokespersons and Muslim organizations fear. Before we do this, we must emphasize that the focus of this chapter is on citizenship and political alienation and so other forms of exclusion suffered by Muslims, such as social deprivation, will not be discussed. This is not to imply that the latter are not important. On the contrary, socio-economic and other structural forms of exclusion are enormously important (Eatwell 2006), to the extent that their description and due consideration is simply too large a task for the purposes of this chapter. Saggar (2008) offers a very comprehensive overview of these in his recent book. However, the link between socio-economic and social deprivation is assumed widely to translate into political 'grievances' linked with British identity and support for British mainstream society and the British state; an assumption that is never tested. Neither is a second assumption: that these grievances then translate into a strengthening of religious identity and therefore increased vulnerability to the attractions of extremism. Hence, in the remaining part of this chapter we will look at these two questions: are Muslims alienated and excluded? And is there any link between alienation and exclusion and religious identity?

To assess the extent of political exclusion among Muslim Britons we will use three widely accepted indicators of political exclusion: (1) trust in institutions; (2) feeling of political efficacy (influence); and (3) political participation; as well as a more direct fourth indicator (4) a sense of belonging to Britain. Trust in institutions is a summary measure of trust in local councils, the police and Parliament. Political efficacy is measured by a single question on whether the respondent feels they have an influence over decisions affecting Britain. Political participation is a summary measure tapping whether respondents engaged in any of a range of civic acts in the last 12 months, including contacting any of their various political representatives and institutions (i.e. local councillor, MP, government official or council official), taking part in protest and demonstrations, signing a petition or attending a public meeting or a rally. Finally the sense of belonging to Britain is measured by a single question: 'Now I would like you to tell me how strongly you feel you belong to each of the following areas: Britain?' There were four available answers ranging from 'very strongly' to 'not at all strongly'. Those who said they 'didn't know' are excluded from the analysis.

These four indicators are presented in Figure 1.1 which compares Muslim Britons and other religious groups, namely Christians, other minority religions and those who declared no religious belonging. Other minority religions mainly comprise of Hindus and Sikhs, and Christians are mostly white. Some Afro-Caribbean minority respondents are also included in the Christian group, but the sheer number of white Christians means that the figures mostly represent white Christian's attitudes. The respondents who do not belong to any religion

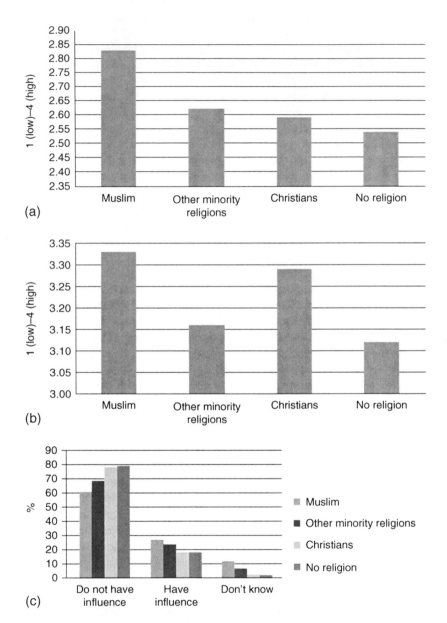

Figure 1.1 Four indicators of political alienation: (a) mean institutional trust; (b) mean sense of belonging; (c) influence on decisions affecting Britain; (d) participation in the last 12 months.

Source: 2007 Citizenship Survey.

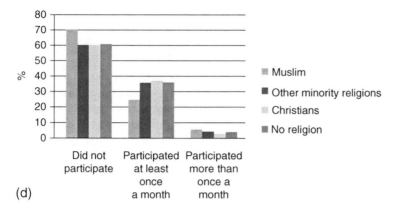

Figure 1.1 Continued

are also predominantly white. Muslims, as described above, are a mixed group of predominantly South Asian origin, but also inclusive of African and other Muslims. This comparison specifically does not look at ethnic differences within various religions as it is meant to investigate the role of religion rather than other aspects of origin and culture. To be clear, ignoring ethnic differences in this context is a result of the way in which the public debate is framed, rather than an expression of the belief that these differences do not matter in reality.

Looking at the distribution of the first of the indicators of alienation – political trust among the main religious groups in the UK – it is striking that against expectations Muslims show the highest rates of trust. We can only speculate about the reasons for this, but one of the most popular perceptions of Muslim communities is their valuing of authority more than others, which could contribute to higher levels of trust. Especially in comparison to the group that professes no religious affiliation, which is most likely to contain disaffected, well educated young people opposed to any kind of authority, including political institutions. Other religious groups, however, also do worse than Muslims on this count. Another reason could be Muslims' tendency to live in areas of high concentration of Muslims, which has been shown to have a positive effect on their levels of electoral participation (Fieldhouse and Cutts 2008), which is often linked with higher political trust. These differences between groups are statistically significant.

In terms of the second indicator of alienation – the feeling of political efficacy – Muslims also do rather well. They were the group least likely to say they felt they had no influence over the decisions affecting Britain. Even though they were also the group most likely to say they do not know whether they have influence, and even if we add those answers to the respondents who said that they have no influence, Muslims are still doing much better than Christians and those with no religious affiliation (i.e. the majority). Those adhering to minority religions fall somewhere between Muslims and the majority on this front. Again, only as a speculation, this could have something to do with the higher electoral participation rates among Muslims living in high concentration Muslim areas, as electoral participation is positively correlated with feelings of efficacy and some argue could result from the act of voting.

It is only when we look at the third indicator of political alienation when we see where the notions of an alienated Muslim community come from. Muslims are much less likely to engage in forms of political (non-electoral) participation than the other minority and majority religious groups, a difference that is statistically significant. They are, however, a little more likely to participate often when they do participate, suggesting that there is a small minority within the Muslim community who are very engaged in civic politics. Despite this poor rate of participation it is not entirely clear whether Muslims are particularly politically excluded. The participation figures do not include voting, which is a fundamental act of citizen engagement. As other research shows (Fieldhouse and Cutts 2008) Muslims living in predominantly Asian communities vote in even greater numbers than the majority population, and since a lot of Muslim communities live in concentrated ethnic neighbourhoods (Mason 2000) their electoral participation rates are likely to be at least as high as the majority, providing little evidence of political disengagement.

Finally, the fourth indicator of alienation, a sense of belonging to Great Britain, presents a picture similar to the first two indicators. Here, Muslims do not show a great difference to a Christian (and mostly white) majority, but they do have a significantly higher sense of belonging than other minority religious groups and those not affiliated with any religion who are, like Christians, a predominantly white group. In the case of the latter group, the reason for this lack of belonging may be similar to the reasons for this groups' low political trust. It is more difficult however to interpret the low levels of belonging among other minority religions. This group mostly consists of South Asians of Indian and African origin, who are often perceived as among the most well integrated British minorities. Muslims' high sense of belonging does not come as a complete surprise, as it has been previously described on the basis of the 2003 CS (Maxwell 2005). It is none the less noteworthy as most of the Muslims in this sample are immigrants and hence perhaps may be expected to have a lower sense of belonging to a country they were not born in. Overall, therefore, the available indicators of political alienation paint a picture of satisfied citizens who feel they belong, a very different image from the overwhelmingly negative picture often presented in the media and literature.

Of course there are many other faces of alienation and exclusion that go beyond the political aspects discussed above. Justifiably a lot of attention is often turned to the social and economic aspects of exclusion and alienation (for the best summary to date see Saggar [2008]). However, because this chapter seeks to offer an overview of claims of Muslims' vulnerability to political forms of Islamic extremism, these remain relevant only as far as they translate into political forms of alienation and exclusion. As we have seen above, this may not necessarily be

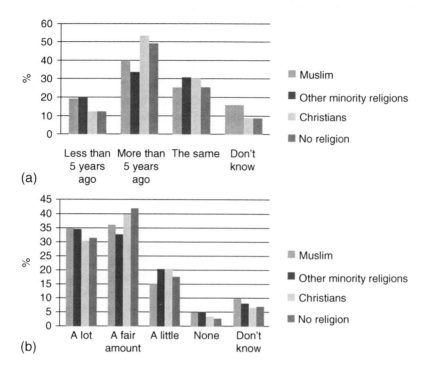

Figure 1.2 Perceptions of racial and religious prejudice: path to exclusion? (a) Amount of racial prejudice in Britain today; (b) amount of religious prejudice in the UK.

Source: 2007 Citizenship Survey.

the case, apart from non-electoral political participation, as Muslims do not appear politically alienated according to most available criteria.

Another often considered aspect of minority exclusion is racial prejudice and, in the case of Muslims, specifically religious prejudice. The importance of existing prejudice for minority groups in areas such as employment and education inequalities is often mentioned yet is rarely investigated in the context of politics. It is clear from Figure 1.2 that Muslims in our sample perceive prejudice to be widespread in Britain. Moreover, they are aware of both racial *and* religious prejudice. However, Muslims are more optimistic about both forms of prejudice than majority Christians and people with no religious affiliation: they are less likely to think that prejudice is rising, and more likely to think it is falling; more Muslims than Christians also think there is no religious prejudice whatsoever. However, they do perceive more prejudice than the other minority religious groups, a difference that is statistically significant. We can only hypothesize here on this curious pattern of majority religious groups, who are predominantly white in our sample, perceiving there to be more prejudice. It may be a sign that they judge the amount of prejudice held nationally by their own levels of prejudice. It may also be a sign of the pressure on political correctness and the idea that any prejudice at all is unacceptable, making the white majority particularly sensitive to it. Either way, what is interesting in the presented figures, at least for the purposes of this chapter, is the clear fact that Muslims are more aware than other minority religions of the possibilities of both racial and religious exclusion. In this sense, they may be at greater risk from alienation.

Thus far the picture of Muslim Britons as a politically alienated and disengaged group is mixed; while Muslims do seem to be relatively disengaged and may feel excluded on the basis of prejudice, they also seem satisfied with their political influence, institutions and their belonging to Britain. However, even the relatively small number of alienated Muslims may become of special interest if in fact they do seem more vulnerable to the attractions of religious extremism and if Islamic identity becomes for them an alternative source of identity and loyalty, thereby replacing the sense of Britishness. Whether they become more focused on religion as a result of alienation, or they are more prone to it because of the often advertised 'clash' between their religion and British (or Western) values, the relationship between religion and forms of exclusion and alienation permeate almost all literature on Islamic identity and extremism. For this reason, we will now explore the relationship between religion and alienation and exclusion, comparing Muslims who declare themselves as practicing with those who said they did not practice their religion. The results are summarized in Figure 1.3.

Looking at the two indicators of exclusion due to prejudice and four indicators of political alienation we can see immediately that there are almost no differences between religious and non-religious Muslims. The only statistically significant difference is the counter-intuitive non-religious Muslims' greater awareness of religious prejudice. It is likely that other reasons lie behind this difference, for example levels of education that may contribute to a greater awareness of prejudice in society and lower levels of religiosity. It could also be the effect of being young and born in Britain, with both of those correlating with lesser religiosity and, as we will soon see, a greater perception of prejudice.

Generally the religious Muslims are not excluded or alienated more than non-religious Muslims, suggesting that Muslim religion and identity is not a replacement for British citizenship engagement and sense of belonging, and does not cause withdrawal from 'Western' political life or society. The picture of alienated Muslim youth seeking solace in the hands of extreme and violent Muslim clerics thus seems to apply only to a marginal minority. While quantitative research can say little about such small minorities, the general link between alienation and religiosity is refuted. The claim that a sizeable number of alienated religious Muslims are providing 'moral oxygen' to Islamic terrorism is a myth. Rather than their political exclusion leading them toward religious extremism, it is much more likely that socio-economic exclusion is driving young British Muslims to a life of poverty or crime, just as it does their white deprived counterparts.

Given that a lot of attention focuses on young Muslim Britons as the group most likely to be alienated and vulnerable to extremism we will now explore this issue in more detail. As we saw above, there is no evidence for a link between

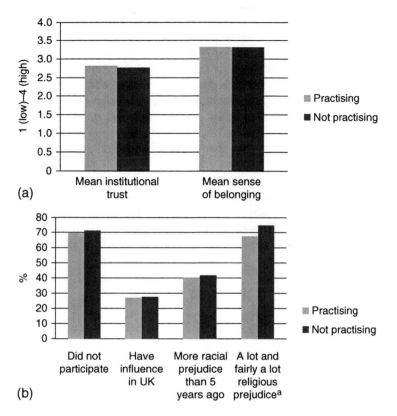

Figure 1.3 (a) Alienation and (b) exclusion of Muslims by religiosity.
Source: 2007 Citizenship Survey.
Note
a Statistically significant.

alienation and religion, but the greater alienation of British-born young Muslims does seem to be worth investigating in its own right, even if it may not drive them to Wahabbi mosques. The vulnerability of Muslim youth may be a result of what is available to them as an alternative to mainstream engagement and identities (i.e. radicalism and perhaps violence) rather than due to a higher level of alienation. However, the current discourse does not differentiate between these two issues and hence creates a misleading impression that both aspects are equally as severe. We can further put it in context by comparing them to British white youths, who are also often portrayed as politically and socially alienated, and vulnerable to certain kinds of anti-social alternative identities and cultures, from criminal gangs to political extremist groups based on non-religious grounds, such as animal rights terrorists.

We will look first at British-born Muslims. There are good theoretical reasons to believe that British-born minorities will be more critical of their place in the society and sensitive to prejudice. Alejandro Portes (1984) described this in his study of second-generation Cubans in the USA. Previous work on immigrants had argued that increased integration of second-generation immigrants into the host society will contribute to their greater solidarity and satisfaction with their position in that society, but Portes ventured that the opposite may be true. Second- and third-generation immigrants compare their position in society with the majority host population rather than their immigrant parents' generation or their own ancestral homeland. As a result, they grow more dissatisfied and alert of the presence of discrimination and prejudice than first-generation migrants. Hence British Muslims born in this country may have good reason to feel more excluded and alienated than their immigrant parents.

Looking at Figure 1.4 we see that there are many differences between British-born Muslims and their immigrant parents and almost all, apart from a sense of belonging to Britain, are statistically significant. On traditional indicators of political alienation, British-born Muslims are slightly more alienated than their immigrant counterparts. They show less trust, have a lower sense of efficacy, on

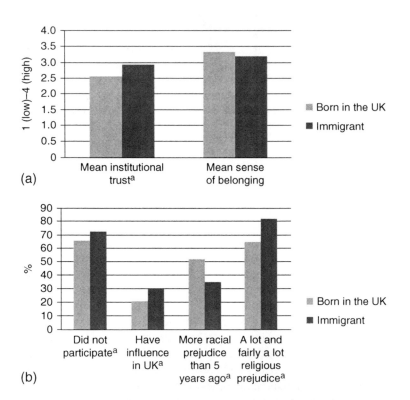

Figure 1.4 (a) Alienation and (b) exclusion among British-born Muslims.
Source: 2007 Citizenship Survey.
Note
a Statistically significant.

the one hand, but, on the other, they do participate more: particularly in forms of protest behaviour such as demonstrations, rallies or other unorthodox forms of participation such as signing petitions. British-born Muslims also express no greater sense of belonging to Britain than Muslim immigrants. A more puzzling picture emerges when looking at the indicators of exclusion: perception of racial and religious prejudice. On the one hand, and as predicted, Muslims born in the UK perceive racial prejudice to be more widespread, but, on the other, they seem to think there is less religious prejudice – a factor that is often assumed to bring them to the brink of extremism – than immigrant Muslims do. It may be linked to the lower levels of religiosity among younger, British-born Muslims, and religiosity was shown to be linked with a higher perception of religious prejudice.

Another theoretical reason to concentrate on young British Muslims as a particularly alienated group is the general trend of young people in society (whether belonging to a minority or the majority) to be more politically disengaged, alienated and excluded (Henn *et al.* 2005). This may be the result of both lifecycle differences, with older people being more interested in politics, more knowledgeable about it and hence more engaged; and a generational decline in political engagement. Do Muslim youth show a particular vulnerability to disengagement, or do they follow the general pattern seen in the white population?

Looking at Figure 1.5 there seem to be many differences between Muslim and non-Muslim young people, and a lot of these are statistically significant, but they do not add up to a clear pattern. Young Muslims have higher levels of trust and belief in their political influence than their majority counterparts. However, young Muslims also participate less. This picture is generally more reminiscent of the initial comparison between Muslims in general and majority Christians and it provides little evidence of particular Muslim vulnerability. This analysis is based on those under the age of 35 years old in order to assure a larger sample, but similar analysis with a younger age groups works in very similar ways.

Conclusion: from questions of integration and religious identity to the problem of religious prejudice and exclusion

The most striking result of the analysis presented in this chapter is the picture of politically well-integrated Muslims, both religious and secular, who express a strong sense of belonging to British society. While this particular research does not look at the very real problems of socio-economic deprivation within Muslim communities (see the Introduction to this volume), the analysis of political indicators presents an optimistic picture that stands at odds with the prevailing public view. In much of the public and academic debate on this issue, it is a standard assumption that Muslims – and especially young Muslims – are facing problems integrating and that as a result of these problems they find release and an alternative in religious identity and observance. Looking at the survey data, for the majority of Muslims it seems to be almost exactly to the contrary. Muslims appear to be very well integrated on most indicators, such as support for democracy

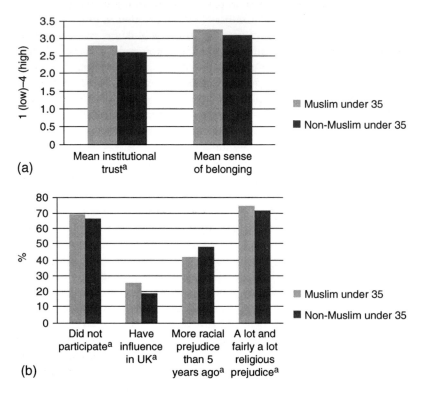

Figure 1.5 (a) Alienation and (b) exclusion of Muslim youth.
Source: 2007 Citizenship Survey.
Note
a Statistically significant.

measures (i.e. trust and efficacy) and sense of belonging to Britain. Moreover, there is no evidence that less-integrated Muslims are turning to religion as a source of an alternative identity.

The two indicators that do affirm the vulnerable position of Muslims in contemporary Britain are their heightened perceptions of religious prejudice and their lower levels of civic activism. Arguably, in terms of addressing these issues, the government's community projects may prove more effective in dealing with lower rates of participation. The perception of prejudice is a more complex problem that may escape any government efforts or community initiatives. It signals a sense of exclusion, rather than alienation, an externally imposed marginalization from mainstream society as it is linked to the perception that the society itself places Muslims at its fringes and there may be little that policymakers or Muslims themselves can do about it. Along similar lines, Saggar (2008) identifies this as one of the most important problems facing the government and British society in respect to their relationship with Muslim communities, as he argues that prejudice against Muslims may turn these communities into social and political pariahs, thereby undermining prospects for integration in the long term. The widespread belief that Islam is functioning as an alternative and oppositional identity to the British one clearly may contribute to the problem.

Religiosity does not exacerbate alienation nor is it a 'replacement' identity for those alienated from British society and citizenship. The debates over tacit or potential support for Muslim extremism should be more carefully separated from the question of Muslims' religious identity and its relationship with Britishness, as the conflation of these issues is both misleading and potentially damaging to the reputation of Islam and hence Muslims' political future. The main question in the light of the findings above is whether the rising political salience of Muslim religious identity has anything to do with religion, or is rather a form of ethnic identity or even a racialized identity. This point has already been made in some literature which argues that religious identity among Muslims may be a replacement for the geographically defined identities of first generation immigrants as British-born Muslims have no experience of their parents' home countries (Jacobson 1998; Samad 1998; Duderija 2008; Meer 2008). Greater religious identification may therefore have little or nothing to do with religiousness and religion itself.

These findings suggest that the government's particular focus on the integration of Muslims, rather than of all ethnic and religious minorities, may in fact lead to the unnecessary problematizing of Muslim identity. This chapter alone cannot inform policy towards the British Muslim community, but similar voices pointing to the 'problematizing' of Muslim community can be found elsewhere (Ameli 2007; Saggar 2008). Without giving explicit advice about what the policy towards the small number of actual violent political extremists should be, it seems worth questioning their current focus on Muslims as a 'problem' community, especially the focus on young British-born Muslims. This chapter sheds an interesting light on the level of alienation among Muslims born in the UK. They are often thought to be more acutely aware than their immigrant parents of their unequal treatment in wider society. As they were born in the UK, they have a reasonable claim to Britishness and equal treatment to people of white British origin, but these expectations are frequently disappointed due to prejudice (racial or religious) and discrimination. As a result, they are more aware of the obstacles before them and their unequal status and hence may feel more alienated, excluded and disaffected. This prediction is borne out to an extent by the data presented in this chapter, as British-born Muslims do score higher on more indicators of alienation than their immigrant counterparts. However, this result seems to be almost entirely a result of the younger age structure of those Muslims. The comparison between young Muslims under the age of 35 and other (mostly white British) young people finds almost no difference in the level of political alienation between these two groups of young people.

These findings undermine the argument that Islam functions as a replacement identity sought by alienated individuals and the general perception that Muslims, and especially young Muslims, are particularly vulnerable to alienation. As a result, public concern about a large or growing number of Muslims supporting terrorism (even if only weakly or tacitly), as reflected in the many opinion polls and a large body of academic work, may hold too much sway over government policy. It may be that it is fuelled more by the spectre of Huntington's 'clash of civilizations' than an understanding of British Muslims and in a way it may be unduly indulged by the authorities, thus exacerbating the problem of 'pariah politics' that now surrounds the question of Islam and Muslims in this country (Saggar 2008).

Of course, the results presented in this chapter do not tackle the problem of the very tiny minority of Muslims who do participate in networks supporting terrorism and perpetrating or planning to perpetrate acts of violence (for a discussion of recruitment to violent Islamism see Chapter 2). These are individuals who attract a lot of media and academic attention, and who government policy cannot risk ignoring. However, the current debate is losing sight of the problem by hunting the ghosts of a supposedly larger circle of 'tacit' or potential supporters of terrorism. The conviction that terrorism can be prevented through ensuring wider integration of Muslims into British society is especially misleading in this context. For one, as was mentioned earlier, it is often committed by new converts rather than lifelong Muslim believers, and hence not possible to prevent through work within these communities. But also, and as argued by Hardin (2002), by the very nature of extremist behaviour and organizations, integration of the majority of the community will not prevent extremists from emerging: individuals who are 'left behind' once the community becomes more integrated into mainstream society are more likely to defend the 'purity' of their original culture or religion and move to extremes to separate themselves from those who are perceived to have integrated and abandon the 'pure' form of their faith (Hardin 2002).

Notes

1 I would like to thank Sundas Ali for her research assistance and Erik Bleich for his helpful comments.
2 A very similar point is made in an analysis of the representation of Muslims in British Media: 'Media depicted the 7/7 suspects as well integrated (normal upbringing, education, job, etc.) upon their (re)discovery of Islam, they were led away from normality into something extreme and sinister. Therefore implying that Muslims in general have a *potential* to develop such extreme views and behaviour regardless of their being integrated in society or their political stance' (Ameli *et al.* 2007).
3 This perspective is similarly evident in the debate over actual or potential support for right-wing extremism (see Chapter 7).
4 A selection has been made for ease of presentation, however all existing polls conducted between July 2005 and December 2006 have been analysed and conform to the patterns shown. For a comprehensive list and analysis see Field (2007).
5 The Citizenship Survey is a biennial cross-section survey. Earlier editions have been used in earlier drafts of this chapter and support the picture presented here.
6 First, by their nature they are minority attitudes and often may not be represented in a survey and, second, extreme attitudes may be concealed in a survey as they may be considered socially undesirable.

Bibliography

Abbas, T. (ed.) (2007a) *Islamic Political Radicalism: A European Perspective*, Edinburgh: Edinburgh University Press.

Abbas, T. (2007b) 'Muslim minorities in Britain: integration, multiculturalism and radicalism in the post-7/7 period', *Journal of Intercultural Studies*, 28(3): 287–300.

Ameli, S.R., Mohammed, M.S., Sameera, A., Seyfeddin, K. and Arzu, M. (2007) *The British Media and Muslim Representation: The Ideology of Demonisation*, Islamic Human Rights Commission.

Awan, A.N. (2007) 'Transitional religiosity experiences: contextual disjuncture and Islamic political radicalism', in T. Abbas (ed.) *Islamic Political Radicalism: A European Perspective*, Edinburgh: Edinburgh University Press, pp. 207–30.

Bawer, B. (2006) *While Europe Slept: How Radical Islam is Destroying the West From Within*, New York: Broadway Books.

Breton, A., Galeotti, G., Salmon, P. and Wintrobe, R. (eds) (2002) *Political Extremism and Rationality*, Cambridge: Cambridge University Press.

Davie, G. (1994) *Religion in Britain since 1945*, Oxford: Blackwell Publishing.

Duderija, A. (2008) 'Factors determining religious identity construction among western-born Muslims: towards a theoretical framework', *Journal of Muslim Minority Affairs*, 28(3): 371–400.

Eatwell, R. (2006) 'Community cohesion and cumulative extremism in contemporary Britain', *The Political Quarterly*, 77(2): 204–16.

Field, C.D. (2007) 'Islamophobia in contemporary britain: the evidence of the opinion polls, 1988–2006', *Islam and Christian-Muslim Relations*, 18(4): 447–77.

Fieldhouse, E. and Cutts, D. (2008) 'Diversity, density and turnout: the effect of neighbourhood ethno-religious composition on voter turnout in Britain', *Political Geography*, 27(5): 530–48.

Giuriato, L. and Molinari, M.C. (2002) 'Rationally violent tactics: evidence from modern Islamic fundamentalism', in A. Breton, G. Galeotti, P. Salmon and R. Wintrobe (eds) *Political Extremism and Rationality*, Cambridge: Cambridge University Press, pp. 183–216.

Hardin, R. (2002) 'The crippled epistemology of extremism', in A. Breton, G. Galeotti, P. Salmon and R. Wintrobe (eds) *Political Extremism and Rationality*, Cambridge: Cambridge University Press, pp. 3–22.

Henn, M., Weinstein, M. and Forrest, S. (2005) 'Uninterested youth? Young people's attitudes towards party politics in Britain', *Political Studies*, 53(3): 556–78.

Huntington, S. (1996) *The Clash of Civilisations and the Remaking of World Order*, New York: Simon and Schuster.

Jacobson, J. (1998) *Islam in Transition: Religion and Identity among British Pakistani Youth*, London: Routledge.

Mason, D. (2000) *Race and Ethnicity in Modern Britain*, Oxford: Oxford University Press.

Maxwell, R. (2005) 'Muslims, South Asians and the British mainstream: a national identity crisis?', *West European Politics*, 29(4): 736–56.

McRoy, A. (2006) *From Rushdie to 7/7: The Radicalisation of Islam to Britain*, The Social Affairs Unit.

Meer, N. (2008) 'The politics of voluntary and involuntary identities: are Muslims in Britain an ethnic, racial or religious minority?', *Patterns of Prejudice*, 28(3): 371–400.

Norris, P. and Inglehart, R. (2004) *Sacred and Secular: Religion and Politics Worldwide*, Cambridge: Cambridge University Press.

Pargeter, A. (2008) *The New Frontiers of Jihad: Radical Islam in Europe*, London: I.B. Tauris.

Phillips, M. (2006) *Londonistan: How Britain has Created a Terror State Within*, London: Gibson Square. [Used 2008 reprint.]

Portes, A. (1984) 'The rise of ethnicity: determinants of ethnic perceptions among Cuban expats in Miami', *American Sociological Review*, 49(3): 383–97.

Saggar, S. (2008) *Pariah Politics: Understanding Western Radical Islamism and What Should be Done*, Oxford: Oxford University Press.

Samad, Y. (1998) 'Media and Muslim identity: intersections of generation and gender', *Innovation*, 11(4): 425–38.

Shore, Z. (2006) *Breeding Bin Ladens: America, Islam and the Future of Europe*, Baltimore, MD: Johns Hopkins University Press.

Spalek, B. (2007) 'Disconnection and exclusion: pathways to radicalism?', in T. Abbas (ed.) *Islamic Political Radicalism: A European Perspective*, Edinburgh: Edinburgh University Press, pp. 192–206.

Voas, D. and Crockett, A. (2005) 'Religion in Britain: neither believing nor belonging', *Sociology*, 39(1): 11–28.

2 Mobilization, recruitment, violence and the street

Radical violent *takfiri* Islamism in early twenty-first-century Britain

Jonathan Githens-Mazer[1]

Introduction

Some of the most basic problems in understanding the impetus and causation of radical violent *takfiri* jihadism[2] (RVTJ) are the lack of empirical data and actor focused 'bottom-up' perspectives of this phenomenon. Academics, policymakers and media commentators all try to make sense of who participates in Islamically inspired violent extremism with limited knowledge and little access to those who are actually participating (or have participated in the past) in this and related phenomena. Scholars such as Marc Sageman have identified the lack of empirics when considering phenomenon such as radicalization, and lamented the affect that this has on useful policymaking to help reduce the threat of Islamically inspired terrorism and political violence (Sageman 2007). The problem, in Sageman's analysis, is due to an overemphasis by funders on 'modelling' violent extremism and radicalization, rather than a more methodologically sound scientifically based derivation of causation in light of observation.

Top-down perspectives, though useful as part of a larger overview of violent radicalization, have several significant blind-spots when deployed to understand radical violent *takfiri* jihadism. Policymakers and the security services have come to increasingly rely on network analysis and profiling to identify relevant cases for observation, in academia, or surveillance, in the security services (Eilstrup-Sangiovanni 2008; Home Office 2009). However, such methods, though indicative, do not provide a causal analysis of the 'why's' of what is happening on the ground. Understanding violent radicalization[3] requires more 'bottom-up' studies. Rather than searching for a structural variable, or a complex combination/interaction between structural variables, this chapter reflects research findings achieved through semi-structured targeted interviews, and to a lesser degree through participant observation, to try to establish how and why Islamically inspired terrorism, and 'radicalization', are occurring on the streets of modern Britain. It seeks an understanding from the perspective of the (potentially) radicalized themselves.

For policymakers, the inability to identify a simple cause for radicalization is problematic. Politicians must appear to be solution-oriented, fully aware and in control of any potential threat to the public. Admitting that causation is beyond immediate policy solutions runs counter to pressure to deliver cause and solution in party manifestos and television sound bites – and 'counter-radicalization' is subject to immediate political pressures defined by occasionally hysterical media and often nervous voters. That this is lamentable is immaterial – it is the reality of the current situation. It will be argued here that radicalization, as a process that explains participation in violent extremism, is subject to extremely complex interactions of variables including broad categories such as ideology, religion, economic factors, global contexts and structural factors. However, from a set-theoretical perspective, such categories appear to be so grand as to potentially lose their meaning – so they can be understood to be broadly at play in any process of radicalization, yet observing them requires in depth case specific examinations (Goertz 2006; Goertz and Mahoney 2005; Mahoney 2000; Mahoney 2007; Ragin 2000, 2008; Ragin and Pennings 2005). The effects of a variable such as class or religion can only be understood to be meaningful in light of the way in which a RVTJ recruiter uses them to recruit from and/or mobilize his target audience (Githens-Mazer 2008a). The RVTJ recruiting process is an important focus for study because it provides an opportunity to examine the content of these macro variables, in terms of how recruiters operate within existing paradigms to coax into and partner with individuals to participate in terrorist acts.

Some problems with radicalization

In the introduction to this volume, Goodwin and Eatwell wrestle with key conceptual problems surrounding the definition of extremism, ultimately settling on a recognition of the use of this word with reference to action and to values. A perfunctory survey of the use of the word of radicalization indicates that there is also a great deal of confusion as to its meaning along similar lines: Does it refer to actions or ideas? Are these mutually exclusive or just distinct and occasionally overlapping categories? What is the relationship between radicalization and Islamically inspired terrorism?

For the EU, radicalization often denotes violence and terrorism, a move from a peaceful perspective to one which encourages and thrives on the use of violence, and the 2005 EU *Strategy for Combating Radicalization and Recruitment to Terrorism* is intended to 'prevent, protect, pursue and respond' to terrorist threats posed by 'violent radicalisation' (Secretariat 2007). For the European Commission, radicalization constitutes 'the phenomenon of the people embracing opinions, views and ideas which could lead to terrorism'.[4] The UK's Department of Communities and Local Government (DCLG) suggests an implicit relationship between Islam and terrorism, which hinges on a vulnerability emanating from identity crises; when a youthful affinity for terrorism meets a search for identity during moments of 'personal crisis'.[5] From the British perspective, as stated in the most recent statement on counter terrorism strategy: *Pursue Prevent Protect Prepare: The United Kingdom's Strategy for Countering International Terrorism* (aka CONTEST 2), successful radicalization hinges on a resonant public narrative which attracts and mobilizes British Muslims to participate in violence (Home Office 2009: 37).

For some academics, radicalization has come to increasingly denote the unstated but implicit correlation between the 'dangers of radical Islam' and violence (Kepel 2005; Kirby 2007). In this context, being radical, or becoming radicalized is rapidly accruing a pejorative connotation. In fact, the term is often being used interchangeably and opaquely with terms such as fundamentalist, Islamist, Jihadist and neo-Salafist or Wahabbist, with little regard for what these terms actually mean, and instead indicate signals about political Islam that the media and politicians wish to transmit (Saeed 2007; Turner 2007).[6] In such cases, Islamic radicalism can mean 'those people who believe that Islam is under threat and that they are sanctioned to defend Islam from that threat' (Lim 2005). Where radical is being used to specifically denote RVTJ specifically, terms such as 'radical activities' are also being used to mean terrorist activities, and indicate not just the perpetration of actual terrorist attacks, but the logistics and training behind them (Cesari 2008). 'Muslim radicals' (here often meaning politicized Muslims) are often understood by many Western politicians and media to be 'anti-Western' – an inherent danger to Western cultural and political values, and distinct from (and a malign influence on) psychologically weak/ideologically feeble 'vulnerable' Muslims in the UK and beyond (Kirby 2007; Lewis 2007).

Research design

Rather than get bogged down in ideologically driven normative debates as to the relative (de)merits of the role of religion, let alone Islam in politics, the study of radicalization should be a matter of examining historical and contemporary cases, and any resulting analysis should be firmly based on this kind of empirical study. An empirical basis for ontological understanding of radicalization is ultimately possible because it is an observable concept. Studies of radicalization may be complex, intimate and methodologically challenging, but suffer neither more nor less from methodological dilemmas than parallel studies of collective political behaviours such as mobilization and recruitment – not least in questions of where agency lies in such behaviours? (in individuals? in 'culture'?) And whether radicalization is a rational choice – and if so, what are the determinants of outcomes here?

The subjects of this study, who were almost entirely based in London, represent a sample population who have experienced recruitment into radical violent *takfiri* jihadist criminal and terrorist activities first hand, and who potentially participated in such activities in the past. These interview subjects came from London, and were associated with the Islamist scene in and around the Finsbury Park Mosque and Brixton since the mid-1990s. This means that the focus for this study was limited to urban experiences of radicalization into participation into Islamically inspired violent extremism. The interview subjects who participated in these semi-structured interviews gave accounts of their experiences of recruitment by recounting past personal experiences, as well as describing observations on current processes of radicalization.[7] Why Britain, and even more specifically why London? In part, this research focus reflects the realities of conducting this kind of research – including long established relationships replete with high degrees of trust with key individuals in London Muslim communities. However, this reality of access was highly fortuitous, as the interview subjects mainly came from North London (the Finsbury Park Mosque area) and South London (Brixton and Streatham), which can be seen as the epicentres of RVTJ in the UK, in Europe, and potentially even in the West since the 1990s (Phillips 2006). The Finsbury Park Mosque was infamously the symbolic power base of the radical Egyptian-born cleric Abu Hamza al-Masri, who provided ideological succour for the 7/7 and 21/7 bombers, as well as playing a major role in other successful and foiled terrorist plots in the UK and beyond. Brixton is home to a large Salafi community of mainly reverts to Islam, and was home to Richard Reid, the shoe bomber. Brixton's importance here is as a key battleground between the most radical and violent of London's RVTJ recruiters and preachers, such as the Jordanian cleric Abu Qatada, spiritual Godfather to the Armed Islamic Group of Algeria (GIA), and the Jamaican-born Abdullah el-Faisal and groups such as the Brixton Salafis, who sought to confront and expel what they viewed as this *takfiri* threat. Both Abu Qatada and el-Faisal, along with many others, were actually repelled by the Brixton Salafi community, who deemed their messages of hate and violence to be an anathema to their understanding of true Islamic practice or *deen*.

This chapter will lay out the basic steps of recruitment to RVTJ as relayed by interview subjects and interspersed with backing from secondary open-source material, such as newspaper articles and other news reports. It will seek to establish the basic framework of recruitment, and discuss the impact of technology on this recruitment process. It will then go on to discuss the significant and fundamental issue of causation – and in this way attempt to move debates and discussions away from the moving target of 'how' radicalization occurs to the more important issue of why it is occurring. In some ways, the research design deployed here has an obvious flaw: this is telling the story after the fact, and does not necessarily reflect experiences at the exact moment of radicalization; it does not engage with individuals who are currently participating in RVTJ. This is for quite obvious reasons. Those currently participating in RVTJ are (1) almost impossible to access and (2) any such research with this specific target population is fraught with ethical, moral, criminal and tangible security concerns. Some have sought to find proxies for this category by studying groups such as *Hizb-ut-Tahrir* (HT). However, such studies often end up illustrating that the HT experience, though potentially 'radicalizing' and/or reflecting aspects of extremism, is quite distinct from a willingness to strap on a rucksack full of explosives and ball bearings to oneself in an attempt to commit suicide-murder on a massive scale in the name of Islam. It is the reality of this kind of research, that to figure out what is happening in this part of the population, the researcher must triangulate this aspect in light of circumstantial and contextual data.

Processes of radicalization

At the outset of this process, there is the basic unit of analysis – the potential radical violent *takfiri* jihadist. This is most often a young male, who feels 'disaffected' for a variety of potential reasons. This notion of disaffection comes up again and again during interviews and participant observation, and subjects relayed that it is key factor that RVTJ recruiters seek to exploit. Disaffection is a sentiment that is described by interviewees, as a failed sense of entitlement, and a general sense of isolation from the rest of society. This sentiment, according to our subjects, was both individually and collectively defined – a function not only of personal circumstance, but also slotted into other contemporary British social and economic categories, such as race, ethnicity and class. The link to RVTJ hinges on the exploitation of this sense of disempowerment and identity.

It is also important to explicitly define what is meant by 'recruiter' here. Sageman (2007) quite rightly distinguishes key phases of the RVTJ threat, referring to the first, second and third waves. In the first wave, threats came from immigrants in Europe who sought to participate in RVTJ to destabilize what they considered to be a Western enemy. During the first wave, foreign recruiters arrived in the UK, identified those individuals who wanted to participate in RVTJ, and helped them to find tactical training in terrorism abroad, so that they could engage in 'Jihad' around the world. In the second wave, individuals born in the UK (or Europe) went abroad to train to participate in terrorism in their countries of birth. During this training, they would make key links with the global jihadi movement, thereby facilitating criminal and terrorist activities in the UK and beyond (in places such as Afghanistan, the Balkans and Chechnya). In the second case, those British born RVTJ participants who returned from their training themselves played key roles in identifying the next generation of RVTJ recruits, and acted as a linking mechanism between home organizations and the global jihadi movement.

In the third phase, traditional recruiting has disappeared, as the global surveillance of al-Qaeda or al-Qaeda-inspired activities have shut down almost any opportunity for training abroad, and removed (through detention and, potentially, rendition) the threat posed by a substantial number of the second wave recruits who had contacts abroad. Sageman argues that the exposure of the second wave of RVTJs, and their subsequent arrest, has meant potential pathways between recruits and training have been lost. Now, for example, a candidate from Britain showing up in Northwest Pakistan would be looked at with suspicion rather than brought into contact with relevant trainers and recruiters, as had been the case during the 1980s and 1990s. Recruiting in the current context, therefore, has a different meaning and feel to what it meant in the past, and here is being used to refer to the attempts by key ideologues to 'light the fuse' in individuals who may be sympathetic to the ideals of RVTJ. Recruitment, in the third wave, has come to mean dispersal of ideas while allowing individuals to use various technological platforms to learn how to make bombs, rather than recruitment into some sort of central al-Qaeda organization.

On the street, such recruiters seem to start out as key neighbourhood figures, men who have the power and legitimacy to inspire young followers to think about the world through a *takfiri* jihadi infused filter. Recruitment into political movements is something that political scientists often attempt to explain – though often in reference to political party recruitment rather than participation in terrorism. Brady, Schlozman and Verba (1999) have identified recruitment patterns in social movements, where elites target those who appear to be 'attractive' prospects, and that these prospects are also engaged in a process of determining which movements appear resonant, rational and likely to achieve their objectives. For other scholars, such as Teske (1997), this orientation to recruitment on the part of prospects reflects the point at which self-interest and moral obligation to participate become one, in a sense creating the basis by which individuals feel that participation is rational, reasonable and necessary (Lichterman 1996; Polletta and Jasper 2001: 290). This process is clearly at play here. There are, of course, siginificant differences between participation in and support for RVTJ – support ranging from vocal, to tactical, to implicit, while participation denotes high risk (potentially fatal) action. Subjects often referred to the way that these recruiters treated recruits with a degree of respect that they had never before experienced – and some referred to it feeling as though these recruiters were acting like a father figure they had never had. In this identification of 'raw talent', and search for empowerment, recruiter and candidate are involved in high degree of reciprocity around searches for legitimacy and empowerment.

Several interviewees explicitly stated that they felt that the power of recruiters stemmed from an absence of father figures among potential recruits, and (especially in the case of Afro-Caribbean convert communities) social praise and the lack of non-Muslim support for individuals who otherwise have little exposure to positive feedback and reinforcement. The London Borough of Lambeth, and the Brixton Hill Ward specifically, have high rates of lone parent households – 17.9 per cent and 17.1 per cent, respectively, compared to a UK national average of 6.5 per cent (ONS 2002; London Borough of Lameth Council 2003). While empirically testable, it is clearly not the only reason for participation in terrorism in the UK; and even where testable, these claims are not true for the 7/7 and 21/7 bombers. Some interviewees couched this lack of positive reinforcement and community empowerment as the difference between 'thug life' and a 'normal' British experience. The term 'thug life' was coined by the late rapper Tupac Shakur, and is an acronym for 'The Hate U Gave Little Infants Fucks Everybody'. It refers to a glamourised gangster-rap defined perception of street life, hustling and drug dealing – which either leads to wealth or death, where reputation is the definition of the moral, and wherein there is no 'mainstream' alternative. Within these interviews, this was often elided with the effects of drug usage in urban communities, where vast swathes of the community members are, apocryphally, assumed to have succumbed to some aspect of the drug trade – as addict or dealer ('the played' or 'the player'). This lack of father figure and lack of praise was expressed differently depending on class and ethnicity, so among Afro-Caribbean converts was described as reflecting a lack of fathers among interviewees' friends, whereas for Asian Muslims, was described more in light of inter-generational conflict, where fathers just did not understand the experiences of their sons. Again, these perceptions may well reflect the impact of stereotypes rather than reality, however, the key aspect here is perception. Such claims dominate community views/perspectives on issues of radicalization and terrorism. While clearly family structure is a factor which should be investigated, and which could clearly could impact on structural factors and psychological orientation, this perception is also symbolically important – rendering recruiters with a power, legitimacy and authority that would otherwise be accorded family members or community elders.

One subject described the approach of recruiters as being unlike anything else he had previously experienced – whereby recruiters make constant reference to the bond between Muslims, and heap praise and responsibility on individuals (here mainly young men) who felt that they were otherwise being told every action they were doing was wrong and/or suspect. In part, the awe and reverence accorded to the recruiters, which means this praise is so highly prized, stems from the sense that these recruiters are the epiphany of an individual who 'has their act together' – having moved beyond the drug trade, and transcended the temptations and dangers of the 'thug life'. One study points out that Muslims in Britain are the most disadvantaged faith group, three times more likely to be unemployed than the Christian majority, have the lowest employment rates of any group and the highest level of economic inactivity (O'Duffy 2008: 40). Recruiters are aware of these disadvantages, and exploit not only the realities on the ground, but also candidates' perceptions of these facts. The process of recruitment, from this perspective, is about empowerment and respect, which is perceived (whether rightly or wrongly) as not being forthcoming from non-Muslim British society. Interviewees felt as though the wider British society only thought about Finsbury Park Mosque and Brixton in terms of terrorism and knife crime, and therefore only with negative perceptions.

From this initial approach the recruiter is described as inviting the RVTJ candidate for a meal and to watch a video. This video is, in every case, reported as showing horrific accounts of anti-Muslim violence in Palestine, Afghanistan, Iraq, and less recently Chechnya and Bosnia. This construction of Islamic struggle through specific 'paradigms' is a theme that was constant in all of the interviews, among old and young, men and women, and in initial interviews beyond the London context this still appears to hold true. At least superficially, these paradigms appear to have been key components of the suicide bombing videos of individuals such as the 7/7 bomber Mohammed Siddique Khan, and more recently were key elements of the apparent suicide tapes left behind by participants in the recent 'Airline Plot'.

The concept of paradigm is intentionally used here, as it denotes the power of a worldview which transcends understandings of narrative and framing. Paradigm, as used by scholars such as Khun (1996) and Geddes (2003) indicates the conditions which not only shape knowledge, but frame further pursuits of knowledge. Scientific theories, as paradigms, shape research and knowledge – what we believe we know to be true shapes our truth and how we seek this and further truths. The construction of knowledge exists within certain parameters, and these parameters in turn structure knowledge. In this context, paradigms emerge from apparently universal interpretations of specific situations of conflict and ideology; religious claims (if not practice) of universality, faith and belief, and the application of these apparently universal perspectives at local levels into sub-*Umma* local drivers. In the British case, because of a variety of factors such as ethnic background, Islamic sect, geographic location, generation, age, sex, class, education, etc., understandings of the past – and of key Muslim related conflicts, not only create mechanisms for framing and understanding current struggles, but also literally contain the shared knowledge and perceptions of truth among specific Muslim communities and the broader British context.

The role of religion

For many individuals undergoing recruitment to a movement, religions (here specifically Islam) provide mechanisms to 'right wrongs', and paradigms by which to understand one's own disempowerment, disenfranchisement and sense of alienation from key political and social processes (Habeck 2006: 161–4; Yates 2007). This may be couched as a search for meaning – and in some cases may include a (re)discovery of religion. In order to end up a radical violent *takfiri* jihadist, this must include not only the (re)discovery of Islam in belief and everyday practice, but also a belief that it justifies terrorism and violence against *kafir* (or non-believers). Many young disaffected individuals (re)discover Islam, and yet do not go on to believe that religious practice justifies violence. However, when pushed, no interviewee felt that recruiters sought to recruit on highly intellectual theological justifications for RVTJ and terrorism. So what is the actual role for Islam here? Islam clearly plays a key role, it is ultimately Islamically inspired terrorism that is being observed here, but there are three different ways which Islam can be understood to matter here: elite, recruiter and street.

First, for elites in movements such as al-Qaeda, Islamically inspired religio-politics is the purpose of their actions. This inspiration is translated into rhetoric about removing non-believers from Muslim soil, re-establishing Islamic political systems in Muslim lands, and/or as a desire to ensure correct Islamic practice, *deen*, among all Muslims. It should be noted that in no case is this elite understanding of Islam millenarian in its intent. At the level of the recruiter, religion is no less observed, but slightly more pragmatic. It is not that Islam is not seen as the reason for recruitment and/or action, but that Islam provides not only the reason for action, but in its ideology and practice the very means for recruiting. In cases like London, this means exploiting resonant senses of difference from non-Muslim Britain, and proclaiming responsibility to participate in direct action as inspired by the *Umma* under threat (which often reflects an extension of the concept of defensive jihad to include attacks against opponents in foreign lands). From his power base at the Finsbury Park Mosque, Abu Hamza al-Masri typified this usage of Islam for mobilization and as a call for an individual defined moral obligation to participate in violent action. Abu Hamza's sermons constantly referred to imminent threats from the West against Islamic culture, society and practice, and how it is that such culture provides the means to resist. From this perspective, Muslims are besieged and must defend their families and their honour from the pervasive threat of a corrupt and comforting *kafir* lifestyle. In one sermon he states that direct action is necessary to prevent the West from 'legislating and existing in our [sic] own land'. Those that do not participate in direct action, as defined by Islamic practice, constitute lesser Muslims, '... he is too coward, he is inexperienced, he doesn't want to take the challenge: this is wrong'.

The role of religion from the street level – from the perspective of the potential recruit, differs from these other two perspectives. Again, our subjects emphasized how Islam has come to have a street credibility, a 'coolness', because of its stark contrast to the experiences and expectation of white 'middle England' and its unpopularity in white British society, and because of factors as banal as Islamic fashion. Interviewees described experiences of individuals first coming to the Mosque to find out how they could buy thobes (the outfit worn by Salafi men), and only subsequently becoming interested in Islam. Several interviewees also describe the importance of books such as the *Autobiography of Malcolm X* in the process of their reversion to Islam.

It is here that the recruiter's pragmatic approach to religion is most apparent. At the street level, there are vast differences in terms of the appeal of Islam; differences which reflect ethnic and/or sectarian orientations, geographic distinctions, and race and class. Al-Qaeda trained and/or inspired recruiters deploy tailored religious narratives, which differ from recruiter to recruiter, community to community, but all of which are unified by their ideologically pitting Islam versus the West/Christianity. Perceptions of injustice were, and continue to be, foci for propaganda by al-Qaeda and other *takfiri* jihadist recruiters seeking new members among immigrants in mosque environments, directly referring to conceptions of 'Muslims under siege' in the flashpoints of Chechnya, Kashmir, Iraq, and most significantly Palestine (Githens-Mazer 2008a, 2008c; Ranstorp 2005: 3).

Take, for example, the case of South London, where recruiters try to target a diverse range of Muslim communities, in terms of ethnicity, generation, class, sect and race. This means operating in an environment where the population includes third or potentially fourth generation South Asians, more recent West Indian and Afro-Caribbean converts/reverts to Islam, and a variety of other smaller communities, including Somalis. In all cases, Islam clearly matters, yet in each group knowledge of Islam may differ widely. For South Asians, Deobandi or Barelvi, or even Sufi, it may be that knowledge of *deen* is a key aspect of their community, and that recruiters have to operate within this existing religiously and ethnically defined paradigm. Recruiters may emphasize perceptions of injustice in Kashmir, and in light of recent events in Pakistan and Afghanistan, and couch them in light of community defined aspects of religious practice, in order to link with the broader theme of an *Umma* under threat. This same tailoring of religion with recruiting messages is apparent amongst South London Somali communities, where local sentiments of deprivation and/or social exclusion are linked by such recruiters to recent Somali history (i.e. its abandonment by the West in the 1990s, and USA/Western support for the recent Kenyan invasion), religiously defined perceptions of injustice, and the legacy of colonialism in Somalia over the course of the nineteenth and twentieth centuries. For West Indian and/or Afro-Caribbean converts/reverts, knowledge of Islam may not be particularly deep or well established amongst certain sections of the community. In such cases, recruiters may emphasize different aspects of disaffection, isolation and exploitation, again linking experiences from the street. An individual like Abdullah el-Faisal typified this approach – attempting to garner support for his brand of RVTJ by using quotations from key historical (and in this case Christian) figures such as Marcus Garvey, and linking his Islamically inspired perspective on participating in violent direct action with the rhetoric of pursuing racial equality and justice in Britain.

This confusing array of approaches, claims and counter-claims of religious and moral legitimacy may in part account for how and why Brixton has become a front line in confrontations between those that support and those that work against RVTJ in Britain. This confrontation plays out in street level struggles between established and theologically nuanced groups, such as the Brixton Salafis, and *takfiri* Imams, such as al-Faisal, who at every turn sought to undermine the theological and street credibility of the Salafis in Brixton who tried to counter his narrative. Such challenges cannot be actually be understood as battles of theological legitimacy, or dismissed as the vagaries of community politics. The key ingredient of the street obfuscates any simple analysis, adding a deep layer of complexity to understanding and decoding messages and the deployment of resonant myths, memories and symbols in these kinds of confrontations. For example, relationships between the Afro-Caribbean community and the police are still infused with memories of the Brixton Riots of 1981, and of later clashes between the police and Rastafarian community in Brixton. Even where Afro-Caribbean reverts seek to assist the police in identifying those who are recruiting for and/or participating in RVTJ activities, these individuals must be careful not to be seen working to closely with the authorities lest they lose their credibility amongst other members of the community.

The key point about the street-level view of religion is that it may, or may not, be family or community instilled, but is unlikely to play the only role in defining contemporary political perspectives. However, the recruiter operating in this environment can use religion to inspire action, by highlighting personal plight, by exploiting the *Umma* under threat, or by combining these two approaches. Ultimately, potential radical violent *takfiri* jihadists are encouraged to become active participants in violence through the translation of empathy into sympathy and ultimately participation – a building of RVTJ strategic capacity. According to our subjects, this is a key moment in the recruitment process – where the recruiter moves from planting ideas and interpretations into actually inviting an individual to participate in something like wilderness/survival training. One significant aspect emphasized in our interviews is that such activities were free – recruiters explicitly refer to the fact that no money is needed, and that ample food and warm shelter will be provided. Our subjects emphasized that the attraction of hearty meals and warm beds cannot be overemphasized in this context – especially for those who may be involved in day to day struggles to find work or productive activity in their neighbourhoods.

Coolness, criminality and the street

Interviewees often make reference to recruiters and those involved in counter-radicalization work being involved in a 'street by street' battle, where they compete to recruit those candidates on each street who care, are reliable, and whom others look up to and admire. This competition is intense, and subject not only to ideological battle, but is often also a source of physical confrontations over turf. This intensity reflects a street level view of key tipping points; where several key individuals, once recruited, can turn an entire peer group in one direction or the other. Often this recruitment competition was described as hinging on what is perceived as being 'cool' within the street culture itself. When pushed, no respondent suggested that theological rigour or inspiration had anything to do with this assessment of what was 'cool'. Respondents also emphasized the importance of previous experience of criminal enterprise and recruitment in this process, with one subject stating that the same processes of inducement to participate in drug-dealing were being used by those who were seeking to find new recruits to RVTJ. Subjects likened this experience to gang recruitment and warfare – with each group seeking to claim separate streets and terraces as their own. Themes of reputation and honour often colour these references. Once a street has 'turned' in one direction or the other, the rewards are large – with sections or even whole communities following the lead of one individual or another. 'Star recruits', while ostensibly representing a specific religious orientation, are subsequently paraded to inspire others to follow in their footsteps, potentially including participation in religious training classes, and peer pressure and group bonding. This can have a significant practical impact whereby ideological perceptions that the Muslim world is under siege from the West are practically cemented in key elements of communities. This competition is based on what are perceived as rational inducements and merits by the participants themselves – but to those outside of this process, whether Muslim or non-Muslim, these issues can appear to be arcane and nonsensical.

This became apparent in the way that interviewees emphasized the link between 'street' culture, criminal enterprise, and the subsequent power of recruitment and efficacy of recruiting structures. Our subjects report that recruiters identify key 'players' on a street, and seek to recruit them first. Key street figures, often in the drug trade, are approached by recruiters who tell them that their criminal enterprises are justified in Islam. One subject reported this as recruiters saying 'we understand how you've come to deal drugs, it is the fault of the *kufar*, and the key is that you continue to do so in the knowledge that you are doing this against them'. This was reported to be a factor which helped both members of the community and security services to identify religious scholars and potentially even Mosques which could be harbouring and supporting terrorist activity. Once the main street players are recruited, interviewees suggested that they brought their entire criminal organization along with them, including both individual members of a gang, and the tactical capacity to operate beneath the police's radar. In part, our subjects stated, this is often perceived as a continuation of previous criminal behaviour in alternative ideological and moral frameworks. Given that by its very nature such actions and behaviours need to be hidden from outsider non-street view, and therefore undetectable to the law, recruiters have, through this process, appeared to have identified key mechanisms and institutions through which to operate in the UK urban environment.

In part, this was reflected in the actions of the Egyptian-born cleric, Abu Hamza al-Masri at the Finsbury Park Mosque. Once he gained a foothold in the mosque, Abu Hamza later used force and intimidation to maintain and strengthen his grip on power. Abu Hamza's circle of close supporters were literally flexing their muscles and threatening anyone who opposed their 'emir'. For many of them, their first experience of adult responsibility was performing tasks on behalf of the *Supporters of Sharia*, such as working in a bookshop on the ground floor of the Mosque and recording, copying, cataloguing and distributing talks by Abu Hamza (including the transcripts cited in this article). At the same time, Abu Hamza was aiding and abetting a variety of criminal enterprises in the basement of the mosque. This was mainly credit card fraud, counterfeiting and low level theft, and these were often enterprises of illegal immigrants who had little or no recourse to legal money making enterprises. However, Abu Hamza not only turned a blind eye to these activities, but explicitly supported them as a way of waging war against the *kafir*, and he won admiration from this growing band of supporters. By the late 1990s Abu Hamza's first-floor office within the mosque had become the hub of his operation, actively promoting, and in turn supported by, the *Supporters of Sharia*, significantly countermanding the official mosque management at every turn and effectively flaunting the inability of the mosque's trustees and the UK Charity Commission to regulate or inhibit his active and explicit financial and tactical support for criminal and terrorist enterprises in the UK and abroad. When Abu Hamza did eventually concede defeat to the Charity Commission, on a point of procedure, agreeing to confine his role at the mosque to certain periods and specific parts of the building, he proclaimed it a tactical victory. He convinced his supporters that he was acting strategically and deceptively in accordance with the teachings he gave them about how Muslims were licensed to behave when confronting their non-Muslim *kafir* enemies.

Taking the next step: self-selection, training and the Internet

Until recently, the moment of truth associated with the process of recruitment into RVTJ was the moment of self-selection by those individuals who travelled abroad to theological and terrorist training facilities in Afghanistan. From 1979 through 2001, and arguably to some degree even until today, Afghanistan (and now Waziristan) provided sanctuary for a variety of jihadist training programmes (pre- and post-Taliban) to facilitate tactical training in conventional and insurgent combat, especially during the conflict with the Soviets (Sageman 2007). The importance of this self-selection had particularly reflected the point where individuals who were experiencing peer pressure at home distinguished their outlook by choosing to go abroad, and once abroad could choose to stay the course away from their 'mates' in local communities and neighbourhoods. In the wake of the British bombings of 7/7 and 21/7, the 3/11 Madrid Train Bombings, and the recent plot in Denmark to kill Kurt Westergaard, the Danish cartoonist who drew depictions of Mohammed, which were considered 'sacrilegious' by large parts of the Muslim world, the importance of this step is now unclear. The key question is: To what extent self-starting radical violent *takfiri* jihadist terrorist cells still undergo processes of self-selection in this process, given that training is no longer dependent on going abroad? This may reflect adaptation in light of new roles for the Internet and technologically based exchanges which facilitate communication of ideology and technically sophisticated tactical knowledge which was impossible three decades ago.

During this process of self-selection, which included going abroad, almost all accounts talk about the 'guest house experience'. Individuals arrived in Pakistan and waited to be transported to training camps in Afghanistan, during which time they waited in guest houses with other individuals waiting to make the same trip. These guest houses provided rooms for individuals from around the world, though there are some discrepancies in the extent to which each guest house reflected ethno-national identity (i.e. whether certain guest houses catered only for 'Arabs' versus others catering only for British/Europeans, or a mix of people). Many recruits left either during or just after the guest house experience, some experiencing injury, others feigning injury because of homesickness. Others describe only just at this point realizing the nature of the endeavour on which they have embarked. Those returning from training, or exiting the training process appear to stay at the same guest houses as those arriving for training. Whether this is for security reasons (i.e. those having completed their training are, in a sense, bona fide, or have been tasked with a mission) or whether this is a construct to maintain high morale among pre-trainees is unclear. From this point, training is the final step, but just like any other military body, training is intended to reflect and build upon a recruits natural abilities and commitment. Whereas technologically complex training, in skills such as bomb making is not universal, basic training in insurgency based infantry warfare, including training in the use of basic weapons such as the AK-47 and RPGs is much more common. From this point, any number of actions are possible. This training may only be an initial part of a bigger mission, such as al-Qaeda infiltration of the USA for flight training previous to the events of 9/11. Alternatively, individuals may leave this training process and await order in other locations (sleeper cells), or be charged with recruiting others to the radical violent *takfiri* jihadist cause.

Recently, foreign sojourns for training in ideology and tactics have become impossible, and to a certain extent, redundant. Ideology is still being disseminated in person, but is also aided by technological tools such as the Internet and DVDs. Individuals who are pre-disposed to becoming radical can now be 'operationalized' over a variety of technological platforms. Shared perceptions of a universal conflict between radical Islam and the West both rely on, and reinforce, linkages that exist not only between committed RVTJs, but also among virtual communities that transcend regional, national and international communities, inherently propagating a belief that where the Muslim experience is 'difficult' (subject to oppression, repression and recrimination), this virtual *Umma* will provide stability and help. These linkages are key in providing support and encouragement for those who seek to perpetrate RVTJ inspired terrorism.

This does not mean, however, that the use of the Internet can be understood as a cause of RVTJ. The Internet is a facilitator, not a cause. In the older process, individuals went abroad to receive training, whether tactical, in the use of weapons/making of explosives and/or ideological, often described as experiences of religious training. This process also was often described as including the reading of specific key texts, such as Syed Qutb's *Milestones* and *Islam and Social Justice*, as well as key passages from *In the Shade of the Qu'ran*, Abdullah Azzam's *Join the Caravan*, Abu Ala Mawdudi's *Let Us be Muslims*, *Jihad in Islam* and *Human Rights in Islam*, and more recently Abu Mus'ab al-Suri's (aka Mustafa bin Abd al-Qadir Sitt Maryam Nasar) *The Global Islamic Resistance Call*. In this older process, recruiters were able to weed out the truly committed from the 'wannabes', and every account gathered during this study emphasized the extremely gruelling nature of this foreign training experience. Homesickness, rough living conditions, lack of facilities, dysentery, etc., all contributed to a process through which only the truly dedicated emerged at the end as fully bona fide RVTJs.

The Internet has, obviously, transformed this process. The use of technology, particularly the Internet, represents adaptation rather than design and it may be possible to compare similar changes in format, if not content, to the recruitment processes of extreme right-wing movements (Goodwin 2010). If candidates are no longer able to travel to training camps, RVTJ elites have sought alternative platforms of 'distance learning' to enable recruits to train. However, for those RVTJ recruits whose experience is limited to the Internet, this has inherently transformed the nature of this process. By its instantaneous nature, the Internet can facilitate those expressing an initial curiosity into RVTJ to be in touch with high level recruiters and trainers. While the language of paedophilia is being used to describe this process (especially with the use of words such as 'grooming') leading to the Internet being understood as a tool by which recruiters prey on the vulnerable, this does not indicate the reciprocity of the recruiter-candidate interaction. It is the technological savvy of foreign based recruiters that has transformed the nature of this threat, but this adaptation can possibly be understood as a simultaneous advantage and flaw. In the past, recruiters identified potential candidates, and helped them through the process, and the human interaction at each step acted as a filtration mechanism by which to identify the better prospects in the RVTJ movement. Now recruiters are confronted with otherwise unknown quantities, such that they cannot be nearly as sure of the quality and ability of these candidates.

Does this in any way reduce the threat of RVTJ terrorism? Most probably not – the most recent example of the product of this form of radicalization occurred in the Southwest of England – in the case of Nicky Reilly (aka Mohamed Abdulaziz Rashid Saeed-Alim). In this case, exchanges on various Internet platforms, chatrooms, social networking sites (and there has even been some suggestion of using gambling websites) helped to facilitate ideological induction and support, and weapons training (Fresco 2008). Conversely, this change in tack does not ensure reliability in recruitment and training – and this was exposed in the Exeter bombing. Reilly, who was described by the police as having been radicalized through the Internet during interactions with foreign handlers, ostensibly in Pakistan, has been reported as being mentally unstable, developmentally disabled, and even more significantly appeared to have botched his attack by setting off his explosives in a toilet while arming the devices, so as to result only in injury to himself (Fresco 2008; Morris 2008; BBCNews 2008). This case epitomizes the threat and shortcomings of Internet radicalization – which allows wider access to potential recruits in the UK, but has none of the in built quality assurance mechanisms of the older foreign-based recruitment process.

So what is to be made of technological adaptation in the recruitment process? The reality is that we do not really know, and there is not enough open-source, publicly available information to say yet. Without enough datapoints, it is methodologically unsound to make a substantial claim one way or the other. There are, however, most probably three reasonable working hypotheses which could be tested in the future: (1) that in time RVTJ elites and recruiters will adapt and evolve the covert use of technology, and that subsequently what was a 'street' process will increasingly become a 'web' process; (2) that the recent use of technology is like the rest of the RVTJ phenomenon – opportunistic – and that while technology facilitates some elements of this process, it has several in-built insurmountable flaws, and that successful/effective RVTJ operations will still require face to face recruitment and training – meaning that episodes such as the attempted Exeter bombing represent crimes of opportunity rather than precision oriented RVTJ plots; and (3) that the reality is a combination of the first two hypotheses, that Internet recruitment, which so obviously 'feels different' than the street paradigm of RVTJ recruitment and action, represents the multi-headed 'Hydra' nature of the contemporary RVTJ threat, where without a unified leadership or agenda for action, individual groups from within the UK and the rest of the world, should be expected to do whatever they can to attempt to destabilize the political, social and economic institutions that form modern Britain.

Disrupting recruitment: positivism and causation in recruitment

There are many superficial and complex implications for policy makers and the security services here. Superficially, but significantly, recruitment needs to be recognized as a dynamic process, and a moving target for the security services.

Those recruiting to, and participating in, RVTJ activities know that they are operating in a globally hostile environment, and are engaged in an on-going struggle to keep ahead of security services around the world who wish to dramatically curtail their activity. This cat and mouse game can be expected to continue for the foreseeable future, and while security measures may at points strike a blow at the ability of RVTJ recruiters to operate effectively, we must expect that they will adapt and return with ever more clever and complex answers to the obstacles placed in their paths.

It needs to be understood that technological adaptation, evolution and potential transformation of the recruitment process indicates the inherently dynamic nature of the action of recruitment. For security services, any knowledge gleaned about past processes reflects past practices, and may have little or no technical relevance for current recruitment and or activities of RVTJ cells and networks. Recruiters are dynamic and willing to adapt messages to succeed – catering to audiences of potential recruits – yet they also operate within ideologically and culturally constructed and community defined paradigms. Recruiting messages must resonate – and resonance, the way in which the myths, memories and symbols that recruiters are invoking to attract and recruit potential candidates require these myths, memories and symbols to have real meaning to the potential recruit – after all 'it is not just in the shape but in the content of what lies within that we need to seek an explanation' (Smith 1998: 83; see also Githens-Mazer, 2008b). The myths, memories and symbols, whether religiously, ethnically or 'street' derived and oriented, must provide a *mise-en-scène* for individual interpretation, providing contexts for individuals to understand participation in and support for RVTJ (Githens-Mazer 2008b: 44). If government and the security services are seeking to disrupt recruitment, they must do more than combat one narrative of recruitment – they must pull the rug out from under the feet of those seeking to foment RVTJ, by substantially addressing local and international grievances that create the basis for resonance.

The distinction between adaptation of recruitment and resonance is crucial, demonstrating the difference between the 'how questions' and the 'why questions' for RVTJ. Causation and ontology are clearly related, but are not at all the same. Observations of the transformation of recruitment to RVTJ from geographically specific training camps to 'virtual' training over the Internet are clearly important, especially for those whose job it is to prevent terrorist attacks in the UK. This is similar to charting the evolution of the use of specific kinds of explosives – a pursuit of forensic history which allows for a positivist-prediction and prevent oriented counter-terrorism strategy. If you know where C4 explosive is coming from, you can close that avenue for terrorists to obtain it, if a website is teaching individuals how to make explosives, you can restrict access to it. However, charting the development of tactics and/or the evolution of training in light of technology should not be confused with causality – the former is the how of RVTJ terrorism, the latter is the why, i.e. why is it happening in the first place? While it is tempting, and methodologically easier to establish the 'how's', by creating large datasets of terrorist attacks, and seeking to identify and code key variables which may help to indicate elements of causality in a 'global' or macro picture of RVTJ, these do not explain the appeal of the recruiter on the street. They aid the security services in knowing how to deploy limited resources in the fight against terrorism, but there is a larger remit for academics and politicians seeking to understand violent radicalization. The why questions are methodologically extremely challenging to chart, and intellectually immensely difficult to understand – but there are many tools that already exist across a variety of academic disciplines. As Sageman alludes to in *Leaderless Jihad*, understanding causation requires greater sharing of knowledge and facts, and it requires creative thinking between scholars of social movement theory, history, psychology, human geography, sociology and anthropology among many other perspectives and disciplines (Sageman 2007: 172). The 'why questions' help to explain the success of RVTJ recruiters because their messages resonate in light of the realities of the street perceptions of thug life, and through successful attempts to elide experiences of disaffection and exclusion with an *Umma* under threat. However, tackling the why questions provides a fundamental and alternative way to understand causation of RVTJ. While the hows of terrorism are a moving target, the whys appear to be somewhat more stable. The 'how questions' may provide a basin, where we can collect the flowing tap of radicalization, but the 'why questions' may serve to turn the tap off itself, by providing us blueprints to prevent successful recruitment. This will require a willingness to work with Muslims (and Islamists) in the UK and around the world, in order to undermine the so far immensely successful perception of an *Umma* under threat.

Notes

1 The author wishes to gratefully acknowledge the support of the ESRC to enable the fieldwork cited here, conducted on a research grant entitled 'Cultures of Repression', RES-181-25-0017.
2 *Takfiri* refers to radicalized Muslims who feel that it is a religious and moral obligation to wage jihad against *kafir* or non-believers. *Takfiri* often feel unconstrained by traditional *fiqh* or Islamic jurisprudence, as they see their goal of attacking apostasy and ensuring the emergence of a Muslim world as ends which can justify almost any means, whether this means violating any element of the *fiqh*, including eating pork, drinking, etc. While some scholars may feel the term radical violent *takfiri* jihadist over-elaborated, the point here is to suggest individuals who are radical, committed to violent political action, and who not only believe that jihad can be waged in Muslim lands of conflict/ occupation, but that this fight can be taken and imposed on non-believers anywhere at any time.
3 Radicalization is defined here as representing the point where commitment to an elite defined rhetoric is transcended by an individual obligation to participate in direct action, the point where there is a rejection of ritual in favour of practice. Within this definition of radicalization, there is no inherent link between radicalization and violence, and the inspired direct action could, in theory and in practice, just as likely lead to participation in pluralistic democratic political activities.
4 Available at http://ec.europa.eu/justice_home/funding/2004_2007/radicalisation/doc/ call_2007_en.pdf (accessed 1 December 2008).
5 Available at http://www.communities.gov.uk/documents/communities/pdf/452628.pdf (accessed 1 December 2008).

6 This is not to tar all recent work on this subject with the same brush: see especially Entelis, J.P. (1997) *Islam, Democracy and the State in North Africa*, Bloomington, IN: Indiana University Press; Esposito, J. (2003) *Unholy War: Terror in the Name of Islam*, Oxford, Oxford University Press; Fuller, G. (2002) 'The future of political Islam', *Foreign Affairs*, 81(March–April); Hafez, M. and Wiktorowicz, Q. (2005) 'Violence as contention in the Egyptian Islamic movement', in Q. Wiktorowicz (ed.) *Islamic Activism: A Social Movement Approach*, Bloomington, IN: University of Indiana Press, pp. 61–88; Hafez, M.M. (2003a) 'The armed Islamic movement in Algeria: from the FIS to the GIA', *International Journal of Middle East Studies*, 35(1): 175–8; Hafez, M.M. (2003b) *Why Muslims Rebel: Repression and Violence in the Islamic World*, London: Lynne Rienner; Kurzman, C. (ed.) (1998) *Liberal Islam: A Sourcebook*, Oxford: Oxford University Press; Wickham, C.R. (2004) 'The path to moderation: strategy and learning in the formation of Egypt's Wasat Party', *Comparative Politics*, 36(2): 205–28. These authors, among others, are often meticulous in defining and using terms to denote specific forms of Islamically inspired politics, and their careful and articulate use of terms allows for the reader to gain complete sense of their analysis and description of the phenomena they are examining.

7 Specifics of the recruitment experience (names, dates, specifics of experiences) have not been included due to substantial concerns for the security and safety of interview subjects, but rather distilled down to basic events and actions so as to illustrate what recruitment into RVTJ, and hence radicalization, look and feel like in modern Britain.

References

BBCNews (2008) 'Nicky was easy prey says mother'.

Brady, H.E., Schlozman, K.L. and Verba, S. (1999) 'Prospecting for participants: rational expectations and the recruitment of political activists', *American Political Science Review*, 93(1): 153–68.

Cesari, J. (2008) 'Muslims in Europe and the risk of radicalism', in R. Coolaset (ed.) *Jihadi Terrorism and the Radicalisation Challenge in Europe*, Aldershot: Ashgate, pp. 97–107.

Eilstrup-Sangiovanni, M. and Jones, C. (2008) 'Assessing the dangers of illicit networks: why al-Qaida may be less threatening than many think', *International Security*, 33(2): 7–44.

Entelis, J.P. (1997) *Islam, Democracy and the State in North Africa*, Bloomington, IN: Indiana University Press.

Esposito, J. (2003) *Unholy War: Terror in the Name of Islam*, Oxford, Oxford University Press.

Fresco, A. (2008) 'Bomber Nicky Reilly was brainwashed online by Pakistani extremists', *The Times*.

Fuller, G. (2002) 'The future of political Islam', *Foreign Affairs*, 81(March–April).

Geddes, B. (2003) *Paradigms and Sand Castles: Theory Building and Research Design in Comparative Politics*, Ann Arbor, MI: University of Michigan Press.

Githens-Mazer, J. (2008a) 'Islamic radicalisation among North Africans in Britain', *British Journal of Politics and International Relations*, 10(4), 550–71.

—— (2008b) 'Locating agency in collective political behaviour: nationalism, social movements, and individual mobilisation', *Politics*, 28(1), 41–9.

—— (2008c) 'Variations on a theme: radical violent Islamism and European North African radicalisation', *PS: Political Science and Politics*, 41(1).

Goertz, G. (2006) *Social Science Concepts: A User's Guide*, Princeton, NJ: Princeton University Press.

Goertz, G. and Mahoney, J. (2005) 'Two-level theories and fuzzy-set analysis', *Sociological Methods Research*, 33(4): 497–538.

Goodwin, M.J. (2010, forthcoming) *The New British Fascism: Rise of the British National Party*, Oxford: Routledge.

Habeck, M. (2006) *Knowing the Enemy: Jihadist Ideology and the War on Terror*, New Haven, CT: Yale University Press.

Hafez, M.M. (2003a) 'The armed Islamic movement in Algeria: from the FIS to the GIA', *International Journal of Middle East Studies*, 35(1): 175–8.

—— (2003b) *Why Muslims Rebel: Repression and Violence in the Islamic World*, London: Lynne Rienner.

Hafez, M. and Wiktorowicz, Q. (2005) 'Violence as contention in the Egyptian Islamic movement', in Q. Wiktorowicz (ed.) *Islamic Activism: A Social Movement Approach*, Bloomington, IN: University of Indiana Press, pp. 61–88.

Home Office (2009) *Pursue Prevent Protect Prepare: The United Kingdom's Strategy for Countering International Terrorism*, London: The Stationery Office.

Kepel, G. (2005) *The Roots of Radical Islam*, London: Saqi.

Kirby, A. (2007) 'The London bombers as "self-starters": a case study in indigenous radicalization and the emergence of autonomous cliques', *Studies in Conflict and Terrorism*, 30(5): 415–28.

Kuhn, T. (1996) *The Structure of Scientific Paradigms* (3ed), Chicago, IL: University of Chicago Press.

Kurzman, C. (ed.) (1998) *Liberal Islam: A Sourcebook*, Oxford: Oxford University Press.

Lewis, P. (2007) *Young, British and Muslim*, London: Continuum.

Lichterman, P. (1996) *The Search for Political Community: American Activists Reinventing Commitment*, New York: Cambridge University Press.

Lim, M. (2005) 'Islamic radicalism and anti-Americanism in Indonesia: the role of the Internet', *Policy Studies*, 18.

London Borough of Lambeth Council (2003) Brixton Hill Ward Data Tables.

Mahoney, J. (2000) 'Path dependence in historical sociology', *Theory and Society*, 29(4): 507–48.

—— (2007) 'Qualitative methodology and comparative politics', *Comparative Political Studies*, 40(2): 122–44.

Morris, S. (2008) 'Nicky Reilly: from BFG to failed suicide bomber', *Guardian*.

O'Duffy, B. (2008) 'Radical atmosphere: explaining jihadist radicalization in the UK', *PS: Political Science & Politics*, 41(1): 37–42.

Office of National Statistics (ONS) (2002) Households: by type, spring 2002: Regional Trends 38.

Phillips, M. (2006) *Londonistan: How Britain is Creating a Terror State Within*, London: Gibson Square.

Polletta, F. and Jasper, J.M. (2001) 'Collective identity and social movements', *Annual Review of Sociology*, 27: 283–305.

Ragin, C.C. (2000) *Fuzzy-set Social Science*, Chicago, IL: University of Chicago Press.

—— (2008) *Redesigning Social Inquiry: Set Relations in Social Research*, Chicago, IL: University of Chicago Press.

Ragin, C.C. and Pennings, P.P. (2005) 'Fuzzy sets and social research', *Sociological Methods Research*, 33: 423–30.

Ranstorp, M. (2005) *The London Bombings and the Broader Strategic Context*, Madrid: Real Instituto Elcano.

Saeed, A. (2007) 'Trends in contemporary Islam: a preliminary attempt at a classification', *The Muslim World*, 97(3): 395–404.

Sageman, M. (2007) *Leaderless Jihad: Terror Networks in the Twenty-First Century*, Philadelphia, PA: University of Pennsylvania Press.

Secretariat, E.C. (2007) FACTSHEET: The European Union and the fight against terrorism in P. O. o. t. C. o. t. E. Union (ed).

Smith, A.D. (1998) *Nationalism and Modernism*, London: Routledge.

Teske, N. (1997) *Political Activists in America: The Identity Construction Model of Political Participation*, Cambridge: Cambridge University Press.

Turner, B.S. (2007) 'Islam, religious revival and the sovereign state', *The Muslim World*, 97(3): 405–18.

Wickham, C.R. (2004) 'The path to moderation: strategy and learning in the formation of Egypt's Wasat Party', *Comparative Politics*, 36(2): 205–28.

Yates, J.J. (2007) 'The resurgence of jihad and the spectre of religious populism', *SAIS Review*, 27(1): 127–44.

3 Faith and state

British policy responses to 'Islamist' extremism

Erik Bleich

Introduction

Islamist extremism has been the focus of intense global scrutiny since September 11, 2001 (9/11).[1] As liberal democracies became the targets of attacks, they have had to respond with policies that have amplified or even dramatically changed their approach to fighting terrorism. In the early days after 9/11, many government leaders continued to view Islamist extremism as originating abroad. However, this evolved quickly in the wake of events such as the 11 March 2004 train bombings in Madrid, the assassination of Dutch filmmaker Theo van Gogh in November 2004 and the London transportation bombings of July 2005, each of which showed the vulnerability of European societies to internal attack.

Many European states have responded to these challenges with a common policymaking pattern. They have adopted an overlapping three-pronged strategy for tackling violence associated with Islam that includes: (1) generic anti-violence policies that consciously avoid mention of Islam; (2) repressive policies that explicitly target Muslim extremists; and (3) policies that seek to integrate Muslims into national societies, either by softly enabling or by firmly compelling such integration.[2]

This chapter explores the British state response to Islamist extremism, using the overlapping three-pronged pattern as a lens through which to view its key strategic elements. This lens illustrates Britain's at-times ambiguous recognition of Islamism as a core element of new terrorist challenges; it highlights the state's focus on repressing Muslim extremists; and it discusses the ambition to integrate Muslims more successfully into British society. Because other contributions to this volume focus attention on the repressive aspect of this balancing act (see Chapter 4), this chapter gives slightly greater emphasis to the integrative aspects of British policymaking. The ultimate goal, however, is to portray an accurate picture of British approaches to Islamist extremism that have been implemented since 2001. To do this, the following section briefly examines the history of Muslim immigration to Britain, highlighting factors that have spurred the state to ramp up its policymaking efforts since the 1980s. The subsequent section introduces the comparative European context before turning squarely to the British case. It analyses Britain's CONTEST strategy as a multiplicity of policies that reflect the overlapping three-pronged strategy.

From immigrants to Muslims to extremists

There are between 1.6 and 2 million Muslims living in Great Britain today.[3] According to the most recent census figures, just over half of the Muslims residing in Britain in 2001 were immigrants, with the majority of those born in South Asia.[4] Significant 'Muslim' immigration began in the 1950s, but for most of the post-Second World War era these immigrants were not primarily defined by their religion. Until recently, it was far more common to identify them by their official status (immigrants, asylum-seekers/refugees or foreigners), or by their race, ethnicity or nationality (Black, Asian, Pakistani, etc.). This was partly a result of state rules and societal perceptions, and partly a result of the way the migrants organized themselves. Over the past 20 years, however, Islam has become an identity consciously deployed by many Muslims in Britain, and it is one that the state and society increasingly use to identify segments of the population. As religious identities have become part of the public conversation, so too have contentious issues surrounding religion. The 1989 Rushdie Affair marked a definitive turning point in the passage from 'immigrants' to 'Muslims', revealing the capacity of significant numbers of British Muslims to mobilize around their religious identity and of the British media, politicians and public to respond on similar terms. Since that time, tensions have cropped up in other areas too, generating debates about funding for religious schools, religious education within state schools, mosque construction, headscarves, ritual slaughter, Islamic rules for burying the dead, sharia courts and national blasphemy laws.

These discussions, and in particular the inflammatory book-burning tactics of the Rushdie protesters, have drawn attention to the potential for extremism among British Muslims. Yet, although Britain has been vocally criticized for harbouring known radicals – creating what has derogatorily been called Londonistan (Kepel 2004: 242–6) – there were no major acts of Islamist extremism in Britain between 1989 and 2001. Following 9/11, British policymakers began to pay attention to the possibility that Muslim citizens might perpetrate acts of terrorism on British soil. The December 2001 attempt by Richard Reid (the 'shoe bomber') to blow up a transatlantic flight highlighted the fact that Islamist terrorism was not confined to people of Middle Eastern or North African origin, and could be carried out just as easily by European citizens.

The November 2003 attacks on British targets in Istanbul and the March 2004 discovery of stocks of ammonium nitrate fertilizer in suburban London – linked to British citizens of Pakistani origin – led to further anxiety about Islamist extremism directed against Britain (Kepel 2004: 245). As a reflection of the winding down of permissive Londonistan policies, in late 2004 British authorities charged Muslim cleric Abu Hamza al-Masri with 'encouraging followers to murder Jews and other non-Muslims' and also charged Abu Qatada, who reportedly was the 'spiritual counsellor' of Mohamed Atta, the principal architect of the 9/11 attacks.[5] The 7 July 2005 (7/7) London transportation bombings and the subsequent incidents of late July 2005 (in London) and of June 2007 (in Glasgow) can thus be seen as the culmination of the increasing concern about domestic Islamist extremism that has taken place since 9/11.

There has undeniably been a transition in Britain since the 1950s, from a broad unease about immigration, to increased attention to Muslims as a specific group, to focused apprehension about Muslim extremists. But to their credit, few British policymakers have made the mistake of simply conflating Muslims with extremists. In fact, in the aftermath of recent attacks, most leaders have gone out of their way to condemn the perpetrators as fringe elements within the broader British Muslim community. In recent years, however, there has been a transition from focusing on the very few individuals willing to carry out attacks toward a broader group – perhaps as much as 10 per cent of the British Muslim population – that comprise what Shamit Saggar (2009) has termed the 'circle of tacit support' that helps to enable the perpetrators to carry out their acts.

Survey evidence lends support to the notion of widespread Muslim integration contrasted with pockets of significant difference (see Chapter 1 in this volume). Two Ipsos MORI polls conducted in the aftermath of the 7/7 attacks, for example, show that feeling strongly Muslim is not incompatible with a strong sense of belonging to Britain.[6] Moreover, the vast majority of Muslims surveyed in 2005 and 2007 agreed that immigrants should learn English, pledge their primary loyalty to Britain, integrate fully into British society and respect the rule of law.[7] Conversely, polls also demonstrate the potential for disgruntlement, cultural disconnects and even extremism. According to the 2005 National Survey on Equality, Diversity and Prejudice in Britain, 46 per cent of Muslims polled reported having suffered from prejudice or discrimination based on their religion (Abrams and Houston 2006: 43); 2005 and 2006 surveys found that 54 per cent of Muslims approved of arranged marriages and 40 per cent of Muslims backed introducing sharia in parts of Britain;[8] and in 2006, one-fifth of British Muslims canvassed expressed sympathy with the 'feelings and motives' of the 7/7 suicide bombers.[9] These surveys therefore reinforce the point that while almost all British Muslims reject extremism, there remain grounds for concern both about the very few willing to carry out attacks, and about those in the circle of tacit support.

European and British state responses to Islamist extremism

Many West European countries have developed an overlapping three-pronged strategy for responding to the threat of Islamist extremism (Bleich 2009). The three elements of the strategy are:

1 generic counterterrorism policies that avoid references to Islam;
2 policies designed to repress Islamist extremism; and
3 policies to enable and to compel integration of Muslims into national life.

Britain, France, Germany, Italy, the Netherlands and Spain have each deployed this strategy in slightly different ways since 9/11 and subsequent events, but almost all of these countries have revamped their anti-terrorism provisions in a manner that downplays the centrality of Muslim extremism as a core concern. Although many recent laws were crafted with Islamist terrorism in mind, most states have opted to minimize the specific connection to Islam by referring to 'international' terrorism and by including at least some non-Muslim groups on their watch-lists or in their public pronouncements. These policy stances self-consciously seek to neutralize tensions associated with religion.

At the same time, European states have not entirely shifted the focus away from Islam. In particular, many countries have stepped up monitoring of suspected radical Muslims. There have been official government investigations into the practice of Islam, increased training and hiring of national security agents with relevant expertise, tape recording of religious services and scrutiny of particular mosques and public statements about tabs kept on potential suspects. There have also been proposals to track more closely foreign imams and foreign funding of domestic mosques and even a governmental proposal to require regular reporting to the police by anyone suspected of radical leanings. Increased monitoring has resulted in raids, round ups, arrests and trials of hundreds of suspected Islamist terrorists. France, Germany, Italy, the Netherlands and Spain have each engaged in active repression of potential perpetrators of religiously motivated violence. In addition, many of these countries have translated the monitoring of mosques into expulsions of so-called 'rogue imams'. France has been among the most active states in this respect, with dozens of religious leaders deported since 2001, but Germany and the Netherlands have also shifted their laws and policies to facilitate expulsions.[10]

Integration of Muslims has been equally high on European agendas. Religious consultation and representation have become a popular way to reach out to Muslim communities, as evidenced both by post-crisis meetings with Muslim leaders and by state encouragement of more formalized bodies, such as France's Council of the Muslim Faith (CFCM), Spain's Islamic Commission or Italy's Consultative Council for Islam, each set up since 2003 (Laurence 2005, 2006).[11] In recent years, European governments have also proven more willing than ever to fund initiatives specifically for the Muslim community. Whether financing privately organized Dutch language and culture training programmes for imams and Muslim chaplains, setting up university degree programmes in 'contemporary French civilization' for future imams, or enabling foundations in Spain and France that aid Muslim communities, these initiatives have taken new forms and deeper roots over the past few years.[12]

European states have balanced policies that *enable* integration of religious minorities with policies that *compel* integration by obliging a degree of cultural conformity. The most notable policy in recent years is undoubtedly the 2004 French law banning religious symbols worn by students in public schools. Although cast in religiously neutral terms that apply to visible symbols of all faiths, the law's purpose was clearly to ban Muslim headscarves. Paralleling the

French policy but on a smaller scale, five of the 16 German federal states have outlawed headscarves for public school teachers, and in the wake of the July 2005 London bombings, the Italian government instituted heavy fines and imprisonment for wearing a burqa in public (Laurence 2006), and both Dutch and French political leaders have voiced support for banning the burqa outside of the home.[13]

Britain's specific approach to countering Islamist extremism fits Europe's general three-pronged pattern quite closely. By early 2003, the government had launched its CONTEST counterterrorism strategy, which encompassed four core strands: PREVENT, PURSUE, PROTECT and PREPARE. In brief, the PREVENT strand reflects the third prong of integrating Muslims into British society through a focus on addressing disadvantages, challenging extremist ideologies and undermining the grounds that give rise to terrorist impulses. The PURSUE angle echoes the second prong of repressing violence by focusing on disrupting Muslim terrorists via intelligence gathering, police work and prosecutions. The PROTECT and PREPARE elements are closest to the first prong of the common state response in that they are generic policies – i.e. not specific to Muslim terrorism – aimed at reducing the vulnerability of targets and enabling a rapid and effective response to an attack.[14]

Generic policies: how much focus on Islam?

Looking more closely at the fit between the strands of the British approach and each prong of the general model reveals the challenges of responding to Islamist extremism. In particular, British policymaking has been quite contradictory and conflicted in the extent to which it acknowledges the Muslim element of extremism and terrorism confronting the state. For example, while the PROTECT and PREPARE policies are the most generic elements of its overall strategy, they form part of the overall CONTEST approach. As such, they are packaged as part of a strategy that describes the 'principal current terrorist threat' to Britain as emanating from 'radicalized individuals who are using a distorted and unrepresentative version of the Islamic faith to justify violence', and which argues that 'the current threat from Islamist terrorism is serious and sustained' (HM Government 2006: 1).

Yet, as this language implies, British governmental officials have carefully chosen their words when discussing the 'Islamist' dimension of the problem. The very same summary of the CONTEST strategy takes pains to emphasize that such perpetrators are 'a tiny minority within the Muslim communities here and abroad' and that 'Muslim communities themselves do not threaten our security; indeed they make a great contribution to our country' (HM Government 2006: 1). This explains the choice of 'Islamist' rather than 'Islamic' to describe such terrorists and the overwhelming use of the euphemism 'international terrorism' to summarize the threat in a way that avoids repetition of the words Islam or Muslim. It also accounts for the complete neutrality of language in the PROTECT and PREPARE elements of the CONTEST strategy. British policymakers very quickly developed an instinct to avoid linkages between terrorism and Islam wherever possible. This is reflected in discussions of protecting public places and preparing for the consequences of attacks, which are framed in the neutral language of dealing with a generic attack. It is also reflected in the Brown administration's transition away from discussing the 'war on terror', which many Muslims had come to see as code for targeting Islam. In the immediate aftermath of the June 2007 attack on Glasgow airport, the new prime minister avoided this catchphrase, as well as any mention of the word 'Muslim,' a studied neutrality that both he and his home secretary repeated when introducing the latest version of the CONTEST strategy in March 2009.[15]

In large part, downplaying the 'Muslim' angle of 'Islamist terrorism' is an element of a conscious strategy of responding to such extremism. However, in some measure, it also reflects the reality that focusing on Muslims is likely to be counterproductive in more ways than one. Apart from demonizing and alienating a faith group within the country and all of the disadvantages that accrue to divided states, a recent report by the British security service MI5 concluded that it is not possible to develop a profile of the typical British terrorist. It found that most are 'demographically unremarkable' and that assumptions cannot be made based on skin colour, ethnic heritage or nationality.[16] At the same time, however, and reflecting the difficulty of calibrating a response to Islamist extremism, the report stressed that the most pressing threat to Britain today is from Islamist extremist groups, while also acknowledging that there are violent extremists in non-Islamic movements.

Repressing Islamist extremism

Britain's contemporary legal arsenal for repressing terrorism was initially for-mulated in the 1970s following the onset of attacks by the Irish Republicanism movements. By the late 1990s, government leaders felt the need to systematize the country's aggregation of piecemeal legislative tools. The Terrorism Act 2000 was designed to alleviate some criticisms of the longstanding Prevention of Terrorism Act,[17] but it contained surprisingly little mention of Islamist terrorism. In a sign of the times, a March 2000 BBC story about the pending legislation described it as covering 'acts by animal activists, direct action by environmental protesters, computer hackers, acts motivated by religious beliefs and action against property such as that in last year's riots and anti-capitalist protests in London'.[18] The fact that Islamist extremism was not a primary factor motivating the 2000 law stands in sharp contrast to legislation passed since that time. Britain has enacted four major laws since 9/11 (see also Gregory, Chapter 4 in this volume). The Anti-Terrorism, Crime and Security Act 2001, the Prevention of Terrorism Act 2005 (enacted prior to the 7/7 bombings), the Terrorism Act 2006 and the Counter-Terrorism Act 2008 have each refined and extended British powers to repress terrorism in ways that enable the PURSUE strand of the country's overall counterterrorism strategy. Although such legislation seldom explicitly mentions religion or Islam, each has been a direct response to the perceived threat of Islamist terrorism and has been used primarily to target Muslim extremists.

Taken together, Britain's anti-terrorism provisions have endowed the country with potent tools for countering extremist acts. They increase police powers for investigation and detention of suspected terrorists; they make it illegal to incite terrorism or to provide training for terrorist purposes; they outlaw statements that involve the 'glorification' of terrorism; they allow the government to freeze and to seize financial assets associated with terrorism or with terrorists; they proscribe organizations deemed by the government to be involved in terrorism, making it an offence to belong to, support or display support for that organization; they enable the government to enforce 'control orders' on suspected terrorists who cannot be convicted or deported, limiting their freedom of movement and association; and they facilitate deprivation of British citizenship and even deportation for those connected to terrorism.[19]

While most of these repressive measures have their roots in legislation, there are also policy programmes that have been deployed as part of the PURSUE strategy. Most importantly, Britain has re-organized its intelligence services to streamline the gathering and analysis of information about terrorist threats. Its Joint Terrorism Analysis Centre (JTAC) was created in 2003 to coordinate the efforts of the intelligence community. It involves members of the Security Service (MI5), the Secret Intelligence Service (SIS), the Government Communications Headquarters (GCHQ), the Defence Intelligence Staff, and representatives from the Foreign and Commonwealth Office, the Home Office and the police services. This group is responsible for assembling and analysing information about potential terrorist threats and for setting the official threat level within Britain.[20] Its explicit focus is on 'international terrorism', which is summarized as 'Al Qaida and related terrorist groups'.[21] As such, it has become a prominent organization in the fight against Islamist extremism.[22] National and local police forces have also been reorganized or reconstituted to improve their ability to address terrorist threats (HM Government 2009: 63–4).

These tools have been applied in practice with significant effect. While data on sensitive or undercover investigations are closely guarded by authorities, official government reports claim numerous disruptions of potential attacks within Britain since 2000 (HM Government 2006: 17, 2009: 62). In 2007/8, the Metropolitan Police Service (Met) reported 3,458 information referrals related to terrorism, all of which were given an initial assessment within the five days called for by intelligence protocols; the Met also reported 13 terrorist network disruptions in that same time period.[23] Between January and May 2008, the Met arrested 46 people based on terrorist investigations, 10 of whom were charged.[24] Nationwide, over 40 people were convicted on terrorism charges in 2007/8, receiving a combined total of 600 years in prison sentences. In one high-profile case, the surviving perpetrator of the Glasgow airport attack was handed down two life sentences in December 2008 for his acts.[25] Also, as of June 2008, 15 control orders were in place, six of which had been served since March 2008 and three of which applied to British citizens.[26] These data demonstrate that the British state is making significant use of its increased powers of repression.

It has also applied its powers to ban Islamist militant groups, enforcing them against Al Ghurabaa and the Saved Sect on the grounds that they glorified terrorism. These groups were the successors to the controversial Al Muhajiroun organization, led by Omar Bakri Mohammad, who has been barred from re-entering Britain, and were seen as mobilizing forces behind the inflammatory protests of the Danish cartoons in February 2006. As of July 2006, it became an offence to belong to, encourage support for, or display clothing or articles that symbolize these groups. In explaining the decision, Home Secretary John Reid said 'I am determined to act against those who, while not directly involved in committing acts of terrorism, provide support for and make statements that glorify, celebrate and exalt the atrocities of terrorist groups.'[27]

While it is not always clear how many terrorism-related arrests, prosecutions, convictions, deportations, bans and control orders specifically target Muslims, virtually all of the individual cases that have come to light involve Islamists.[28] A 2006 government report lists five successful prosecutions, including those of Mohammed Ajmal Khan, Abu Hamza, Andrew Rowe (a British Muslim convert), Saajid Badat and Kamel Bourgass, who received combined sentences of 61 years for offences such as conspiracy to provide money for a terrorist attack, solicitation to murder, possession of an article for a terrorist purpose, conspiring to destroy an aircraft and plotting to manufacture homemade poisons and explosives (HM Government 2006: 18). In two other prominent cases, six Muslim men were convicted in April 2008 of incitement to terrorism or of inviting others to provide money to support terrorism,[29] and the four Muslim suspects in the 21 July 2005 attempted bombing were sentenced in June 2008 to a combined total of 44 years in prison.[30] The British state has thus shown itself to be aggressive in surveillance, arrests, convictions and control of suspected Islamist extremists in a way that has undoubtedly saved lives and provided a significant deterrent to acts of violence.

Yet the PURSUE element of the CONTEST strategy has had notable and sometimes tragic setbacks. The day after the 21 July 2005 attempted attacks on the London transportation system, the police shot and killed Brazilian electrician Jean Charles de Menezes, mistaking him for a dangerous suspect. In June 2006, claiming specific intelligence gleaned from months of surveillance, police raided a home in the Forest Gate section of London.[31] They shot 23 year old Mohammed Abdulkahar in the process of arresting him. He and his brother were released a week later without charges and with the apologies of the police.[32] The final bill for the failed operation was over £2.2 million.[33]

There have also been significant failures in applying the terrorism laws. In spite of the government's insistence – over heated objections – that 2006 provisions banning the glorification of terrorism were necessary, they have seldom been applied. Although they were part of the justification for banning Al Ghurabaa and the Saved Sect, they have not proven enforceable against other controversial groups that Prime Minister Blair explicitly vowed to disband – such as Hizb-ut-Tahrir[34] – nor against the sole individual against which they have been tested.[35] Moreover, in a September 2008 decision which *The Times* described as 'a severe blow to Britain's anti-terrorist campaign', a jury failed to convict eight defendants of an August 2006 plot to blow up transatlantic flights.[36] The Crown

Prosecution Service immediately vowed to retry seven of the eight defendants – the eighth having been found not guilty – as part of an effort to salvage the £10 million, two-year-long case, and in September 2009 it obtained three convictions of the men involved.[37]

In sum, British authorities have endowed themselves with potent resources for pursuing Islamist extremists, and have shown a readiness to use these tools. There have been stepped up surveillance, arrests, prosecutions, convictions, deportations and other forms of repression of extremists in recent years. While authorities have at times encountered major problems in enforcing their PURSUE strategy, there can be no doubt that increasing repression has been a major axis of activity since the events of 9/11 and especially since the attacks of 7/7. In spite of some high profile failures, this effort to repress has to be seen at least as a qualified success in that it has undoubtedly thwarted a number of attacks, and inasmuch as it reassures the public that the government is active and capable of protecting its citizens from great harm.

Integrating Muslims into British society

British leaders have been at the forefront of developing policies designed to facilitate Muslim integration. From the outset of the CONTEST strategy, the PREVENT element has focused centrally on five key strands that aim to stop people from 'becoming or supporting terrorists or violent extremists' (HM Government 2008: 6):

1 challenging violent extremist ideology and supporting mainstream voices;
2 disrupting those who promote violent extremism;
3 supporting individuals who are being recruited to terrorism;
4 increasing communities' ability to respond to challenges of violent extremism; and
5 addressing grievances exploited by extremist ideologues.

From the government's point of view, the goal is 'winning hearts and minds' of people who might be attracted to terrorism or extremism. To do this, officials try to distinguish between those who are committing terrorist acts, those sympathizers who are in the circle of tacit support, and those who reject extremism and fully embrace life in Britain. It aims to isolate the active extremists, sway the fence-sitters, and support mainstream Muslims. The government's rhetoric serves to reinforce these points:

> This is not about a clash of civilizations or a struggle between Islam and 'the West'. It is about standing up to a small fringe of terrorists and their extremist supporters. Indeed, Government is committed to working in partnership with the vast majority of Muslims who reject violence and who share core British values in doing this.
>
> (Communities and Local Government 2007: 4)[38]

This strategy of integration has two main axes. It seeks to discipline Muslims that are susceptible to terrorist activities as well as to encourage all Muslims to take part in British society. It is a dual strategy of repression and accommodation that in itself entails a stick and a carrot, thereby supplementing the pure stick of repression embodied in the PURSUE strand of the CONTEST strategy.

A major part of the effort to delegitimize extremists involves fostering acceptable Islamic discourse within the country. One of the government's leading initiatives in this respect is its funding of *The Radical Middle Way*, which bills itself as 'a revolutionary grassroots initiative' whose goal is to bring young British Muslims into contact with Islamic scholars from around the world.[39] Since being founded in 2005, it has served as an independent, government-funded bridge between British Muslims and authoritative, anti-extremist Islamic scholarship. With government support, the Radical Middle Way has organized a number of 'roadshows' in which respected Islamic leaders from the Middle East and other regions travel around Britain speaking to public forums.

Additionally, the government has stepped up efforts to introduce citizenship instruction in local mosque schools (*madrassahs*). Approximately 100,000 children between the ages of five and 14 attend *madrassahs* in Britain, typically for two hours after school each day (Communities and Local Government 2007: 5). The Department of Communities and Local Government and the Department for Children, Schools and Families are coordinating with Muslim communities to develop an understanding of best practices and best curricula and to push for wider adoption of citizenship programmes in *madrassahs* across the country (Communities and Local Government 2007: 5–6; HM Government 2008: 22).[40] In undertaking these steps, the government is also attempting to provide a more prominent platform for mainstream views in order to marginalize extremist ones.

The strategy is complemented by a concerted effort to foster moderate leadership in the British Muslim community. The central government and local partners have created a wide variety of schemes for identifying those least likely to tilt toward extremism, and then for building their skills in ways that are calculated to discourage extremist activities among the community as a whole. The clearest examples of this policy involve establishing criteria and training for imams. Just before leaving office, Prime Minister Blair announced an additional £1 million in funding for Islamic Studies at UK universities, designating the topic a strategically important subject. This decision was based on the logic that such courses can help produce British-trained imams and undermine extremism.[41] Like most programmes in the UK, its application often differs by locality. The accent on training imams, for example, has taken a more specific form through the Black Country Imams project, which focuses on developing language and other skills for 36 imams from Dudley, Wolverhampton, Sandwell, Walsall and Birmingham (HM Government 2008: 18–19). These programmes are often piloted in specific regions or by local governments, and then heralded as potential models from which others can learn.

While there is significant local variation in how such programmes are developed and applied, there are also national standards that increasingly govern imams in Britain. As of August 2004, for example, the British government mandated that anyone entering the UK to work as a minister of religion prove a command of the English language.[42] Prison Service imams have received national training in an effort to help them work with convicted terrorists or those susceptible to radicalization while in prison (HM Government 2006: 13). As government-paid employees, these imams are subject to the new minimum standards for all Muslim chaplains employed by the state, whether in prisons, healthcare, the Ministry of Defence or in educational institutions (Communities and Local Government 2007: 11–12, 2008: 45).

Beyond improving the skills of imams, the government has also made an effort to reach out to women and faith-based organizations. The National Muslim Women's Advisory Group focuses on thinking through ways to empower Muslim women by increasing their role in 'civic, economic and social life'. According to one government publication, 'women can play a vital role in building strong communities and tackling violent extremism' (Communities and Local Government 2007: 9–10). This is a fascinating and innovative gamble by the government in a number of respects. It is an attempt to hear the voices of average Muslim women through moderate leaders, an effort to spur women to dispel stereotypes about their role in Islam, and a concrete initiative to empower Muslim women at the local level.[43] Women as a class of people are thus being cultivated as strategic actors that can turn others away from extremism. Given that most extremists are men, this may be an effective strategy if it is not seen as patronizing or as an effort to recruit informants. The government has also set aside £600,000 to establish a Faith and Social Cohesion Unit, designed to support the governance and effectiveness of faith-based community oriented groups, and to encourage unregistered groups to register themselves in order to take advantage of tax breaks (Communities and Local Government 2008: 45).[44] Of course, the government's stake in registration is better knowledge of such groups' activities and a certain amount of oversight.

Muslim youths have also been the target of a number of government schemes, although in this case the goal appears to be equal part leadership training and diversion of at-risk individuals from less desirable activities. In two examples of touted local initiatives, the Leytonstone Muslim Community Centre has provided a leadership programme for youth in higher education who were 'at risk of isolation and detachment from their previous support networks', while another organization worked with younger men in a deprived ward in the London Borough of Waltham Forest, dealing with a range of issues surrounding citizenship, conflict resolution, and coping skills for managing the risks of antisocial behaviour, including extremism (HM Government 2008: 33). Because one of the government's stated objectives is to support individuals vulnerable to terrorist recruitment, it has encouraged local communities to sensitize service providers – such as teachers, social workers, and law and order employees – to the potential radicalization of individuals they come into contact with. In October 2008, to give one example,

Secretary of State Ed Balls announced a £4.68 million initiative to disseminate an anti-extremism toolkit in schools, with advice for teachers trying to deal with students exhibiting extremist tendencies.[45] The government has also pushed to develop referral networks that can further assess the danger of radicalization, as well as programmes such as mentoring services that can be deployed to help deter any further slide toward extremist sympathy or behaviour (HM Government 2008: 27–9).

The steps listed thus far have been aimed principally at promoting moderate Islamic thought and mainstream Muslim leaders and at diverting potential extremists in the direction of a less radical path. It is no accident that this range of policies dovetails with a renewed emphasis on 'Britishness' as a way to cement a common identity and with a corresponding de-emphasis of 'multiculturalism' on the grounds that it may undermine community cohesion.[46] Although the concrete steps outlined above – like almost all undertaken under the integration umbrella – have both a repressive and an accommodating aspect, they are closer to the repressive end of the spectrum in their primary focus on curbing negative behaviour. Policies falling under this umbrella are designed less to reach out to Muslims on their own terms than they are to discourage discourse, activities and leaders judged to have failed the test of integration.

By contrast, there have also been a host of policy initiatives that reflect a softer side of the push to integrate Muslims into British society. In particular, the government has approached Muslim communities in an effort to encourage dialogue surrounding issues high on their agendas. Immediately following the July 2005 attacks, the prime minister and the home secretary hosted two meetings with Muslim leaders and agreed to establish community-led working groups to recommend ways to tackle extremism. Various ministers also hosted or attended meetings over the course of the next year in an effort to open lines of communication with Muslims and to engage in outreach to Muslim communities. For example, the government supported several regional 'Muslim Forums against Extremism and Islamophobia', which brought together Muslim community members, law enforcement officials, and public service providers to discuss not only how to curb extremism, but also a range of issues relevant to Muslims themselves (HM Government 2006: 13–14) and they have encouraged local authorities to conduct similar forums in order to field Muslim grievances (HM Government 2008: 36–7).

Efforts to facilitate communication with Muslims are also reflected in on-going groups such as the Muslim Women's Network and its successor the National Muslim Women's Advisory Group, which have been facilitated and at times chaired by ministers who are seeking to connect with the Muslim community (HM Government 2006: 13, 2008: 31, 34).[47] While these groups are partly intended to strengthen actors deemed less extremist, they also serve as direct conduits for Muslims to voice their concerns to high government officials. Similarly, the Muslim Safety Forum coordinates meetings between Muslim leaders and police representatives to discuss community concerns, mainly related to extremism but also touching upon other issues (HM Government 2006: 22).

The PREVENT initiative has also instituted a public relations campaign in the wider Muslim world, and has sent delegations of British Muslims abroad to help refute the image of Britain as being anti-Islam (HM Government 2006: 16). Through these initiatives, the government hopes to show that it is listening to and taking seriously Muslim voices.

The outreach to Muslim communities involves several highly symbolic changes to the criminal code that are meant to show that the state is not just listening but also acting upon Muslim concerns. Britain's Anti-Terrorism, Crime and Security Act 2001 included provisions outlawing religiously aggravated offences which extended the Crime and Disorder Act's 1998 concept of racially aggravated offences. As of the 2001 law, crimes motivated by or displaying hostility against people because of their faith are subject to additional penalties. Given that there was tremendous concern about anti-Muslim attacks in the wake of 9/11, this move was meant to take the edge off what was otherwise a very repressive law. The government also made several attempts to broaden incitement to racial hatred provisions to cover incitement to religious hatred. Although these were hotly contested, much delayed, and eventually watered down, they were implemented in 2006 through the Racial and Religious Hatred Act.

In a civil law vein, prominent figures such as the Archbishop of Canterbury and the Lord Chief Justice have bucked public and elite political opinion by endorsing adaptation of certain elements of sharia law within Britain.[48] In spite of vociferous criticism of the idea from many quarters – including from Sadiq Khan, a junior minister in the Department of Communities and Local Government as of October 2008 – sharia courts began passing binding judgments in 2007 under the auspices of the Arbitration Act 1996 (which also governs the use of Jewish Beth Din courts), *The Times* reported in September 2008.[49] While some of these steps may backfire by arousing public resentment or even outrage – especially in the case of sharia courts – such legal developments in the criminal and civil spheres constitute signals to Muslims that they are protected on a par with analogous groups.

The effort to integrate Muslims into mainstream policymaking extends to programmes aimed at fighting socioeconomic disadvantage, to programmes aimed to help faith groups, and to citizenship education about Britain's multicultural composition. For example, the government's broad social cohesion plans focus not just on racial issues, but also explicitly on reducing inequalities associated with faith, and even more specifically on steps that can help Muslims improve their educational, employment and housing situation (HM Government 2006: 11; Home Office 2005). The government also launched a Faith Communities Capacity Building Fund in early 2005 which by mid-2006 had already spent £7.7 million, of which £1.5 million went to Muslim organizations (HM Government 2006: 11). And the Department for Education and Skills recently published Sir Keith Ajegbo's *Curriculum Review on Diversity and Citizenship*, which recommends – among many steps – extending an understanding of Islam and Islamic culture, society and history across all communities in an effort to diminish misunderstandings and prejudices in the broader population (Department for Education and Skills 2007: 18; HM Government 2008). These efforts run parallel to those designed to promote inter-faith dialogues and understanding that have been popular in Britain and many other countries since 9/11 (Home Office 2005: 46).

Most broadly, the government has taken up the banner of Islamophobia as a major cause for national concern. It has used this term as a way to signal to Muslims that it is aware of a problem faced by their community, and as a rationale for broad outreach that includes public statements and symbols of support by high government officials (Joppke 2009). State officials have translated the abstract concern about Islamophobia into concrete policy initiatives, such as the late 2004 Association of Chief of Police Officers joint initiative 'Islamophobia – Don't Suffer in Silence', which distributed 50,000 information packets to Muslim community venues and to police stations that were designed to encourage reporting of anti-Muslim incidents.[50] While some critics (Joppke 2009) charge that this platform has promised Muslims more than it can deliver – thereby arousing resentment and a quest for ever-greater recognition – its ambition is to demonstrate clearly that British government officials are ready, willing and able to divert energy, attention and resources toward fostering integration in the Muslim community.

The goal of integrating Muslims more firmly into the British national community has thus been pursued through a number of avenues and through a wide variety of policy initiatives. Some are small-scale, local projects that vary by region or city, and others are national in scope. In total, the government has allocated tens of millions of pounds, hundreds of personnel and countless hours to the task.[51] While integration efforts at times have their repressive side, they also represent an honest effort to reach out to Muslims.[52] Naturally, the government is not undertaking these initiatives out of the goodness of its heart. Attempts to integrate Muslims would not have been nearly as extensive were it not for the government's fear of extremism and its calculated strategy that integrating Muslims into British society is a necessary for the security of the country as a whole.

Conclusion

British state responses to Islamist extremism have conformed to an overlapping three-pronged strategy of consciously downplaying the Islamic element of the threat, repressing Muslim extremist activity and integrating Muslims through a dual strategy that itself involves elements of repression and accommodation. It is worth emphasizing that many of the specific policies deployed embody more than one of the three prongs. The notion of community-based counter-terrorism policing, for example, involves outreach to community members in order to gather better information about potential threats. This strategy encompasses both an effort to repress terrorism, as well as an attempt to integrate communities as sympathetic stakeholders in the policing process (Klausen 2009; also Chapters 4 & 5, this volume).

There have also been dynamic elements to British state responses that suggest limits to any completely static interpretation of the three-pronged framework. The scope of repression and especially of integration efforts has greatly expanded over time. This is true comparing developments pre- and post-9/11 and even more so for those pre- and post-7/7. There have also been small recalibrations of government terminology when discussing extremism. Most official publications dance around the Islamic or Muslim nature of the threat by referring briefly to Islamist terrorism before recasting the analysis in more faith-neutral terms. However, Gordon Brown has gone further than Tony Blair in emphasizing that terrorism is a criminal undertaking, and not one necessarily associated with any particular faith community. His avoidance of catchphrases like the 'war on terror' suggests the government may increasingly shy away from terms that imply a connection to Islam, at least in events for public consumption.

Framing British responses to Islamist extremism as an overlapping three-pronged strategy remains very useful for grasping the main axes of Britain's policies, however. It has the additional advantage of unveiling many of the internal tensions between the constituent parts of the overall approach. Is it possible, for instance, to both strong arm and to reach out to Muslims in an effort to encourage integration? How can the state walk the fine line between repressing certain members of a community and encouraging others to feel fully part of British society? And rhetorically, is it logical to say in the same breath that Islamist extremism is the biggest security problem in Britain, but then stress that Muslims are not a threat and to euphemize the challenge as one of 'international' terrorism?

Although these internal contradictions may raise questions about the effectiveness of the overall strategy, examining Britain's approach in comparative perspective suggests that it fits squarely into a common European pattern among states coping with Islamist extremism. European countries must balance competing ideas and interests in crafting their policy responses, and it has been the competition among these forces that have propelled all nations to adopt an overlapping three-pronged strategy. States such as Britain have to acknowledge that Islamists are perpetrating deadly attacks, but also reassure the public that most Muslims reject such actions. They must demonstrate to the general public that they are capable of disrupting terrorist networks and promoting national cohesion, while also showing Muslims that they can be full citizens and not simply national pariahs.

These competing tasks are undeniably in tension with one another. As a result, liberal democratic states such as Britain are forced to develop policies that attempt to target each issue and each constituency as precisely as possible. Among European countries, Britain has been at the forefront of devoting time, energy and resources to this conundrum in a way that makes it a model from which other states can learn a great deal. Not all of its specific policies will have the intended effect, and the effect of many programmes will be impossible to judge by any standard policy yardsticks. But this may be the nature of dealing with problems that will inevitably vex policymakers trying to walk the fine line required to maximize cohesion and undermine extremism.

Notes

1 The author would like to thank Roger Eatwell, Matthew Goodwin and Shamit Saggar for their helpful input in the planning and execution of this essay, as well as Francesca Lambert for exceptional research assistance.
2 For an expanded discussion see also Bleich (2009).
3 The 2001 Census records 1.6 million Muslims, but a 2008 statement by the Home Secretary places the number closer to 2 million (*Guardian*, 8 April 2008).
4 Available online: http://www.statistics.gov.uk/cci/nugget.asp?id=958 (accessed 4 November 2008).
5 *New York Times*, 20 October 2004. Abu Hamza Al-Masri was the imam of the Finsbury Park Mosque, which both Richard Reid and Zacarias Moussaoui reportedly attended before their arrests.
6 See Ipsos MORI 'Attitudes of British Muslims' and 'Muslims "Take Pride" in British Way of Life.'
7 Ipsos MORI 'Muslims "Take Pride" in British Way of Life' and 'Muslim Attitudes – The Real Story'.
8 Ipsos MORI 'Attitudes of British Muslims' and *Telegraph*, 20 February 2006.
9 *Telegraph*, 20 February 2006.
10 For an extended discussion of developments across Western Europe, see Bleich (2009).
11 US Department of State. Available online: http://www.state.gov/g/drl/rls/irf/2004/35485.htm (accessed 19 December 2008).
12 *New York Times*, 18 October 2004; *Le Figaro*, 10 March 2005; *New York Times*, 24 October 2004.
13 BBC News, 16 January 2006; Aljazeera, 9 March 2006; BBC News, 17 November 2006; BBC News, 22 June 2009. Local authorities in Belgium and Italy had also previously enacted or enforced bans on burqas, justifying the move by arguing that appearing masked in public presents a threat to security (IHF 2005: 46, 100–1).
14 For the most recent assessment of the CONTEST strategy, see HM Government (2009).
15 *Washington Post*, 4 July 2007; *New York Times*, 4 July 2007; *New York Times*, 22 July 2007; HM Government (2009: 4–5).
16 According to a classified internal research document on radicalization reported in *Guardian*, 21 August 2008.
17 The Prevention of Terrorism Act was passed in 1974 and was renewable annually.
18 BBC News, 15 March 2000.
19 The Immigration, Asylum and Nationality Act 2006 facilitates deprivation of citizenship, the right to abode and refugee status.
20 For the government's summary of JTAC, see http://www.intelligence.gov.uk/agencies/jtac.aspx (accessed 29 October 2008).
21 See http://www.mi5.gov.uk/output/international-terrorism.html (accessed 21 October 2009).
22 Britain's strategy also has an international dimension. In the fiscal year 2005/6, the UK spent over £7 million helping other nations with their counter-terrorism programmes; for example, it provided training and liaised with authorities in places such as Pakistan, Malaysia and North Africa (HM Government 2006: 22).
23 See Metropolitan Police Authority, Report 7b of the 24 July 2008 meeting, at http://www.mpa.gov.uk/committees/mpa/2008/080724/07b.htm (accessed 30 October 2008).
24 Ibid.

25 BBC News, 17 December 2008.
26 See Control Orders Update, Statement by Tony McNulty to Parliament, 12 June 2008, at http://security.homeoffice.gov.uk/news-publications/news-speeches/control-orders-update-0608 (accessed 30 October 2008).
27 *The Times*, 18 July 2006.
28 As of December 2008, there were 45 groups proscribed in the UK under the Terrorism Act 2000, the vast majority of which are Islamist groups. There are also 14 Irish groups proscribed under earlier legislation. See http://www.homeoffice.gov.uk/security/terrorism-and-the-law/terrorism-act/proscribed-groups (accessed 18 December 2008).
29 See http://cms.met.police.uk/news/convictions/six_men_convicted_of_terrorism_offences (accessed 30 October 2008).
30 See Metropolitan Police Authority, Report 7b of the 24 July 2008 meeting, at http://www.mpa.gov.uk/committees/mpa/2008/080724/07b.htm (accessed 30 October 2008).
31 BBC News, 2 June 2006.
32 BBC News, 10 June 2006; BBC News, 14 June 2006.
33 BBC News, 3 October 2006.
34 *Observer*, 24 December 2006.
35 This is the case of Abu Izzadeen, aka Omar or Trevor Brooks. See *The Times*, 9 February 2007.
36 *The Times*, 9 September 2008.
37 *The Times*, 9 September 2008; BBC News, 7 September 2009.
38 For more information on the strategy, and on the Preventing Violent Extremism Pathfinder Fund launched in October 2006, see Lowndes and Thorpe (Chapter 6, this volume).
39 http://www.radicalmiddleway.co.uk/about_us.php (accessed 10 November 2008).
40 See also http://theiceproject.com/ (accessed 10 November 2008).
41 BBC News, 4 June 2007.
42 The mandate also requires them to prove that they are ordained or have been practicing as a minister for at least 12 months out of the preceding five years. See http://www.workpermit.com/news/2004_08_23/uk/immigration_rules_for_ ministers_of_religion.htm (accessed 18 December 2008).
43 The multiple justifications for the initiative were given in January 2008 when the NMWAG was officially launched by Prime Minister Brown: http://www.communities.gov.uk/news/corporate/680335 (accessed 18 December 2008).
44 See also http://www.charity-commission.gov.uk/tcc/faithsc.asp (accessed 10 November 2008).
45 See *The Times*, 8 October 2008; see also the website of the Department for Children, Schools and Families, http://www.dcsf.gov.uk/publications/violentextremism/toolkitforschools/(accessed 12 November 2008).
46 See the 2006 statements by then head of the Commission for Racial Equality Trevor Phillips in response to Gordon Brown's call for a national 'proud-to-be-British' day (*Guardian*, 14 January 2006).
47 See also http://www.communities.gov.uk/news/corporate/680335 (accessed 11 November 2008).
48 BBC News, 8 February 2008; BBC News, 4 July 2008; *Guardian*, 4 July 2008.
49 *The Times*, 14 September 2008.
50 See the Forum Against Islamophobia and Racism's 16 November 2004 press release 'Police and Muslim Communities Work Together to Tackle Islamophobia', http://www.fairuk.org/pressreleases/2004/20041116FAIRUK_Press_Release.pdf (accessed 12 November 2008).
51 See speech by Rt Hon Hazel Blears, MP, Secretary of State for Communities and Local Government, speech 31 October 2007 to the Preventing Extremism Conference, at

http://www.communities.gov.uk/speeches/corporate/preventingextremism   (accessed 12 November 2008).
52 This is not to imply that they have all been successful, nor that the government's strategy is the best possible one. For a thoughtful critique, see Thomas (2009).

References

Abrams, D. and Houston, D.M. (2006) *Equality, Diversity and Prejudice in Britain: Results from the 2005 National Survey*, Canterbury: Centre for the Study of Group Processes, University of Kent.

Bleich, E. (2009) 'State responses to "Muslim" violence: a comparison of six West European countries', *Journal of Ethnic and Migration Studies*, 35(3): 361–79.

Department for Education and Skills (2007) *Diversity and Citizenship Curriculum Review*, London: Department for Education and Skills.

Department of Communities and Local Government (2007) *Preventing Violent Extremism – Winning Hearts and Minds*, London: Department of Communities and Local Government.

—— (2008) *Preventing Violent Extremism: Next Steps for Communities*, London: Department of Communities and Local Government.

HM Government (2006) *Countering International Terrorism: The United Kingdom's Strategy*, London: HM Government.

—— (2008) *The Prevent Strategy: A Guide for Local Partners in England*, London: HM Government.

—— (2009) *The United Kingdom's Strategy for Countering International Terrorism*, London: HM Government.

Home Office (2005) *Improving Opportunity, Strengthening Society: The Government's Strategy to Increase Race Equality and Community Cohesion*, London: Home Office.

IHF (2005) *Intolerance and Discrimination against Muslims in the EU: Developments since September 11*, Vienna: International Helsinki Federation for Human Rights.

Joppke, C. (2009) 'Limits of integration policy: Britain and her Muslims', *Journal of Ethnic and Migration Studies*, 35(3): 453–72.

Kepel, G. (2004) *The War for Muslim Minds: Islam in the West*, trans. P. Ghazaleh, Cambridge: Harvard University Press.

Klausen, J. (2009) 'British counter-terrorism after 7/7: adapting community-policing to the fight against domestic terrorism', *Journal of Ethnic and Migration Studies*, 35(3): 403–20.

Laurence, J. (2005) 'From the elysée salon to the table of the republic: state–Islam relations and the integration of Muslims in France', *French Politics, Culture & Society*, 23(1): 37–64.

—— (2006) *Knocking on Europe's Door: Islam in Italy*, US–Europe Analysis Series, Washington, DC: The Brookings Institution.

Saggar, S. (2009) 'Boomerangs and slingshots: radical Islamism and counter-terrorism strategy', *Journal of Ethnic and Migration Studies*, 35(3): 381–402.

Thomas, P. (2009) 'Between two stools? The government's "Preventing violent extremism" agenda', *Political Quarterly*, 80(2): 282–91.

4 Policing the 'new extremism' in twenty-first-century Britain

Frank Gregory

Introduction

Since the development of Britain's modern police system in the nineteenth century the policing of suspect or actual criminality related to a political purpose as opposed to private gain has tended to reflect the dominant concerns of each time period. Thus, at the end of the nineteenth century there was a pre-occupation with anarchists and Irish republican groups (Clutterbuck 2006). In the period from 1917 to 1939 the preoccupation was with 'bolsheviks', 'communists' and 'fascists'. Post-1945 the spectrum has included 'communists', Irish groups such as the Provisional Irish Republican Army (PIRA), nationalist terrorist groups such as the Popular Front for the Liberation of Palestine (PFLP) and the Palestinian Liberation Organization (PLO), animal-rights groups, anti-capitalist groups, anarchist groups such as the Angry Brigade, right-wing extremist groups and now Islamist extremists. However, until the development of the UK response to the events of 9/11 and the London bombings in July 2005, the policing requirements were more limited in nature in terms of operational policing except during periods of terrorist activity by Irish groups. Essentially, the police Special Branch (SB) structure dealt with the investigation of suspect behaviour that might lead to breaches of the Official Secrets Act or ordinary crimes with a political motivation. The police, other than the SB personnel, in any given local area would mostly become involved if any of the activities pursued for political purposes that caused either public order problems (e.g. violence at political rallies) or the commission of other crimes such as break-ins to animal-testing laboratories.

By contrast the Prevent strand of the UK Government's post-9/11 CONTEST counter-terrorism strategy (HMG 2006, 2008a, 2009) has emphasized 'community-policing principles and partnerships with Muslim groups' (Klausen 2007). Community-policing is a resource significant pro-active policing task and, moreover, one that is always at risk from demands for police resources for re-active policing (for detailed studies of community policing in the UK see Fielding 1995; Grabosky 2008; Skinns 2008). In addition, the current Prevent strategy lays heavy emphasis on the inter-agency aspect of community-policing in respect of the police working with local authorities and educational and youth organizations. This emphasis on community engagement and empowerment, or in other words a 'community-based "bottom-up"' ' (Wilton Park 2006) approach to counter-terrorism, has evolved from the conclusions (Home Office 2005a) of seven 'Preventing Extremism Together Working Groups' set up by the Home Office after the July 2005 London bombings. The strategy's age group focus reflects the fact that the Muslim community is 'a very youthful one' (WPS06/5 March 2006) with 37 per cent of Muslims in the 16–34 age group and 34 per cent aged under 16.

The UK's perception of this terrorist threat recognizes its international dimension and the UK's response also takes place within the context of its obligations as an EU member state with regard to the relevant EU policies and strategies. The EU policies are articulated in the 'Strategy' and 'Action Plan on combating terrorism' (EU 2007) and the 'European Union Strategy for Combating Radicalisation and Recruitment to Terrorism' (EU 2005). The 'Strategy on Radicalisation' recommends 'Member States to take forward work at national level based on a common understanding of the factors and of principles and actions for countering them' (EU 2005: para 16). However, the EU (2005) also recognizes that 'The challenge of combating radicalisation and terrorist recruitment lies primarily with the Member States, at a national, regional and local level'.

In developing the analysis contained in this chapter it has been necessary to take account of the following factors. First, the implementation of the policy delivery aims of the 'Prevent' strategy part of CONTEST and the development of the related neighbourhood policing response systems are both still in their very early stages. Second, the evaluation of actual outcomes in relation to the goals set is still dependent upon the development of well grounded performance indicators. It is also important to note that one of the potential consequences of the current economic downturn, both in the UK and globally, may well be some expansion in the numbers of individuals and groupings that may resort to violent extremism. In that context, the current MI5 Director-General, Jonathan Evans, noted that 'Social, foreign policy, economic and personal factors all lead people to throw in their lot with extremists' (Telegraph.co.uk 2009).

The chapter is structured into four main parts: a consideration of the policy and legislative context for the policing of extremism in twenty-first-century Britain; issues related to performance indicators for policing extremism under Prevent; counter-terrorism (CT) and counter-extremism policing structures in Britain; and finally case studies of Prevent in four CT 'hub' police forces and conclusions.

In terms of the discourse on the topic there is clearly a division between those, as in the EU, using 'radicalization' (O'Duffy 2007) to describe the problem, or in the USA, which uses the term 'violent radicalization' in its 'Violent Radicalization and Homegrown Terrorism Prevention Act 2007' (US House of Representatives 2007) and the UK government which seems to prefer 'extremism' or 'violent extremists' as descriptive labels for this form of terrorism. This latter terminology does have a particular Prevent import in terms of UK specialist policing because 'extremism', in the context of Prevent is of primary concern to the SB in the provincial police forces and the Counter-Terrorism Command in the Metropolitan Police. However, the policing of other forms of 'extremism', such as animal-rights extremist groups is still a residual SB responsibility and at national level it comes within the remit of the units under the National Coordinator for Domestic Extremism (NCDE). A form of co-ordination exists in the sense that the Association of Chief Police Officers (ACPO) 'bridge between Government direction on counter terrorism and the operational implementation' (ACPO 2008) is the ACPO (TAM) Committee, which not only oversees the work of the National Coordinators for SB, terrorist investigations, ports policing and community engagement but also covers the work of the NCDE.

One could also argue that any emphasis on a 'community-policing' response should in fact be sufficiently flexible as to engage with a range of extremist behaviour, not least because of the potential for violence from far right political activity and the personal and economic harm caused by animal-rights extremists. This issue seems to be recognized in the broader approach to extremist behaviour, in public policy terms, as seen in the US 'National Strategy for Homeland Security' (US HS Council 2007: 10), which uses a more all-embracing terrorism threat framework 'The terrorist threat to the Homeland is not restricted to violent Islamic extremist groups. We also confront an ongoing threat posed by domestic terrorists based and operating strictly within the United States. Often referred to as "single-issue" groups, they include white supremacist groups, animal rights groups, and eco-terrorist groups among others'.

It could be suggested that the UK might benefit from a similarly broad policy approach to extremism with reference to the following cases. For example, in December 2008 seven animal-rights extremists were convicted of conspiracy to blackmail with menaces after a six-year campaign against Huntingdon Life Sciences (HLS). The group targeted hundreds of businesses linked to HLS, ranging from small transport firms to pharmaceutical giant GlaxoSmithKline (Sky News 2008). The police mounted a two-year operation ('Achilles') costing £3.5 million into the group who used the cover name of SHAC (Stop Huntingdon Animal Cruelty). The culmination of Operation Achilles came in May 2008 with 700 police officers being involved in raids in Britain, Belgium and the Netherlands that led to the arrest of 32 people (Timesonline 2008). Another example is the case of far-right extremist, Martyn Gilleard, who was convicted at Leeds Crown Court in June 2008 of terrorist offences and possessing child pornography. Peter McDonagh of the Crown Prosecution Service's Counter Terrorism Division is quoted (Telegraph.co.uk 2008) as saying that Gilleard was 'actively planning to commit terrorist acts against people and communities that he hated with a bigot's zeal – black and Asian people, European immigrants, Jews, Muslims and anyone he regarded as a political opponent'. The existence of a more widespread threat from right-wing extremism seems to be indicated by a series of right-wing related arrests and property searches in the Yorkshire area in June and July 2009. The West Yorkshire Chief Constable, Sir Norman Bettison, reported (Leppard 2009) that 300 weapons and 80 bombs were recovered. This haul represents the largest seizure of suspected terrorist weapons in the UK since the early 1990s.

The UK Prevent strategy has a very clear focus upon 'Al-Qaida-influenced terrorism' which, as far as the Government is concerned, is de facto the 'new extremism' and that focus also includes 'violent extremism' (HMG 2008a: 5, 4).

'Violent extremism' is not actually defined per se but by reference to what Her Majesty's Government sees as the causal factors of 'violent extremism' it can be understood as any conduct that promotes, justifies, supports or carries out acts of or related to terrorism, as defined in the current anti-terrorism legislation and related laws.

For the police forces there is an inevitable tension in relation to the community-orientated multi-agency 'soft' policing engagement with Muslim communities, under Prevent and the more 'hard' policing requirement of intelligence gathering, under the lead of MI5, investigations and arrests under Pursue, with its focus on stopping terrorist attacks. The inherent tensions between Pursue and Prevent forms of CT policing were identified in academic studies well before the events of 9/11 in the context of the impact of the Prevention of Terrorism Act (PTA) on Irish communities (Hillyard 1993). Post-9/11 a number of studies have also looked at these same tensions in the UK in respect of relations between different policing strategies and Muslim communities (Spalek and Lambert 2007; Lambert 2008).

The local and indeed national reactions to the, apparently inconclusive, raid in Forest Gate, London, in June 2006 are illustrative of the potential tensions between Pursue and Prevent (IPCC 2007; MPA 2008). Referring to the IPCC Report into Forest Gate, Deputy Assistant Commissioner Alf Hitchcock, of the MPS Diversity and Citizen Focus Directorate said 'The MPS learned a great deal from Forest Gate about community consultation and engagement ...' (MPS 2007). Hopefully this was indeed a timely lesson in the context of the 2008 Prevent strategy aims.

Policy and legislative context for policing extremism in twenty-first-century Britain

The policy context is provided for the police in three strategic-level policy documents: the 'National Policing Plan (NPP) 2005–8', the 'National Community Safety Plan 2008–11' and 'The Prevent Strategy – A Guide for Local Partners in England' (Home Office 2004). Under the (Home Office 2005b), CT is not one of the five key policing priorities but is described as an 'overarching imperative' (NPP 2005: paras 1.3–1.4) and the linked importance of community engagement in CT is set out in paragraph 3.60 of the NPP. Interestingly, the NPP, written in 2005, does not use the terms 'extremism' or 'violent extremism' in the context of its discussions of the terrorist threat. When the NPP does refer to 'extremism' it does so by reference to situations where 'domestic extremism, including animal rights extremism, moves beyond the boundaries of legitimate protest to intimidate individuals engaged in lawful activity and to impose economic costs on legal businesses' (Home Office 2005b: para 3.56). The requirement laid on police forces in respect of this form of 'extremism' is to 'give their support to national units co-ordinating the law enforcement response to such threats and make full use of the powers available to them' (Home Office 2005b: para 3.56). This requirement is clearly very different from the explicit requirement for community engagement with respect to 'extremism' linked to terrorism.

In 'The Prevent Strategy' the stress is on tackling 'violent extremism' via multi-agency partnership groups in which it is expected that 'local authorities and the police should take the lead' (HMG 2008a: 8). For the police, this task is also linked to their existing work in the Crime and Disorder Reduction Partnerships, which are a requirement under section 17 of the Crime and Disorder Act 1998. For all the public sector partners, including the police, the Prevent strategy has five key strands (Prevent 2008: 16): (1) challenging the violent extremist ideology; (2) disrupting the promoters of violent ideology; (3) supporting vulnerable individuals; (4) increasing community resilience; and (5) addressing grievances being exploited by extremists. These strands are to be supported by two cross-cutting work streams: developing understanding, analysis and information and strategic communications.

Within the police, key roles are identified for the basic or borough command unit (BCU) commanders, force counter-terrorism intelligence officers (CTIOs) and force counter-terrorism security advisors (CTSAs) (Home Office 2008a). At the national level forces and BCUs are supported by the work of the inter-Ministry Research, Information and Communications Unit (RICU – drawn from the Home Office, Department of Communities and Local Government and the Foreign and Commonwealth Office), which is 'hosted' (Prevent 2008: 44) by the Home Office's Office for Security and Counter Terrorism (OSCT) and the ACPO National Communities Tensions Team (NCTT), which is headed by a senior officer (see http://www.acpo.police.uk/NCTT/Teamprofiles.asp). Their CTIOS are supported nationally by the office of the National Coordinator Special Branch and the CTSAs are supported by the National Counter-Terrorism Security Office (NaCTSO), which works with the MI5 led Centre for the Protection of the National Infrastructure (CPNI) (Gregory 2007, 2008). At the regional level forces will be supported by regional Prevent teams including regional CT units.

For individual police forces, one of the main means of engagement with this multi-partnership community engagement strategy is through 'the embedding of neighbourhood policing teams' (Home Office 2008a) and the use of 'key individual networks' and independent advisory groups. It is important to note that, for policing purposes, 'neighbourhoods' are defined not by reference to any ethnographic or faith group notion of 'communities' but rather by reference to local government wards (House of Commons 2008: para 248, p. 73). This neighbourhood policing work may be supported, in areas identified as having a high priority for tackling 'violent extremism', by 'dedicated Prevent policing resources' (House of Commons 2008: para 248, p. 47). At the strategic level the 'National Community Safety Plan 2008–11' notes (p. 15) that ACPO's Terrorism and Allied Matters Working Group (ACPO-TAM) was 'developing an operational delivery strategy to embed tackling violent extremism into mainstream policing across the country'. Guidance for BCU commanders on consequence management of counter-terrorism operations is available through 'The BCU Commanders Guide to CT Operations'.

It is important to note that forms of Prevent-related community policing initiatives existed before the government's promulgation of this requirement for policing in its 2008 strategy document. For example, in 2007 the Lancashire Police SB was already involved in the force's community engagement strategy that included working with key community 'stake holder' groups and neighbourhood policing teams (ACPO-TAM [RIU] 2007). In 2007, the Metropolitan Police Service's (MPS) seven-point CT community cohesion plan – 'Operation Delphinus' – was also being rolled out across the MPS BCUs (MPA 2008).

The primary legislative bases for the policing of 'violent extremism', as understood in Prevent, are the Terrorism Acts 2000 and 2006 and the Racial and Religious Hatred Act 2006 (c.1) (which provides for amendments to the Public Order Act 1986 (c.64)). For the purposes of the Prevent strategy, the offence categories should be seen not so much as providing criteria for the purposes of arrest and charge but rather as offering guidance to the police on types of potential offending behaviour and activity that might be identified early enough for interventions to change potentially illegal behaviour and activity. Thus, for example, under the provisions of the Racial and Religious Hatred Act 2006 (c.1) a new 'Part 3A' is inserted into the Public Order Act 1986 (c.64) defining criminal acts that may constitute 'Hatred against persons on religious grounds', which may include the possession of 'inflammatory material' (s.29G). As further examples, the Terrorism Act 2000 (s.58) defines the offence of possessing information likely to be of use to a person committing acts of terrorism and the Terrorism Act 2006 created the new offence (s.5) of committing acts preparatory to terrorism.

The investigation, arrest, charge, prosecution, conviction and subsequent successful appeal of Samina Malik, aged 23, who described herself as 'the lyrical terrorist', provides a good illustration of the types of behaviour and activity that the Prevent strategy seeks to address (RUSI 2007; BBC News 2008). This case involved a British-born Muslim of Asian origin from Southall, West London who formerly worked at Heathrow. Among her activities Samina Malik published poems on the Internet praising Osama Bin Laden and some reporting gave the impression that she was arrested for publishing poetry expressing views related to 'violent extremism'. However, in 2007 she was in fact charged with, and convicted, of offences under section 58 of the Terrorism Act 2000, namely collecting information such as the 'al-Qaeda Manual' and 'The Mujahideen Poisons Handbook' likely to be useful to those preparing for a terrorist act. Subsequently, in 2008 the Court of Appeal held that the conviction was unsafe as the jury might have been confused by the fact that the prosecution submitted in evidence 'a large number of documents' (Lord Phillipps, Lord Chief Justice), possessed by Malik but the content of which did not fall within section 58 of Terroism Act 2000, being propagandist or theological material. Malik was also a member of the extremist organization Jihad Way that had been 'set up to support al-Qaeda and disseminate terrorist propaganda' (RUSI 2007).

A second relevant case relates to the conviction in September 2008 of Hammaad Munshi of Dewsbury, West Yorkshire, aged 18 years, for offences under sections 57 and 58 of Terrorism Act 2000 and his sentence to two years imprisonment.

Munshi has been described as Britain's 'youngest convicted terrorist', as he first became involved in activities related to terrorism at the age of 15 (CPS 2008; Guardian.co.uk 2008; Timesonline 2008b). His conviction related to both possession of materials likely to be useful in carrying out terrorist attacks (e.g. a guide to making napalm) and making a record of information for terrorist purposes. In his sentencing comments at the Old Bailey, Judge Timothy Pontius said 'I have no doubt that you, amongst others of similar immaturity and vulnerability, fell under the spell of fanatical extremists ... your codefendent Aabaid Khan in particular' (Timesonline 2008b). Munshi's grandfather said in a statement 'this case demonstrates how a young impressionable teenager can be groomed through the internet to associate with those whose views run contrary to true Muslim beliefs and values' (Timesonline 2008b). In relation to the Prevent strategy one can ask how might the strategy have altered their behaviour patterns and actions and what do parents or elders actually know about young people's environment?

Performance indicators

As yet Britain's CONTEST strategy has only some general performance indicators. For example, in terms of the robustness of investigations and the presentation of evidence in criminal cases, the percentages of those arrested under the Terrorism Act 2000 who went on to be charged, as of 2005, was said by the Director of Public Prosecutions, Mr Macdonald, to be 50 per cent or roughly equivalent to the rate for other categories of serious crimes (HAC 165.ii 2005). The multi-agency Prevent strategy is clearly a policy with wide performance related implications for a range of policy actors.

Currently the Prevent strategy's performance is, or is planned to be, measured within the following frameworks. At central government level Prevent outcomes will be measured via the CT Public Service Agreement (PSA26). At local government area levels Prevent outcomes will be measured through local area agreements (LAAs) based upon APACS (Assessments of Policing and Community Safety). The APACS will use National Indicator 35 (NI35) 'Building Resilience to Violent Extremism' and APACS 63. The work to prevent violent extremism will also form part of the Comprehensive Area Assessment (CAA).

With regard to performance indicators for the police, first, during summer 2008 HM Inspectorate of Constabulary (HMIC) has visited a number of police forces 'as part of a Prevent learning and development exercise' (MPA 2008) and HMIC will produce a report in late 2008 which will identify 'good practice/what works' (MPA 2008). Second, and for the first time, CT performance measures are to be included within the national police performance frameworks (MPA 2008). Importantly, from the perspective of the police role it has been decided that as a 'result of the difficulty in measuring the effectiveness of police activity in contributing to Prevent the Police Counter Terrorism Board has decided that HMIC will play a key role in providing an independent, professional and rounded assessment of the progress made in the first year' (MPA 2008). Performance indicators for the police will certainly reflect performance related to:

> Prevent outcome 1 – 'Increase the extent to which domestic Muslim communities reject and condemn violent extremism'.
> Prevent outcome 2 – 'Reduce the risks of individuals who come into contact with key sectors/services becoming or remaining violent extremists'.

The police performance measures are also likely to reflect the assessment framework for NI35, which examines work programmes on a 1–5 scale against four main criteria: understanding of, and engagement with Muslim communities; knowledge and understanding of the drivers and causes of violent extremism and the Prevent objectives; the development of a risk-based preventing violent extremism plan in support of the Prevent objectives and effective oversight.

What is very evident from this summary of the relevant performance indicators is that the focus has been on generic matters, structures and processes and that the question of measuring effectiveness in tackling violent extremism still remains under consideration. With reference to concerns about linkages between Prevent and Pursue, one proposed performance indicator makes that link in quite specific terms. Charles Farr, the Head of the OSCT, has said, if

> you create, as we are able to, an intelligence baseline to establish how much radicalisation is going on in those places at the moment, you then look at the programmes you are trying to introduce in those areas to stop radicalisation, and then you check your intelligence the following year, you can get an idea, albeit an imperfect one, of whether the risk of radicalisation in those areas … has reduced or increased.
>
> (House of Commons Home Affairs Committee 2009:
> Ev 25–26, Q 153)

The current proposed performance indicators are used in this chapter to provide a general background to the case studies of Prevent strategy understanding and implementation in key CT 'hub' police forces. The four selected are: the MPS, Greater Manchester Police (GMP), West Yorkshire Police (WYP) and the West Midlands Police (WMP). Before introducing the case studies the general structure of CT and extremism policing will be outlined.

Counter-terrorism and domestic extremism policing structures

Counter-terrorism policing

CT has its origins, for the police service, as mentioned earlier, in the late nineteenth century with the need to tackle the mainland manifestations of the Irish problem of the period. The present system comprises, under the strategic oversight of the ACPO-TAM and the more tactical oversight of the ACPO-TAM Advisory Group, a number of central police services and the specific Metropolitan Police Counter-Terrorism Command (SO15 or CTC – formed in 2006 by the merging of the Metropolitan Police Special Branch [SO12] and the Anti-Terrorist Branch [SO13]) plus the associated special units, the provincial police forces SBs and those other provincial police force assets that may be deployed, from time to time, in CT operations (HMG 2009). Central coordination of non-operational SB work is provided by the National Coordinator Special Branch (NCSB) and the National Coordinator Ports Policing (NCPP) who also oversees the dissemination of the police intelligence products from the National Ports Analysis Centre (NPAC) (Cabinet Office 2007: 36).

To date, only a few individual police forces, other than the MPS, on the basis of either a threat assessment or a risk assessment (e.g. North Yorkshire, West Midlands, City of London and Greater Manchester Police) have brought all the relevant specialist sections together in a single CT unit or other form of centralized structure. The MPS continues to play its leading role in CT operations in London and a significant role nationwide and internationally, especially through the role of the Senior National Coordinator for Terrorist Investigations (NCTI).

Moreover, CT requires that the SB and CT units work under the tasking direction of MI5 to develop intelligence, ideally, into evidence that may be presented in court and where MI5 officers may have to give evidence themselves, under cross-examination. MI5 also has to work very closely, at senior level, with the ACPO rank officer designated as the Senior NCTI who chairs the Executive Liaison Group, which agrees operational priorities, the ACPO rank officer who chairs the National Counter Terrorism Tasking and Coordinating Group and with chief constables in the development of anti-terrorist operations. In October 2007, MI5, after having assumed lead-agency responsibility for intelligence gathering related to mainland operations against Irish related terrorism in 1992, also took over responsibility from the PSNI for national security tasks in Northern Ireland. However, the MPS CTC still receives copies of all intelligence on Irish republican terrorism in the UK as the CTC retains a police national responsibility in this area under the lead responsibility of MI5.

New guidelines on the work of the police SBs were issued in March 2004 (Home Office 2004: paras 20–1) and these make it clear that 'counter terrorism remains the key priority for Special Branch' and that 'All intelligence about terrorism obtained by Special Branch is provided to the Security Service ... (as the lead agency) ... (and) ... The Security Service sets the priorities for the gathering of counter terrorist and other national security intelligence by Special Branch'. The SB's intelligence collection role is further defined by the 'requirements set out in the National Police Counter-Terrorism and Extremism Strategic Assessment and Control Strategy' (Cabinet Office 2007: 98).

Following the post-2003 introduction of the SB Regional Intelligence Centres (RICs), MI5 has recently developed nine 'regional offices' (about 25 per cent of MI5's staff will eventually work outside London) to promote even closer cooperation between itself and the police. These stations now work with the regional counter terrorism units (CTUs) or 'hubs', created following a decision by ACPO-TAM in 2006 in Birmingham, Leeds, Manchester and Thames Valley (the CTC in the MPS is the 'fifth' English 'hub') following the abandonment of more ambitious government plans for police force amalgamations. The provincial CTUs have absorbed the relevant RICs and some of these are now referred to as Counter-Terrorism Intelligence Units (CTIUs). Much of the organizational effort, described above, has been primarily focused on the Pursue CONTEST objective. Similar CT structures are also to be found in Northern Ireland, Scotland and Wales.

The more recent emphasis within CONTEST (Prevent) on the necessity to engage closely with communities in tackling terrorism has seen the development of more overt forms of engagement by the police SBs with communities in the process of information gathering – under MI5 tasking – which may produce more usable intelligence. This joint effort is known as the 'Rich Picture' approach (*Independent* 2006; MPA 2008). In this area of intelligence gathering, the MPS has a very wide-ranging strategy related to 'Community Engagement to counter terrorism' (MPA 2008) including the BOCU based 'Operation Delphinus' and the deployment of BOCU-based CTIOs. The locally based CTIO approach is also developing within the provincial forces. The latest stage in this area of joint working was the announcement by the prime minister in November 2007 of the formation of 'a new unit bringing together police and security and intelligence research which will identify, analyse and assess not just the inner circle of extremist groups but those at risk of falling under their influence – and share their advice and insights' (BBC News 2007). As a consequence of the prime minister's announcement, and after inter-agency discussions, a new team has now been established within the Joint Terrorism Analysis Centre (JTAC) based in Thames House which focuses on producing Prevent-relevant reporting for policymakers and deliverers tasked with implementing the relevant strategy under CONTEST (Home Office 2008). Within all these structures there is an inherent possibility for a conflict of interest or at least tension between the Prevent and Pursue elements of CONTEST and this will be considered further in the case studies.

Extremism policing

By contrast to the relatively well defined spatial and population group focus within the Prevent emphasis on countering violent extremism, the policing of non-CT related extremism is much more diverse in character. It may be target specific in relation to the physical assets (laboratories or animal farms) targeted by animal-liberation groups but very geographically dispersed in terms of the individual locations of these assets. Alternatively, the focus might be spatially specific but of varying time durations, as in the cases of the construction of a bypass, the location of a G8 Summit or BNP activities.

A brief examination of the history of the UK police public order intelligence system provides some basic understanding of a national response in this area.

The catalyst for the evolution of the UK National Public Order Intelligence Unit (NPOIU) was concern about the effects of the threatening behaviour and actions of animal-rights groups in the early 1980s. This led to the creation of a unit to establish and manage an intelligence source known as the Animal Rights National Index (ARNI). The ARNI had originally been based upon open-source research but later also utilized police SB human intelligence sources. By the 1990s, with the rise of environmental protest groups, the ARNI unit was also logging information and intelligence on non-animal-rights extremist groups. In 2000, ARNI was merged into a new police central facility, the NPOIU, which has now evolved into a much broader structure. This is headed by an ACPO rank officer as the National Coordinator Domestic Extremism (NCDE). Under the NCDE are three specialized units: (1) NPOIU; (2) NDET (National Domestic Extremism Team), which coordinates the national implications assessments of extremism criminal cases across the UK police forces; and (3) NECTU (National Extremism Tactics Coordination Unit). NECTU has domestic extremism specialist officers in each of the police regional intelligence centres. NPOIU is also the UK contact point for queries relating to extremist threats to any non-football major sporting event.

The NPOIU has no website system for sharing information but it does produce a hard copy 'Weekly Overview' report for UK official use and it also produces, as an open source shareable on request resource, a 'Protective Tactics Manual'. This can be shared with EU partners and others in the Police Working Group on Terrorism (PWGT) network. However, in 2006, the NCDE did participate in the first animal-rights policing meeting at Europol and this has led to the consideration of Europol undertaking an analytical work file (AWF) project on animal-rights groups.

Thus it can be seen that, in terms of police tasks, policing 'extremism', as opposed to 'violent extremism' or 'violent extremists' as expressed in Prevent (2008), is a completely separate police task albeit one that is still within the remit of SB. It might be argued that the Prevent approach could be applied to this area of police work. A counter-argument would run that the participants in the types of extremism represented by, for example, elements in the anti-capitalism movements, animal-rights groups and environmental movements, do not live in the kind of communities that are the focus of Prevent but are much more widely dispersed by age group, ethnicity and geographical location. Indeed the case of the right-wing extremist Martyn Gilleard referred to earlier, only came to light as a result of a police raid on his flat to search for child pornography materials.

Police force case studies

For all the forces studied the general policing background stems from the piloting of the National Reassurance Policing Programme (NRRP) between April 2003–2005. This led ACPO to launch the neighbourhood policing (NHP) programme in April 2005. The four large forces studied – the Metropolitan Police Service, Greater Manchester Police, West Yorkshire Police and West Midlands

Police – are all CT 'hub' forces, that is, they are the locations of major CT units with regional roles and a national role in the case of the MPS. From a general local authority and force perspective it is now accepted, as a report from South Yorkshire Police Authority notes (20 July 2008), that the Association of Police Authorities expects all Police Authorities to 'recognise that CT policing is fundamental to their responsibilities and treat this as mainstream business ... (and) ... proactively engage with communities on counter-terrorism, and integrate this activity into local community engagement strategies'.

Metropolitan Police Service

The MPS Prevent strategy response was set out in some detail by the Assistant Commissioner (Specialist Operations) (ACSO) in a Report to the MPA in July 2008 (MPA 2008). The Prevent strategy is led, on behalf of the ACSO, by an MPS Commander who also chairs the Prevent programme board. Currently the MPS has 41 staff in Prevent delivery posts and this number is scheduled to increase to 93 by 2010/11. Delivery is the responsibility of territorial policing and partners, via the BCUs in a phased series of sites (Phase One sites are: Hounslow, Tower Hamlets, Newham and Waltham Forest) with support from SO in matters such as intelligence management. The MPS vision 'is to embed Prevent activity within core Safer Neighbourhood policing as part of "business as usual" ' (MPA 2008: para 10). However, it is very noticeable that the Report makes little early reference to countering radicalization but *does* emphasize the intelligence gathering aspect alongside community engagement.

Nonetheless, the specific activities referred to in the MPS Prevent Report *do* reflect some of the letter and spirit of Prevent as is shown below (MPA 2008: para. 12). Operation Nicole (originally developed by the Lancashire Constabulary (Home Office 2008a)) is a table top exercise undertaken with community representatives to explain the police role in Prevent and Pursue. Operation Delphinus emphasizes BCU work in connection with disrupting terrorist activity. The operation also seeks to use community engagement, especially with 'key groups, young people and women, and offers 'safe places' for discussions on community safety and violent extremism. The Channel Project (originating from the ACPO NCTT, (Home Office 2008a)) uses existing police, local authorities and community group links to develop and deliver partnership intervention strategies to those identified by a MAPPA process 'who might be vulnerable to becoming involved in violent extremism' (Home Office 2008a). A Channel Project pilot is running in Lambeth and another pilot is planned for Waltham Chase. However, 'Rich Picture', referred to in the same paragraph of the MPS Report and which has MI5 involvement, is described as both 'a mechanism to gather National Security intelligence to identify investigative opportunities for both local and regional levels ... [and] ... "neighbourhood policing intelligence for counter terrorism" ' (Prevent 2008). This does seem to further express the tensions between Pursue and Prevent objectives of CONTEST.

West Yorkshire Police

This force had CT as part of its 'Strategic Priority 2', (Chief Constable's Annual Report 2005–6: 4) and was devoting considerable resources from post-July 2005 into Operation Theseus, which was a joint MPS-WYP investigation linked to the London bombings. Its 'Strategic Priority 1' was as required by the NPP. Neighbourhood Policing, via Neighbourhood Policing Teams (NPTs) was launched in West Yorkshire in January 2005, on a 'roll-out' basis and was fully in place during 2006 and the force bid successfully for additional PCSOs. The NPTs work in partnership with local communities and agencies and the force has established police contact points in all NPT areas.

The current Chief Constable of West Yorkshire, Sir Norman Bettison, described, in April 2008, his force's response to Prevent as 'the *new face* of Neighbourhood Policing in West Yorkshire' (JustWestYorkshire.org 2008, emphasis added). He referred to the period 2006–7 being more devoted to the capacity building in respect of the Protect and Pursue parts of CONTEST but that it was now time to address Prevent as he noted that 'Here in West Yorkshire, we have seen the evidence. People born and educated in our towns, people who lived as our neighbours, have gone on to be at first attracted to and then directly involved in violent extremism' (www.justwestyorkshire.org.uk 2008). But Sir Norman acknowledges that the police service has, historically, been low on the list of public agencies in terms of how well it is trusted by Muslim communities. Importantly, he also recognizes that, whatever the nature of the contribution that the police can make to Prevent, the 'police are not the appropriate agency to challenge warped ideology' (www. justwestyorkshire.org.uk 2008; see also, Bettison 2009).

The new police response from West Yorkshire comprises 47 teams 'to work at the heart of communities tackling the issues that affect people every day at local level' (Bettison 2009). In practice this scheme is actually operating initially only on a 'roll-out' basis with four pilot sites and really depends upon the specially funded post in each team of an officer 'to take responsibility for building local coalitions and providing a "channel" for information and referrals and to build a repertoire of multi-agency interventions with the partners involved' (Bettison 2009). It would appear, from a West Yorkshire Police Authority Report (WYPA, Specialist Policing Committee 20 June 2008, Minute 82) that the police teams will be working with local 'Guardianship Groups' who would be receiving Prevent briefing items.

Greater Manchester Police

This force is one of the CT 'hub' forces (CTUs), which can provide 'resilience and investigative capacity to support and deliver counter terrorist policing at a wider level' (Greater Manchester Police 2005: 14). It has a strategy, at force level, to ensure 'that counter terrorist work is embedded into all of its policing divisions' (Greater Manchester Police 2005), which stresses intelligence gathering from local communities and identifying and addressing threats to community safety as early as possible. On a force and North West regional level, the CTU work includes: standardization of processes including those related to building neighbourhood profiles, making Prevent part of everyday policing, developing local and sub-regional projects, partnership building and the development of intelligence sharing protocols. The strategy is backed up by the use of a single CT briefing message (Operation Sentinel) 'delivered to all ... front line officers and staff' (Greater Manchester Police 2005) and dedicated CT field intelligence officers are appointed for each BCU. Operational Sentinel also provides a mechanism for developing tasking processes. The implementation of Prevent-related NP in GMP has provided some useful learning experiences in police-community relationships. For example, in the Bolton area Operation Windsor targeted human trafficking in what is described as 'the Pakistani Heritage community in Bolton' (HMIC 2008: 18). A result of this operation was that it 'significantly developed the force's relationship in the community as well as the division's understanding/interpretation of related neighbourhood intelligence' (HMIC 2008: 18).

What is particularly helpful to this analysis is that HMIC carried out a focused inspection in this force in 2008 on 'Neighbourhood Policing Developing Citizen Focus Policing' (HMIC 2008). The Report, citing an assessment of GMP's NHP by the NPIA, draws attention to an issue which is both a general policing issue and one of particular relevance to attempts to deliver community-based Prevent policing. HMIC reported the NPIA as finding 'that while NHP staff receive Rich Picture briefings with interest, the relevance of the briefings to their role is not always recognised ... (and) ... Rich Picture activity is considered as an area traditionally dealt with by specialist officers, e.g. special branch (SB)/CTU staff' (HMIC 2008: 20).

West Midlands Police

Unlike the other CT 'hub' forces studied the WMP seem to be more reticent in their publications about their response to Prevent. They do, however, stress that they were one of the first forces to introduce neighbourhood policing 18 months before the government's April 2008 deadline and the force records (West Midlands Police 2007) that it has 297 experienced neighbourhood policing teams in place. The force also notes that 45 per cent of its budget for police officers goes on neighbourhood policing.

That the force area does encompass CT issues in respect of both Pursue and Prevent can be easily demonstrated. In 2007–8 the WMP was involved in Operation Gamble, a major investigation into the planned abduction and murder of a serving soldier by Islamist extremists, who also planned to film these actions and post them on the Internet. In January 2008, at Leicester Crown Court, four of those arrested in connection with this case pleaded guilty to various related offences under the Terrorism Act 2000 (West Midlands Police 2008). In relation to Prevent, the WMP area features a number of times in reports on 'Preventing violent extremism Pathfinder Fund case studies' (DCLG 2007). The case studies referred to the following projects: 'Black Country Imam' (supporting existing and new generation mainstream/moderate imams), 'Birmingham Study Circles' (helping young people to a better understanding of Islam) and 'Birmingham Young Muslim Leadership Programmes and Green Light Resources' (which includes how to respond to signs of radicalization among young people). This latter Pathfinder Project could clearly feed into WMP neighbourhood policing Prevent work.

Conclusion

Because the embedding of the Prevent CT strategy into neighbourhood/community policing is still in its early or 'roll-out' stages, much of this study has had to focus on outlining the development of the relevant organizational structures, processes and planned performance indicators. Though notwithstanding the key role the police play in the Prevent partnerships via neighbourhood policing teams, the comment cited earlier on the inherent limitation on the police capability in respect of Prevent made by the Chief Constable of West Yorkshire is worth repeating; whatever else the police can do by way of engagement with communities the 'police are not the appropriate agency to challenge warped ideology'.

However, this study has been able to identify three potential problem areas. First, the Prevent CT intelligence gathering aim of 'Rich Picture' may produce conflicts of interest in the delivery of some aspects of the police part of the prevent partnerships approach. Second, one can ask whether the emphasis on tackling the variety of extremism defined in (Home Office 2008a) may produce some relative neglect, in terms of the allocation of police resources, of the forms of extremism coming within the remit of the NCDE. Third, there is the problem of CT performance measurement which, under Prevent, applics to all the Prevent partner agencies including the police. The Security Minister Lord West noted that measuring the effectiveness of counter-terrorism measures 'is extremely difficult ...' and that the authorities were trying to still 'work out what we can use as empirical evidence' (House of Commons, Defence Committee 2008: Q.64). Perhaps, therefore, it is not surprising to also find ACPO making the general comment that 'The service is grappling with an expanding, yet imprecise, mission ... (with) ... a lack of shared clarity among stakeholders about what is expected of it in relation to the breadth of the challenge' (House of Commons, Home Affairs Select Committee 2008: para. 14, p. 10).

References

National Counter Terrorism Policing Structure – Building Capability.
ACPO (2008) *National Community Tension Team*, available at: http://www.acpo.police.uk/NCTT/Teamprofiles.asp (accessed 12 September 2008).
ACPO-TAM (RIU) (2007) 'Academic outreach – radicalisation: its impact on UK counter terrorism', Report of a Workshop 11–12 May 2006. (Limited circulation.)

ACPO (2009) Memorandum submitted by Association of Chief Police Officers (ACPO) on the police and terrorism to House of Commons Home Affairs Committee inquiry on 'Project Contest', February 2009, availale at: http://www.parliament.the-stationery-office.co.uk/pa/cm200809/cmselect/cmhaff/212/ (accessed 25 October 2009).

BBCNews (2007) 'In full: Brown anti-terror speech', 14 November, available at: http://newsvote.bbc.co.uk/mpapps/pagetools/print/news.bbc.co.uk/l/hi/uk_politics/70 (accessed 24 November 2009)

BBCNews (2008) 'Lyrical terrorist wins appeal', 17 June, available at: http://newsvote.bbc.co.uk/mpapps/pagetools/print/news.bbc.co.uk/1/hi/uk/7459180.stm (accessed 25 September 2008).

Bettison, N. (2008) Statement on Prevent and West Yorkshire, available at, www.JustWestYorkshire.org, (accessed 29th April 2008).

Bettison, N. (2009) 'Preventing violent extremism – a police response', *Policing*, 3: 129–38.

Cabinet Office (2007) *Security in a Global Hub – Establishing the UK's new border arrangements,* London: Cabinet Office.

CPS (2008) 'Terrorist "Mr Fix-It" convicted with two others of terrorist offences', press release 18 August, available at: http://www.cps.gov.uk/news/pressreleases/154_08.html (accessed 9 October 2008).

Clutterbuck, L. (2006) 'Countering Irish Republican terrorism in Britain: its origins as a police function', *Terrorism and Political Violence*, 18: 95–118.

Department of Communities and Local Government (DCLG) (2007) 'Preventing violent extremism pathfinder fund 2007/08 Case Studies', London: DCLG.

—— (2008) 'Key Communities, Key Resources – Engaging the capacity and capabilities of faith communities in civil resilience', London: DCLG.

European Union (2005) Council of the EU, Presidency Note to COREPER/Council 'The European Union Strategy for Combating Radicalisation and Recruitment to Terrorism', EU Council Doc. 14781/1/05, REV 1, LIMITE, JAI 452. 24 November 2005 and see also Council of the EU, COREPER to COUNCIL "A" Item Note, 'Revised EU Strategy for Combating Radicalisation and Recruitment to Terrorism', EU council Doc. 15175/08, LIMITE, JAI 597, 14 November 2008, Brussels: European Union.

—— (2007) Council of the EU 'EU Action Plan on combating terrorism', 7233/07, March 2007 and see also EU Council (2009), 'Policy recommendations on counter-terrorism', EU Council Doc. 8205/06, ENFOPOL 63, 26/1/09, Brussels: European Union.

Fielding, N. (1995) *Community Policing*, Oxford: Oxford University Press.

Grabosky, P. (2008) 'Community policing in an age of terrorism', *Crime, Law and Social Change*, 50(1–2): 1–6.

Greater Manchester Police (2005) 'Policing Strategy 2005–8 – Year Three 2007–8', Manchester: Greater Manchester Police.

Gregory, F. (2007) 'Police and Counter-terrorism in the UK: a study of 'one of the highest and most challenging priorities for police forces nationally'[Home Office, NPP 2003–2004]' in P. Wilkinson (ed.) *Homeland Security in the UK*, London: Routledge.

—— (2008) 'The police and the intelligence services: with special reference to the relationship with MI5', in C. Harfield, A. MacVean, J. Grieve and D. Phillips (eds) *The Handbook of Intelligent Policing : Consilience, Crime Control and Community Safety*, Oxford: Oxford University Press.

Guardian.co.uk (2008) 'Yorkshire teenager becomes Britain's youngest convicted terrorist', 18 August, available at: http://www.guardian.co.uk/uk/2008/aug/18/security.alqaida/print (accessed 9 October 2008).

Hillyard, P. (1993) *Suspect Communities: People's Experience of the Prevention of Terrorism Acts in Britain*, London: Pluto.

HM Government (HMG) (2007) *Countering International Terrorism: The United Kingdom Government Strategy, (CONTEST)* Cm 6888, London: The Stationery Office.
—— (2008a) 'The Prevent Strategy: A Guide for Local Partners in England – Stopping people becoming or supporting terrorists and violent extremists', London: Home Office.
—— (2008b) 'National Community Safety Plan 2008–11', London: Home Office.
—— (2009) *Pursue, Prevent, Prepare, Protect. The United Kingdom's Strategy for Countering International Terrorism*, Cm 7547 , London: Home Office.
HM Inspectorate of Constabulary (HMIC) (2003), 'HMIC Thematic Inspection of Special Branch and Ports Policing – a Need to Know', Home Office Communications Directorate.
—— (2008) 'Greater Manchester Police Neighbourhood Policing – Developing Citizen Focus Policing', London: Home Office.
Home Office (2005a) 'Preventing Extremism Together', Working Groups, August – October 2005, London: Home Office.
—— (2005b), 'National Policing Plan 2005–8 – Safer, Stronger Communities', London: Home Office, NPP3, London: Home Office.
—— (2008), Speech by Jacqui Smith, Home Secretary, at the BCU Commanders Conference on 16 April 2008, http://press.homeoffice.gov.uk/Speeches/bcu-conference-speech, accessed 29/9/08.
Home Office, Scottish Executive, Northern Ireland Office (2004) *Guidelines on SPECIAL BRANCH WORK in the United Kingdom*.
House of Commons, Defence Committee (2008) Minutes of Evidence, 'UK National Security and Resilience', 21/10/08, HC 718-ii, Q.64.
House of Commons, Home Affairs Select Committee (2005) Minutes of Evidence, 'Terrorism and Community Affairs', 25 January, HC 165-ii, Q 368 [DPP].
—— (2008) 7th Report, Session 2007–8, 'Policing in the 21st Century', HC 364-I, November 2008.
House of Commons, Home Affairs Committee (2009), 9th Report of Session 2008–9, 'Project CONTEST: The Government's Counter-Terrorism Strategy', HC 212, 7th July.
IPCC (2007) *IPCC concludes Forest Gate Inquiries*, 13 February 2007, full reports available at: http://www.ipcc.gov.uk/index/resources/evidence_reports/investigation_reports.htm (accessed 16 October 2008).
Justwestyorkshire.org (2008) 'West Yorkshire Police chief: local heartbeat of fight against terror', by Sir Norman Bettison, 29 April 2008, available at: http://www.justwestyorkshire.org/News/local/11.html (accessed 26 October 2009).
Klausen, J. (2007) 'British Counter-Terrorism After the July 2005 Attacks: Adapting Community-Policing to the Fight Against Domestic Terrorism', USIPeace Briefing, available at: http://www.usip.org/pubs/usipeace_briefings/2007/0205_terrorism_html (accessed 11 September 2008).
Lambert, R. (2008) 'Empowering Salafis and Islamists against al-Qaida: a London counter-terrorism case study', *PS: Political Science and Politics*, 41(1): 31–5.
Leppard, D. (2009) 'Bomb seizures spark far-right terror plot fear', *Sunday Times*, 5 September, available at: http://www.timesonline.co.uj/tol/news/uk/crime/article 6638139.ece.?print=yes&radn (accessed 26 October 2009).
Metropolitan Police Authority (MPA) (2008) 'MPS Prevent delivery strategy', Report: 8, Date: 24 July 2008 By: Assistant Commissioner Specialist Operations on behalf of the Commissioner, available at: http://www.mpa.gov.uk/committees/mpa/2008/080724/08. htm (accessed 17 September 2008).
MPS (2007) 'IPCC Report into Forest Gate', MPS, Bulletin 0000000631, 13 February.
O'Duffy, B. (2007) 'Radical atmospheres: explaining jihadist radicalization in the UK', *PSOnline*, available at: http://www.apsanet.org, January, 37–42.

RUSI (2007) ' "Lyrical terrorist" avoids jail', available at: http://www.rusi.org/go.php? structureID=S4459CODF31D9A&ref=C475D20974C2F1 (accessed 25 September 2008).

Skinns, L. (2008) 'A prominent participant? The role of the state in police partnerships', *Policing and Society*, 18(3): 311–21.

Sky News (2008) 'Animal rights activists guilty', 23 December, available at: http://wwwnews.sky.com/skynews/Home/UK-News/Animal-Gights-Activists-Found-Guilt, (accessed 5 January 2009).

South Yorkshire Police Authority (2007) 'Counter Terrorism Developments', Report of the Clerk and Treasurer, 20 July, available at: http://www.southyorks.gov.uk/embedded_digest.asp?docid=3975 (accessed 25 October 2009).

Spalek, B. and Lambert, R. (2007) 'Terrorism, counter-terrorism and Muslim community engagement post 9/11', in R. Roberts and W. McMahon (eds) *Social Justice and Criminal Justice*, pp. 202–14. London: Centre for Crime and Justice Studies.

Telegraph.co.uk (2008) 'Nazi sympathiser Martyn Gilleard jailed for 16 years', 25 June, available at: http://www.telegraph.co.uk/news/uknews/2193160/Nazi-sympathiser-Martyn-Gillear (accessed 5 January 2009).

—— (2009) 'MI5 chief warns of threat from global recession', 7 January, available at: http://www.telegraph.co.uk/news/newstopics/politics/defence/4144460/MI5-chief-war (accessed 23 January 2009).

Timesonline (2008a) 'Hammaad Munshi, schoolboy terrorist, given two-year sentence', 20 September, available at: http://www.timesonline.co.uk/tol/news/uk/crime/article4786555.ece?print=yes&randn (accessed 9 October 2008).

—— (2008b) 'Animal rights extremists guilty of campaign to blackmail Huntington Life Sciences', 22 December, available at: http://www.timesonline.co.uk/tol/news/uk/crime/article5384003.ece?print=yes&randn (accessed 5 January 2009).

US Homeland Security Council (2007) 'National Strategy for Homeland Security', available at: http://www.dhs.gov/xlibrary/assets/nat_strat-homelandsecurity_2007.pdf (accessed 25 October 2009).

US House of Representatives (2007) 'Understanding H.R.1955: The Violent Radicalization and Homegrown Terrorism Prevention Act of 2007', Committee on Homeland Security, Fact Sheet, available at: http://homeland.house.gov/sitedocuments/hr1955factsheet.pdf (accessed 25 October 2009).

West Midlands Police (2007) 'Annual Review 2006–7', available at: www.west-midlands.police.uk/pdf/corporate-publications/annual-reports/AnnualReview2006-2007.pdf

—— (2008) 'Chief Constable's Information Report to the Police Authority', 14 February. www.west-midlands-pa.gov/downloadchecklink.asp?filename

West Yorkshire Police (2005) 'Chief Constable's Annual Report 2005–6', available at: http://www.westyorkshire.police.uk/files/docs/annualreport20052006.pdf, (accessed 25th October 2009).

West Yorkshire Police Authority (2008) Specialist Policing Committee, Minutes of Meeting, 20 June, available at: http://www.wypa.org/access-file?filemane=pa-m-200608.pdf (accessed 11 October 2008).

Wilton Park Conferences Report (2006) 'Towards a community based approach to counter-terrorism', WPS06/05, available at: http://www.wiltonpark.org.uk/documents/conferences/WPS06-05/pdfs/WPS06-05.pdf (accessed 25 October 2009).

5 Policing within a counter-terrorism context post-7/7

The importance of partnership, dialogue and support when engaging with Muslim communities

Basia Spalek and Robert Lambert

Introduction

Within the Prevent strand of the government's counter-terrorism strategy, CONTEST2, the police and local authorities are seen to be taking the lead in any strategies aimed at preventing violent extremism (PVE), working with wide-ranging bodies, including representatives from the education sector, children's and youth services, probation and prison services, and with Muslim communities being viewed as key partners (HM Government 2008). The prevention of violent extremism is being integrated into mainstream policies and practices of a wide range of statutory and non-statutory organizations since 7/7 and the heightened threat of homegrown terrorism. The central role of the prevention of terrorism within policing is helping to blur distinctions between the role of the police and the security services (Lowe and Innes 2008), with community policing being viewed as an important resource for counter-terrorism policing (Gregory Chapter 4, in this volume). These developments raise many questions for both policing and for the prevention of violent extremism, some of which are raised by Gregory in the previous chapter.

This chapter draws upon the results of two interrelated research studies that examined police engagement with Muslim communities for the purposes of counter-terrorism: the first study was carried out by Robert Lambert between 2006 and 2007; the second comprises a study carried out between 2007 and 2008 by a team of researchers under the auspices of the Religion and Society programme within the Arts and Humanities Research Council (AHRC). Both studies focus on engagement in a counter-terrorism context in the period since the events of 9/11. As such, they offer insights into police and community experience that pre-date the launch of the government's PVE strategy. Whereas both research projects draw out first hand experiences of successful and problematic engagement, Lambert's research has an additional interest in describing challenges to the legitimacy effectiveness of such activity. In consequence, this chapter comprises important sources of knowledge to draw upon in order to raise questions for contemporary developments.

Within policing and policy contexts, much attention is being placed upon developing and implementing an infrastructure for PVE, consisting of a wide range of actors and agencies. In relation to policing, this infrastructure is vast and multi-layered, consisting of local community liaison and neighbourhood policing officers, regional counter-terrorism units and national units such as the National Communities Tension Team, with Prevent indicators and police performance measures being used to assess the effectiveness of any initiatives and engagement work that is being undertaken (see, for example, Chapter 4). This chapter raises the concern that in formulating and implementing models of engagement for the purposes of the prevention of violent extremism, and in using performance indicators to measure effectiveness, it may be that the human aspects and dynamics to engagement are overlooked, and yet engagement necessarily involves interaction between people – and in the case focused upon in this chapter, between police officers and members of Muslim communities. Moreover, this interaction takes place within a highly politicized context, with power processes and intra-community and individual dynamics at play, which may have historical, political or emotional roots, and so there are many tensions that those involved in interaction have to confront and effectively negotiate through, or distance or disengage themselves from.

The studies drawn upon in this chapter comprise of small-scale qualitative research that focused on engagement at a micro rather than macro level, highlighting that engagement is complex and multi-layered and in constant flux. This chapter discusses some of the key issues raised for engagement work by police officers and community members who have been engaging in a counter-terrorism environment. In highlighting the micro-level processes and aspects to engagement, a key concern for us is that we provide an account of police–community interaction that can inform current and future policy and practice on the Prevent agenda so that community policing does not merely become a tool through which to secure intelligence, whereby communities are viewed as suspects or informants rather than as minorities, and which may have the effect of alienating community members. The approach taken in this chapter therefore reflects the approach taken by Githens-Mazer (Chapter 2 , this volume), in terms of highlighting the importance of micro-level analyses within a counter-terrorism context. First, the notions of 'community', engagement, disengagement and partnership will be discussed before we look at the importance of, and dynamics to, partnership, support and dialogue with Muslim communities in a post-7/7 context.

Community, engagement, partnership and violent extremism – complexities inherent to the Prevent agenda

The notions of community, engagement, partnership and violent extremism feature explicitly and implicity within the Prevent agenda. The complexities inherent to these notions really highlight the complexity of the Prevent agenda, and raise significant questions about the appropriateness of using performance indicators to evaluate the effectiveness of initiatives. Put simply, terms like 'community', 'engagement' and so forth are fluid and have contested meanings, and so are unlikely to be amenable to measurement by performance indicators which, rather than reflecting reality, reflect an over-simplified and overly static view of the social world in general and the Prevent agenda in particular.

Although the notion of 'community' is contentious and open to many different interpretations, often in government discourse the notion of community tends to be treated in rather unproblematic terms, as both subject and object of policymaking and intervention (Prior *et al.* 2006). This is clearly the case in the Prevent agenda, where, as in other social policy contexts, dialogue has often taken place with community leaders who can, in fact, be out of touch with, or ignorant of the concerns of those on whose behalf they are supposed to be speaking. Community leaders are often middle-aged (or older) males who have very little comprehension of the viewpoints of younger community members or of females, whose voices may therefore remain unheard by those who are supposedly consulting them.

Active engagement might be thought of as involving individuals, organizations and communities achieving power not for domination but to act with others to implement change. Partnership might be defined as involving equality, transparency and legitimate cooperation between partners. Partnership work has a number of inherent difficulties. For example, there may be differences in the resources available to different groups in the engagement process, and different organizations are also likely to have different sets of priorities, so that there can be considerable difficulties arising from, and tensions within, partnership approaches. At the same time, partnership work can be difficult as it involves power differentials and so community groups may not feel that they are actual partners in the policy process. In cases where there are power imbalances between partners, it is important for those partners in positions of relative power to create spaces within which all partners are equals, equally included and respected (Thacher 2001; Friedman 2003). This is especially important in the context of police–community engagement as police officers are in positions of relative power over community members. For Cook (2006) community participation often falls short so that supporting independent community interests, is rarely put into practice. Importantly, managerial imperatives and strategic decisions on what can and cannot be done influence the scope of community participation. Moreover, market research-type consultation is often used, which for Cook (2006: 125) 'masks a patronising and complacent attitude to service users'.

With these complexities in mind, the following sections highlight key issues for policing in a post-7/7 environment, drawing upon two interrelated and innovative studies that explore police–community engagement in a counter-terrorism context. One is a PhD study by Lambert (2009 forthcoming), entitled 'The London Partnerships: An Insider's Analysis of Legitimacy and Effectiveness'. The other is a project funded by the AHRC under the auspices of the Religion and Society programme, headed 'An Examination of Partnership Approaches to Challenging Religiously-Endorsed Violence involving Muslim Groups and Police'.[1] Before setting out the key findings we first discuss the wider context to the research.

Wider context to the research

Prior to the events of 7/7, within the government's counter-terrorism strategy, CONTEST, the Pursue strand was dominant, involving 'hard' policing and engagement tactics that consisted of surveillance, intelligence gathering, the use of informants and the implementation of a number of anti-terror laws. 'Softer' approaches, on the other hand, which might be viewed as the development of ongoing dialogue, participation and community feedback between Muslim communities and state agencies, including the police, were marginalized (Spalek and Imtoual 2007). Nonetheless, more recently, 'softer' approaches to countering terrorism have gained increasing prominence as the Prevent strand within the government's CONTEST strategy has gained in significance. With respect to policing, the model of community policing within counter-terrorism is receiving more attention, as exemplified by the work of the Muslim Contact Unit (MCU) in London, but is also seen in other international contexts. For example, in the USA and Canada there are community policing-based initiatives that work towards engaging with Muslim, Arab and Sikh communities for the purposes of counter-terrorism. US-based researchers argue that police–community partnerships can provide police officers with important cultural and linguistic insights and crucial information while also enabling hate crimes to be properly investigated and prosecuted (Ramirez 2008). These initiatives are different from the dominant model of neighbourhood policing in the UK (which attempts to combine neighbourhood policing with intelligence-gathering models of policing) in that they are initiatives which are grounded specifically within a counter-terrorism context and consist of ongoing interaction and, in some cases, sustained partnership work between Muslim communities and the police (Hanniman 2008; Spalek 2009).

Key findings: Muslim communities as suspect

A key theme emerging from interview data was the experiences of Muslim communities as suspect communities. In both research studies, a common finding was that stories of individuals being treated by state authorities as 'suspect' emerged. This involved people being stopped and searched by police or being detained over a number of days without charge, having serious consequences for them in terms of the effects on their family, personal and professional lives, and being approached by the security services to act as informants. Individuals also spoke about being stopped and searched at airports:

> The other day I had a flight, a one hour flight to Paris, I spent two hours just being searched. Standing in a line and being stripped. And it was ridiculous.

These dynamics, alongside cases of heavy-handed policing responses such as the Forest Gate incident, have created distrust in Muslim communities. Moreover, the 'War on Terror' as constructed by the Bush regime has been viewed as a war against Islam by many Muslim minorities, and the torture and mistreatment of those labelled as 'enemies' has helped to create deep-seated mistrust, impacting significantly on some individuals' desire to engage with the authorities, as the following quotation from an interview illustrates:

> but now suspicion means five years in Guantanamo. It's not just okay, let's keep on eye on that person. It's not let's go and, and have a friend go and have a word with him so that ... it's not that anymore. It's go raid their house, break down their doors, you know, tie them up in front of their children. Dehumanise them in whatever time they spend in Belmarsh or Guantanamo and then just tag for the rest of their lives. That's what suspicion means. So who in their right mind would go and say 'hang on, I think ...?' Who would do that? And we all lose out.

A key finding from both studies is that those experiencing anti-terror measures have argued that they are less likely to engage with state authorities in the future, this being significant for the Prevent agenda in which communities are being placed at the centre of the fight against violent extremism. This is also significant for policing, given that previous research has established that trust and confidence in the police can be seriously undermined in situations where communities feel that they are being over-policed (MacPherson Inquiry 1999; Jones and Newburn 2001), and that, moreover, this can have serious consequences on the flow of information from communities, considered a key issue within the CONTEST strategy (Hillyard 1993, 2005).

Collectively, individuals' narratives illustrate the kinds of frustration and anger that 'hard' approaches to counter-terrorism generate within Muslim communities, significantly compromising efforts to engage with communities to reduce the terror threat. Individuals' stories powerfully illustrate that any initiative set up to counter terror involving state authorities and Muslim communities will have to be sensitive to, and be able to negotiate through, the negative and painful experiences that individuals have suffered, either individually or at the group collective level, in order to build an effective project whereby Muslim communities feel that they are stakeholders and equal partners in the initiative. A defensive response from state authorities, one which denies people's frustrations or one which tries to silence or marginalize people's experiences or dissent, will only serve to further compound individuals' anger and distress and sense of grievance, thereby placing limitations on any project trying to counter terrorism through engaging with Muslim communities. At the same time, some individuals spoke about their experiences of racism and Islamophobia, including experiences of being verbally or physically assaulted and their property being attacked:

> Muslims are being ghettoised, there is a huge amount of Islamaphobia in Britain, we are at the receiving end of attacks and bully boy tactics.

Importantly, both research studies have found that within this difficult context, trust-building activities by the police are crucial. Our research studies highlight that while engagement in the context of counter-terrorism can often be experienced by communities in negative ways, when 'hard' approaches to policing, that are dominant within a counter-terrorism context, are applied, some pioneering work in some local areas suggests that building trusting relationships between police and communities is feasible despite the difficult climate. Our research studies illustrate that spaces for effective dialogue, support and trust-building activities are being created by some pioneering police officers and Muslim community members, where partnership work serving to prevent violent extremism is taking place. As discussed below, this work is grounded in principles of community policing and is resource-intensive in that the trust that is necessary as the social glue for ongoing engagement and partnership work is often a result of individuals balancing and negotiating pathways through conflicting values, whether at the individual, personal (including religious) level, or at the community or national security levels, and where individuals challenge dominant norms their personal security may be compromised. At the same time, our studies illustrate the importance of reassurance policing, and that although community policing has generated much criticism, both from within a counter-terrorism context and from a wider policing context, where community policing is used to serve minority communities by empowering them and by supporting independent community interests this may yield important intelligence from which to prevent violent extremism.

In this context, MCU police officers are shown to utilize high levels of what Thomas and Inkson (2003) call cultural intelligence to empathize and communicate effectively with each other in what is essentially a cross-cultural dialogue. For Thomas and Inkson (2003: 14), cultural intelligence consists of 'being skilled and flexible about understanding a culture, learning more about it from your ongoing interactions with it, and gradually reshaping your thinking to be more sympathetic' to it. It is important to highlight the key role that Muslim police officers deployed on the MCU have played in developing and nurturing this skill to the benefit of police colleagues and community partners alike. The same officers are also described as having made a significant contribution to trust building between MCU and Muslim community partners. In addition, the Muslim police officers are shown to have played a vital role in introducing non-Muslim police colleagues to the religious and cultural differences of richly diverse and often competing Muslim community groups in the capital. However, it is important to point out that Muslim police officers working within the MCU have straddled the artificially constructed yet dominant societal binary oppositions of state (police)–community and as such have experienced distrust from within both policing and community arenas. They have, therefore, shown a significant ability to negotiate through this difficult context by drawing upon their own personal and professional resources.

This kind of approach is also significant given the lack of cultural empathy and trust that has characterized the wider engagement between Western officialdom and Muslim communities in the first six years of the 'War on Terror'. Throughout the period under review, the MCU partnership's two-way cultural empathy and trust building stands in marked contrast to prevailing attitudes of confrontation and suspicion variously explicit and implicit in the wider war on terror. One Muslim community leader in East London compares the courteous partnership approach of the MCU with his degrading treatment at the hands of immigration and security officials at a US airport where he was detained overnight in a cold cell pending further enquiries into his visit (both to lecture and to see his son at university). When he was asked at 2 a.m. whether he had any tattoos by a security official with a form to fill in it struck him that he was unwittingly on the wrong side of a war between 'us and them' – a thought that has occurred to London Muslim community leaders on numerous occasions during the period under review. Subsequently, on his return to the UK the MCU sought to explain the community leader's value as a community partner against al-Qaeda to US officials – with limited success. Attempts to broker a meeting between US officials and the community leader were unsuccessful. In this case, as in so many others, the MCU partnership approach towards Muslim figures with uncompromising religious and political beliefs failed to inspire confidence in the wider war on terror. In consequence MCU officers became concerned that their ability to win over suspicious community leaders would be undermined. As one MCU officer notes, 'it is hard to think of someone less likely to have a tattoo and less important in persuading local Muslim youth that al-Qaeda is the wrong way to go'.

Policing within counter-terrorism: supporting communities through partnership, dialogue and reassurance

Within a counter-terrorism context, one marked by mutual suspicion and ongoing tensions between police and communities, building trust is essential in engagement work. Our research studies have shown that trust-building activities can include ongoing interaction between police officers and communities where there are opportunities for dialogue regarding community, policing and other affairs, and for reciprocal exchanges. This might involve police officers attending seminars on terrorism organized by community members as part of a wider methodology of attempting to understand terrorism and counter-terrorism from community perspectives as part of a broader remit in relation to a critical counter-terrorism discourse based on voices from 'grassroots level' rather than those defined as 'experts'. It might also include police officers visiting people in their homes for social gatherings, participating in weddings or death ceremonies, visiting people in hospital, being interested in wider community activities that individuals are organizing and so forth. This kind of activity, while not necessarily producing immediate 'results' of the kind that policymakers and senior police officers are concerned with in terms of uncovering violent extremist activities and preventing them from occurring (so-called crime reduction strategies), is of high value within a counter-terrorism context as it helps build trust between communities and police. Trust should be viewed as an important aspect of the social capital that is necessary for initiatives that are developed for preventing violent extremism that involve communities.

A further important component to trust-building is in relation to providing reassurance policing – and our research identifies two important strands/aspects to this. First, in a context of fear due to the dominance of 'hard' policing strategies and also the risk that some communities run of racist and Islamophobic attacks, counter-terrorism police officers can play an instrumental role in providing reassurance policing in terms of being accessible to communities and providing them with support if they experience hate crimes, which is important in a context generally characterized by secrecy. Second, it is important to highlight the politicized nature of the government's Prevent agenda, whereby initiatives that are being developed involving Muslim communities may be creating division among community members. It appears that engagement is often dominated by government-led (mis)understandings of Islam and the UK Muslim population, whereby those Muslim groups seen as 'moderate' are viewed as being allies in the prevention of terrorism (Spalek and Imtoual 2007; Lambert 2008; Spalek and Lambert 2008). Other, more 'radical' Muslim groups are deemed illegitimate, as radicalism is often conflated with violent extremism, and so these Muslims are often marginalized and excluded from policymaking processes. Within this context, building trust with members of marginalized communities through ongoing dialogue and support, notably with Salafis and Islamists, contains elements of reassurance policing in the sense that police officers are engaging with minority sections of the Muslim population who have been stigmatized by government discourse and by popular commentators, and so engagement work here involves police officers going against the grain of dominant socio-political norms and discourses and reassuring stigmatized communities that they will continue to support them in any projects aimed at PVE, despite running the risk of criticism from the media, policymakers, senior police officers and so forth. This kind of work illustrates that although community policing has been criticized for being nothing more than a public relations exercise, or for being a form of 'soft power'; getting communities to follow wider policing or political agendas (Innes 2006), it may, in an alternative form, involve a high degree of community participation or even community empowerment, and it may include police officers having to balance conflicting values. For example, drawing upon the work of Murphy (2005), Hanniman (2008) argues that national security policing derives its authority from a state or government. Therefore, national security policing traditionally employs policing strategies that are secret, meaning they do not require public consent or support and are not open to public or legal scrutiny. Furthermore, the national security-based version of community policing may see communities as merely a source of security information and criminal intelligence. In this context, community members are encouraged to watch and share information on suspicious neighbours or friends with police – viewed as informants rather than partners. Local police may also be encouraged to use their community-policing programmes and relationships to penetrate local communities and provide intelligence. These strategies, Hanniman (2008) argues, can rapidly alienate a community. Our research studies suggest that counter-terrorism police officers can facilitate community participation at the highest level, by supporting independent community interests, and providing advice or other forms of support to help communities develop their own projects aimed at PVE. For example, officers can help to provide advice on sources of funding and the writing of applications for project ideas that community members approach them with. Police officers can help facilitate a change of leadership within mosques under the influence of extremists by working with members of the mosque communities, including brokering meetings between influential individuals to facilitate change. At the same time, counter-terrorism officers can work to help communities in gaining permission to organize political demonstrations. Both research studies illustrate the numerous ways in which counter-terrorism police officers have supported independent community interests within a counter-terrorism context, this being a significant achievement given that the theory of community participation often falls short (Cook 2006).

However, supporting independent community interests may be difficult given that the wider social and political context may be unhelpful to police officers engaged in such sensitive areas. Therefore, rather than working in isolation, it is useful for police officers to build links with wider society in order to help facilitate work around the Prevent agenda, building links with government departments, think tanks, academics and policy analysts who may hold similar views in relation to the importance of engaging with those communities labelled as 'radical' so that police officers can draw on any social and political capital that these institutions and individuals bring. According to Oppler (1997), this form of policing can be linked to a multi-agency approach, whereby the police, communities, elected officials, statutory and other agencies work in partnership to address crime and community safety, underpinned by a principle of finding local solutions to address local issues.

Importance of building competencies for policing within a counter-terrorism context

Within trust-building activities between police and communities, our studies suggest that it is important for space to be given for police officers to develop a range of cultural, religious, political and emotional competencies. The Muslim population in the UK is extremely diverse; ethnically, culturally, religiously and politically, therefore posing significant challenges for engagement. It may be that some groups place higher value on organizing demonstrations and vociferously expressing their concerns to the police, whereas other groups prefer an approach that involves implicitly expressing their concerns while maintaining good relationships with police. These different styles and viewpoints of engagement inevitably lead to tensions between groups and individuals and may lead to some groups and individuals partially disengaging from established police–community structures. It is important to point out, however, that this kind of disengagement is not necessarily negative because those individuals/groups who disengage from existing structures of engagement may continue engaging with police, albeit in new ways. Other intra-community tensions that may impact upon community–police engagement include; the lack of representation and the perception that this has been reduced through intra-community dynamics and political manoeuvrings, including the marginalization of certain ethnic and religious groups from engagement, competition between groups for voice and influence, internal leadership disputes, and in some cases ineffective grassroots communication so that any engagement between community members and police does not filter down onto a wider population. Community members have described a variety of motivations and goals as underpinning their active engagement and partnership with police: primarily as part of their dedication to preventing violence underpinned by feelings of social justice, protection and security of British society, diverse communities and future generations; as a religious duty, which includes factors such as a feeling of being able to affect social change, to help bring communities together, to improve the image of Muslims and Islam; to represent a particular ethnic, religious, gender, political or ideological perspective; and to contribute a community voice to debates. These motivations and goals may at times be shared, and at other times be very different to those of police officers, illustrating the importance of shared goals, but also to the possibility of there being fundamental differences between individuals involved in engagement that can be overcome within partnership work.

The above discussion highlights the central importance for police officers to develop a nuanced and culturally, politically and religiously sophisticated understanding of the Muslim communities that they are engaging with. Added to this, our research also highlights the importance of police officers developing skills in relation to emotional competence. The intangibility and central importance of emotion in understanding socialities renders it complex and challenging for study and for engagement work. Nonetheless, there is growing research attention upon emotions, which might be viewed as being active stances towards the world, as well as being responses to situations (Woodhead 2009: 1). Some academic work has focused upon emotions in a criminal justice and policing context. For example, both Karstedt (2002) and Spalek (2006) have discussed the ways in which emotions pervade the criminal justice system as issues of crime and justice elicit powerful emotional reactions within both 'victims' and offenders' as well as from within wider society. With respect to policing, according to Drodge and Murphy (2002: 421), 'police organizations and police work are affect laden because of cultural and social rules and because of the nature of the work itself, particularly as it occurs at the interface with public law and order'. However, it seems that within policing, detached rationality is generally valued whereby 'neutrality, objectivity and impartiality are viewed as necessary antecedents in policing' (Drodge and Murphy 2002: 425).

Our studies highlight a number of issues in relation to emotions within a counter-terrorism policing context. First, individuals that police officers might be engaging with in this context may have directly experienced state repression (including torture) before their arrival to the UK. As such, individuals have a set of experiences, histories and emotions which may impact upon the ways in which they engage with counter-terrorism police officers in the UK. When engaging with individuals, it is therefore helpful for police officers to be aware of these contexts as an individual's history and set of emotional reactions to their experiences can impact significantly upon any interaction that takes place between police officers and community members. It may be the case, for example, that a person is so traumatized and has experienced such marginalization in the past that they feel extremely disempowered and unable to engage with police officers. It may be that police engagement re-awakens a person's prior experiences with police from within their country of origin, thereby bringing about a set of emotional and psychological processes that are painful and extremely difficult for the individual to negotiate through. At the same time, those individuals that police officers approach may previously have experienced particularly 'hard' policing tactics within the UK, and so may be extremely fearful of having any kind of interaction with police officers, or they may be extremely angry with police.

Interestingly, our studies highlight that some community members may feel that policing culture and practice is hindered by a police service that is viewed as being overly bureaucratic and emotionally distant. Our studies further highlight that some groundbreaking police officers have shown what might usefully be referred to as 'emotional intelligence'. In these cases, an acknowledgement and awareness of emotions has been used by officers as a way of helping to build effective partnerships grounded in empathy, reciprocity and in emotional connections between partners. Indeed, it might be argued that within the counter-terrorism context it is important for those working on counter-terrorism to emotionally connect with those individuals deemed at risk from violent extremism. This is because it may be that individuals linked to, or inspired by, al-Qaeda networks draw upon their emotional intelligence to influence individuals emotionally and thus encourage engagement in extremist activities. Within such a context, practitioners need to be able to empathize and make those deemed at risk feel comfortable with them in order to allow for effective prevention work to take place. This reflects current thinking within cognitive psychology whereby emotions are viewed as being intertwined with human thinking and behaviour (Goleman 2003). Therefore, it might be suggested that a way of altering cognitions and transforming how individuals relate to, and interact with, the world is through an awareness of, and working with, emotions.

Muslim Contact Unit and legitimacy

Lambert's research study consists of an insider's analysis of the London-based MCU and Muslim community partnership initiative intended to counter the influence of al-Qaeda propaganda and recruitment activity. It researches the London partnership initiative from January 2002 to October 2007 and draws on prior police and community experience. A significant part of the police experience was that counter-terrorism policing against the Provisional IRA (PIRA) became counter-productive when it lost focus on legitimate terrorist suspects and drifted into the targeting of Irish Catholic communities in London as 'suspect communities' (see Lambert 2008). In contrast, the MCU drew on its experience of effective counter-terrorism policing where Sikh community leaders and others were treated as partners.

Expertise emerges as the defining feature and a key ingredient in the rich experience that police and community partners bring to the London partnership initiative. Two case study sites in London – Brixton and Finsbury Park – provide the community settings within which the London partnership initiative and the issues surrounding its legitimacy and effectiveness are elucidated. 'Al-Qaeda' is used to denote a loose and adaptive terrorist movement that developed a distinctive brand in London from the early 1990s, due in part to the activities of Abu Qatada, Abu Hamza and Abdullah el Faisal. At both of these sites, the partnership initiative was effective in securing its explicit purpose of countering the impact of al-Qaeda propaganda and recruitment activity within local Muslim communities.

In terms of scale, however, MCU partnership activity represented less than 0.0001 per cent of the Metropolitan Police Service's (MPS) investment in counter-terrorism[2] and far less than 0.00001 per cent of the national financial investment in UK counter-terrorism during the period under review.[3] Operating with between two and eight officers the unit was an equally small part of MPS human and administrative resources.[4] One officer recalls how the first four years of the MCU were spent without an office, shuffling from one temporary venue to another while significant resources were poured into operational counter-terrorism activity:

> With one or two notable exceptions counter-terrorism management was reluctant to invest in the MCU. It was either viewed as a side-show or a complete waste of time. Had we packed it in some managers would have been pleased.

It is also important to note research that has shown police have a tendency to control and manage partnerships (Balloch and Taylor 2001). In addition, one Muslim community leader who rejected an approach from detectives to become an informant has commented on the pervasive nature of what he calls the 'informant culture' in policing. On the one hand, his prior experience of resisting what he describes as a concerted attempt to recruit him as making him wary of entering into a subsequent partnership relationship with the MCU. On the other hand, he describes how one senior police officer who formed a local partnership with Muslim community groups continued to adopt a management rather than a partnership style in his discussions with community representatives:

> In some ways the MCU has broken police stereotypes. When I was growing up in we had a few encounters with the CID. Some of them really did behave like they were in the *Sweeney*. And I had one friend who got pressured into being an informant and he was always regretting it. Instead of making him

feel safe, it made him feel anxious all the time. So when detectives wanted to recruit me I was experienced enough to say no. But I had to be very firm and stand up for myself. So I was initially very wary of the MCU partnership thing but I could see it was different and was prepared to give it a chance. And it has been unusual to be listened to so much. It's been good to be a real partner.

Nonetheless, expert skill in countering al-Qaeda influence emerges as a necessary but insufficient factor in determining the partnership's legitimacy and effectiveness. Principally, notwithstanding a benign objective and some demonstrable success in achieving it, the legitimacy and effectiveness of the partnership endeavour is a contested issue because of the problematic identities of the two Muslim communities at each location – Brixton Salafi and Finsbury Park Islamist. By empowering Salafi and Islamist communities the London partnership initiative was at odds with influential academic, practitioner, popular and community discourses that conflate Salafism and Islamism with terrorism, extremism and sectarianism (Cox and Marks 2006; Gove 2006; Phillips 2006; Desai 2007).

The core objection to the partnership between the MCU and Brixton Salafi community leaders is that Salafism is a key ingredient in al-Qaeda terrorism and should therefore be discouraged rather than empowered and legitimated by police. The core objection at the second case study site is that the police partners – Finsbury Park Islamist community leaders – are linked to the Muslim Brotherhood and Hamas, both of which condone suicide terrorism against civilians in Israel and should not therefore be empowered and legitimated by police. By exploring these and related objections the case study encounters grass roots perspectives that challenge conventional terrorism studies accounts that generally support the objectives and the underlying rationale of the war on terror. Moreover, it follows from both objectives that any proven effectiveness against al-Qaeda propaganda and recruitment activity at either site might still be outweighed and countermanded by a charge of illegitimacy. Both objections also encourage an analysis of the nature of the chosen relationship between police and the two Muslim community groups – partnership. Elsewhere in counter-terrorism, the identities of both community partners – Salafi and Islamist – are generally sufficient to preclude them from partnership status and to confine them instead to the role of police informants.

In contrast, both our studies provide empirical evidence that speaks directly to the question of the legitimacy and effectiveness of London-based police and Muslim community partnership activity intended to counter the adverse impact of al-Qaeda terrorist propaganda and recruitment strategies in Muslim communities. Principally, the question of legitimacy and effectiveness turns on the identity of the Muslim community partners. Police have a clear duty to prevent and reduce the threat of terrorism and to work with community leaders who may be able to help in that task and to that extent no research question of interest arises. It is the trenchant view of politicians, including Michael Gove and Pauline Neville-Jones, academics following Daniel Pipes and Gilles Keppel, think tanks, including

Rand, the Hudson Institute, Policy Exchange and the Centre for Social Cohesion, and media commentators, including Melanie Phillips, Charles Moore and Dean Godson (2005), that certain kinds of Muslim identity are anathema to British (or Western) identity that provides a basis for research interest. The more so when the Muslim participants in the London partnership initiative fall precisely into the two categories that are most commonly described by these influential voices as being antithetical to a liberal democracy – Islamist and Salafi. Thus, from this authoritative perspective, the police side of the partnership has made the grave mistake of conferring legitimacy on community partners who do not warrant it. Effectiveness, advocates of this school argue, insofar as it might be achieved at all, should be sought instead by the traditional and tested coercive relationship of police or security officer and informant rather than by recourse to a partnership approach that confers legitimacy on community partner. More than sufficiently powerful to marginalize the work of the London partnership initiative, this school of thought was nonetheless bolstered by Muslim opponents of Salafis and Islamists with axes to grind. In response, both the police and community partners have at times felt marginalized, a familiar experience for some of the community partners (Garland *et al.* 2006).

Of its own volition, the London partnership initiative raised important questions about its legitimacy and effectiveness, especially as both the police and community partners found themselves vulnerable to institutional and community scepticism about the legitimacy and effectiveness of their chosen endeavour. That is to say, while the partnership was isolated from disapprobation of the kind highlighted for a significant period, it encountered local resistance from the outset. On the police side, the initiative was hampered by a lack of senior support and a failure to bridge two competing policing models – counter-terrorism and community policing. Indeed, the police unit involved in the initiative faced opposition from senior police officers who favoured a neighbourhood policing model as a preferred approach to counter-terrorism intelligence gathering (Innes 2006).

On the community side, the distinction between working in partnership with police and performing the role of police informant was vulnerable to claims that it was artificial and contrived. For some Muslim community groups, no attempt to dress up a relationship with police in partnership clothes could hide the unacceptable nature of being a traitor to the community; a 'grass', a 'snitch', an 'informant'. These commonplace concerns became heightened in the wake of the 'War on Terror' when the government's international counter-terrorism strategy became viewed with deep distrust in Muslim communities. One community leader characterized a more prevalent position for Muslim communities and their representatives as 'passive disengagement', capturing the sense in which the full impact of the war on terror militated against active participation with its agents. Another Muslim community leader in West London voiced his frustration with the situation in 2005 in these terms:

> I have struggled continuously to convince young members of the community that they should help the police to fight extremism. They believe George Bush

is fighting a war against Islam not a war against terrorism and I have given up trying to disabuse them of this idea. Instead I try to reassure them that the British police have got a difficult job to do and should be supported when they are investigating terrorist attacks like 7th July. Unfortunately there have been too many occasions when the British authorities have been seen to be puppets of the US for my words to be heeded. It has become a very difficult issue.

In particular, Muslim partners expressed concern about the approach adopted by Tony Blair. Thus, typically, in a speech to the World Affairs Council in Los Angeles on Monday, 1 August 2005 Tony Blair described the War on Terror as a 'struggle between what I will call Reactionary Islam and Moderate, Mainstream Islam'.[5] In consequence, whenever the MCU reported and endorsed the views of its community partners that directly contradicted the prime minister's analysis it faced the prospect of marginalization itself. This became particularly acute after 7/7 when the Association of Chief Police Officers (ACPO) became even less inclined to challenge government orthodoxy on the topic. Which raises an additional question concerning MCU legitimacy and effectiveness when the unit's rupture with government policy extends to acknowledging Richard Jackson's claim that the language of the war on terror 'prevents rather than facilitates' the search for solutions to terrorism (Jackson 2005: 4). This entailed the MCU explaining both that government policies and the manner in which they were expressed ran the risk of being counter-productive. Certainly, when discussing the problem with their community partners it became increasingly clear to the MCU that the terrorist threat had to be understood in terms of the war on terror, the killing of civilians by 7/7 suicide bombers alongside US helicopter gunships attacking insurgents on the streets of Fallujah.

Somewhat predictably, al-Qaeda propagandists sought to capitalize on the situation both to increase recruitment and tacit support – success that would be made clear in the statements made by the 7/7 bombers. However, the post 9/11 Washington–Whitehall view that al-Qaeda comprised such a new and exceptional threat as to license unbridled counter-terrorism measures paid no heed to the risk that the measures might be counter-productive (Lambert 2008). Moreover, such was the skill with which neo-conservative politicians mobilized a global response to 9/11 that academic disapprobation was confined to the margins. Still less were the concerns of two police officers in London about the risk of alienating the very communities whose support was most needed, understood or acknowledged. Positing a case that lessons learned during the long counter-terrorism effort against the PIRA should not be ignored, the police officers launched the local partnership initiative with Muslim communities as bombing raids took place in Afghanistan for the same ostensible purpose. While the local initiative gained some crucial support at senior police level it was never able to impose its rationale on the wider strategic machinery of government.

For both police and community partners, therefore, the London partnership initiative entailed trust building in a hostile and negative climate. As such, the study illuminates qualities that enabled the partners to achieve effective outcomes in spite of the obstacles that surrounded them. Of particular significance was a shared assurance that the influence of al-Qaeda propaganda and recruitment in communities was best tackled by community voices that understood the problem and had credibility amongst target audiences. Launched in the shadow of the militarized global war on terror, the locally negotiated partnership initiative was out of kilter with a counter-terrorism strategy driven by Washington and Whitehall that sought unconditional support from its citizens, Muslim or otherwise. When 7/7 switched the focus of government attention to 'home grown radicalisation' the partnership initiative was seen to be further out of step – especially comprising as it did Salafis and Islamists who were now being portrayed as stepping stones on a route to violent extremism. Ironically, as community partnerships against violent extremism came into vogue the ground breaking work of the London partnership initiative simultaneously failed to capitalize on its success because of the weight of allegations against its Salafi and Islamist partners. Instead, alternative Whitehall friendly projects took centre stage, lauded by Timothy Garten Ash and other champions of liberal democracy as the perfect tools with which to counter violent extremism and the evil ideology that was understood to underpin it.

Nonetheless, according to both sides of the partnership, increased mutual respect was achieved during the course of demanding, sometimes dangerous, pro-active engagement. As one community partner explains:

> I got a phone call from someone I didn't know very well asking me to help with their son who had joined Abu Hamza's circle. It didn't sound altogether genuine and it just made me concerned that it might be some kind of trap. I went to the house at 9pm but on the way I let the MCU know what was happening and agreed to phone later if everything was ok. As it turned out everything was genuine but it was reassuring to know I had support if I needed it.

This kind of work sits at the heart of the London partnership initiative and is presented in detail at both community sites – Brixton and Finsbury Park. To illuminate the nature of pro-active London partnership initiative work in a counter-terrorist arena it helps to describe key events as they have unfolded. Thus, for example, events and partnership responses in relation to complex negotiations to reclaim de facto control of Finsbury Park Mosque[6] from the adverse influence of Abu Hamza[7] and his hardcore supporters are charted by observing a strict chronology and faithfulness to street-level community politics during the period 2002–2005. This perspective helps illuminate features that distinguish the activities of the London partnership initiative from negative accounts of security and police engagement with Abu Hamza in popular accounts such as *The Suicide Factory* (O'Neil and McGrory 2006). Pro-activity is characterized as being firmly grounded in a partnership where community interests are paramount whereas in traditional counter-terrorism decisions are often made without direct engagement with the community representatives most closely affected. Pro-activity, it emerges, is also what separated the two case study sites (Brixton and Finsbury Park) from other sites of dialogue between the MCU and Muslim community groups in London that did not progress beyond cordial exchanges.

Conclusion

This chapter raises some important issues in relation to policing within a counter-terrorism context. While individual police officers and Muslim community members can engage and indeed partner with each other in order to reduce the threat from al-Qaeda inspired/connected violence, and the studies drawn upon in this chapter illustrate some of the bravery and commitment of the individuals concerned, nonetheless, the wider political, social and cultural context within which they operate creates significant difficulties for any engagement and partnership work to take place. The dynamics of this problematic context are multiple and over-lapping, consisting of 'hard' policing strategies and their impacts upon Muslim communities, Islamophobia and religious racism, the political, bureaucratic and militaristic machinery of the 'war on terror', as well as political and socio-cultural structures that view particular Muslim minorities, notably Salafis and Islamists, through the homogenized all-encompassing lens of 'suspect'. As a result, those individuals wishing to create space for dialogue, interaction and partnership have to draw upon significant personal and professional resources in order to effectively negotiate their ways through the difficult terrain. It is only with sustained commitment from government and from senior police officers that the work highlighted in this chapter can grow.

Notes

1 Both studies examined a series of similar questions, including: What are the key components to effective partnership work between police and Muslim groups for counter terror purposes? What is meant by 'partnership work', and how does this differ from other forms of engagement? How do different participants view partnership? How, and in what ways, might partnership work be compromised? How, and in what ways, are the experiences and religious knowledge of Muslim groups working with the police important to the development of counter terror strategies? How do Muslim groups challenge religiously or other endorsed violence in counter-terrorism partnerships developed between themselves and the police? And what are the structures and processes of Muslim/police partnership? With respect to the AHRC funded study, in total 42 individuals were interviewed. Thirteen of these participants were police officers (MCU, NCTT and ACPO officers) and 29 were members of Muslim communities and organizations involved, to varying levels, in partnership/engagement work with the police, either through the MSF or directly with the MCU or NCTT. Interviews took place between December 2007 and July 2008. At the same time, researchers attended and observed MSF community meetings and MSF meetings with senior police officers in Scotland Yard. The minutes of meetings were also examined.
2 'The budget also includes £30 million extra for counter terrorism measures (rising to £45 million in 2007/8) bringing the level of specific counter terrorism funding for the

Met to £257 million in 2006/7. This is a substantially increased budget and will be fully spent on strengthening the Met's capability to counter the terrorist threat', Len Duval, Metropolitan Police Authority (MPA). Available at: http://www.met.police.uk/ job/job970/live_files/1.htm (accessed 29 December 2007).

3 In answer to a question during a pre-budget statement to the House of Commons on 6 December 2006 the Chancellor Gordon Brown announced 'an additional £84 million directed to intelligence and counter-terrorism ... our budget for security, which was just £1 billion in 2001, will now be more than £2 billion for 2007–8', see http://www.theyworkforyou.com/search/?s=terrorism&pid=10068&pop=1 (accessed 29 December 2006).

4 The MPS is far and away the largest police service in the UK and its head, the Commissioner, from 2005 Sir Ian Blair, is accorded the status of the country's leading police voice. London's largest employer, the MPS was staffed by 31,141 police officers, 2,106 police community support officers (PCSOs) and 13,661 civil staff in 2006. See http://www.met. police.uk/about/ (accessed 30 December 2006). In addition the MPS serves citizens in 32 London Boroughs estimated to number 7.2 million, plus 3 million daily commuting capital workers and over 30 million annual tourists. See http://www.london.gov.uk/gla/ publications/factsandfigures/factsfigures/population.jsp; http://www.lda.gov.uk/upload/ pdf/Evidence_Base_Section_5.pdf (accessed 30 December 2007).

5 http://www.number10.gov.uk/output/Page9948.asp (accessed 2 August 2006).

6 The Finsbury Park Mosque is officially known as the North London Central Mosque.

7 For the major part of the case study Abu Hamza has been in UK prisons, both on remand and then serving a sentence for incitement to murder. He is also subject of ongoing extradition proceedings to face terrorism charges in the USA.

References

Alderson, J. (1979) *Policing Freedom*, Plymouth: Macdonald & Evans.

Balloch, S. and Taylor, M. (eds) (2001) *Partnership Working: Policy and Practice*, Bristol: Policy Press.

Breen Smyth. M. (2007) 'A critical research agenda for the study of political terror', *European Political Science*, (6): 260–7.

Briggs, R., Fieschi, C. and Lownsbrough, H. (2006) *Bringing it Home: Community-Based Approaches to Counter-Terrorism,* London: Demos.

Bunyan, T. (1977) *The History and Practice of the Political Police in Britain*, London: Quartet Books.

Campbell, A. and Stott, R. (2008) *The Blair Years: Extracts from the Alistair Campbell Diaries*, London: Arrow Books.

Cook, D. (2006) *Criminal and Social Justice*, London: Sage.

Cox, C., and Marks, J. (2006) *The West, Islam and Islamism: Is Ideological Islam Compatible with Liberal Democracy?*, London: Civitas.

de Guzman, M.C. (2002) 'The changing roles and strategies of the police in time of terror', *ACJS Today*, 1: 13.

Desai, M. (2007) *Rethinking Islamism: The Ideology of the New Terror*, London: I. B. Taurus.

Drodge, N. and Murphy, S. (2002) 'Interrogating emotions in police leadership', *Human Resource Development Review*, 1(4): 420–38.

Garland, J., Spalek, B. and Chakraborti, N. (2006) 'Hearing lost voices: issues in researching hidden minority ethnic communities', *The British Journal of Criminology*, 46: 423–37.

Godson, D. (2005) 'You'll never guess who's to blame for 7/7', *The Times*, 13 December, Available at: http://www.timeonline.co.uk/article/0,1922518,00.html (accessed 2 August 2008).

Goleman, D. (2003) *Destructive Emotions: How We Can Overcome Them*, London: Bloomsbury.

Gove, M. (2006) *Celsius 7/7*, London: Weidenfield & Nicholson.

Hanniman, W. (2008) 'Canadian Muslims, Islamophobia and National Security Royal Canadian Mounted Police', *International Journal of Law, Crime and Justice*, 36(4): 271–85.

Hillyard, P. (1993) *Suspect Community: People's Experience of the Prevention of Terrorism Acts in Britain*, London: Pluto Press.

—— (2005) 'The 'War on Terror': lessons from Ireland' *Essays for civil liberties and democracy in Europe*, Available at: http://www.ecln.org/essays/essay-1.pdf (accessed 12 July 2008).

HM Government (2008) *The Prevent Strategy: A Guide for Local Partners in England: Stopping People Becoming or Supporting Terrorists and Violent Extremists*. London: HMSO.

Innes, M. (2006) 'Policing uncertainty: countering terror through community intelligence and democratic policing', *Annals of the American Academy*, 605(May): 1–20.

Jackson, R. (2005) *Writing the War on Terrorism: Language, Politics and Counter-Terrorism*, Manchester: Manchester University Press.

Jones, T. and Newburn, T. (2001) *Widening Access: Improving Police Relations with Hard to Reach Groups*, Police Research Series Paper 138, London: Home Office.

Karstedt, S. (2002) 'Emotions and criminal justice', *Theoretical Criminology*, 6(3): 29–317.

Lowe, H. and Innes, M. (2008) 'Countering terror: violent radicalisation and situational intelligence', *Prison Service Journal*, 179: 3–10.

Lambert, R. (2008) 'Salafi and Islamist Londoners: stigmatised minority faith communities countering al-Qaida', *Crime, Law & Social Change*, 50: 73–89.

Lyons, W. (2002) 'Partnerships, information and public safety: community policing in a time of terror', *Policing: an International Journal of Police Strategies & Management*, 25(3): 530–42.

Lustick, I.S. (2006) *Trapped in the War on Terror*, Philadelphia, PA: University of Pennsylvania Press.

Macpherson Inquiry (1999) *The Stephen Lawrence Inquiry, Report of an Inquiry by Sir William Macpherson of Cluny*, Cm 4262-I, London: Stationery Office.

Moore, C. (2008) 'How to beat the Scargills of Islam', *The 2008 Keith Joseph Memorial Lecture*. Centre for Policy Studies, 10 March, available at: http://www.policyexchange.org.uk/images/libimages/362.pdf (accessed 2 September 2008).

Murphy, C. (2005) Securitizing community policing: towards a Canadian public policing model, *The Canadia Review of Policing Research* 1.

O'Neil, S. and McGrory, D. (2006) *The Suicide Factory: Abu Hamza and the Finsbury Park Mosque*, London: Harper Perennial.

Phillips, M. (2006) *Londonistan: How Britain Is Creating a Terror State Within*, London: Gibson Square.

Prior, D., Farrow, K., Spalek, B. and Barnes, M. (2006) 'Can anti-social behavior interventions help to contribute to civil renewal?', in T. Brennan, P. John and G. Stoker (eds) *Re-energizing Citizenship: Strategies for Civil Renewal*, pp. 91–111. Basingstoke: Palgrave.

Ramirez, D. (2008) 'Partnering for Prevention', available at: http://www.ace.neu.edu/pfp.

Reiner, R. (2000) *The Politics of the Police*, Oxford: Oxford University Press.

Spalek, B. (2006) *Crime Victims*, Basingstoke: Palgrave.

Spalek, B. (forthcoming, 2009) 'Muslim communities, policing within a counter-terrorism context and the prevention of violent extremism', *British Journal of Criminology*.

Spalek, B. and Imtoual, A. (2007) ' "Hard" approaches to community engagement in the UK and Australia: Muslim communities and counter-terror responses', *Journal of Muslim Minority Affairs*, 27(2): 185–202.

Spalek, B. and Lambert, B. (2008) 'Muslim communities, counter-terrorism and de-radicalisation: a reflective approach to engagement', *International Journal of Law, Crime and Justice*, 36(4): 257–70.

Thacher, D. (2001) 'Conflicting values in community policing', *Law & Society Review*, 35(4): 765–98.

Thomas, D. and Inkson, K. (2003) *Cultural Intelligence*, San Francisco, CA: Berrett-Koehler.

Tupman, B. and Tupman, A. (1999) *Policing in Europe: Uniform in Diversity*, Exeter: Intellect.

Woodhead, L. and Riis, O. (2009) *A Sociology of Religious Emotions*, Oxford: Oxford University Press.

6 'Preventing violent extremism' – why local context matters

Vivien Lowndes and Leila Thorp

Introduction

In the wake of the 7/7 bombings in London (2005) the Government stated the need for a measured, community-led response. As the then Prime Minister, Tony Blair put it:

> We will seek to debate the right way forward in combating this evil within the Muslim community with Muslim leaders, and it's our intention to begin this process immediately ... In the end, this can only be taken on and defeated by the community itself, but we all can help and facilitate and we will do so.
>
> (Blair 2005)

The call for a calm and measured community-based response was immediately placed in tension with the need for security against an unknown enemy (see Bleich, Chapter 3 in this volume). This tension was graphically played out by a number of incidents, perhaps most prominently the accidental fatal shooting of a young Brazilian man by the security services, which took place in the wake of further terrorist activity on the 21 July 2005. At first the government's preference for a community-led approach appeared to waiver (see DEMOS 2006; McGhee forthcoming). This was in spite of the establishment of 'Muslim working groups' to inform policy on how to *Prevent Extremism Together* (Home Office 2005). But the approach was given new impetus in April 2007 when, following pilot work and consultation, the Department of Communities and Local Government (DCLG 2005b) produced an action plan, *Preventing Violent Extremism – Winning Hearts and Minds*, and guidance to support Preventing Violent Extremism (PVE) Pathfinders in selected local areas (DCLG 2007a). The PVE policy framework emphasized 'local solutions to local problems', with a focus upon local authority engagement with Muslim communities in order to build collective resilience to terrorism. The challenge for Pathfinder projects was to enable local communities 'to challenge robustly the ideas of those extremists who seek to undermine our way of life' (DCLG 2007b: 4). Tensions between a locally driven, community-focused approach and a nationally led, security-oriented agenda (Home Office/Cabinet 2006) have been ongoing.

Indeed, since 2005 there has been much debate in the media and academia about the nature and wisdom of the government's approach (for example: Blick *et al.* 2006; Brown 2008; Ellery 2009). But, despite extensive speculation on the topic, there has been very little substantive analysis of practice on the ground. This chapter addresses the gap by providing a case study analysis of a regional PVE Pathfinder, involving three unitary city councils working with a range of local agencies and community groups. Using action research methods, the chapter identifies the important role of local context in shaping policy outcomes, despite the intensity of national debate and the apparent 'top-down' character of the agenda (see McGhee's discussion of governmentality, forthcoming, and Brown 2008). We explore the role of both local level policymakers and Muslim communities themselves in interacting with the government agenda. Our research shows how 'governance strategies' (Newman 2005) emanating from the centre have been interpreted in different ways locally, and explores the creative and often surprising interplay between such strategies and local political agency. Our evidence also points to the inadequacies of any crude distinction between risk reduction strategies and community capacity building in PVE policy. The case study shows how this binary thinking was increasingly challenged over the Pathfinder year, as local actors reflected critically on new information, experiences and relationships.

The chapter starts by explaining our action research approach. We then look at the role of the region as a contested 'governance space' (Newman 2005) in which government discourses were debated and renegotiated, and in which city-level actors came to reflect critically upon their own policy assumptions. We then look in detail at how city-level contexts shaped the development and implementation of the PVE agenda. We show how Pathfinder activities varied between the three cities, and were expressive of distinctive, and highly dynamic, 'settlements' between the local state and Muslim communities.

An action research approach

The PVE Pathfinder fund for 2007/8 provided £6 million to local authorities with populations comprising at least 5 per cent of Muslims. The government explained the purpose of the programme as being to develop a community in which Muslims:

- Identify themselves as a welcome part of a wider British society and are accepted as such by the wider community.
- Reject violent extremist ideology and actively condemn violent extremism.
- Isolate violent extremist activity, and support and co-operate with the police and security services.
- Develop their own capacity to deal with problems where they arise and support diversionary activity for those at risk (DCLG 2007a: 3).

The government's action plan set out four key approaches for Pathfinder authorities:

1   Promoting shared values – through better citizenship and Islamic education.
2   Supporting local solutions – through the setting up of Muslim forums to address concerns of extremism and Islamophobia.
3   Building civic capacity and leadership – through ensuring that women's and young people's voices are heard, helping to remove barriers to inclusion in Mosques, and developing leadership and mentoring schemes.
4   Strengthening the role of faith institutions and leaders – by supporting Imam education and skills development and improving Mosque governance (DCLG 2007a: 3).

Pathfinders were required to undertake evaluation activity and, in the case under investigation, an action research approach was agreed upon. Given the novel and sensitive nature of the policy arena, conventional evaluation techniques had major limitations. Practice was evolving on a daily basis, and was being shaped by community dynamics, ongoing learning among partners, and a fast changing national policy context. The Pathfinder did not have a clear starting-point or 'baseline' and lacked obvious measurable outputs. Moreover, it was established on a regional basis, in recognition of the fact that Muslim communities, and the connections between them, cross local authority borders. Thus the Pathfinder was not 'owned' by a single local authority but led and implemented by a complex (and shifting) partnership of actors from three different cities and a myriad of statutory and community-based agencies. There were few fixed points for evaluation. Rather, the action research approach allowed us to:

- Record the experience of the programme as it happened.
- Gather evidence from all stakeholders to get a multi-dimensional picture of the programme as it unfolded.
- Facilitate critical reflection among stakeholders to support problem-solving and innovation.
- Compare experience in the three cities and maximize learning across city boundaries.
- Identify and communicate lessons from the Pathfinder for other cities/regions and for national policy development.

As Denscombe (2003: 73) notes, action research is practical, change-oriented and prioritizes the active participation of practitioners in the research process.

The approach provided almost unlimited research access. Building relationships of trust with the full range of stakeholders (including community actors) was facilitated by the recognition that we were contributing to the development of the Pathfinder. Partners commented that we were able to play an 'honest broker' role in facilitating critical discussion and problem-solving because we had combined an in-depth knowledge of local dynamics but were not aligned with any particular part of the Muslim community, or with a local authority or other local agency. However, negotiating the insider–outsider boundary had its challenges, for instance when certain actors sought to mobilize our expertise in support of particular positions, or when we had to set limits on our involvement given finite research resources. As Denscombe (2003: 78) observes: 'The participatory nature of action research brings with it a question mark about who owns the research and its outcomes'. Our own identity also imposed some constraints, for instance in accessing male-only arenas in the Muslim communities. Finally, ongoing tensions around the language and focus of PVE meant that maintaining a neutral but approachable position as researchers was not always an easy task. Anonymity and confidentiality were also vital for some participants, sometimes to protect their personal safety. The informal, even invisible, nature of the action research process precipitates complex ethical issues of authorization and consent (Denscombe 2003: 79).

The research had three main elements. First, using interviews, observation and documentary analysis, PVE strategies, structures and activities were mapped across the three cities, analysing distinctive local responses to a common policy agenda. Second, case studies of key initiatives were produced to communicate good practice within the region and to a wider audience (via a national, local government sponsored 'Community of Practice'). Third, special events brought partners together to share experience and, using action learning techniques, to work on problem solving and action planning.

Data were collected through in-depth qualitative interviews with senior managers and front line workers from local agencies, and with community leaders and 'ordinary' participants in events and activities (with a particular focus on Muslim women and young Muslim people). We also facilitated learning events and undertook extensive participant observation of strategy meetings and community activities, which involved a rich diversity of casual encounters and informal conversations as well as structured observations. We look first at the regional policy arena, and then in more detail at PVE activities in the three cities.

The regional context – a contested governance space

A regional steering group was established, comprising strategic and operational leads (police and local government) from the three cities along with regional police and security personnel. The group was supported by a regional PVE coordinator and chaired by the Senior Director to the Home Office (at the Government Office of the Region [GOR]). Steering group meetings were on occasion attended by representatives from central government in order to facilitate a direct dialogue (for instance on the Local Area Agreement PVE indicator). The coordinator also organized conferences and training sessions to build the capacity of the cities, and of GOR staff (e.g. Islamic Awareness Workshops).

The steering group faced the challenge of spanning the different cultures and perspectives associated with a diverse range of partners – local authority senior managers, community cohesion officers, police and security officers, and staff from youth services and youth justice. Not only was it an opportunity for people from the three different cities to exchange experience; sometimes regional activities were the only occasion when partners from *within* the same city came together. The regional steering group provided a pressure valve for releasing some of the underlying tensions within the PVE agenda – there were heated discussions about the language of PVE (did it stigmatize Muslim communities?) and the relationship to community cohesion policies (was PVE an essential element of, or a distraction from, cohesion goals?). Outside their day-to-day environment, actors literally let off steam and tried out different positions on one another.

However, at the heart of most debates was a common tension between, on the one hand, working to build trust with marginalized Muslim communities and, on the other hand, working to gather intelligence to reduce the risk of acts of violent extremism (see also Lambert 2008). This was clearly illustrated in an ongoing discussion about potential security risks associated with the funding of local Muslim community groups from PVE funds. Funds were distributed by different mechanisms in each of the three cities but, in each case, there were efforts to involve representatives from Muslim communities themselves in the commissioning process. The Counter Terrorism Unit's (CTU) offer to provide a regional screening service for funding bids was interpreted by some local actors as Home Office vetting. Outrage turned to laughter when the CTU proposed words like '*youth*' and '*mosque*' as 'trigger terms' which, if found in funding bids, would lead to screening. Given that such terms appeared in 90 per cent of bids, local actors felt that this level of suspicion would jeopardize their ability to work with Muslim community groups.

For their part, regional police and security sought to express the gravity of the threat to local actors who, at the same time, lacked the security clearance to receive detailed intelligence. While security could warn that city X was 'hot', they could not provide the detail to help local actors review their relationships and participate in joint action. As these frustrations became more apparent, the GRO sought to act as a broker, initiating a series of briefings by the CTU for local authority chief executives, and developing a process for collating 'sanitized' intelligence information for wider local circulation, especially where threat levels were high.

The regional government office also played an important role in Local Area Agreement (LAA) negotiations, which resulted in the inclusion of the new PVE indicator (NI35) in 2008/9 LAAs for two of the three cities in the region. The PVE steering group provided a forum for consultation with DCLG personnel over the content of the indicator, in which opinions from the three cities were heard. The process-based nature of the indicator and the language around it was discussed in relation to the experiences within the three cities. Having said this, the final version of the indicator was Home Office-led and therefore incorporated new elements as well as those discussed at the regional steering group.

Our research revealed the region to be a 'contested governance space' (Newman 2005). A wide range of actors engaged at the regional level, but brought with them diverse understandings of the role and purpose of the 'region' in the PVE agenda. Given its ambiguous constitutional and political status, the idea of 'region' is relatively un-fixed within governance and public policy; hence it became the perfect terrain on which to act out various positions within the PVE policy debate. Acting as a 'floating signifier', different (and often conflicting) meanings and actions became attached to the idea of the 'region'. An analysis of steering group minutes, notes and interviews reveals the co-existence of at least three different perspectives on the role of the region in relation to PVE:

- *Government broker* – the GOR translated government policy to local level actors and sought to ensure policy was properly understood; it monitored implementation and supported local actors through the provision of extra information and resources; on occasion, it transmitted back to Government the concerns and questions of local actors.
- *City coordinator* – the GOR brought together key people (at different levels and from different agencies) from the three cities to ensure that they shared information, experience and emerging good practice.
- *Holistic overview* – the concern of GOR was with Muslim communities across the whole region, regardless of city boundaries, and with connecting regionally based security approaches with local capacity building projects.

These perspectives tended to be associated with central government, local government and regional officers, respectively; but on a daily basis they became intertwined, having different resonance in the context of different projects, and at different points in time over the Pathfinder year. We now take a closer look at how city-level contexts have shaped the PVE agenda.

Local approaches to PVE – communities, contexts and responses

Although neighbours, the three cities covered by the Pathfinder varied in important respects: the demographics of their Muslim communities; the nature of community activity and community relationships; the level of risk from violent extremism; and the institutional arrangements put in place to support the PVE agenda. Distinctive approaches to PVE emerged in each of the three cites, which we can characterize as based, respectively, upon community safety, community cohesion and community development. Table 6.1 summarizes the main differences.

City A – a 'community safety' approach

Despite relatively high levels of community cohesion (according to national indicators), City A was judged by security services in the region to face the greatest threat from Muslim related violent extremism in 2007/8. The majority of Muslims in the city were of Pakistani (Mirpuri) heritage; community organization was largely on ethnic lines and Biraderi (clan) networks were strong. There were eight different mosques in the city and a lack of coordination across Muslim communities. Geographically, the Muslim population was relatively concentrated in one main area of the city. There was a positive correlation between levels of

Table 6.1 Variation in local contexts: a summary

	City A	City B	City C
Profile of Muslim communities	Relatively homogenous, concentrated, ethnic-based organization	Relatively diverse, dispersed, range of community organizations	Relatively fragmented, dispersed, low level of organization
Level of deprivation	Highest	Lowest (but pockets of high)	Mix of high and low levels
Level of security threat	Highest	Lowest	Medium
PVE approach	Community safety	Community cohesion	Community development
Institutional arrangements for PVE	Partnership – city council, police, others	City council – strategic leadership	City council – departmental activities
Consultation arrangements	New Muslim forum	Existing Muslim groups	Work with Muslim clients
Activity focus	Capacity building with forum, youth, women, tension monitoring	Youth, women, capacity building with groups, inter-community relationships	Youth (projects with boys/girls), community mapping

deprivation and those parts of the city with a high Muslim population. Educational achievement among Pakistani heritage boys was lower in City A than in the other two cities.

Responsibility for PVE was located in the Community Safety Partnership (CSP). PVE funds were used to establish a new Muslim forum, working through existing ethnic associations, which was run by community members supported by CSP staff. The intention was for the Muslim forum to become both a representative body for Muslim communities and a commissioning body for projects funded under PVE. Clearly acknowledging the risks from criminal activity associated with Islamic radicalization, City A used the language of PVE right from the start and pioneered a protocol for 'community tensions monitoring'. Openness to government discourse on PVE and PREVENT made it relatively unproblematic for City A to adopt the new LAA indicator in 2008/9, although the new Muslim Forum did debate the issue of language at length.

City A's approach to PVE was distinctive in three ways. First, it was partnership-led rather than directed by the city council. Second, it was located within a 'community safety' paradigm, which prioritized joint working with local police and specifically sought to combine risk reduction with community capacity building. Third, it built upon an established system of neighbourhood working that facilitated in-depth knowledge of local communities and provided a framework for multi-agency initiatives.

City B – a 'community cohesion' approach

With the highest levels of community cohesion (according to national indicators) of the three cities, City B was judged by regional security services to have the lowest level of threat from Muslim related violent extremism in 2007/8. The majority of Muslims in the city were of East African Indian origin, but there were also significant Somali, Bangladeshi and Pakistani communities. Of the three cities, City B had the highest percentage of young Muslim men. Despite the relatively affluent status of Muslims in the city, there was still a correlation between levels of deprivation and areas of the city with a significant Muslim population, although the population was relatively dispersed (four particular areas). There was a relatively low level of gang-related crime, compared with the other two cases. City B had more than 30 different mosques and a plethora of Muslim community-based organizations. A local federation had more than one hundred members and was affiliated to the Muslim Council of Britain.

Responsibility for PVE was located in the city council's Community Cohesion Team, which had a central location in the Chief Executive's Department. There was an initial reluctance to use the language of PVE, which was felt to stigmatize Muslim communities, detract from other sources of violent extremism (notably the BNP presence in the city) and re-direct funds and attention from cohesion initiatives involving a range of different communities. City B's approach was distinctive within the region for being strongly led by the city council and embedded in a well-established 'community cohesion' narrative. A city-wide rather than a neighbourhood approach was prioritized, and projects focused on work with young people and Muslim women, building on links with existing Muslim community organizations. Progress was slow on community safety and intelligence monitoring activities.

At the end of the Pathfinder year, City B announced its intention to adopt NI35, reflecting both government pressure (via the GOR) and the city council's growing awareness of the security threat (via engagement in the regional PVE steering group). But this also became possible in the context of a gradual 'sanitization' of the PVE discourse within the city, as Muslim community organizations themselves adopted an increasingly pragmatic and assertive stance towards accessing, even controlling, PVE funds.

City C – a 'community development' approach

City C had particularly low levels of community cohesion, high incidences of gun crime, drugs and gang culture, and was judged by regional security services to have the second highest risk of Muslim related violent extremism. The majority of Muslims in the city were of Pakistani (Mirpuri) heritage, but the city also had smaller Bangladeshi and Somali communities, and 19 mosques in total. There were strong Birardari (clan) networks, which supported and sponsored Muslim councillors, all of whom were of Pakistani origin. Geographically, the Muslim population was more dispersed than in cities A and B, with five distinctive clusters across the city. Levels of deprivation were particularly high in City C and, as elsewhere, there was positive correlation between levels of deprivation and parts of the city with a high Muslim population. There was a high degree of fragmentation among Muslim communities, along the lines of ethnicity and faith tradition.

Responsibility for PVE was in a division of the city council dealing with communities, leisure and culture. The city council was reluctant to highlight PVE as a discrete policy area. Like City B, the council preferred to see the work as part of the broader community cohesion agenda; but, unlike City B, there was an absence of strong strategic leadership or established good practice in this area. Community divisions, alongside organizational instability in the city council (restructuring and staff changes), led to a slow process of community capacity building. Towards the end of the Pathfinder year, the city council completed a mapping of Muslim communities. A coordinator was appointed to develop relationships with community leaders, including exploring the possibility of establishing a Muslim forum for the city. The youth service was active in developing projects with young women and young men from Muslim communities, but there was poor communication with the broader community cohesion agenda.

The strengths of City C's approach lay in traditional youth and community work. PVE funds were used to tackle particular pockets of deprivation and disengagement in the city. But as a policy area, PVE was not well developed. The city had a relatively low level of involvement in regional initiatives (particularly among senior officers), and did not engage in the critical reflection that led City B to reassess aspects of its initial approach. City C also saw its community safety priorities as relating to gun and knife crime, rather than Islamic extremism, and – unsurprisingly – did not agree to adopt NI35 in its 2008–9 LAA, despite regional pressure.

PVE activities – coercive policy, creative outcomes?

Having explored the community dynamics and institutional context of each of the three cities, this section elaborates on the local distinctiveness of PVE activity within what is generally regarded as an imposed, top-down (even coercive) policy agenda. It explores the interaction of the national policy framework with local political agency, both on the part of elected local authorities and Muslim communities themselves.

As such, our work makes an important contribution to an area of research that is both conceptually and empirically underdeveloped. Although both Brown (2008) and McGhee (forthcoming) acknowledge the potential scope for Muslim community empowerment within the PVE Pathfinder process, they each conclude that the securitization of the agenda renders such an outcome impossible. This conclusion is reached through a focus on national level discourses, and is grounded in a Foucauldian approach to power as an inevitably top-down process. Bleich (see Chapter 3, in this volume) does allow for the existence of contradictions within government strategy, but does not provide any empirical elaboration of how these play out in practice.

Our case study analysis, and action research methodology, allows us to explore the role of both local level policymakers and Muslim communities themselves. The evidence reveals surprisingly creative outcomes, reflecting locally specific and highly dynamic 'settlements' between the local state and Muslim communities. Within Muslim communities, such outcomes are illustrative of the three elements of 'social resilience' identified by Briggs:

> First, resistance, which equates to the degree of disruption that can be accommodated without undergoing long-term change. Second, recovery, the ability to 'pull through' or bounce back. Third, and most important in the context of social resilience and national security is creativity. In other words, resilience is not just about returning to an initial equilibrium. Rather, by adapting to new circumstances and learning from the experience, higher levels of functioning (and thereby resilience) can be attained.
>
> (Briggs 2008: 5)

We look at the connections between such practices through an analysis of PVE activities in the following areas, comparing policy interventions in the three cities:

- representation and partnership: setting up Muslim forums;
- 'empowerment' and capacity building: working with young people and women;
- community tensions monitoring: monitoring and responding to tensions.

Representation and partnership

National guidance on the PVE Pathfinder described the concept of Muslim forums as a crucial mechanism for supporting the Muslim community in developing skills and capacity to combat extremism and Islamophobia (DCLG 2007a: 12). The idea of forums was derived from the Local Government White Paper as a hub for local community and partnership empowerment and engagement. In addition to this, the forums were described as a 'safe space' for local communities to openly debate the issues that mattered to them (DCLG 2007b: 8).

In City A, setting up a Muslim Forum was the key priority. As a first step, the CSP worked with a community centre (which served the dominant Muslim ethnic group) and associated community leaders to secure a meeting place. This centre was centrally located within the main Muslim community. With the CSP, the community centre played an active role in the selection of a chair and project co-ordinator for the forum.

The early forum meetings were publicized within the community (on community radio for example). A mixture of group representatives and individuals went along to meetings. Although some statutory body representatives attended at relevant times, this membership was limited in order to build community trust and ownership. The new Muslim forum debated the issue of language at length, and came up with its own phrasing, 'preventing violent behaviours associated with Islam' for the official terms of reference. The ongoing debate reflected the community's active and critical engagement with the government's PVE agenda, which was not simply imposed from above. Debate in the forum led to the generation of an organic discourse that sought to dissociate 'extremism' and 'violence', and to specify 'behaviours' rather than beliefs as problematic.

As the discursive frame became more settled, the group went on to draw up action plans for work with Muslim women and young people and to allocate PVE resources, alongside the identification of additional sources of funding. As such, the forum was empowered both through identifying its own terms of reference and gaining control over government funds for work in Muslim communities. The forum's project coordinator sought to increase representation from all parts of the Muslim community, and to forge networks with other local organizations (such as the college and inter-faith body). The CSP assisted in this work, at times able to appear more neutral and to play a valuable mediating role between different groups. The longer term aim was to develop an elected steering group, alongside an open community forum.

In City B an already professionalized Muslim community had organized youth forums (with the direct support of DCLG) prior to the instigation of the local PVE Pathfinder. These forums took place through a large umbrella organization representing Muslim groups in the city. Rather than creating a new forum, the city council decided to work though this federation. But a coordinating body, with membership from statutory organizations and Muslim organizations, was also set up to oversee the allocation of PVE funding. Chaired by the council cabinet lead for community cohesion, the work was firmly situated within the council's dominant cohesion discourse, initially leaving little room for the re-negotiation that happened in City A. City B's arrangements also led to a separation of the representative and funding functions associated with PVE, which produced over time a suspicion on the part of many in the Muslim community that the city council was holding on to the 'real power'.

City B was determined to direct at least some of the PVE funds to support inter-community cohesion related projects. The central focus was youth, citizenship and empowerment. Funding was allocated to several projects run by non-Muslim organizations, and included work with the wider community in addition to Muslims. This became a source of tension within the co-ordinating body: as one Muslim community representative put it: 'Hands off – this is Muslim money'. As in the case of City A, the role of local political agency was clear. There were those in the Muslim community who were not content for the city council to re-frame the PVE agenda towards broader cohesion aims, and to influence funding decisions accordingly. Muslim representatives' initial distaste for the PVE agenda was overcome in a struggle to access resources for their community, precipitating another reconstruction of PVE as 'money for Muslim communities'.

In City C the overriding concern of the local council was that their involvement in the Muslim community may exacerbate divisions and disillusionment as well as potentially alienate key political Muslim allies. In an attempt to avoid this situation, detailed research and relationship-building work was undertaken in advance of establishing any specific forum. This work tried to engage those in the community with a low-resource base as well as those with more power and influence. The softly-softly approach was inspired in part by the low starting point in terms of council–community relationships, and partly by the council's opposition to high profile PVE policies and projects. The appointment of a 'Muslim communities' coordinator' from 'inside' the city council proved controversial, as many thought the funding and position should go to someone from a Muslim community group. Indeed, the approach contrasted with that in City A, where established community leaders were funded in the roles of both project manager and forum chair.

The PVE agenda, and the potential opportunities it presented, was never really accepted by City C's Muslim communities during the Pathfinder year. There was not the sort of active, critical engagement with the agenda that occurred in Cities A and B, nor the accompanying renegotiation of the PVE discourse. This related to the council's own hostility to the government agenda and its determination to keep PVE below the public radar. Because of the council's lack of strategic leadership on PVE, new 'governance spaces' were not opened up in the same way as in the other cities. Muslim communities were less able to engage – either constructively or opportunistically – with the discourse, practices and resources of PVE.

'Empowerment' and capacity building

National guidance on the PVE Pathfinder does not explicitly refer to work with women and young people in terms of empowerment and capacity building.

Instead the guidance suggests that activities need to: 'encourage greater engagement in community voluntary activities', and promote 'democratic participation,
engagement and civic involvement in particular by 'allow(ing) voices to be heard'
(DCLG 2007a: 10). Broader documentation makes a more explicit reference to
the role of women in this agenda in terms of 'enabling their voices to be heard
and empowering women to engage with disillusioned youths'. Activities such
as leadership training, are recommended in order for women to develop the
confidence and skills to play such a role in their communities (DCLG 2007a: 9).
Broader documentation similarly expands on the role of young people beyond that
of proposing activities to support 'at risk groups' from resisting violent extremism
(DCLG 2007b: 11). Instead, documentation refers to young people in the context of
broadening and deepening the civic participation of those who are often excluded
(DCLG 2007a: 9).

In City A, the Muslim forum had an informal women's sub-group, which worked
on capacity building projects with a number of newly formed Muslim women's
groups. Outcomes included initiating access for women to Islamic education
provided by the city's largest mosque, supporting women's participation in
Muslim media outlets, and a programme of events designed to increase awareness
of Muslim women's social contribution and to build knowledge and confidence
among Muslim women. A series of events provided information on local services,
skills workshops (e.g. on writing CVs), taster sessions for leisure and fitness
activities, and Islamic poetry readings and music. The events also included
facilitated discussions and presentations on the role of women in Islam and fighting
extremism (including Islamophobia). City A also developed a 'buddying scheme'
to support Muslim women attending committees and other formal meetings in the
community.

In a similar approach, the forum commissioned a local Muslim community
organization to set up leadership coaching workshops with young people, using
personal development techniques to develop positive self-esteem. The main
themes of the workshops were around: identity, citizenship, access to services
and civic participation. The work also provided qualitative data on the opinions of
young people on these issues. The workshops were run in three sessions aimed at
men or women and particularly tried to engage with those who may be at risk of
radicalization (and more general social marginalization). These were not flagged
as PVE events but as community activities, in an attempt to maximize trust among
vulnerable young people, but this did lead to some tensions around obtaining the
need for openness and accountability when receiving public funding. City A's
activities with women and young people reflected another recasting of the PVE
agenda – this time in terms of personal development and self-esteem.

City B funded community-based mapping work that identified 35 Muslim
women's organizations in the city and started to develop a capacity building
and networking programme for participants. But the focus during the Pathfinder
year was on working with young people. A Muslim youth awards ceremony
was organized by a committee of young volunteers under the aegis of the
city's federation of Muslim community groups. Nominations were requested

via advertising on local Muslim radio and in schools and *madrassahs* (mosque schools). The prestigious event was well attended by the community, local dignitaries and media, and aimed to build the self esteem not just of those who won awards, but young Muslims across the city. For young Muslims involved in the organization of the awards, the outward-facing image of the community that was presented by this event was key. They saw this as righting the many negative images that appear in the media regularly in relation to Muslims. For the community therefore the event was as much about building community self-esteem as it was about individual self-esteem.

City B also funded the development of a comic style publication, created by young people, about preventing violent extremism. This project was conducted in a school setting and engaged teenagers with a variety of backgrounds, including Muslims. The children were selected by teachers on the basis of the additional skills they would develop as a product of the sessions. Following initial discussions, the story-line selected focused on attitudes of extremism and racism between East European arrivals and others in the community. Openness on the topic was encouraged through role playing techniques and the use of comedy, allowing stereotypes and assumptions to be questioned, alongside developing ideas about how to develop better relations in a plural society. The young people proposed that learning to speak English, sharing activities and respecting one another were key. The children worked with an artist and journalist (who was also a community leader) to improve literacy and design skills, as well as awareness of community issues. Both the youth awards and the comic project provided examples of how the PVE agenda was successfully reconstructed through the city's dominant community cohesion narrative.

In City C, youth workers used PVE funding to develop a Muslim girls' residential weekend, which aimed to build self-esteem and awareness skills among the group, and also improve the take-up of youth services by an under-represented group. The youth workers collaborated with community leaders to recruit the girls, who received an AQA award for their participation. The weekend included invited speakers and workshops on matters including health and relationships, domestic violence, mental health, and Islamophobia, as well as sports and dance activities and a chance to meet new people and socialize with them in a safe environment. Several of the girls continued to work with the youth service, contributing (for instance) to the development of new school-based projects to support and empower young Muslim women. Youth workers in City C also ran a Muslim boys' course teaching young people about anger management, co-ordination and discipline through coaching in boxing. Boys were drawn from clubs or voluntary organizations as well as others being selected from those who are not engaged in youth club activities in general. City C recorded a dramatic 87 per cent increase in the uptake of youth services by Muslim young people: from 231 in February 2007 to 432 in February 2008.

In its work with women and young people, City C interpreted PVE in terms of self-development opportunities – as in City A. But, in contrast, the approach was professionally and service-led, rather than community owned. City C's approach lacked the connections to broader issues of community representation and capacity building provided by the Muslim Forum leadership in City A.

Community tensions monitoring

National guidance set out a number of policy intervention objectives relating to 'increasing the resilience of key organizations and institutions and supporting early interventions' (DCLG 2007b: 11). These were:

- Activities that improve intelligence gathering and sharing at a local level, to create systems in their own services/institutions (or with partners) for enabling concerns/intelligence to be reported and acted on and to promote effective working with local police/regional security services.
- Activities that seek to provide mechanisms to identify vulnerable communities, groups and individuals in local areas and strategies by which to address such at risk groups.
- Activities to develop targeted programmes of counter- and de-radicalization work in local areas, particularly in key institutions – such as universities, colleges and schools – and key locations (DCLG 2007b: 11).

Across the three cities, there was a broad acceptance of the Institute of Community Cohesion's (2007) definition of community tensions as: 'A state of community dynamics, which may potentially lead to disorder or threaten the peace and stability of communities'. Within the community-based paradigm of the PVE Pathfinders (in contrast to Home Office-led Prevent policies), community tensions monitoring was considered the 'sharp end' – the point at which capacity building intersected with intelligence gathering, and where interventions were focused specifically on latent or emerging conflicts, and the risk of violence. This area of work also required the closest liaison between city councils and police and security forces, and put the most strain upon statutory/community relationships. These challenges were negotiated differently in each of the three cities, reflecting once again the different contexts, relationships and discourses around PVE work.

In tune with its community safety approach to PVE, City A was a pioneer in this field, piloting and then implementing a tensions monitoring protocol, which involved referral, risk assessment and action planning for response. The approach enabled multiple reporting routes for those in the community prepared to highlight tensions (via the police, neighbourhood teams and the central CSP community cohesion team) and a multi-agency approach to assessment and response (involving these core agencies, along with health, police, education and youth services). The secondment of a police officer to City A's central cohesion team ensured that community tensions monitoring remained at the heart of the PVE strategy, and embedded the partnership approach from the top-down. Challenges remained in City A in terms of improving ongoing data sharing (rather than incident-based information) between agencies, with a view to identifying trends and developing preventative action. Like the other two cities, there were vexed issues of tone and language – not just in communicating with communities about tensions monitoring, but also with frontline service workers, who did not wish to be seen to be 'spying' on clients and community members, or doing the work of the police (without appropriate training and, indeed, protection).

City B relied on informal arrangements for tensions monitoring, operating at a city-wide level. The city's multi-cultural advisory group and faith leaders' forum had an excellent record of meeting to discuss high profile incidents, either in the city itself or on the international stage, and work through community networks to diffuse sustained tension or related violent behaviours. City B's reluctance to develop a more systematic framework related to an overriding concern not to 'contaminate' the community cohesion discourse in which its approach to PVE was embedded. Highlighting community tensions, and seeking to improve 'soft intelligence' via community routes, was seen as potentially jeopardizing the 'good relations' message, and undermining interventions aimed at celebrating diversity and mutual respect. Lacking City A's neighbourhood approach, it was also harder for City B to develop a more systematic approach on the ground. But, by the end of the Pathfinder year, City B was considering a more formal multi-agency framework, and was seeking actively to learn from City A's experience, via action learning events and regional workshops.

City C had developed a tensions monitoring protocol on paper, but was experiencing difficulty in rolling this out across the city, due to poor coordination between council departments and under-developed partnership working with other agencies. Police-led 'local issue updates' were discussed at area committees, but their political composition led to some sensitivities on the part of local councillors. City C's community development approach to PVE led to a lack of comfort around the collection of 'soft' data, and a slow take-up of the tensions monitoring agenda on the ground. Like City B, the profile of this work increased over the course of the Pathfinder year, underpinned by regionally based interactions with police and security services, and opportunities to explore with other cities the challenge of improving tensions monitoring while protecting fragile relationships of trust with Muslim communities.

Conclusion

This chapter set out to address important gaps in the, albeit small, body of research on policy to 'prevent violent extremism'. This tends to focus on the international level, or on interventions with targeted individuals, and to prioritize security oriented responses (Sageman 2007; Eilstrup-Sangiovanni and Jones 2008). There is a lack of academic studies on initiatives designed to build community resilience to the threat of violent extremism. What commentary does exist tends to be journalistic, or fatalistic (or both). Academic sources have stressed the top-down, coercive nature of the government agenda, portraying local authorities as passive implementers, and Muslim communities as 'under siege'. Conceptually, there has been a reliance on a 'governmentality' frame. Empirically, the field is quite simply under-developed. As Githens-Mazer argues in Chapter 2, we need to build a better understanding of 'the "why's" of what is happening on the ground' through more 'bottom-up studies'. Our study starts to develop the evidence base in this direction, whilst exploring the theoretical significance of local context.

Our chapter presents a case study analysis of a regional PVE Pathfinder, involving three unitary city councils working with a range of local agencies and Muslim community groups. Using action research methods, we were able to explore the role of both local level policymakers and Muslim communities themselves. The evidence revealed surprisingly creative outcomes, reflecting locally specific and highly dynamic 'settlements' between the local state and Muslim communities. The three cities covered by the Pathfinder varied in relation to their demographics and community profiles, their level of risk from violent extremism, and the institutional arrangements they put in place to support the PVE agenda. Distinctive approaches to PVE emerged in each of the three cites, which we characterized as based, respectively, upon community safety, community cohesion and community development. No doubt other Pathfinder localities have developed their own PVE approaches, perhaps including elements of those we observed, but alongside locally specific, and unanticipated, elements. Further research is required to elaborate this range of possibilities.

The distinctive local settlements we observed challenged the assumption that centralized government power was uniformly enacted; instead, each city incorporated PVE into its own 'governance story' (Bevir and Rhodes 2006: 166). Rather than revealing a stark stand-off between risk reduction strategies and community capacity building, local PVE 'stories' revealed distinct (and changing) blends of both – albeit in uneasy tension. At the same time, the region served as an ambiguous governance space (neither central nor local), where government discourses could be debated and renegotiated, and where city-level actors could reflect critically on their own policy assumptions.

We also explored what Modood (2007) calls the 'emergence of Muslim agency', which has produced a rapid growth in civil society activity of all sorts as well as forms of 'corporatist' engagement with government – and, of course, the political radicalization and criminalization of small numbers of extremists. PVE policy at the local level provides an excellent example of what Newman (2005: 2–4) calls 'the contradictory and contested process of remaking governance'. A policy which sets out to build resilience via 'capacity building' and 'empowerment' has implications for how citizens 'are constituted as actors in the public sphere'. Using Newman's language, we can see that, on the one hand, the PVE agenda seeks to construct 'new governable subjects' ('Muslim communities', 'moderate Muslims', 'faith leaders'); but, on the other hand, 'opens up new sites of agency'. These new governance spaces (Muslim Forums, women's networks, youth forums) enable what Newman calls 'performing citizens' to become directly involved in the co-production of particular policy outcomes that matter to them. These contributions to specific policy projects can potentially combine to generate a system of co-governance, especially where 'invited spaces' (in which citizens enter at the behest of the state) are combined with 'popular spaces ... arenas in which people come together at their own instigation' (Cornwall 2004: 2).

Of course, PVE also seeks to 'responsibilise' Muslim citizens (Clarke 2005). Does the policy do no more than draw citizens 'freely' into responsibilities that they may have previously resisted, and to implicate them in new governance forms that de-legitimize social and political conflict? Newman (2005) argues that the instability of the new governance strategies means that they are continually subject to challenge and contestation, inevitably generating new sources of agency for citizens to act on their own terms. Looking at policing in a counter-terrorism environment, in Chapter 5 Spalek and Lambert observe that the engagement of Muslim communities is 'complex, multi-layered and in constant flux'. As John Clarke (2004: 158) explains, new subjects may be called but not respond, choosing instead to 'refuse to listen, or tune into alternative hailings that speak of different selves, imagined collectivities and futures'. And, in the case of PVE, these 'alternative hailings' and 'imagined collectivities' may be associated with violent Islamism.

The response of Muslim communities in the PVE Pathfinder we studied can best be described in terms of 'social resilience' (Briggs 2008: 5), a process that included 'resistance' to coercive policy elements, 'recovery' from experiences of both shock and stigmatization, and 'creativity' in accessing (and shaping) new governance spaces and resources. However, the future of local PVE programmes is in doubt. Two factors threaten to undermine the creative agency of both local policymakers and local communities. First, the replacement of PVE with the Home Office-led Prevent agenda signals a strengthening of the security dimension vis-á-vis community capacity building, and a greater focus on 'at risk' individuals rather than 'mainstream' Muslim communities. Second, the introduction of NI35 requires local authorities to measure the outcomes of their PVE policies against nationally agreed indicators, potentially undermining the distinctive 'governance stories' described above. As Spalek and Lambert argue in this volume (Chapter 5), the use of performance indicators in this area risks overlooking the 'human' and 'dynamic' aspects of community engagement. These two developments are symptomatic of a growing unease with government as to whether the PVE Pathfinder programmes have 'made a difference'. Such a critique, however, is accompanied by a continuing lack of clarity about what difference PVE was intended to make, and a lack of imagination as to how a quality like 'community resilience' might reasonably be assessed.

Bibliography

Bevir, M. and Rhodes, R. (2006) *Governance Stories*, Abingdon: Routledge.
Blair, T. (2005) 13 July speech in the aftermath of 7/7 London bombings, as reported by CNN news 14 July 2005, available at: http://www.cnn.com/ (accessed November 2008).
Blick, A., Choudhury, T. and Weir, S. (2006) 'The rules of the game: terrorism, community and human rights', Democratic Audit, Human Rights Centre, University of Essex for the Joseph Rowntree Trust, available at: http://www.jrrt.org.uk (accessed 4 February 2009).

Briggs, R. (2008) 'Building strong communities to tackle the terror threat', paper presented at BISA Annual Conference, Exeter University, 15–17 December 2008. Available at: http://www.bisa.ac.uk/2008/online08.html (accessed 4 February 2009).

Brown, K. (2008) 'The promise and perils of women's participation in UK mosques: the impact of securitisation agendas on identity, gender and community', *British Journal of Politics and International Relations*, 10: 472–91.

Clarke, J. (2004) *Changing Welfare, Changing States: New Directions in Social Policy*, London: Sage.

—— (2005) 'New Labour's citizens: activated, empowered, responsibilized, abandoned?', *Critical Social Policy*, 25(4): 447–63.

Cornwall, A. (2004) 'New democratic spaces? The politics and dynamics of institutionalised participation', in A. Cornwall and V. Coelho (eds) *New Democratic Spaces?*, *Institute of Development Studies Bulletin*, 35(2): 1–10.

Denscombe, M. (2003) *The Good Research Guide*, Maidenhead: Open University Press.

DCLG (2007a) *Preventing Violent Extremism Pathfinder Fund: Guidance Note for Government Offices and Local Authorities in England*, London: Department for Communities and Local Government.

—— (2007b) *Preventing Violent Extremism: Winning Hearts and Minds*, London: Department for Communities and Local Government.

DEMOS (2006) *Bringing it Home: Community-based Approaches to Counter-terrorism*, available at: http://www.demos.co.uk (accessed May 2008).

Eilstrup-Sangiovanni, M. and Jones, C. (2008) 'Assessing the dangers of illicit networks: why al-Quaida may be less threatening than many think', *International Security*, 33(2): 7–44.

Ellery, S. (2009) 'Extreme measures', *Guardian*, 28 January: 3.

Home Office (2005) *Preventing Extremism Together: working groups August – October 2005*, London: Home Office.

Home Office/Cabinet (2006) *Countering International Terrorism: The United Kingdom's Strategy*, London: Home Office/Cabinet.

Institute of Community Cohesion (2007) *Understanding and Monitoring Tension and Conflict in Local Communities: A Practical Guide for Local Authorities, Police Service and Partner Agencies*, Coventry: iCoCo.

Lambert, R. (2008) 'Salafi and Islamist Londoners: stigmatised minority faith communities countering al-Qaida', *Crime Law and Social Change*, 50(1–2): 73–89.

McGhee, D. (forthcoming) 'From hate to PREVENT – community safety and counter-terrorism', in N. Chakrabarti (ed.) *Hate Crime*, Devon: Willan Publishing.

Modood, T. (2007) *Multiculturalism: A Civic Idea*, Cambridge: Polity Press.

Newman, J. (ed.) (2005) *Remaking Governance: Peoples, Politics and the Public Sphere*, Bristol: Policy Press.

Sageman, M. (2007) *Leaderless Jihad: Terrorist Networks in the 21st Century*, Philadelphia, PA: University of Philadelphia Press.

Part II

7 Who might vote for the BNP?

Survey evidence on the electoral potential of the extreme right in Britain

Robert Ford

Introduction

When Tony Blair first assumed office Richard Barnbrook was an unknown secondary school arts teacher. Little more than a decade later he has become the most successful extreme-right political candidate in British electoral history. He first stood for the British National Party (BNP) in the 2005 general election and secured nearly 17 per cent of the vote in the east London constituency of Barking, the strongest ever constituency performance by an extreme-right candidate. The following year, Barnbrook was elected to the Barking and Dagenham council as one of 12 victorious BNP candidates, making the BNP the second largest party represented on the council. Two years after this, Barnbrook became the first ever BNP member of the London Assembly after the party secured over 130,000 Assembly votes in the 2008 elections, over 5 per cent of the total cast. Nearly 70,000 Londoners also voted for him personally as their first choice for London mayor, another record for an extreme-right candidate.

Barnbrook's startling series of victories illustrates the renewed vigour of the extreme right in Britain since the 1982 emergence of the BNP. The BNP's total vote and their average vote per candidate has increased in every general election since 1987, culminating in a record performance in 2005, when the party secured nearly 200,000 votes in a total of 119 constituencies, an average of over 1,600 votes per candidate. In the 2009 European Parliament elections, the BNP continued its upward trajectory by securing nearly one million votes, and sending the first ever British extreme-right representatives to Strasbourg. Britain is far from unique in having seen a resurgence in right-wing extremism; indeed until recently it was considered an anomalous case of extreme-right failure (Ignazi 2003a) in a Europe where rising support for the extreme right has become a worrying general trend (Ignazi 2003b; Mudde 2007). Even after its recent strong performances, the electoral successes of the BNP are minor compared with parties such as French National Front (FN), the Austrian Freedom Party (FPÖ) and the Flemish Interest in Belgium (VB), which have regularly secured more than 10 per cent of the popular vote in national elections (Ignazi 2003b; Norris 2005).[1]

Academics trying to account for these trends have pointed to the importance of both *demand* and *supply* in the electoral market (Eatwell 2003). Early scholars examining the electoral breakthroughs of parties such as the FN and VB in the 1980s and early 1990s pointed to the emergence of a growing constituency of disaffected 'losers from modernization': less educated, poorer and older working-class voters who felt that their economic and social position was under threat from the transformations associated with globalization (Kitschelt and McGann 1995) and that the national culture they valued was under threat from sharp increases in immigration from outside Europe (Sniderman *et al.* 2004; Ivarsflaten 2005). The anxieties and demands of such voters were not addressed by mainstream parties, which appeared unwilling or unable to mitigate economic change and mass migration, so these voters instead turned to the extreme right who articulated their concerns and offered (often simplistic) solutions. Later scholars have pointed out that such demand-based explanations for the extreme right are too simplistic, and cannot explain large variations in the success of the extreme right among countries in which social circumstances and public attitudes are quite similar (Norris 2005; Van Der Brug *et al.* 2005; Ivarsflaten 2006). These newer accounts have emphasized the importance of supply from the party system; extreme-right success also requires the existence of cohesive and accepted party organizations that can crystallize and mobilize inchoate public demands.

The analysis of the British extreme right in this volume takes an integrated approach, examining levels of public support for extreme right ideology and policy, the changing organization and strategy of the BNP in attempting to mobilize that support and the interaction between these two factors to explain current patterns of extreme-right success. This chapter will focus on the issue of public demand, examining how much electoral potential there is for extreme-right parties in Britain in the form of public support for their ideas and policies, and dissatisfaction with the existing political system. Supply-side issues will be taken up by Goodwin (Chapter 8) in examining the organization of the modern BNP, while the interaction between supply and demand is addressed in Chapter 9, which investigates the nature of contemporary support for the BNP.

In this chapter, I will examine two potential sources of potential public support for the extreme right. First, I will look at popular agreement with extreme-right ideology and policy proposals. Extreme-right ideology is built around three pillars: authoritarianism, ethnic nationalism and xenophobia (Mudde 2007). Authoritarianism emphasizes the need for law and order and respect for tradition and authority. Authoritarians have been found to be much more sensitive to and concerned about perceived threats to the established social order, such as migration, crime and ethnic diversification (Adorno *et al.* 1950; Altemeyer 1988, 2007). Ethnic nationalism equates the national in-group with an ethnic group with a shared ancestry and culture, and seeks to restrict the privileges of national membership to members of this group. Xenophobia is a fear of and hostility towards foreigners, in this case focused on recent immigrants to Britain. All three of these ideological orientations have featured strongly in BNP literature and campaign appeals, and form the foundation for most of their policy proposals.[2] This analysis will cast some light on the levels of *potential* support for the extreme right in Britain by showing what proportion of voters agree with the ideas and policies associated with the extreme right in general and the BNP in particular. Agreeing with the extreme right's ideas, however, is unlikely to be sufficient to encourage voters to defect to the BNP: voters who dislike immigrants will not vote for the BNP if what they care about most is healthcare and education, or if they believe the Labour government is doing a good job dealing with immigration. I therefore also look at the importance voters assign to the issues closely related to the extreme right's agenda, and at how well they think the Labour government is performing on these issues.

Second, I will examine the appeal of the extreme right as a tool for expressing profound dissatisfaction with the existing political and social order. Many writers analysing new extremist parties in Europe have argued that they draw particularly strong support from disaffected sections of the electorate, who register their dissatisfaction at the ballot box by 'protest voting' for extreme parties (Betz 1994; Swyngedouw 2001; Norris 2005). Extreme-right parties recognize this motivation in their supporters, and frequently engage in populist criticism of the existing political system. The BNP is no exception: their 2005 general election manifesto was titled 'Rebuilding British Democracy' and is peppered with observations such as 'genuine democracy … is starkly absent from Britain' (BNP 2005: 1) and 'our dearly bought birthright of freedom is under mortal threat once more' (2005: 5). I will look at levels of public dissatisfaction with the party political status quo, to get a sense of how many politically disaffected voters there are in the contemporary British electorate who might be receptive to such populist messages.

To examine the levels of potential public support for the extreme right, I draw upon a range of survey data collected in the last few years, by academic survey organizations such as the National Centre for Social Research and by commercial polling organizations such as Ipsos-MORI and YouGov. The data are the most up to date available on each subject area. When looking at each particular facet of extreme-right appeal, I examine the level of overall public support and the level of support among the group who have so far provided the core support for the BNP: the white, working-class,[3] to see if the ideas and priorities of the extreme right hold a particularly strong appeal for this group of voters. It is not always possible to break down the survey data by ethnicity, however, and where such breakdowns cannot be made I instead look at support levels in the working class as a whole. Analysis of surveys with ethnic data suggest that in most cases non-white, working-class respondents are less likely to agree with extreme-right ideas which are often hostile to their interests so these results can be considered as, if anything, conservative estimates of the extreme-right appeal among white, working-class voters.

Extreme-right ideology: authoritarianism, ethnic nationalism and xenophobia

While there is considerable debate about what constitutes the ideological core of the extreme right (Mudde 2000, 2007; Rydgren 2007) three features have been identified by Cas Mudde as being associated with most, if not all, extreme-right parties in Europe: authoritarianism, ethnic nationalism and xenophobia. Authoritarian ideology emphasizes the need to maintain law and order and defend traditions, and supports harsh action against individuals or groups who are perceived as a threat to order and tradition. Authoritarian attitudes have been shown to correlate significantly with Conservative voting in Britain (Evans *et al.* 1996) and with support for extreme-right parties in many other European nations (Billiet and Witte 1995; Lubbers and Scheepers 2000). As Bob Altemeyer (1988, 1996, 2007) has emphasized in a series of publications, authoritarianism is also a monistic belief system of the kind Eatwell and Goodwin identify as potentially threatening to democracy (see Introduction to this volume).

Those with strongly authoritarian values tend to regard people who dissent from the conventions and established values of their societies as threats who should be silenced, if necessary using violence (Feldman 2003). Authoritarian ideas are strongly emphasized in the 2005 campaign literature from the BNP. The 2005 BNP manifesto emphasizes deference to British culture and traditions, which it calls a 'precious inheritance', and calls for various actions to defend this inheritance. The BNP manifesto also reveals the classic authoritarian preoccupation with external threats, characterizing Britain as 'embroiled in a long term cultural war' (BNP, 2005: 3) and emphasizing the manifold threats to traditional British society from immigrants, Muslim terrorists and the European Union among others.

Ethnic nationalism defines the national unit ascriptively, in terms of birth and ancestry. To the ethnic nationalist, national identity is not a matter of choice, and can be neither acquired nor abandoned. Individuals remain 'ineluctably, organically, a member of the community of their birth ... forever stamped by it' (Smith, 1991: 11). In extreme-right ideology, a strong belief in ethnic nationalism is usually joined to a belief in ethnocracy, that the proper political unit is the ethnic group and that non-members of the ethnic group should be denied rights of settlement and citizenship (Minkenberg 2000; Betz and Johnson 2004). The BNP places a very strong emphasis on ethnic nationalism in its literature, referring repeatedly to the British 'tribes', British 'ancestral peoples', even the British 'aboriginal peoples' (BNP, 2005: 21–3). While taking greater care than in the past to emphasize the rights of ethnic minorities, the BNP continue to call for policies designed to favour these ethnically defined groups, such as a 'Sons and Daughters' preference policy, which would give priority in housing and schooling assignments to ethnically British people.[4]

The centrality of xenophobia to extreme-right ideology is very clear (Ivarsflaten 2005; Van Der Brug *et al.* 2005). All extreme-right parties expend a great deal of ink and energy worrying about threats from outsiders both abroad and within the nation, and the BNP is no different in this respect. The BNP manifesto calls immigration 'a crisis without parallel' (BNP, 2005: 13) and blames 'foreign ethnic groups' for, among other things, 'unemployment, welfare dependency, educational failure, and other social pathologies'. The BNP concludes that allowing significant immigration means 'choosing to become a poorer, more violent, more dependent and worse educated society' (BNP, 2005: 13). The BNP also regularly expresses hostility towards Muslims in Britain, whom it has linked with social problems such as drug dealing[5] and rape.[6]

These three ideological pillars – authoritarianism, ethnic nationalism and xenophobia – constitute the core of European extreme-right ideology. All these ideas are plainly antithetical to pluralist, multicultural democracy and as such constitute a threat to the proper functioning of democracy in open, diverse societies. All are also clearly emphasized by the BNP, currently the dominant force in the British extreme right. But how much appeal do these values, and the policies they inspire, have to the British electorate?

Public support for extreme-right ideology and policies

In Britain, support for many authoritarian ideas is widespread. Over 90 per cent of Britons polled by Populus in 2008 agreed that there was insufficient respect for traditional authorities such as teachers, parents and the police in modern Britain, while 85 per cent of those polled by the British Social Attitudes survey in 2006 agreed that schools should make a greater effort to teach obedience to authority. A majority of British respondents also believe that minority groups should assimilate into the existing British culture rather than preserving their own values and traditions, with 58 per cent in a 2005 BBC poll emphasizing a preference for assimilation over multiculturalism, and 73 per cent agreeing that immigrants should be made to integrate fully into British society.

Anxieties about possible threats to social order, and a desire to inflict stronger punishments on those who engage in threatening behaviour, are also widespread. An average of around 60 per cent of Britons support the reintroduction of the death penalty in five polls by different organizations fielded since 2005, and large majorities of between 70 per cent and 90 per cent of respondents support longer prison sentences for criminals in 11 polls conducted during this period. Large majorities also support expanding the powers of police to enforce the law, with 70 per cent backing 'zero tolerance' policing (ICM, June 2006), and 60 per cent backing providing more firearms to police (Populus, June 2007). Sixty-five per cent also supported giving police whatever powers they need, even if this put civil liberties at risk (Populus, June 2007).

The desire to expand the powers of authorities also extends beyond the police: majorities of respondents in a series of polls by different organizations backed the proposed expansion of the government's power to detain terror suspects without charge, both to the 90 days called for by Tony Blair in 2005 and the 42 days called for by the Brown administration since 2007, and 65 per cent of respondents in the 2006 British Social Attitudes survey favoured allowing the authorities to detail terror suspects for as long as they want without a trial. Legislators who twice voted down these extensions were therefore acting *against* the expressed will of the British public. Many voters would go further still: half of respondents polled by the British Social Attitudes in 2006 would prevent revolutionaries from holding public meetings, and 40 per cent would deny them the right to publish their views.

The polling evidence thus suggests that public support for the established policies of multiculturalism and the protection of civil liberties is actually rather thin. A desire for conformity, order and protection is very widespread in Britain, and voters are perfectly willing to sweep aside concerns about the rights of individuals or groups when they consider themselves to be threatened. Seemingly radical BNP proposals, such as the reimposition of the death penalty, the abolition of all multicultural policies in favour of coercive assimilation, or large expansions in police powers, enjoy support from majorities of British survey respondents. The authoritarianism of the extreme right, while 'extreme' in the sense that it is threatening to the liberal values of modern British democracy, is not 'extreme' in the sense of being the position of a small minority of voters. Instead, such ideas could easily pass into law if put to the public via direct referenda.[7]

Mainstream political elites are, however, aware of the popularity of authoritarian ideas on crime, terrorism and civil liberties and have pursued policies reflecting the public preferences. Both Labour and Conservative governments have in the last 20 years adopted authoritarian approaches on issues such as crime and terrorism, such as tougher sentencing, ASBOs and the recent push for expanded police anti-terrorism powers. Therefore, while the authoritarianism of the extreme right is popular, it is also shared in many aspects by mainstream parties and is not a unique source of appeal for parties such as the BNP.

The promotion and defence of an ethnically defined national culture is a much more distinctive extreme-right ideological proposition, as no other significant political party would be willing to regularly propose ethnicity and descent as legitimate criteria for deciding whether someone is British. The BNP, however, regularly celebrate white British traditions and history and promise in their 2007 manifesto to defend the 'culture and identity of the indigenous peoples of the British Isles' (BNP 2007: 5). Nationalist beliefs are very complex, and have unfortunately only been examined on a few occasions using survey data. However, in those surveys which have been carried out there is evidence that many white Britons do consider their culture, heritage and race to be important aspects of their national identity (see Table 7.1). There is widespread public support for birth and long-term residence as criteria for membership of the national in-group, with over 70 per cent of white Britons polled in 2003 by the British Social Attitudes survey considering these to be either 'fairly' or 'very' important markers of Britishness. Half of Britons in the same sample were willing to go further and argue that following British customs and having British ancestry are also important criteria for being considered British, and 42 per cent of respondents polled in 2006 denied that even permanently settled immigrants could describe themselves as British. A significant minority were willing to go further still, and impose religious or racial criteria for national membership: 32 per cent of respondents believed being Christian was fairly or very important as a prerequisite to Britishness, and 15 per cent saying that being white was at least 'fairly' important for being regarded as British. The white, working-class 'core constituency' of the BNP consistently applied a more strongly ethnic

Table 7.1 Ethnic nationalism and national pride in Britain (white respondents only)

Statements about being British	All (%)	Working class (%)
National identity: how important are the following to being truly British? (respondents answering 'very' or 'fairly')		
Being born in Britain	73	81
Living most of one's life in Britain	72	76
Having British ancestry	50	59
Being Christian	33	40
Being white	15	20
Citizenship and Britishness (% agree)		
People who do not share British customs and traditions are not truly British	53	57
Immigrants who settle permanently in the UK are not entitled to call themselves British (BSA, 2006)	42	49
Legal immigrants should not have the same rights as British citizens	37	43
British citizenship should be denied to people born in Britain if their parents are born abroad	19	23

Source: British Social Attitudes 2003, except where indicated.

understanding of their national identity on all of these items, suggesting that an exclusive ethnic and cultural understanding of Britishness is particularly strong among this group.

While most Britons have become more accepting of ethnic minorities (Ford 2008), the popular understanding of British identity continues to incorporate ideas about culture, heritage and religion, which are particularly strongly held among the white working class. Perceptions that the distinctive cultural heritage of the ethnic majority group is under threat from migration and multiculturalism have been one of the strongest predictors of extreme-right voting in other European countries (Ivarsflaten 2005). A similar anxiety is likely to be felt by the many white Britons who continue to take pride in their cultural heritage, and feel that it is being neglected by mainstream politicians in multicultural Britain. Proposals for defending white British culture are therefore likely to resonate with an electorate far beyond that which is currently mobilized by the extreme right: over one-third of British voters agree that legal migrants should not have the same rights as British citizens, and one-fifth would deny citizenship rights even to the British-born *children* of such migrants. Persuading such voters of the benefits of migration and the rights of British migrants is likely to be a tough challenge.

Such hostility to immigrants and other outsiders is of course the most widely discussed aspect of the extreme-right political programme, and can take forms far more extreme than the denial of equal citizenship rights. Xenophobic hostility in contemporary Britain is focused particularly on two groups: immigrants and Muslims. Immigrants have been attacked by the extreme right for allegedly stealing British jobs and welfare resources, and failing to integrate adequately into British society. Since September 11 2005 (9/11) British Muslims have also come under pressure, being criticized by right-wing journalists as a potentially disloyal 'fifth column', fostering extremist intolerance and more loyal to Muslims abroad than their compatriots in Britain (Phillips 2006).

While similar attacks on immigrants and ethnic minorities have in the past been made by Conservative politicians such as Enoch Powell, and continue to be vigorously made in right-wing British newspapers such as the *Sun* and the *Daily Mail*, they are no longer considered acceptable by the leadership elites of the mainstream political parties. Even relatively moderate expressions of concern about the impact of immigration have become highly controversial; Labour politicians such as Margaret Hodge and Frank Field who express sympathy for the anxieties of their constituents about immigration have been criticized by their party's leadership,[8] while Michael Howard was also attacked for pandering to extremism by promoting, in the run up to the 2005 General Election, Conservative proposals to limit migration.[9] The Conservatives' subsequent abandonment of immigration as part of David Cameron's centrist makeover have left the BNP as the main outlet for the political expression of growing public anxiety about record migration rates and Muslim terrorism (Brown 2006).

Table 7.2 provides an insight into the extent of such anxieties, drawing upon the most recently available public opinion survey data. It is clear from this table that negative views about both immigrants and Muslims are widespread in contemporary Britain. Immigrants and asylum seekers are regarded by a majority of the British public as economically and socially costly, undercutting British workers, draining government resources, and encouraging crime and social disorder. Large majorities of British respondents also believe that immigrants and asylum seekers receive special treatment from the government; a dramatic demonstration of the perceived injustices resulting from the government's needs-based resource allocation policy.[10] While there is also evidence that this anti-immigrant sentiment is stronger in the working classes, who express more hostility to migrants on every item recorded here, most of these xenophobic sentiments attract widespread public support.

The possible influence of the media on public opinion in this area can be seen when we contrast public views about the national effect of immigration, as shown in Table 7.2, with judgements of the local impact of migration. For example, 58 per cent of respondents in an April 2008 MORI poll agreed that 'parts of this country don't feel like Britain any more', but only 25 per cent agreed that 'my area doesn't feel like Britain any more'. Similarly, while 77 per cent of respondents to a November 2007 MORI poll expressed little or no confidence that their local public services can cope with the added pressures of migration, the number reporting direct experience of problems with such services are much lower: 18 per cent claim they had difficulty getting an appointment with a doctor, and 10 per cent reported problems getting their child into their first choice school. While the anxieties may thus be as much a reaction to media reporting as the result of direct experience of difficulties arising from immigration, there is little doubt

Table 7.2 Xenophobia in contemporary Britain: hostility to Muslims and immigrants

Attitudes to immigrants and Muslims	Agree (%)	Working class agree (%)
Immigrants		
Government has been dishonest about the scale of immigration (MORI, Nov 2007)	80	81
Special treatment of immigrants means ordinary people are losing out (YouGov, Jan 2008)	69	72
Government spends too much money assisting immigrants (MORI, Apr 2008)	64	71
Immigration is making Britain a more dangerous place in which to live (YouGov, Jan 2008)	60	64
Most asylum seekers contribute nothing to the British economy and are a drain on resources (YouGov, Jan 2008)	59	62
Immigrants pay less in taxes than they receive in benefits and public services (YouGov, Jan 2008)	59	66
There are too many immigrants in Britain (MORI, Apr 2008)*	59	63
Parts of the country don't feel like Britain any more due to immigration (MORI, Apr 2008)*	58	62
Asylum seekers get more generous benefits than UK natives (ICM, Apr 2005)	57	64
Migrant workers are undercutting British workers in terms of pay and taking our jobs as a result (YouGov, Jan 2008)		
Immigration levels are making me feel like a stranger in my home town (YouGov, Jan 2008)	47	53
Most migrant workers contribute nothing to the British economy and are a drain on resources (YouGov, Jan 2008)	37	44
Immigration is bad for Britain (MORI, Nov 2007)	36	45
Muslims		
British Muslims more loyal to Muslims abroad than to other Britons (BSA, 2003)*	62	68
Muslims need to do more to integrate into British society (ICM, Jan 2008)	56	54
Britain in danger of losing its identity if more Muslims come to live here (ICM, Jan 2008)	48	57
Islamic extremists have created 'no go' areas which are dangerous for non-Muslims to enter (ICM, Jan 2008)	35	42
Unhappy if a mosque built in your neighbourhood (ICM, Jan 2008)	33	40
Unhappy if a close relative married a Muslim (BSA, 2003)*	25	31
Muslims come to Britain to take jobs, housing and health care (BSA, 2003)*	20	25
A large proportion of British Muslims feel no sense of loyalty to this country and are prepared to condone or even carry out acts of terrorism (YouGov, Aug 2006)	18	20

Note
* White respondents only.

that public concern about immigration is real, intense and widespread, making it a potent political issue.

Public hostility to Muslims is also widespread. Even before the 7/7 terrorist attacks, six in 10 Britons believed British Muslims were more loyal to Muslims abroad than to non-Muslim Britons. In more recent polling, similar proportions have agreed that Muslims need to do more to integrate into British society, while around half of respondents express concern that the growth in the Muslim population is threatening British identity. A significant minority of respondents – between one-fifth and one-third – also agree with much stronger anti-Muslim statements, opposing Mosque construction and white-Muslim intermarriage and agreeing with strongly anti-Muslim arguments such as the claim that most British Muslims feel no sense of loyalty to Britain and condone Islamic terrorism (see also the discussion by Sobolewska in Chapter 1). Once again, these hostile sentiments are more pronounced among working-class respondents.

What sort of policies do British voters favour to deal with the problems they believe immigrants and Muslims are generating? There is unfortunately little polling evidence on public views of policies relating specifically to Muslims and Islam, rather than the issues of security and civil liberties raised by terrorism in general, so it is not possible to gain much of a sense of public opinion in this area. However, the British public have been asked on a number of occasions about immigration policy. Their responses are summarized in Table 7.3. The polling reveals widespread support for a reduction in immigration, with between 75 per cent and 85 per cent of respondents to polls by four different companies favouring a reduction or strict limit to immigration. The polls also suggest that many Britons are in favour of more draconian measures of the kind regularly proposed by the BNP, such as a complete halt to migration, the denial of benefits to migrants and even measures to encourage the repatriation of settled migrants. While most of these policies enjoy somewhat stronger support from the working classes, the desire for more restrictive policies on immigration is widespread.

There is evidence, however, that public opinion on this issue is volatile, and can be influenced by the frame of reference immigration is presented within. For example, the proportion favouring a complete halt to migration varies from 12 per cent in a November 2007 Ipsos-MORI poll to 47 per cent in a Populus poll conducted six months earlier, with a January 2008 YouGov poll falling in between at 23 per cent. These variations correspond to how the issue is framed and the alternative options that are offered. The MORI poll with the lowest figure also presented respondents with the alternative option to make laws on immigration 'much tougher', which large majorities favoured. The YouGov poll offered the weaker 'reduce immigration but not stop it altogether' as an alternative, and puts its question after a long series of items asking about negative effects of immigration. The more negative frame and weaker alternatives seem to have boosted support for a halt to migration. The Populus poll, which records the highest level of support, only allowed respondents to agree or disagree with a total halt to immigration, and framed the issue around Margaret Hodge's comments concerning the restriction

Table 7.3 British public views of possible immigration

Statements about immigration	Agree (%)	Working class agree (%)
Reduction in immigration		
Government should reduce immigration levels (YouGov, Jan 2008)	84	86
It should be made harder for immigrants to come to Britain (ICM, Jan 2008)	78	82
There should be a strict limit on immigration set by the government (Populus, Oct 2007)	77	81
Support much tougher laws on immigration, or a complete halt to immigration (MORI, Nov 2007)	76	80
Total halt to immigration and other more draconian policy options		
British citizens should always get priority for social housing ahead of immigrant families (Populus, May 2007)	69	76
People who have grown up in an area should get preference for council housing (Populus, Feb 2008)	67	69
Benefits should be restricted to those born or brought up in the UK (Populus, Feb 08)	58	60
Government should encourage immigrants to return to their country of origin (MORI, Apr 2008)*	49	56
We should not allow any more migrant workers into this country (Populus, May 2007)	47	57
Government should halt immigration to Britain altogether (YouGov, Jan 2008)	23	30
Immigration should be stopped altogether (MORI, Nov 2007)	12	18

Note
* White respondents only.

of immigrant access to council housing. The lack of alternatives and the framing of the migration question around a housing policy widely perceived to be unjust, result in a much higher public demand for a total halt to immigration.

What these differences suggest is that, while a significant minority of British respondents support draconian action against immigrants in all circumstances, many others are swayed by how immigration and immigrants are presented, and what other options they are offered. This may be because, as discussed earlier, much public hostility to immigration does not seem to be strongly grounded in direct experience of its effects. Therefore, the successful communication of negative narratives about the dangerous consequences posed by immigrants, and the promotion of drastic solutions as the only way to protect from these dangers, may inflame public hostility and encourage support for radical policies. If extreme-right politicians succeed in gaining office, they may be better able to use their position to further promote negative messages about immigration and escalate the very public hostilities which secured their election.

The political relevance of extreme-right issues: salience and dissatisfaction

The evidence from recent public polling therefore suggests that all three aspects of the extreme-right programme – authoritarianism, ethnic nationalism and xenophobia – enjoy widespread public support that far outstrips existing levels of extreme-right voting. However, while support for ideas and policies in principle is a necessary condition for winning votes it is not a sufficient one. It will matter little electorally that over three-quarters of voters agree with the BNP over immigration restriction if what most of them actually care about is the NHS or the state of the economy. Similarly, mainstream voters are unlikely to defect to the extreme right if they remain at least modestly satisfied with the performance of the current government in these policy areas. A truly potent combination of circumstances obtains if the BNP prove to be on the right side of public opinion on issues that are also highly salient and where many voters are very unhappy with current public performance.

Figure 7.1 shows the proportion of citizens rating issues central to the extreme-right appeal – crime, immigration and terrorism – as among the most important facing the country. In the early years of the Blair government, when the political agenda was focused on the economy and public services, very few respondents were concerned about immigration or terrorism while around 20 per cent were worried about crime. From 2000 onwards however, the issue agenda shifts steadily in favour of the extreme right. Britons have become sharply more anxious about

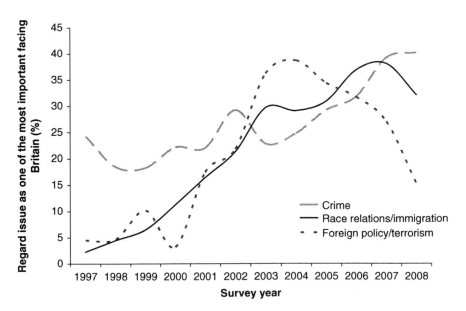

Figure 7.1 Salience of extreme-right issues since 1997.
Source: MORI; figures are annual averages.

terrorism and foreign policy since the 9/11 attacks; crime has risen up the agenda in every year since 2003 and worries about immigration have risen even more sharply, with the proportion naming it as a top issue rising from less than 5 per cent in 1997 to over 40 per cent 10 years later. The salience of all three of these issues has, since 2006, been at or near the highest levels ever recorded by MORI since it began tracking public political priorities in 1974.

In the early years of the New Labour administration it was unlikely that the extreme right could win the attention of many voters, as the issue agenda was dominated by the economy and public services (Clarke *et al.* 2004), issues in which parties like the BNP had little to offer. By the third Labour term in office, however, the public's attention had shifted decisively to the 'security agenda' issues that form the core focus of extreme-right attention: migration, terrorism and crime (Whiteley *et al.* 2006). As we have seen, public opinion is also broadly sympathetic to extreme-right positions on these issues. These figures have fallen back somewhat as the 'credit crunch' has unfolded since 2008, but public concern with all the issues most strongly associated with the extreme right remains well above the levels seen in the late 1990s. If economic difficulties lead to a rise in crime, or more intense conflicts between migrants and natives over resources, then the current crisis could lead to a further increase in public anxiety. The current political issue environment is very favourable to the agenda of the extreme right, with public attention to extreme right issues at or close to historic highs.

As well as becoming rapidly more concerned with these issues, the polling evidence suggests that the British public are growing more dissatisfied with the performance of the Labour government in dealing with them, as shown in Table 7.4. When the percentage of voters who disapproved of Labour's performance in these areas is subtracted from the percentage who approved, Labour held negative net approval ratings on both crime and immigration in the 2005 British election study, though the public did at that point have a positive

Table 7.4 Net dissatisfaction with Labour government performance on extreme-right core issues

Ratings of Labour government performance since 2005	All (%)	Working class (%)
Crime		
British Election Study Jun 2005*	−18	−24
Populus Mar 2008*	−60	−63
Immigration/asylum seekers		
British Election Study Jun 2005*	−56	−63
MORI Nov 2007	−57	−55
Terrorism		
British Election Study Jun 2005*	+31	+31
YouGov Aug 2006	−11	−9

Note
* White respondents only.

view of the government's performance on terrorism. The most recent polling figures available on each of these issues suggests public appraisals of crime and terrorism performance have become sharply more negative at −60 and −11, respectively, while net approval ratings of immigration performance remain below −55. Negative performance appraisals of the government in these areas are seen across the electorate, with no consistent evidence that the white working class have a more negative view of Labour's record than others. There is also evidence from recent opinion polls that the Conservatives, who gained a reputation for being 'tough' on immigration and race issues in the time of Enoch Powell and Margaret Thatcher, no longer enjoy such a strong public image on the issue. While in the 1970s more than six in 10 voters considered the Conservatives the best party to deal with race and immigration issues,[11] as Table 7.5 shows, this figure has fallen to the mid-30s. Around the same number of voters do not think any of the parties offer good policies on immigration, and may therefore be willing to consider new alternatives such as the BNP.

The polling evidence suggests that the extreme right in Britain is currently only realizing a fraction of its electoral potential. There is a large potential constituency of voters who agree with extreme-right ideas but do not currently vote for parties such as the BNP. Extreme-right ideology enjoys particularly strong sympathy among the white working class, which may explain why they have been the first to defect to the BNP in large numbers, but support for these ideas is by no means limited to this group. In addition, the polling evidence has made clear that the current political context offers an unprecedented opportunity for the BNP

Table 7.5 Which party has the best immigration policies? Polling since 2005

Month, year and source	Con (%)	Lab (%)	Lib Dem (%)	None/don't know (%)
February 2005 (Populus)	36	28	16	19
March 2005 (ICM)	30	24	11	32
1 April 2005 (5 poll avg)	36	25	10	26
2 April 2005 (6 poll avg)	35	26	11	25
2005 average	**35**	**26**	**11**	**25**
April 2006 (ICM)	37	27	11	25
April 2006 (YouGov)	35	13	10	40
May 2006 (ICM)	36	18	11	29
June 2006 (YouGov)	29	12	8	48
2006 average	**34**	**18**	**10**	**36**
August 2007 (YouGov)	34	17	7	40
September 2007 (Populus)	35	26	14	24
December 2007 (Populus)	36	20	10	33
2007 average	**35**	**21**	**10**	**32**
June 2008 (Populus)	38	19	15	28
Average since 2005	***35***	***22***	***12***	***31***

to realize some of this potential, as record numbers of voters rate core extreme right issues such as immigration, crime and terrorism as top concerns and express dissatisfaction with their government's current record in these areas. Voters are particularly unhappy about high immigration levels and as many as one-third have lost faith in the ability of all the main parties to resolve this issue for them.

Resentment and disillusionment: the potential for extreme-right protest voting in Britain

Voters may be attracted to extreme parties by their ideologies or by their policies, but they may equally be driven towards extremist groups as a way of expressing profound dissatisfaction with the existing political system and the choices it offers. Much extremist support may thus be as much about voting against the mainstream political parties as it is voting for the extremists. A populist critique of the liberal democratic status quo is a central part of most extreme-right parties' appeals (see Mudde 2007: ch. 6, for a longer discussion). Extreme-right parties regard liberal democracy, as currently practiced, to be a failure and a fraud, an argument that can have considerable appeal to those who feel the current system ignores their interests. This criticism can attract the attention of voters who do not endorse extreme-right ideology, but who do want to express profound discontent with the status quo, for as Van Der Brug and Fennema (2007: 478) observe: 'Since radical-right parties are treated as outcasts by a large part of the elites in their countries, votes for these parties frighten or shock these elites, which is exactly what the protest voter wants to accomplish'. This populist critique is a strong theme in the most recent BNP general election manifesto, which begins with the claim that British electoral democracy is 'a sham and an illusion' (BNP 2005: 1).

Is there a significant audience for such populist attacks? Table 7.6 shows levels of dissatisfaction with the existing party political elite at the time of the 2001 and 2005 general elections. The surveys reveal a startling level of public dissatisfaction with the existing 'political class' (Oborne 2007) even before the scandal over MPs' expenses claims broke in the summer of 2009. Over 8 in 10 respondents agree that there is a big difference between what parties promise and what they deliver, and more than 7 in 10 agree that parties are more interested in winning votes than in representing their constituents or governing effectively. Six in 10 believe that the main parties do not talk about the most important national problems when campaigning, half argue that the parties offer no real choice as their policies are all the same, and more than 4 in 10 believe that (despite their apparent similarity) the existing political parties do more to divide the country than unite it.

Similar cynicism prevails in attitudes to politicians, with 70 per cent of respondents agreeing that MPs quickly lose touch with those who elected them, more than half believing that MPs will habitually lie under pressure, more than 40 per cent believing MPs make no effort to keep the promises they make on the campaign trail and a quarter believe their MPs are corrupt. Again, there is some evidence of higher support for all of these sentiments among the white working

Table 7.6 Dissatisfaction with politicians and political parties (white respondents only)

Statements about parties and politicians	Total (%)	Working class (%)
Parties		
Big difference between what parties say and what they do (British Election Study (BES), 2005)	85	84
Parties are only interested in people's votes, not their opinions (BSA, 2005)	70	74
Parties more interested in winning elections than governing (BES, 2005)	70	71
In elections, parties don't talk about the really important problems facing the country (BES, 2005)	61	63
The average citizen has little influence on politics (BSA, 2006)	56	59
The main political parties offer no real choice; their policies are all the same (BES, 2005)	49	57
Parties do more to divide the country than unite it (BES, 2005)	45	47
Politicians		
MPs lose touch with people pretty quickly (BSA, 2006)	70	71
Politicians almost never tell the truth when in a tight corner (BSA, 2006)	57	59
MPs don't try to keep promises (BSA, 2006)	44	47
'Quite a lot' or 'almost' all British politicians are involved in corruption (BSA, 2006)	26	27

class but the differences are not major, as disaffection with politics was widespread across the whole electorate even before the expenses scandal.

These findings fit with a broader range of evidence of public dissatisfaction and disengagement, including declines in major party identification, activism and membership levels; falling trust in the political system and in expectations that it can deliver desired outcomes; and a long-term downward trend in electoral turnout, which accelerated after 1997 (Dunleavey 2005; Hay 2007). Public satisfaction with democracy, however, remains quite high, and levels of civic participation away from the ballot box have been stable or rising for 20 years (Curtice and Seyd 2003). It seems, therefore, that voters have not lost faith in the democratic system of representative government, but they have become unhappy with the existing party political options available for representing their opinions. This dealignment from, and hostility to, the existing party system provides an opening for new parties who campaign against the existing system and mobilize issues that the main parties have ignored. The past 20 years has seen an unprecedented fragmentation in British voting patterns, with new political forces such as the Celtic nationalist parties, the Respect party, the Green party and the anti-European Union Referendum and UK Independence Parties securing record votes and electoral successes (Dunleavey 2005). It is thus no wonder that the BNP devotes so much attention to attacking the political status quo: the populist extreme-right message that the 'system is broken' commands a great deal of public support.

The extreme-right electoral challenge: past its peak or just beginning?

All three aspects of the extreme-right core ideological agenda enjoy considerable public support in Britain. While authoritarian policies are also offered by the other main parties the other two aspects of extreme-right agenda – ethnic nationalism and xenophobia – are not promoted or supported by any parties but the BNP. The levels of public agreement with ethnic ideas of nationalism and of public hostility to immigrants and Muslims suggest that the BNP could appeal to an electorate far larger than it currently wins over – at least 15–20 per cent of voters, perhaps even more. The current environment is also exceptionally favourable to the BNP, as the issues it focuses upon are attracting record levels of public interest and voters are not impressed by the policies offered by the main parties in these areas. The potential for a continued expansion in BNP support is very high, as plenty of public demand for the politics of the extreme right remains unmet. The chances of more extreme-right electoral breakthroughs are also enhanced by the high and rising levels of voter dissatisfaction with the existing political system. Voters are not impressed with the main political parties, and are losing faith in their ability to respond to and resolve the problems they care about. The scandal over MPs' expenses claims, which tainted a large section of the Westminster political class, has further entrenched this hostility. Party identification, membership and activism are at their lowest levels for decades, and voter volatility is at a post-Second World War high, all of which mean the British electoral market is more open to new entrants than it has been in modern history.

The BNP is very far from realizing the electoral potential suggested by the polling data reviewed here. While BNP support has risen sharply since 1997, even in their all time best general election performance in 2005 they received only 0.7 per cent of the total vote. The analyses here suggest these voting levels could be 10 or 20 times higher, even if we focus only on those voters who agree strongly with all aspects of the BNP platform.[12] Given this wide pool of potential support, the BNP's success in the 2009 European Parliament election, when the party secured its first ever European Parliament seats by winning 6.2% of the vote, looks less shocking than many found it at the time. Despite this signal success, the BNP still fall short of realizing the considerable potential that exists for its brand of politics, with record levels of public concern and dissatisfaction in its core issue areas of immigration, crime and terrorism. As the reason for the current low levels of extreme-right support is not lack of demand for BNP policies in the electoral market, this suggests that considerable supply constraints may still be operating.

The constraints that operate on the BNP, and the party's efforts to overcome them, will be discussed at greater length in the following two chapters, so I will only touch upon a few institutional and public opinion issues here. Some of the chief barriers facing the BNP in their efforts to convert public demand into electoral success include poor organization and limited resources; difficulties mobilizing their potential electorate; the low levels of competence of their candidates and party functionaries; and the poor public image of the party, which limits its legitimacy with many voters. In all of these areas, the BNP currently suffers considerable disadvantage when competing with the mainstream political parties. However, the growing success of the BNP at the local level and the constitutional reforms enacted by Labour since 1997, which have multiplied the number of competitive electoral arenas, may have provided the party with opportunities to overcome many of these obstacles. As Goodwin notes in Chapter 8, the BNP have redirected their strategic focus to local contests, where the electoral terrain is more favourable and where the potential for success is higher.

Local electoral politics provide a valuable opportunity to the BNP for several reasons. First, the electoral districts (wards) are smaller and more socially homogenous than in other elections, allowing the party to target wards with high concentrations of the voters who most strongly share their concerns: the white working class. Second, 'rotten boroughs' are much more common at the local level. By 'rotten boroughs' I mean wards or councils dominated for long periods of time by one party, which has, as a result, little incentive to govern or campaign effectively. The BNP has particularly focused on councils dominated for long periods of time by Labour, such as Stoke, Barking and Dagenham and Burnley. In these councils, the BNP can mobilize the resentments of working-class voters who have lost faith in the hegemonic Labour party without facing any serious competition from other opposition parties. Third, limited resources disadvantage the BNP less in local elections. The party can focus on local issues, reach electorates effectively even with small teams of canvassers, and generate interest through local disputes about immigration or Islam, which are often highlighted in the local media. Finally, local elections provide the BNP with an opportunity to overcome its serious image problems. Doorstep meetings and local canvassing can demonstrate to voters that their BNP candidates are not the stereotypical 'skinhead thugs', while elected BNP councillors have an opportunity to prove their competence and gain valuable experience in representation and administration. The BNP clearly recognizes the value of local elections, and has increased the number of candidates it stands in these elections from 50 in 1997 to over 600 in 2008. The BNP now holds over 50 local council seats, providing a potentially valuable cadre of experienced candidates to put forward to higher office.[13]

The devolved electoral offices set up by Labour's constitutional reforms in the late 1990s have also provided the BNP with new opportunities not available to previous right-wing extremist parties. As well as providing smaller constituencies on average, elections for the Scottish Parliament, and the Welsh and London Assemblies also provide multiple opportunities to vote, with voters able to either cast ballots for constituency candidates and for party list candidates. This more proportional system multiplies the options for the BNP, as two examples will illustrate. Voters with multiple preferences can use their different voters to express these preferences: Labour loyalists angry about immigration could vote Labour in their constituency while registering a BNP preference in the list vote. Voters who favour the BNP but live in 'safe' districts where the party stands little chance of winning can still assist the party's prospects by voting for the party in the list election. The evidence suggests that the BNP has indeed benefited from the additional electoral options provided by these semi-proportional systems: its list vote in London Assembly, Welsh Assembly and Scottish Parliament elections has risen steadily and far outstrips its constituency vote. The party has succeeded in electing a list member to the London Assembly in 2008, and fell narrowly short of achieving the same in Wales in 2007.

The proliferation of devolved elections may also benefit the BNP because these elections, along with the longer standing European Parliament elections, are treated by many voters as 'second order elections': elections where less is perceived to be at stake and which they therefore tend to treat as opportunities to express preferences for minor parties and to register 'protest votes' against the existing political establishment (Heath *et al.* 1999). Both these 'second order' motivations are likely to benefit the BNP, which on issues such as immigration, crime and the European Union is emerging as the principal vehicle for expressing such dissatisfaction, as the NF did in France in the 1980s (Ignazi 2003c). Other populist right parties such as the Referendum Party, UKIP and Veritas, which have exploited discontent on these issues, have failed to build effective lasting organizational structures, and the BNP is well placed to pick up many of their voters (Margetts *et al.* 2004).

[handwritten margin note: Ooops! #2014.]

The BNP has indeed performed much better in these 'second order' elections than in general elections, as was dramatically demonstrated in the 2009 European Parliament elections, where an unprecedented wave of public hostility to the political establishment helped the BNP secure 940,000 votes and two seats in the Strasbourg legislature.[14] The success of the BNP in acting as a vehicle for voter protest in these elections may have lasting ramifications, as it will assist its efforts to attract mainstream media attention and build legitimacy. The sheer size of the protest vote in the 2009 European elections, held as a scandal over MP's expenses raged, has also presented the BNP with a unique opportunity to build links with an expanded electorate: never before had so many voters paid attention to an extreme-right party, even if they only turned to it as a way of attacking the establishment. BNP leaders will hope that many of those who came to the party for the protest can be persuaded to stay for the policies.

Of all the barriers facing the BNP, the most serious is what might be called its 'legitimacy deficit' (Goodwin 2007; also Chapter 8). More than two-thirds of British voters polled in 2004 had a very negative view of the BNP, and had resolved never to vote for it, by far the highest figures recorded in the poll (Dunleavey 2005). Similar figures were found in a large YouGov poll conducted on the eve of the 2009 European Parliament election, with more than 70 per cent of supporters of all the other parties (major and minor) holding negative views of the BNP. Comparative European evidence suggests it is very difficult for extreme-right parties with a reputation for extreme racism and xenophobia to achieve electoral breakthroughs, even when many voters agree with their policies (Ivarsflaten 2006). Evidence that the negative public image of the BNP, which continues to be associated with skinheads, fascism and extremist violence, hampers its ability to win over voters who agree with its policies, has recently been provided by an ingenious 2006 YouGov survey experiment. Respondents in the survey were randomly split into two equal groups: all were asked if they agreed with a range of policies from the BNP manifesto, but one half were shown the policies by themselves while the other half were told these were 'BNP policies'. Once voters became aware of the BNP connection, a 'forked tail' effect kicks in (Heath *et al.* 2001):[15] otherwise identical voters became significantly more reluctant to support a policy once they know it is endorsed by the BNP.

The BNP still face a tough challenge in getting an audience with many voters who still associate them with the violent extremism of racist skinheads. Candidates like Richard Barnbrook, who we considered at the beginning of this chapter, may prove to be a template for the party in overcoming this barrier. An effective communicator from a middle-class background, Barnbrook moved from a strong but unsuccessful general election bid to incumbency on both his local council and the London Assembly. He has since used these posts effectively to promote and communicate the concerns of the BNP and bolster its legitimacy. There are many British voters who share the concerns of the extreme right but do not currently vote for it. If they are offered more candidates like Barnbrook, they may well start doing so.

Note on polling sources

The surveys cited here are a mix of academic studies and commercial polls. The academic surveys used here – the British Election Studies and the British Social Attitudes surveys – can be accessed at the UK data archive in Essex, which is available at http://www.data-archive.ac.uk/ (accessed 27 January 2009). The Internet archives for the commercial polling organizations are available at the following addresses:

> ICM: http://www.icmresearch.co.uk/media-centre-polls.php (accessed 27 January 2009).
> Ipsos-MORI: http://www.ipsos-mori.com/reportsandpublications/research-archive.ashx (accessed 27 January 2009).
> Populus: http://www.populuslimited.com/poll-archive.html (accessed 27 January 2009).
> YouGov: http://www.yougov.co.uk/extranets/ygarchives/content/ (accessed 27 January 2009).

Notes

1 The French FN peaked in legislative elections in 1997, when it received over 3.8 million French votes, nearly 15 per cent of the total. It has since declined, but still secured over one million votes in the 2007 first round of National Assembly elections, and Jean-Marie Le Pen won the support of 3.8 million in the first round of Presidential voting

that year. The FPÖ has secured over 10 per cent of the Austrian vote in every national legislative election since 1990, and won over 850,000 votes (17.5 per cent of the total) in the most recent 2008 poll. Support for the Vlaams Blok/Vlaams Belang in Belgian national elections has steadily increased from 400,000 in 1991 to 800,000 in 2007, over 20 per cent of the total. The party performs even more strongly in Flemish regional elections, winning nearly one million votes in the 2004 election, when it became the second largest party in the Flemish parliament.

2 See http://bnp.org.uk and www.britishpride.org/ (both accessed 25 October 2009) for numerous examples.

3 'Working class' is in this case defined using the Registrar General's definition of social class, which attempts to group together occupations with similar levels of occupational skill. While this definition has been criticized by many academics (Goldthorpe *et al.* 1987) it continues to be the classification most widely employed by polling organizations. Analysis of the breakdown in attitudes using the Goldthorpe class schema, where this was possible, revealed very similar patterns of results.

4 *Daily Mail* (2008).

5 BBC (2004).

6 A policy which the BNP, perhaps not coincidentally, strongly supports (BNP, 2005: 11).

7 Frank Field's concerns, expressed in 2006, that Labour was 'living on borrowed time' over immigration were dismissed out of hand by Tony Blair, who emphasized the economic benefits from migration. Margaret Hodge was attacked by other prominent Labour politicians for proposing local preference in housing allocation in 2007. John Cruddas, MP for neighbouring Dagenham (where the BNP are also strong) and Deputy Leadership candidate at the time of the Hodge controversy, attacked his fellow MP for 'racializing arguments over housing allocation'.

8 Michael Portillo was one prominent critic during the election campaign, noting: 'The most important thing for the Tories to prove to people is that they have changed. I think that by having immigration as such a prominent part of the campaign it suggests to people they haven't' (Younge 2005).

9 Stories of injustices resulting from this system and its alleged abuse abound in both the right-wing press and BNP literature. A search of 'asylum seekers' on the *Daily Mail* website returns 52 pages of results, including articles such as 'Free housing for asylum seekers from EU' (7 April 2006); 'Asylum seekers gang made £200,000 in insurance cash scam' (10 July 2008); and 'Failed asylum seekers paid £36 million to set up vineyards, ostrich farms and beauty salons in their own countries' (16 December 2007). A search of the BNP website yields similar results, such as 'Somali asylum seekers use your tax money to win fight for bigger houses' (21 December 2008) and '£200 minimum per week: what each failed asylum seeker costs the British tax payer' (5 November 2008).

10 In the 1970 British Election study, 58 per cent of voters rated the Conservatives best on immigration; in 1979 61 per cent did.

11 The 2009 European Parliament elections provide a clear demonstration of this potential for expansion. The BNP polled 943,000 votes, easily the largest total vote ever for a British extreme-right party. While the party's two MEPs were elected from its recent strongholds of Yorkshire and the Humber, and the North West, its strongest vote increases were registered in regions where it has traditionally been weak, such as Wales and the East of England. European Parliament elections function as 'second order elections' for most voters – an opportunity to register annoyance with the existing government – and many 2009 BNP voters will doubtless stay at home or choose another party in 2010. Nevertheless, the fact that nearly a million voters considered the BNP as a legitimate outlet for their frustrations shows how far the party has come in establishing itself as part of the British political landscape.

12 It is worth pointing out, however, that local political experience can cut both ways for the BNP. Several BNP councillors have featured in locally prominent stories concerning incompetence or open racism. For example, Terry Farr from Epping Council was suspended in 2005 for writing abusive letters to Trevor Phillips, then head of the Commission for Racial Equality (CRE) and James Lloyd of Sandwell Council failed to attend a single council meeting in the six months following his election.

13 The regional list proportional representation system used in European Parliament elections, which greatly assisted the BNP in winning seats by allowing it to focus efforts on its strongest regions, was another Labour constitutional innovation, introduced in 1999.

14 I borrow the terminology employed by Heath *et al.* (2001), who identified a similar effect handicapping the Conservatives' efforts to win over voters after 1997: because voters perceived the Conservatives as the 'nasty party', they were more likely to oppose policies it endorsed even if they agreed with these policies when they were presented without an endorsement.

References

Adorno, T., Frankel-Brunswick, E., Levinson, D. and Sandford, R. (1950) *The Authoritarian Personality*, New York: Harper.

Altemeyer, R. (1988) *Enemies of Freedom: Understanding Right Wing Authoritarianism*, San Francisco, CA: Jossey-Bass.

—— (1996) *The Authoritarian Specter*, Cambridge, MA: Harvard University Press.

—— (2007) *The Authoritarians*, available at: http://home.cc.umanitoba.ca/~altemey/ (accessed 25 October 2009).

BBC (2004) 'BNP leader repeats Islam attack', available at: http: http://news.bbc.co.uk/1/hi/uk/3898695.stm (accessed 22 January 2009).

Betz, H. (1994) *Radical Right Wing Populism in Western Europe*, Basingstoke: Palgrave Macmillan.

Betz, H. and Johnson, C. (2004) 'Against the current, stemming the tide: the nostalgic ideology of the contemporary radical populist right', *Journal of Political Ideologies*, 9(3): 311–27.

Billiet, J. and Witte, H. (1995) 'Attitudinal dispositions to vote for a 'new' extreme right party: the case of "Vlaams Blok" ', *European Journal of Political Research*, 27(2): 181–202.

BNP (2005) *Rebuilding British Democracy: 2005 General Election Manifesto*, Powys: British National Party.

—— (2007) '2007 Mini-Manifesto', available at: http://bnp.org.uk/2008/08/policies-manifesto/ (accessed 22 January 2009).

Brown, M. (2006) 'Margaret Hodge is right about the BNP', *Independent*, 18 April.

Clarke, H., Sanders, D., Stewart, M. and Whiteley, P. (2004) *Political Choice in Britain*, Oxford: Oxford University Press.

Curtice, J. and Seyd, B. (2003) 'Is there a crisis of political participation?', in A. Park, J. Curtice, K. Thompson, L. Jarvis and C. Bromley (eds) *British Social Attitudes: the 20th Report*, London: Sage.

Daily Mail (2008) 'BBC in race row after BNP leader blames Muslims for Britain's drug problems'. http://www.dailymail.co.uk/news/article-528427/BBC-race-row-BNP-leader-blames-Muslims-Britains-drug-problems.html (accessed 25 October 2009).

Dunleavey, P. (2005) 'Facing up to multi-party politics: how partisan dealignment and PR voting have fundamentally changed Britain's party systems', *Parliamentary Affairs*, 58(3): 503–32.

Eatwell, R. (2003) 'Ten theories of the extreme right', in P. Merkl and L. Weinberg (eds) *Right Wing Extremism in the 21st Century*, London: Routledge.

Evans, G., Heath, A. and Lalljee, M. (1996) 'Measuring left-right and libertarian-authoritarian values in the British electorate', *British Journal of Sociology*, 47: 93–112.

Feldman, S. (2003) 'Enforcing social conformity: a theory of authoritarianism', *Political Psychology*, 24(1): 41–74.

Ford, R. (2008) 'Is racial prejudice declining in Britain?', *British Journal of Sociology*, 59(4): 609–36.

Goldthorpe, J., Llewellyn, C. and Payne, C. (1987) *Social Mobility and Class Structure in Modern Britain (2nd edition)*, Oxford: Oxford University Press.

Goodwin, M. (2007) 'The extreme right in Britain: still an "ugly duckling" but for how long?', *Political Quarterly*, 78(2): 241–50.

Hay, C. (2007) *Why We Hate Politics*, London: Polity Press.

Heath, A., Jowell, R. and Curtice, J. (2001) *The Rise of New Labour: Party Policies and Voter Choices*, Oxford: Oxford University Press.

Heath, A., McLean, I., Taylor, B. and Curtice, J. (1999) 'Between first and second order: a comparison of voting behaviour in European and local elections in Britain', *European Journal of Political Research*, 35: 389–414.

Ignazi, P. (2003a) 'Britain: a case of failure', in P. Ignazi (ed.) *Extreme Right Parties in Western Europe*, Oxford: Oxford University Press.

—— (2003b) *Extreme Right Parties in Western Europe*, Oxford: Oxford University Press.

—— (2003c) 'France: the prototype of the new extreme right', in P. Ignazi (ed.) *Extreme Right Parties in Western Europe*, Oxford: Oxford University Press.

Ivarsflaten, E. (2005) 'Threatened by diversity: why restrictive asylum and immigration policies appeal to Western Europeans', *Journal of Elections, Public Opinion and Parties*, 15(1): 21–45.

—— (2006) 'Reputational shields: why most anti-immigrant parties failed in Western Europe, 1980–2005', paper presented at the Annual Meeting of the American Political Science Association, Philadelphia, PA, 31 August–3 September.

Kitschelt, H. and McGann, A. (1995) *The Radical Right in Western Europe: A Comparative Analysis*, Ann Arbor, MI: University of Michigan Press.

Lubbers, M. and Scheepers, P. (2000) 'Individual and contextual characteristics of the German extreme right-wing vote in the 1990s: a test of complementary theories', *European Journal of Political Research*, 38(1): 63–94.

Margetts, H., John, P. and Weir, S. (2004) 'The latent support for the far right in British Politics: the BNP and UKIP in the 2004 European and London elections', paper presented to the 2004 Elections, Public Opinion and Parties Conference, Oxford, 10–12 September.

Minkenberg, M. (2000) 'The renewal of the radical right: between modernity and anti-modernity', *Government and Opposition*, 35(2): 170–88.

Mudde, C. (2000) *The Ideology of the Extreme Right*, Manchester: Manchester University Press.

—— (2007) *Populist Radical Right Parties in Europe*, Cambridge: Cambridge University Press.

Norris, P. (2005) *Radical Right: Voters and Parties in the Electoral Market*, Cambridge: Cambridge University Press.

Oborne, P. (2007) *The Triumph of The Political Class*, London: Pocket Books.

Phillips, M. (2006) *Londonistan: How Britain Created a Terror State Within*, London: Gibson Square Books.

Rydgren, J. (2007) 'The sociology of the radical right', *Annual Review of Sociology*, 33: 241–63.

Smith, A. (1991) *National Identity*, London: Penguin.

Sniderman, P., Hagendoorn, L. and Prior, M. (2004) 'Predisposing factors and situational triggers: exclusionary reactions to immigrant minorities', *American Political Science Review*, 98(1): 35–49.

Swyngedouw, M. (2001) 'The subjective cognitive and affective map of extreme right voters: using open-ended questions in exit polls', *Electoral Studies*, 20(2): 217–41.

Van der Brug, W. and Fennema, M. (2007) 'What causes people to vote for a radical right party? A review of recent work', *International Journal of Public Opinion Research*, 19(4): 474–87.

Van Der Brug, W., Fennema, M. and Tillie, J. (2005) 'Why some anti-immigrant parties fail and others succeed: a two step model of aggregate electoral support', *Comparative Political Studies*, 38: 537–73.

Whiteley, P., Stewart, M., Sanders, D. and Clarke, H. (2006) 'The issue agenda and voting in 2005', *Parliamentary Affairs*, 58(4): 802–17.

Younge, G. (2005) 'The boundaries of race in Britain today', *Guardian*, 25 April.

8 In search of the winning formula

Nick Griffin and the 'modernization' of the British National Party

Matthew J. Goodwin

Introduction

In the Austrian national election held in October 1999, the Freedom Party of Austria (FPÖ) polled 27 per cent of the vote and subsequently joined a government coalition with the centre-right People's Party (ÖVP). The result received worldwide attention and was followed by EU Member States imposing diplomatic sanctions against Austria. At the same time as these events, in Britain the British National Party (BNP) quietly elected Cambridge-graduate Nick Griffin as its new party Chairman. In stark contrast to the FPÖ, in 1999 the BNP remained in the electoral ghetto, having polled just 1 per cent of the vote in elections to the European Parliament held that year. While founded in April 1982, over the next two decades the BNP languished on the lunatic fringe, electing only a single local councillor. Against this backdrop of electoral failure, the election of Griffin (who became only the second Chairman in the BNP's history following John Tyndall who had led the party for 17 years), was heralded as marking 'a new beginning for British nationalism'. With Griffin at the helm, the BNP announced that it would embark on a more 'media-friendly' approach, develop a more professional electoral strategy and shift its programmatic emphasis toward 'mother-hood and apple pie topics such as calling for the strengthening and extension of democracy'. Looking toward the events in Austria, the BNP encouragingly informed its footsoldiers that 'Haider is living proof that sensible politics can work for nationalism'.[1]

The electoral ascendency of the Austrian FPÖ formed part of a broader upsurge in support for parties on the radical and extreme right-wing.[2] While some of these parties have recently suffered electoral losses, over the past quarter-century parties such as the French National Front (FN), Flemish Interest (VB) and Danish People's Party (DFP) have scored impressive and often durable electoral gains. Yet as reflected in the divergent trajectories of the FPÖ and BNP, not all of these parties have enjoyed as much success as others; while some participate in government coalitions, others struggle to enter the local council chamber. The extreme right in Britain is typically viewed as a case of failure. Although from 2002 onward the BNP has gained elected representation in several local authorities, one seat on the Greater London Assembly in 2008 and two Members of the European Parliament in 2009, it is important not to overstate the party's success, a point underscored by two observations.

First, despite recent gains the BNP's attempt to engineer a wider breakthrough at the national level has been met with only limited success, as reflected in the fact that (at the time of writing) the party has never finished above third place in a parliamentary election. Moreover, even under a more proportional system such as that which was used for elections to the European Parliament in 2009, the number of votes polled by other minor parties such as the UK Independence Party (UKIP) was more than two-fold greater than the number received by the BNP. In the midst of severe economic recession, scandal over MPs' expenses, continued public concern over immigration (see Chapter 7) and more general signs of voter dissatisfaction with the incumbent Labour government, compared to its result in 2004 the BNP only managed to attract an additional 135,000 voters nationally while in the two regions that elected BNP MEPs (the North West and Yorkshire and Humber) the party's total number of votes declined. Far from signalling the BNP's breakthrough into the political 'mainstream', most of the party's gains have remained confined to the local level and pockets of support in outer-east London and the North West, West Midlands and Yorkshire regions.

Second, the party's limited success becomes especially apparent when we consider the level of electoral potential for the extreme right in Britain which, as discussed in Chapter 7, currently far outstrips the BNP's actual level of support. As Ford highlights, evidence from polling data suggests that in modern Britain all three aspects of the extreme right's core ideological agenda (i.e. ethnic nationalism, xenophobia and authoritarianism) enjoy widespread public support, and that consequently the BNP could potentially appeal to an electorate far larger than it currently wins over. Nor is this evidence of there being a sizeable reservoir of latent support for the extreme right unique to early twenty-first-century Britain; rather, these findings should be set alongside two literatures. The first is earlier research in Britain that similarly pointed toward a significant reservoir of public support for policies associated with the BNP's predecessor, the National Front (NF), such as the compulsory repatriation of 'non-white' immigrants (Sarlvik and Crewe 1983: 243; see also Eatwell, 2000).[3] The second is more recent comparative research on the European extreme right, which demonstrates that, although these parties often experience quite divergent electoral fortunes, the underlying voter demand (i.e. xenophobic attitudes, levels of political discontent, etc.) has remained relatively constant across most European states (see Rydgren 2004; Van der Brug *et al.* 2005).

As these opening remarks suggest, the failure of the BNP to more effectively mobilize its underlying electoral potential and achieve a wider breakthrough is not due to lack of demand for policies and ideas associated with the extreme right bur rather supply factors, such as the characteristics of the party itself (i.e. its ideology, strategy, organization and leadership), as well as the reaction of other political actors. In other words, the ability of parties such as the BNP to successfully mobilize their electoral potential depends much on the role of agency, with factors such as a strong internal organization, the presence of an efficient and/or charismatic leader and the nature of the ideological 'package' that is offered to voters all being identified as important predictors of election success.[4]

In elaborating on the importance of the supply-side, one useful starting point is the pan-European literature on right-wing extremism that identifies two party-centric factors as being particularly important: a party's ideological formula and its origins. According to the first, in broad terms the most successful extreme-right parties are those that have (at least publicly) largely abandoned the 'old' ideological formula that combined crude biological racism (that was often accompanied with pseudo-scientific claims over the racial superiority of the white race), anti-Semitism and radical opposition to the liberal democratic system. As Rydgren (2005) notes, in the post-1945 political environment these highly stigmatized 'old' ideological components garnered little support among voters and the few neo-fascist parties that clung to vote-seeking strategies had effectively been rendered obsolete by the outcome of the Second World War. Consequently, toward the end of the twentieth century and inspired by 'New Right' theorists, parties such as the Austrian FPÖ and French FN developed a 'new' radical right formula that downplayed these earlier components and instead combined ethno-nationalist xenophobia (or the new 'cultural racism') and anti-establishment (but not overtly anti-democratic) populism.[5] This exoteric ideological 'makeover' has enabled some parties in Europe to tone down their extremist baggage and, in the process, distance themselves from the stigma of being perceived by voters as undemocratic organizations that operate beyond the borders of the 'normal' democratic arena.

Yet according to a second approach, one important factor that will determine the extent to which a party is able to undertake this transition and, in turn, encourage more favourable perceptions among voters and less hostile reactions from other political actors, will be its own history. The argument here, and which will be developed throughout this chapter, is one of path dependency; like most political organizations, the contemporary behaviour of parties such as the BNP is shaped strongly by the movements and waves of mobilization that preceded them.[6] Seen from this perspective, the ability of a party to change its ideology, strategy and/or organization and in turn promote a more positive and 'democratic' image to voters will be influenced strongly by its origins.

In seeking to explain the limited success of the BNP, in this chapter attention turns to supply factors, in particular the party's attempt to 'modernize' with the aim of mobilizing its electoral potential and achieve a wider breakthrough. The chapter proceeds as follows: section one provides an overview of the BNP's ideological origins; section two focuses on the ascendancy of Nick Griffin who has assumed an instrumental role in the party's strategy of 'modernization'; section three examines the main changes that have been implemented in Griffin's post-1999 BNP but also highlights evidence to question the extent of 'modernization' and presents findings to suggest that voters remain largely unconvinced by these changes.

History matters: the BNP's ideological roots

The extreme right in Britain is heavily indebted to the ideological tradition of racial nationalism. In contrast to more diverse ideological currents that have underpinned 'new' radical right parties such as the Austrian FPÖ, the racial nationalist tradition has placed much heavier emphasis on crude biological racism, conspiratorial anti-Semitism and fascist nostalgia (on the racial nationalist tradition see Copsey 2008: 76–99; also Thurlow 1987). In electoral politics racial nationalism was most clearly expressed in the NF that was founded in 1967. While the NF's outwardly-directed exoteric appeals sought to downplay fascist nostalgia, the party's inner esoteric core remained firmly committed to racial nationalist ideology (Eatwell 1996). The influence of interwar fascism on the NF was reflected in publications such as *Spearhead*, the political journal of John Tyndall, who led the NF twice during the 1970s and who would later establish the BNP. While presenting the magazine as 'an organ of National Socialist opinion in Britain', Tyndall was firmly committed to biological racism and belief in a Jewish-led conspiracy, as reflected in the following extract: '[I]f Britain were to become Jew-clean she would have no nigger neighbours to worry about ... It is the Jews who are our misfortune: T-h-e J-e-w-s. Do you hear me? THE JEWS.'[7] Aside from blatant anti-Semitism, the NF retained the core policy of the British extreme right, namely the compulsory repatriation of immigrants and individuals of non-European origin. At various other times, the Front also hinted at the need to replace democratic institutions with a corporate system and criticized liberalism on the grounds that it undermined national interest and obscured racial awareness (Eatwell 1998: 146–7). The NF's pursuit of electoral credibility was further undermined by its strategy of using confrontational rallies as a means to attract publicity (often in alliance with other extremist groups such as British Movement).

Following the NF's disintegration, by the mid-1980s the BNP had monopolized the extreme-right milieu. In terms of ideology, the BNP saw little reason to depart from the guiding tenets of racial nationalism, as Tyndall underscored in the early 1990s: 'British nationalism inherited from the 1970s an ideology that was quite adequate to all demands'.[8] This strong sense of continuity with previous waves of mobilization owed much to the fact that many of the leading activists in the early BNP had been socialized in the NF. Although these links have been documented by the party (Tyndall 1998: 483), they also become evident when we examine the 54 BNP parliamentary candidates who stood in the 1983 general election, at least two-fifths of whom had stood on behalf of the NF in the previous election of 1979 (Goodwin 2010a).[9]

While activists provided structural linkage to earlier waves of mobilization, ideological continuity was also reflected in the BNP's campaigning literature. As it would do so through much of the 1980s and 1990s, in 1983 the BNP offered voters traditional policies from the extreme right stable; closer links with white Commonwealth countries, pledging 'a complete end to coloured immigration and to work for the gradual resettlement overseas of Britain's coloured community', and complaining that 'the Government's grovelling attitude towards Jewry seems to be boundless'.[10] References to the fascist tradition and Holocaust revisionism were also explicit, with the party's recommended reading for supporters in 1992 including the publications *Did Six Million Really Die?* and *Is the Diary of Anne Frank Genuine?*[11] As discussed in greater depth below, the BNP's roots in this right-wing extremist subculture has exerted a profound influence on the party's more recent attempts to 'modernize'.

The roots of 'modernization'

While the party remained committed to racial nationalism, in the early 1990s a group of activist 'modernizers' began advocating a change of strategy. Modernizers sought to modify the BNP's exoteric ideological appeals in order to improve the prospect of election success. Pointing toward debates over the European Economic Community (EEC), the Channel Tunnel, immigration, the electoral rise of the French FN and the growing salience of Islamic fundamentalism (e.g. the burning of copies of Salman Rushdie's *The Satanic Verses* in Bradford in 1989), these activists called for a new approach. Moreover, legislative revisions to the Public Order and Race Relations Acts, combined with a decline in the number of solidly working-class constituencies, effectively rendered the party's traditional strategy of 'march and grow' obsolete.

At the core of the proposed 'modernization' strategy lay two components. First, rather than sporadically contest costly general elections modernizers urged the party to focus instead on establishing a grassroots presence, enabling local branches to cultivate an image of legitimacy and electoral credibility in carefully selected areas (though in reality most of these areas were in London's East End). Inspired by the community politics campaigning of the Liberal Party, these activists sought to 'localize' the party message and utilize intensive community-based activism as an opportunity to offer a new image of the BNP to a hitherto disinterested British electorate.

Second, modernizers sought to distance the BNP's exoteric appeals from the underlying tradition of racial nationalism, criticizing for example the 'stupid' statement by the NF that it would 'kick its way into the headlines'.[12] Instead, it was argued that the BNP should emulate the example of Jean-Marie Le Pen's French FN by exploring ways of jettisoning its extremist baggage, abandoning confrontational tactics and adopting a more voter-friendly approach. Particularly important in this respect was the call to replace the core policy of the compulsory repatriation of immigrants with a more 'moderate' voluntary version that was based on financial incentives for returning immigrants. More generally, by adopting populist-style themes such as 'freedom', 'identity' and 'democracy', it was argued that the BNP would be able to extend its appeals beyond the traditional recruiting ground of the alienated urban working-class fringe toward a wider audience.

Initial experimentation with the embryonic strategy first took place in the East End in the period 1990–1993. Though these local campaigns did not signal a radical overhaul of BNP strategy, they did introduce a more professional approach to the fledgling party. Much heavier emphasis was placed on targeting local issues in an articulate manner and making contact with local residents, a community-based strategy that assumed an important role in the election of the first BNP local councillor in Tower Hamlets in 1993, a key watershed in the development of the party.[13]

Following this isolated 'success', the party's development was set back when an internal schism erupted between the BNP and Combat 18, a more extreme extra-parliamentary grouping that sought to redirect the attention of activists back toward more confrontational tactics. While causing severe internal discord, the challenge would eventually fade and by the late 1990s modernizers were further encouraged by trends elsewhere in Europe. The high profile electoral advance of similar but more successful parties such as the French FN provided a 'demonstration effect' for BNP activists in search of a new approach (Kitschelt 1995: 253–4). Influenced by these events, modernizers encouragingly informed activists how parties such as the Italian Social Movement (later renamed the National Alliance) had replaced the 'old stale and unsaleable fascism' with a 'modern nationalist policy suite'.[14] These activists subsequently sought to adopt elements of the 'new' radical right approach, for example looking toward the FN's proposal to provide financial incentives to returning immigrants when attempting to revise the BNP's repatriation policy. However, the ageing leadership of John Tyndall remained hostile to calls for change and when the BNP's general election campaign in 1997 revealed no significant change of direction and ended with a disappointing result (the BNP's 56 candidates averaged only 1.4 per cent in the seats they contested), modernizers and their supporters began calling not only for a change of direction but also leadership.

Nick Griffin and the 'hunt for fool's gold'

With the support of key modernizers, in October 1999 Nick Griffin polled over 60 per cent of the membership vote and was elected chairman. Though Griffin himself was still relatively new to the party (see below), his ascendancy to the peak of the British extreme right marked the latest episode in a much longer affiliation with the milieu. Influenced by the politics of his parents, Griffin first entered politics by becoming involved with the Young Conservatives (his father had been a Conservative Party councillor and member of the ultra right-wing Monday Club). Griffin was introduced to organized right-wing extremism in 1974, when his family attended a meeting of the NF which, at that time, was enjoying a growth of support. Griffin enrolled and progressed quickly through the ranks, becoming national organizer for the NF student division in 1978, member of the NF Directorate in 1980, NF parliamentary candidate in 1981 (in the Croydon North West by-election) and deputy NF chairman in 1985 (during this period Griffin also graduated from Cambridge University with an honours law degree).[15]

Whilst the NF's electoral returns ultimately failed to match the party's ambitions, the Front did experience two 'peaks' in support that coincided with the high-profile arrival of immigrants from Uganda (1972–1973) and

Malawi (1976–1977). Various polls at the time pointed toward a significant reservoir of public support for the Front. In one poll conducted in the late 1970s, approximately one-quarter of respondents agreed with the statement that the NF expressed the views of 'ordinary working people', while slightly over one-fifth agreed that it would be 'good for Britain' if the NF was represented in Westminster (Harrop *et al.* 1980). Observing an influx of previously unaffiliated new recruits into the party, Griffin became critical over their lack of ideological awareness and commitment to 'the Cause' and began to develop ideas around the need for an elite cadre of 'political soldiers': an inner core of ideologically educated and highly committed activists who would spearhead national renewal.

Following the demise of the NF and a brief hiatus from politics, Griffin returned to activism in the early 1990s, a decision he traces to hearing of plans by a local school to celebrate a 'multi-faith' Christmas. Griffin sought to draw on the earlier experiences of the NF and International Third Position (ITP) in order to construct a more closely knit, ideologically coherent and electorally successful movement.[16] After temporarily becoming a freelance writer on the extreme-right circuit and disseminating his ideas to various organizations, Griffin was introduced to the BNP in 1992 when he was invited to speak at a meeting of BNP Croydon branch. While considering the BNP both ideologically and organizationally 'primitive', Griffin nonetheless viewed the party as a useful vehicle through which the lessons of the previous two decades could be applied.[17] Griffin subsequently began to edit *The Rune*, a quarterly publication of Croydon BNP, and a position that would result in his conviction in 1998 of publishing material likely to incite racial hatred. The first issue of *The Rune* was unabashedly fascist, advertising Waffen SS posters, watercolours by Adolf Hitler and describing Gregor Strasser as 'one of the greatest of all National Socialist leaders'.[18] Slightly later, Griffin also began contributing to *Spearhead* and a pamphlet entitled *Who Are the Mindbenders?*, the latter being described by Griffin as an examination of the 'over-representation of Jews and Zionists in the media'.[19]

As the above suggests, at least until 1998 both the ideas and tactics espoused by Griffin placed him in direct opposition to those activists calling for a more moderate approach. One example was Griffin's interpretation of the BNP's earlier 'success' in London's East End, which he argued owed less to the party's transformation into a 'post-modernist rightist party' than to what local residents perceived as a 'strong disciplined organisation with the ability to back up its slogan "Defend Rights for Whites" with well-directed boots and fists'.[20] These statements formed part of Griffin's broader critique of a more populist-style approach, as he made clear: '[W]e must seek to recognise that populism – which starts with thoughts of trimming policies, avoiding holding election rallies in areas which might cause Asian riots, sneering at skinheads and acquiescing in the Holocaust lie – is the kiss of death'.[21] Rather than downplay extremist baggage, Griffin labelled the quest for legitimacy a 'hunt for fool's gold' and warned activists against a 'wild goose chase after acceptability'.[22] Under the influence of modernizers, the party's increasing emphasis on electioneering and grassroots activism was similarly criticized; there is more to a revolution, wrote Griffin, 'than plonking a couple of hundred nationalist bottoms on the plush benches of Westminster'.[23] Instead of wasting scarce resources on fighting elections, Griffin argued that the BNP would be better situated by directly confronting opposition from left-wing and anti-fascist organizations, writing that 'it is more important to control the streets of a city than its council chamber'.[24] Rather than advocating a more moderate approach, statements such as this appeared more reminiscent of Goebbel's dictum: 'Whoever conquers the street can also conquer the masses, and whoever conquers the masses thereby conquers the state' (cited in Benewick 1969: 15).

Like Tyndall, Griffin aligned himself with activist hardliners by vigorously opposing calls to sideline extremist elements within the party. Griffin also continued to espouse virulent anti-Semitism and Holocaust revisionism, writing for example: 'And throughout the White world there can no active nationalist who has not found those piles of "gassed" Belsen typhus victims to be by far the biggest propaganda obstacle ... The New World struggling to be born cannot do so until this lie is publicly exposed, ridiculed and destroyed.'[25] While some activists had begun to voice their concern over the continued presence of revisionist literature, Griffin was emphasizing the benefits of having students read postwar fascist 'theorizing', such as the writing of Francis Parker Yockey. Griffin even took issue with the historian David Irving's position on the Holocaust, arguing that Irving was too moderate and challenging the assertion that four million Jews had been victims of the Nazi regime: 'True revisionists would not be fooled by this new twist to the story tale of the Hoax of the twentieth century.'[26]

Through the mid-to-late 1990s, Griffin's articles and speeches played to his role as the wild-eyed extremist who had been promoted by Tyndall in an attempt to balance the growing influence of modernizers. Yet toward the late 1990s Griffin's personal ambitions led him to dramatically modify his views toward party strategy, in the process aligning himself more closely with influential modernizers, such as Lecomber, who despite holding several convictions was one of several activists calling for a new approach. Describing this apparent conversion as turning him from a 'heart on a sleeve hardliner' into a 'born-again modernizer',[27] Griffin subsequently began distancing himself from earlier statements while making the case for a new approach:

> [T]he more then I spent time with people like Tony Lecomber who'd already realized that we had to get out of the ghetto, and had some success breaking out of it because it was their operation that had won in Millwall ... The more I looked at that, the more I thought, 'yeah, we've got to change'.[28]

Though previously critical of populism, Griffin now urged activists to 'forget the ideas for a few minutes and think purely about selling them'.[29] Aware of the changing balance of power within the party, Griffin switched his allegiance by encouraging activists to become better dressed and more willing to learn new tactics. In order for the BNP to become a mass movement, wrote Griffin, the party would need to 'forget about racial differences, genetics, Zionism, and historical revisionism' and instead keep things 'simple'.[30] Such statements reflected Griffin's apparent decision to swing his support behind those activists calling for a more voter-friendly approach.

In some respects, Griffin's 'conversion' was aided by the fact that the arguments put forward by modernizers did not signal a complete break from past practice. Rather, the emphasis on community-based activism and a more moderate approach to issues of race and immigration could be seen as a return to ideas that had been introduced by activists in the NF but which subsequently lay dormant within the British extreme right. For example, in the mid-1980s NF activists had emphasized the usefulness of 'community action' as a means of countering the Front's negative image, while others advocated that the NF adopt New Right ideas such as 'differentialist racism' which, instead of stressing biological inequality between racial groups, argues that they must be kept separate in order to preserve ethnic diversity (for a discussion of these ideas in the NF see Goodwin 2010a).[31] Yet like other activists, in the 1990s Griffin was especially inspired by the electoral rise of the French FN, leading him to meet with then-leading FN elites such as Bruno Mégret and be strongly influenced by the journalist Jonathan Marcus' (1995) detailed analysis of the FN's rise, entitled *The National Front and French Politics: The Resistible Rise of Jean-Marie Le Pen*. By the end of the decade, Griffin and activist modernizers seemingly reached a consensus on the need to transform the BNP into party that, while remaining committed to the underlying racial nationalist tradition, would modify its exoteric appeals in order to pursue wider election success. In the next section our attention turns to some of the key changes that have been implemented within the party under Griffin's leadership.

Ideology, strategy and organization in Griffin's BNP

From 1999 onward, the BNP embarked on a strategy of 'modernization' by downplaying its ideological roots, adopting a more moderate stance toward issues of race, embracing community-based activism and attempting to improve the respectability of its grassroots activist base. Yet as the next section highlights, while this strategy has entailed significant changes to supply factors the party's ability to present itself as a more 'normal', democratic alternative has been severely constrained by its roots.

Ideological appeals

Similar to both the earlier NF and the electorally successful 'new' European radical right, the BNP frames immigrants, ethnic minority groups and asylum-seekers as a 'threat' to national identity, a major cause of crime and social unrest, and as a burden on the welfare state and local resources (on the wider radical right see Rydgren, 2008). While stressing the detrimental impact of various ethnic 'out-groups' on labour and housing markets, the BNP's nativist appeals are also frequently imbued with a survivalist and apocalyptic style, for example the party's repeated claim that white Britons will soon become a minority ethnic group, that interethnic conflict or a race war is inevitable, and that 'Britain's very existence today is threatened by immigration' (BNP 2005: 13).

Historically, the extreme right in Britain has utilized similar frames that seek to embellish perceptions of ethnic threat and competition (e.g. Taylor 1982: 96–9). To a certain extent, however, the post-1999 BNP has sought to moderate its official discourse. First, the party has implemented a revised repatriation policy, through which 'those non-white immigrants who are legally here will be encouraged, but not compelled, to return to their lands of ethnic origin' via financial incentives.[32] Second, and more fundamentally, Griffin's BNP has attempted to replace crude claims over the genetic superiority of the white race with an emphasis on the new cultural racism based on the ethnopluralist doctrine (Taguieff 1988). By formulating a more elaborate critique of multiculturalism the party downplays biological arguments in favour of stressing the need to keep different ethnic groups separate and to avoid race-mixing in order to protect and preserve ethno-cultural diversity: citizens might enjoy other cultures, but they must stick to their own 'or "diversity" will be but a short-lived stepping stone to nothingness' (BNP 2005: 20).

The party has attempted to publicize this more 'moderate' approach by establishing links with members of minority groups. In elections to the European Parliament in 2004, the BNP election broadcast was presented by a member of the Sikh community. The party also established an 'Ethnic Liaison Committee' with the aim of cultivating similar links and although the BNP continues to adhere to a 'whites-only' membership policy in recent years the party has fielded Jewish and half-Turkish Cypriot candidates in an attempt to counter charges of anti-Semitism and racism (though links with members of minority ethnic groups should not be exaggerated).

While downplaying these 'old' ideological components, like other parties on the extreme right the BNP has embraced anti-Islamic nativism. In the aftermath of 9/11, the BNP quickly launched a 'Campaign against Islam', which was presented as a New Crusade for the survival of Western civilization and an attempt to counter the Islamification of Britain. The religion of Islam (referred to in one BNP leaflet as Intolerance, Slaughter, Looting, Arson and the Molestation of women) is portrayed as a threat to the national community, whilst Muslim males are often linked to criminality though particularly of a sexual nature: '[T]he hidden epidemic of molestation, abductions and rape of scores of white girls in northern English cities … show the inherent tendency that the teachings of the paedophile Mohammed have had on some of his followers'.[33]

The adoption of anti-Islamic nativism marks an important stage in the evolution of postwar right-wing extremism. In contrast to crude racism or anti-Semitism, anti-Islamic sentiment is more widespread in established Western democracies and has some support in sections of the media and political establishment, both of which may inadvertently legitimize claims by the BNP (Betz 2007: 47–8). Indeed, the BNP often seizes upon statements by mainstream commentators in an attempt to legitimize its own campaigns. The party regularly cites academic studies such as Samuel Huntington's (1996) *The Clash of Civilizations*, aiming to attach a façade of intellectual legitimacy to its claim that Islam is unable to conform to Western or British values. Similarly, the party quotes columnist Melanie Phillips (*Daily Mail* Online, 10 February 2009) as providing evidence that 'Britain is being Islamised', and cites a study by the Equalities and Human Rights Commission (EHRC) when claiming that 67 per cent of Muslims would not be happy for their child to marry someone of a different religion.[34] However, while there is some evidence to suggest that the BNP's anti-Islamic campaigns are having an impact in some areas (see Chapter 9) it is important not to overstate their significance. In areas where the BNP has been most successful, its local campaigns have centred not so much on Islam as exploiting locally based anxieties over the allocation of scarce resources such as housing and regeneration funding, as well as other often disparate local grievances. For example, the election of a BNP councillor in Blackburn in 2002 was preceded by a campaign that focused on claims that an elderly person's home was to be turned into a hostel for asylum-seekers, while in the outer-London borough of Barking and Dagenham and the borough of Burnley in Pennine Lancashire the party has focused more heavily on exploiting pressure on social housing and regeneration.

More fundamentally, the BNP's claim that it has abandoned 'old' ideological components such as biological racism is highly questionable. Although we would ideally undertake a survey of BNP members and activists in order to fully probe their belief system, evidence of the party's continued adherence to these ideological components can be gleaned from analysis of internally directed literature and highlighted by several illustrative examples. One article that appears in the BNP magazine in 2005 suggests that a drug designed to remedy heart failure among African Americans would 'supply the concept that there are biological differences between the races'.[35] Two years later, the editor of the magazine and long-term extreme right stalwart John Bean draws attention to the 'substantial difference between the world's main racial strains', writing that 'the sub-Saharan African has a brain weighing just under 1 kg, compared with 1240 gms for Europeans and 1300 gms for East Asians'.[36] Activists have also made explicit references to key events in the collective psyche of the extreme right, such as comparing the Asian tsunami with the Allied attack on Dresden during the Second World War (events such as Dresden are typically cited by extreme right groups in an attempt to reduce the significance of Nazi atrocities).[37]

Albeit presented in more subtle terms, anti-Semitism also remains evident within the party. Though advising activists not to subscribe to conspiracy theories, in one article Griffin simultaneously writes 'that certain minority groups do punch far above their weight when it comes to influence within the media', making specific reference to his anti-Semitic pamphlet *The Mindbenders* and stating: 'The formative views of those controlling the media have been moulded by events such as … seeing Schindler's List'.[38] These references within the BNP to the anti-Semitic tradition are often identical in nature to conspiratorial arguments that were advanced by the NF in earlier decades, such as the claim put forward in one article in 2005 that a sinister organization named the 'Bilderberg Group' controls world affairs:

> Do not allow any of this argument to be dismissed as cranky 'conspiracy theory', for this is REAL ... The Bilderberg Group exists ... it includes some of the most influential people in the world whose thirst for absolute power is insatiable: All this is FACT ... they gnaw away at the very foundations of western civilisation like rats behind a skirting board.[39]

Strategy and organization

As noted above, in recent years the BNP has sought to cultivate an image of electoral credibility from the 'ground up'. While the party has not completely abandoned the old tactic of using confrontational rallies,[40] in some areas the BNP has successfully utilized targeted and intensive campaigns to establish a strong grassroots presence, gain representation in local council chambers and take steps toward overcoming the 'credibility gap' that confronts most small parties (Russell and Fieldhouse 2005: 254–6). In addition to localizing the BNP message, party strategists have also redirected their energy away from traditional bastions of support for the extreme right such as London's inner East End, instead shifting their focus toward deindustrializing districts and traditional heartlands of the Labour Party in England's North West, West Midlands and Yorkshire, a shift in emphasis that is reflected in the changing social bases of support for the extreme right in twenty-first-century Britain (see Chapter 9).

Yet in organizational terms the party continues to adhere to the leadership principle, an authoritarian internal structure that awards complete power to the party chairman. Although Griffin's BNP has taken some steps toward promoting intra-party democracy (e.g. by establishing an 'Advisory Council' that offers guidance to the chairman and developing an embryonic voting membership scheme) the BNP retains a heavily centralized structure. Also like its predecessors, the party relies on a small membership base. It is estimated that prior to 1999 membership of the BNP is unlikely to have surpassed 2,500, though in recent years there has occurred some growth to approximately 3,000 members in 2002, 6,500 members in 2005 and 12,000 in 2008 (at the time that the party's membership list was leaked by renegade activists onto the Internet). One qualitative study of BNP activists suggests that different 'types' of activist are drawn into the party: while senior positions are largely dominated by long-term members of the 'old guard' who have been socialized in the racial nationalist tradition, Griffin's BNP has also attracted a layer of 'new recruits' who possess little or no prior experience in politics and 'political wanderers' who have previously been active either in the Conservative Party or in parties such as the UK Independence Party (UKIP; see Goodwin 2010b).

However, it is difficult to asses how many of the party's foot soldiers are active on a regular basis. What is certain is that Griffin's BNP has devoted more effort than their predecessors to the retention, training and overall image of its activist base. Beyond the occasional training session and rally, neither the NF nor early BNP invested much effort into sustaining the loyalty of activists. In contrast, the contemporary BNP has developed a range of initiatives designed to cultivate a sense of collective identity among party foot soldiers. Aside from more regular activist training sessions and summer schools, the party has established several extra-parliamentary organizations that include a youth and student wing, record label, trade union, annual party festival and an association for ex-servicemen, all of which form part of Griffin's goal of developing a broader 'cultural offensive':

> The great failing of the BNP is that it focused almost exclusively on elections ... the idea that we can merely be elected to power, and that the establishment will simply say 'here are the keys, good-bye we're off' is simply not going to happen. The road to power for nationalists in Western Europe is very similar to that which we've seen in Eastern Europe where you have mass support expressed through the ballot box but also you have in the end to have such a weight of public opinion on your side that the other parties simply dare not tear up the rule book and say, 'well we're going to ban you', as for instance they'd done with the *Vlaams Blok*.[41]

Clearly, one additional motivating factor is the need for finance, something the extreme right in Britain has historically lacked. In 2006, the party was forced to raise membership fees as a result of expenditure being 'cut to the very bone' (in the same period auditors raised concern over the longer-term financial survival of the party).[42] The arrival of significant funds as a result of the party gaining two Members of the European Parliament in 2009 will most likely quieten such concerns, yet there is no question that the BNP relies almost exclusively on its membership base as the main source of finance.

In an attempt to jettison extremist baggage the BNP has also encouraged followers to become better dressed and more 'respectable'. For example, one 'language and concepts discipline manual' advises followers to avoid terms such as 'fascist', 'racialist' and 'white' in favour of 'right-wing populist' or 'ethno-nationalist'.[43] However, despite such attempts the BNP has found it difficult to fully abandon its status as a refuge for members of the extreme-right fringe, as several examples reveal. In 1998, the BNP newspaper continued to carry advertisements asking all skinhead and white power bands to write to the Ian Stuart Fan Club (prior to his death in 1993 Ian Stuart Donaldson was a member of the skinhead band Skrewdriver and leading activist in the neo-Nazi Blood and Honour network).[44] In the year prior, the Coventry and Warwick branch of the BNP hosted a benefit gig that included bands from the Bloor and Honour music circuit, with funds raised directly contributing to the BNP's European election campaign in 1999.[45] In the same year, it was reported that David Copeland, who planted three nail bombs in London that killed three people, held links to the BNP.[46]

In more recent years, Griffin's BNP has been careful to publicly reject violence and downplay links with the extremist fringe. Yet as noted by Art (2008), in contrast to 'new' radical right parties which are often able to take advantage of broader and historically rooted nationalist subcultures, parties that emerge from a narrow right-wing extremist subculture such as the BNP are unable to draw followers from more legitimate nationalist networks and will therefore find it difficult (if not impossible) to avoid becoming a bastion of unreconstructed fascists, individuals with links to criminality and violence, neo-Nazis and Holocaust deniers. In turn, the composition of these parties results in them being widely condemned by political actors and media and becoming highly stigmatized, thereby fuelling a perception among voters that the organization lays beyond the borders of 'normal' democratic politics.[47]

Although more research on voters' perceptions of the extreme right is required, the detrimental impact of the BNP's grassroots activist base can be highlighted by several examples. First, the BNP refutes links with violence but there is evidence to suggest that a 'culture of violence' continues to surround the party. In 2007, a former BNP candidate was jailed after having stockpiled explosive chemicals in anticipation of a forthcoming race war.[48] Similarly, in July 2009 it was reported that counter-terrorism officers had uncovered a network of suspected extreme-right activists who had access to 300 weapons and 80 bombs, and that at least one BNP membership card had been recovered at the home of one suspect who was charged under the Terrorism Act.[49] Second, although not implicated in violence BNP supporters have been publicly linked to other extremist acts. In 2002, one party activist in Scotland was convicted of inciting racial hatred and in 2004 over four million viewers watched the television documentary *The Secret Agent* in which BNP activists described attacking Asians, pushing dog excrement through their letter boxes and stated that they wanted to 'shoot Pakis [Pakistanis]'. Shortly afterward, Nick Griffin was (again) arrested on suspicion of incitement to racial hatred. During the campaign for elections to the Greater London Assembly (GLA) the respectability of BNP members was questioned when it was widely reported that one of the party's candidates had stated: 'To suggest that rape, when conducted without violence, is a serious crime is like suggesting that forcefeeding a woman chocolate cake is a heinous offence' (*London Evening Standard*, 1 April 2008).

At the same time, the composition of the party's membership base appears to impose limits to the extent of 'modernization'. Initiatives such as the selection of Jewish candidates or the suggestion of allowing 'non-white' members have also (as in 2004) sparked intense debate within the party. Some activists loyal to the BNP founder John Tyndall (now deceased) have subsequently exited the party to join rival groups such as the England First Party (EFP). Meanwhile, more recent joiners who have been attracted by the party's electoral growth have voiced criticism over the BNP's lack of professionalism, its policy of 'whites-only' membership and the absence of genuine intra-party democracy and transparent financing (see Goodwin 2010a). In areas such as Bradford, some activists have left the party to form a rival grouping, standing candidates against the BNP in six out of eight wards in the local elections in 2008. Other disillusioned activists flocked to an umbrella group named the 'Voice of Change' that sought to campaign for greater 'reform and democratisation' within the BNP and mounted an unsuccessful leadership challenge in the spring of 2008. This internal trade-off between ideological purists and new joiners is especially problematic for minor parties such as the BNP, which despite its claims of sidelining extremist elements simply cannot, for organizational reasons, fully purge its membership base, as the following extract from an interview with Griffin underscores:

> We've lost a number of people who are from the old days ... But at the same time we can't afford to just alienate everyone there from the past, or who regards themselves as a principled nationalist, we simply can't afford to do that; the organizational costs would be too catastrophic. But as a result of that, because we're not changing as some of the newcomers would like to see us change, they want to in effect see us not being nationalists at all, or they think that if we have a few blacks in the party it will do away with the racist smear ... So they want to take us too far the other way.[50]

In this respect, it is also important not to lose sight of the non-electoral (and potentially more violent) right-wing extremist fringe, in which some groups subscribe to concepts such as leaderless resistance through which they adopt a loose phantom cell structure and eschew ties to formal electoral politics. In July 2009, a 'white supremacist' and unemployed electrician, who had been inspired by groups such as Combat 18 and the Ku Klux Klan, was arrested as he was attempting to commence a terrorist bombing campaign.[51] The previous year, a forklift truck driver from East Yorkshire who possessed membership cards for the NF, British People's Party (BPP) and White Nationalist Party (WNP) was charged with terrorism offences and sentenced to 16 years in prison after stockpiling and making small explosives.[52] Particularly at the local level, it remains unclear the extent to which there exists overlap between membership of small extra-parliamentary formations and the more organized electoral extreme right.

Beyond its membership base the BNP has also cultivated strong links at the transnational level. Delegates from the French FN and Swedish National Democrats (ND) regularly attend the BNP's annual festival; additionally in 2004 Jean-Marie Le Pen assisted the launch of the party's European election campaign. In September 2008, the BNP's representative on the Greater London Assembly (GLA) – Richard Barnbrook – was scheduled to speak at a demonstration in Germany against the construction of a mosque that brought together an assortment of European extreme-right movements, and in April 2009 the deputy leader of the party attended a rally alongside representatives from the Italian New Force (Forza Nuova) and French FN. Some of these links undermine claims of 'modernization', notably the BNP's ties with the National Democratic Party of Germany (NPD), an organization that has strong associations with openly neo-Nazi groups.

Perceptions of the BNP

How do voters in the twenty-first century perceive the BNP? Before addressing this question, it is first important to note that as a result of its origins the BNP has been widely condemned in British society, and by numerous actors. In the media the party's stigmatization is aptly reflected in the front-page headline of the *Sun* newspaper that read: 'Bloody Nasty People' (15 July 2004). There is a need for more research on the relationship between, for example, media coverage and the response of mainstream party actors to the extreme right on the perception of voters. Three sources of data shed some light on the question of how voters view the modern BNP. First, focus groups that were undertaken in Barking and Dagenham in 2005 reveal that although immigration was the major issue of concern for local residents the BNP was still viewed by most participants as being clearly racist; some who had voted BNP expressed regret at having done so, particularly after watching *The Secret Agent* documentary (JRRT 2005). Second, an experiment on BNP support undertaken by YouGov the following year suggested that the perceptions of voters reduced support for various policies when they were identified as being the policies of the BNP. As highlighted in Table 8.1, participants were less inclined to support propositions when they were identified with the party, such as that all further immigration to the UK should be halted (in this case support dropping by 11 per cent).

Third, more recent data similarly indicate that despite attempts at 'modernization' the BNP has been unable to shed its 'pariah' status. When voters were asked about their views toward the party just prior to elections to the European Parliament in June 2009, 70 per cent of mainstream party supporters felt 'very negative' toward the party, and almost four-fifths of all party supporters (i.e. supporters of mainstream parties, the Greens and UKIP) expressed 'fairly negative' or 'very negative' feelings toward the party (YouGov 2009). While it is notoriously difficult to probe right-wing extremist sympathies through survey data, these findings suggest that few voters in twenty-first century Britain currently perceive the BNP as a 'normal' player in the political process.

Conclusion

The limited electoral success of the BNP is not due to lack of demand. As highlighted in the previous chapter, there exists in twenty-first-century Britain a sizeable level of support for the core ideas and policies associated with the extreme right. Yet as noted in the wider academic literature, even if a large number of citizens support policies associated with the extreme right, the transformation of electoral potential into actual support at the ballot box will depend heavily on the ability of the party to present itself as a 'normal' and non-violent organization that adheres to the democratic rules of the game (Van der Brug *et al.* 2005: 545–6).

Recent years have seen significant changes within the BNP that should not be ignored. The strategy of 'modernization' is integral to Nick Griffin's goal of transforming the BNP from a fringe extremist sect into a serious political challenger. This strategy has entailed a modification to the party's publicly disseminated ideology, an emphasis on community-based activism and much greater effort being devoted to the recruitment and retention of active followers.

Table 8.1 Perceptions of the BNP

Sample A Do you support or oppose the following propositions?
Sample B Here are some propositions that have been put forward by the British National Party (BNP). In each case, please say whether you support or oppose them?

		Sample A (BNP not mentioned)	Sample B (BNP mentioned)	The 'BNP effect' (B - A)
Criminals sent to jail should serve their full sentence, and their sentence should be lengthened if they behave badly in jail				
	Support	91	87	-4
	Oppose	4	8	4
	Don't know	5	5	0
The UK should withdraw completely from the European Union				
	Support	35	32	-3
	Oppose	36	42	6
	Don't know	28	26	-2
All further immigration to the UK should be halted				
	Support	59	48	-11
	Oppose	29	39	10
	Don't know	13	13	0
All immigrants to the UK should be denied the right to bring further members of their families to this country at a later data				
	Support	52	43	-9
	Oppose	28	34	6
	Don't know	20	22	2
The UK should accept fewer asylum seekers				
	Support	77	74	-3
	Oppose	14	18	4
	Don't know	9	8	-1

(Continued)

Table 8.1 Cont'd

	Sample A (BNP not mentioned)	Sample B (BNP mentioned)	The 'BNP effect' (B - A)
British families should take priority over newly arrived immigrants in the allocation of housing			
Support	83	77	−6
Oppose	9	12	3
Don't know	8	10	2
Non-white citizens are inherently 'less' British than white citizens			
Support	16	11	−5
Oppose	68	76	8
Don't know	15	13	−2
The government should encourage immigrants and their families to leave Britain (including family members who were born in the UK)			
Support	29	22	−7
Oppose	52	58	6
Don't know	19	20	1
Average			
Support	55	49	−6
Oppose	30	36	6
Don't know	15	15	0

Each of these developments warrants the close attention of researchers and policymakers alike.

However, the findings above suggest that the BNP – which holds its roots in the narrow right-wing extremist subculture of racial nationalism – has remained too closely aligned with the fascist tradition to alter the negative perceptions of voters toward the extreme right. In other words, the ability of the BNP to fully mobilize its electoral potential has owed much to what we might term a 'legitimacy deficit'. One of the major obstacles confronting a minor party operating in a majoritarian electoral system is to convince voters that they are a credible electoral alternative or, in other words, that they can win (Russell and Fieldhouse 2005: 6). Yet a more pressing obstacle that confronts a party on the extreme right is to convince voters not merely that they are electorally credible but that more fundamentally they are a 'normal', non-violent and democratic organization.

In some localities, the BNP's change of strategy has enabled the party to present itself as a credible political alternative, particularly in areas where other political parties have abandoned labour intensive forms of activism and where genuine party competition is either weak or absent. However, in path-dependent fashion the BNP's broader attempt to reposition itself in the electoral arena and present a 'new face' to the British electorate has been severely constrained by its roots in the racial nationalist subculture, a particular ideological tradition within British politics that has been consistently condemned by mainstream political actors, media and leaders of various faith communities. As reflected in the political trajectory of Nick Griffin, many of the party's leading activists have been socialized in a strong right-wing extremist subculture that has been characterized by conspiratorial anti-Semitism, biological racism and nostalgia for historic fascism. As a consequence, the contemporary BNP remains highly stigmatized in wider society and, in turn, has found it difficult to attract more experienced and 'respectable' activists that are required to extend the party's appeal beyond the margins toward the mainstream. Instead, the party has been forced to rely upon members of the extremist fringe for resources, individuals who have at various times undermined the party's quest for respectability. While it should not be overlooked that there exists a sizeable reservoir of potential support for an extreme-right party that proves able to overcome this legitimacy deficit (Chapter 7), and that a growing number of citizens are prepared to lend their vote to the extreme right (Chapter 9), the future development of the BNP will depend much upon the party's ability to reconcile the internal trade-off between, on the one hand, widening its electoral appeal and, on the other, the legacy of history.

Notes

1 'Time for a new beginning', *British Nationalist* (Oct), 1999, p. 2, 8.
2 This chapter will focus extensively on the debate over terminology. On 'extremism' see the Introduction and for a wider discussion of terminology and conceptual debates see Mudde (2007).

3 Nor is Ford alone in highlighting latent support for the extreme right. See also P. John and H. Margetts (2009) 'The latent support for the extreme right in British politics', *West European Politics*, 32(3): 496–513.

4 For one example of a study that takes supply-side factors more seriously see Carter (2005).

5 As noted by Rydgren (2005: 416), by adopting a discourse of cultural racism – which maintains that different ethnic groups must be kept separate in order to preserve ethnic diversity – and populist rhetoric directed toward the political establishment, the new radical right parties have been able to free themselves of enough stigma to attract voter groups 'that never would have considered voting for an "old" right-wing extremist party promoting biological racism and/or antidemocratic stances'. On the distinction between 'extreme' versus 'radical' right-wing see also the Introduction to this volume.

6 For studies that similarly stress the importance of party history see for example Art (2008). For a discussion of the path dependence approach see A. Messina (2007) *The Logics and Politics of Post-WWII Migration to Western Europe*, Cambridge: Cambridge University Press.

7 *Spearhead* no. 4, p. 5, cited in Billig (1978: 128).

8 J. Tyndall (1992) '1992: Time to face reality', *Spearhead* (Jan).

9 For a longer discussion of links between the earlier NF and contemporary BNP see Goodwin (2010).

10 BNP (1983) 'Vote for Britain: Vote BNP', *British Nationalist* (May): 1–3.

11 On recommended reading see Spearhead (1992) 'Books', *Spearhead* No. 278 (April): 16.

12 A. Lecomber (1997) 'Success and failure – the new politics and the old', *Patriot*, No.1 (spring): 16–19.

13 For a detailed account of the BNP's campaigning in this period see N. Copsey (1996) 'Contemporary British fascism in the local arena': The BNP and 'Rights for Whites', in M. Cronin (ed.) *The Failure of British Fascism: The Far Right and the Fight for Political Recognition*, pp. 118–41, Basingstoke: Macmillan.

14 See Lecomber, 'Success and failure', 11.

15 Interview two with Nick Griffin, conducted by author October 2006.

16 Interview one with Nick Griffin, conducted by author March 2006.

17 Interview one with Nick Griffin.

18 *The Rune*, Issue 1 (n.d.) contact author.

19 Interview two with Nick Griffin.

20 N. Griffin, 'Editorial', *The Rune*, No. 11 (n.d. 1996?): 2–4.

21 Griffin, 'Editorial' (*The Rune*).

22 N. Griffin (1996) 'Populism or power?', *Spearhead* (Feb): 11–13; see also *Spearhead* (1996) (Dec): 13.

23 N. Griffin (1997) 'A battle for hearts and minds', *Spearhead* (Feb): 14–16; also see Griffin, 'Editorial'.

24 See Griffin, 'Populism or power', 11–13.

25 Ibid.

26 N. Griffin (n.d. 1996?) 'Not such a crazy conspiracy', *The Rune*, No. 11.

27 Interviews one and two with Nick Griffin.

28 Interview two with Nick Griffin.

29 On the 'kiss of death' see Griffin, 'Editorial' (*The Rune*); on the latter see N. Griffin (1997) 'Hard times, soft soap', *Spearhead*, 14–15.

30 N. Griffin (1999) 'BNP – freedom party!', *Patriot*, No. 4(Spring): 5.

31 For example J. Pearce (1985) 'The way forward' and 'Community action', *Nationalism Today*, 11.

32 BNP (2001) 'Time to declare: where we stand!', *Identity*, Issue 9 (May): 6–7.

33 'The Islamic menace'. Available at: http://www.bnp.org.uk/articles/islamic_menace. htm (accessed 26 October 2007).
34 On Melanie Phillips see 'Britain is being Islamised through Sharia banking, admits leading *Daily Mail* writer', available at: http://bnp.org.uk/tag/islamification-of-britain/ (accessed 15 February 2009). On the EHRC see 'Islamification of Britain: Muslims want "Own Society" research confirms', available at: http://bnp.org.uk/tag/islamification-of-britain/ (accessed 15 February 2009).
35 BNP (2005) 'Septembers news', *Identity* Issue, 58: 2.
36 'How small genetic differences give racial diversity', available at: http://www.bnp/org. uk/articles/beans_genes.html (accessed 26 October 2007).
37 J. Bean (2004) 'John Beans nationalist notebook', *Identity*, Issue 52 (Feb): 20.
38 N. Griffin (2005) 'Career opportunities?', *Identity*, Issue 53 (March): 4.
39 P. Flavelle (2005) 'The hidden hand', *Identity*, Issue 51 (Jan): 14–15. On conspiratorial anti-Semitism and the NF see Taylor (1982: 71).
40 For example in September 2008 BNP activists rallied in protest following the death of a BNP member and in February 2009 the party planned to rally in Liverpool city centre.
41 Interview one with Nick Griffin.
42 See N. Griffin (2006) 'Facing the end of liberalism', *Identity*, Issue 70 (Sep): 5.
43 BNP 'Language and Concepts Discipline Manual', available at: http://www.bnp.org.uk/ organisers/store/general_guides/language_discipline.pdf (accessed 1 February 2009).
44 *British Nationalist*, Feb. 1998: 4.
45 *British Nationalist*, May 1998: 6.
46 On the link between organized electoral right-wing extremism and terrorism see for example 'Right-wing terrorism still alive and plotting', *Searchlight* November 2005, available at: http://www.searchlightmagazine.com (accessed 11 March 2009).
47 One example cited by Art (2008) is Flemish Interest (VB), a party that holds its origins in a rich nationalist subculture comprised of an array of diverse organizations (i.e. both right-wing extremist and Flemish nationalist), and which has provided a stream of activists and sense of historical continuity. In contrast, in neighbouring Wallonia the FN has been burdened by its history, coming from a subculture dominated by fringe right-wing extremist groupuscules and thus being forced to rely heavily on activists with links to violence and criminality who, in turn, have contributed to the party's 'pariah' status.
48 'Ex-BNP man jailed over chemicals', BBC News Channel Online, available at: http://news.bbc.co.uk/1/hi/england/lancashire/6923933.stm (accessed 20 July 2009).
49 'Bomb seizures spark far-right terror plot fear', *Sunday Times*, 5 July 2009.
50 Interview two with Nick Griffin, October 2006.
51 'Neo-Nazi convicted of planning terrorist bombing campaign', *Guardian*, 15 July 2009.
52 'Bomb seizures spark far-right terror plot fear', *Sunday Times*, 5 July 2009.

References

Art, D. (2008) 'The organizational origins of the contemporary radical right: the case of Belgium', *Comparative Politics*, 40(4): 421–40.
Benewick, R. (1969) *Political Violence and Public Order: A Study of British Fascism*, London: Allen Lane.
Betz, H.G. (2007) 'Against the "green totalitarianism": Anti-Islamic nativism in contemporary radical right-wing populism in Western Europe', in C.S. Liang (ed.) *Europe for the Europeans: The Foreign and Security Policy of the Populist Radical Right*, Aldershot: Ashgate.

Billig, M. (1978) *Fascists: A Social Psychological View of the National Front*, London: Academic Press in co-operation with European Association of Experimental Social Psychology.

BNP (2005) *Rebuilding British Democracy: British National Party General Election 2005 Manifesto*, Welshpool, Powys: British National Party.

Copsey, N. (2008) *Contemporary British Fascism: The British National Party and the Quest for Legitimacy*, New York: Palgrave Macmillan.

Eatwell, R. (2000) 'The extreme right and British Exceptionalism: the primacy of politics', in P. Hainsworth (ed.) *The Politics of the Extreme Right: From the Margins to the Mainstream*, pp. 172–92, London: Pinter.

—— (1996) 'The Esoteric Ideology of the National Front in the 1980s', in M. Cronin (ed.) *The Failure of British Fascism*, pp. 99–117, Basingstoke: Macmillan.

Goodwin, M.J. (2010a) *The New British Fascism: Rise of the British National Party*, Oxford: Routledge, forthcoming.

—— (2010b) 'Activism in contemporary extreme right parties: The case of the British National Party (BNP)', *Journal of Elections, Public Opinion and Parties*, 20(2): forthcoming.

Harrop, M., England, J. and Husbands, C. (1980) 'The bases of National Front support', *Political Studies*, 28(2): 271–83.

Huntington, S.P. (1996) *The Clash of Civilizations and the Remaking of World Order*, New York: Simon & Schuster.

JRRT (2005) *The Far Right in London: A Challenge for Local Democracy?*, York: Joseph Rowntree Reform Trust.

Kitschelt, H. (in collaboration with McGann, A.) (1995) *The Radical Right in Western Europe: A Comparative Analysis*, Ann Arbor, MI: University of Michigan Press.

Marcus, J. (1995) *The National Front and French Politics: The Resistible Rise of Jean-Marie Le Pen*, New York: New York University Press.

Mudde, C. (2007) *Populist Radical Right Parties in Europe*, Cambridge: Cambridge University Press.

Phillips, M. (2006) *Londonistan: How Britain Created a Terror State Within*, London: Gibson Square Books.

Russell, A. and Fieldhouse, E. (2005) *Neither Left nor Right? The Liberal Democrats and the Electorate*, Manchester: Manchester University Press.

Rydgren, J. (2008) 'Immigration sceptics, xenophobes or racists? Radical right-wing voting in six West European countries', *European Journal of Political Research*, 47(6): 737–65.

—— (2005) 'Is extreme right-wing populism contagious? Explaining the emergence of a new party family', *European Journal of Political Research*, 44(3): 413–37.

Sarlvik, B. and Crewe, I. (1983) *Decade of Dealignment*, Cambridge: Cambridge University Press.

Taguieff, P.-A. (1988) *La Force du préjugé. Essai sur le racisme et ses doubles*, Paris: La Découverte.

Thurlow, R.C. (1987) *Fascism in Britain: A History, 1918–1985*, Oxford: Blackwell.

Tyndall, J. (1998) *The Eleventh Hour*, 2nd edn, London: Albion Press.

Van der Brug, W., Fennema, M. and Tillie, J. (2005) 'Why some anti-immigrant parties fail and others succeed: a two-step model of aggregate electoral support', *Comparative Political Studies*, 38(5): 537–73.

9   Who votes extreme right in twenty-first-century Britain?

The social bases of support for the National Front and British National Party

Matthew J. Goodwin, Robert Ford, Bobby Duffy and Rea Robey

Introduction

In the European elections of 2009 almost one million citizens cast their vote for the British National Party (BNP), in the process sending the first ever representatives from the extreme right-wing in Britain to the European Parliament. Overall, the BNP polled 6.2 per cent of the vote, an increase of 1.3 per cent on the party's performance in the previous contest of 2004 and a considerable improvement on the 101,000 votes the party received in 1999. The party's record result extends the recent rising trend in electoral support for the extreme right in Britain. In terms of national elections, the general election of 2005 was the most successful for the BNP. The 119 BNP candidates averaged 4.3 per cent of the vote in the seats they contested, an increase of 0.4 per cent on the party's average result in the general election in 2001. When all votes had been counted over 192,000 citizens had voted BNP, over four times the number who supported the party in 2001. While a national breakthrough into Westminster remains elusive, the BNP saved a record 34 deposits, as compared to five in 2001, three in 1997 and zero in 1992. In 31 constituencies BNP candidates surpassed the 5 per cent threshold and in a further three seats they polled over 10 per cent of the vote. To a certain extent the party's ability to retain more deposits reflected its use of more targeted campaigning. By focusing on areas where the party had obtained a minimum of 8 per cent in the 2004 European elections, or where there were already elected BNP councillors, party strategists aimed to maximize the average share of the vote and use the general election as a springboard to local election success the following year. The effect of this more professional strategy was particularly apparent in the outer-east London constituency of Barking where BNP candidate Richard Barnbrook polled 16.9 per cent of the vote, the best result for an extreme right parliamentary candidate in British history. The result followed a particularly intensive campaign by BNP activists that highlighted the party's strengthening grasp of community-based politics. In contrast to the majority of the BNP target seats which prior to election day received two election addresses, residents in the carefully selected wards in Barking received up to seven different leaflets that were distributed by weekend canvassing teams of between 20 and 50 activists.[1] In the local elections held the following year, the BNP became the main opposition group on Barking and Dagenham Borough Council when 11 of its 13 candidates were elected (more generally the party more than doubled its number of local councillors to 44). One headline that followed the result read as follows; 'Welcome to Barking – new far right capital of Britain' (*Guardian*, 6 May 2006).

While not signalling the party's breakthrough into the mainstream the results above form part of a more general upward trend in BNP support. As highlighted in Table 9.1, over the past two decades the number of citizens voting BNP in general elections has risen sharply, from 7,000 in 1992 to almost 200,000 in 2005. The party has also experienced significant increases in support at the local level where it has gained a foothold in local government and established a significant electoral presence in areas such as Barking and Dagenham, Bradford, Burnley, Epping Forest and Stoke-on-Trent. As discussed by Robert Ford in Chapter 7, there is also evidence to suggest that a sizeable reservoir of further potential support exists in Britain for some of the core ideas associated with right-wing extremist ideology.

Despite the BNP's electoral gains and the often alarmist publicity that follows, actual supporters of the extreme right in twenty-first-century Britain remain under-researched. Research on the BNP has tended to focus more on the party's historic development (Copsey 2008), strategy (Eatwell 2004) and support in specific localities (Rhodes 2006; Goodwin 2009). Meanwhile, though useful the few studies that do examine BNP voters (John *et al.* 2006; Bowyer 2008) rely heavily on aggregate-level data and tell us little about the individuals who actually vote BNP. Finally, within this academic literature even less attention has focused on the question of the extent to which the BNP's base of support is similar to that which underpinned the only other extreme-right party in postwar Britain of any electoral relevance, namely the National Front (NF) during its heyday in the 1970s. In recent years BNP activists have compared their party's performance with the earlier NF,

Table 9.1 General election performance of the British National Party, 1983–2005

Election year	Vote received	Number of candidates	Average vote per constituency	Deposits retained
1983	14,621	54	271	0
1987	553	2	277	0
1992	7,005	13	539	0
1997	35,832	57	629	3
2001	47,129	33	1,428	7
2005	192,746	119	1,620	34

Sources: Eatwell, R. (2000) 'The extreme right and British exceptionalism: the primacy of politics', in P. Hainsworth (ed.) *The Politics of the Extreme Right: From the Margins to the Mainstream*, p. 173, London: Pinter; Electoral Commission.

dismissing followers of the latter as 'boneheaded Nazi cranks' and 'perpetual losers' (despite the fact that many leading BNP activists were previously leading foot soldiers in the NF; see Goodwin [2010]).[2] But to what extent do these different manifestations of organized right-wing extremism recruit support from a similar social base?

In this chapter we draw on individual level data to examine extreme right party supporters in contemporary Britain. Rather than present only a snapshot of BNP support we also compare our findings with earlier research on NF voters, which allows us to investigate the broader evolution of support for organized right-wing extremism in postwar Britain. The chapter is organized as follows: first, we provide an overview of explanations put forward to explain support for extreme-right parties in Britain; second, we discuss our data and methods; third, we examine the characteristics of self-identified BNP supporters including their gender, age, social class and geographic location, and compare this group with supporters of the earlier NF; fourth, we examine what drives extreme right party support by investigating the characteristics and concerns of BNP supporters in a local case study of Barking and Dagenham.

Who votes extreme right? An overview

Prior to the rise of the BNP the only electorally relevant party on the extreme right was the NF. Founded in 1967, the NF experienced two peaks in support: the first followed the high-profile arrival of Ugandan Asians in the period 1972–1974; the second followed the arrival of Malawian Asians in 1976–1977. Following a parliamentary by-election in West Bromwich in which the NF candidate polled 16 per cent of the vote, the NF contested both general elections held in 1974: in the first (February) contest 54 NF candidates averaged 3.3 per cent of the vote; in the second (October) contest 90 NF candidates averaged 3.1 per cent. In the period 1976–1977 the NF also performed relatively well in local elections, most notably in elections to the Greater London Council in 1977 in which 120,000 Londoners voted for the extreme right party. Yet this 'success' would be ephemeral in nature. Weakened by continued internal factionalism and constrained by the rightward shift of the Conservative Party under Margaret Thatcher, by the late 1970s the NF was on its way back to the political fringe. In the general election in 1979 the 303 NF candidates averaged just 1.3 per cent of the vote.

While the NF did prove able to mobilize an appreciable level of support, most notably in parts of Greater London and the West Midlands, the party ultimately failed in its quest to secure elected representation.[3] Nonetheless, the growth of NF support was the focus of several studies, most of which traced support to citizens who felt threatened by rapid change in post-industrial Britain and, move specifically, the arrival of New Commonwealth immigrants. From this perspective, it is the less well educated and economically more insecure groups who are more likely to be in actual or perceived competition with other ethnic groups over scarce resources such as jobs and housing and who are therefore more responsive than other groups to the nativist and anti-immigrant themes espoused by the extreme right. Across Europe more generally, parties on the extreme right wing have proven to be particularly effective in framing immigrants, minority ethnic groups and increasingly Muslims as 'the problem'; as a threat to national identity, a strain on national and local resources and as the main cause of crime and social unrest (Rydgren 2008). Individuals in lower social classes and who have a lower level of education are more likely to respond to these campaigns because they pledge to prioritize native white citizens in terms of housing, jobs and welfare benefits, which are salient issues to poorer and more deprived white voters. Indeed, seen through a comparative lens much of the support for contemporary extreme-right parties has arrived from male manual workers, the unemployed and from those with lower levels of education (Betz 1994; Lubbers et al. 2002; Arzheimer and Carter 2006; Mudde 2007).[4]

Findings from research on support for the National Front are generally consistent with the above approach. Focusing on support for the NF in the GLC elections in 1977 the aggregate-level study by Whiteley (1979: 375; also Lipset and Raab 1971) drew attention to the prevalence of manual workers, interpreting the NF vote in terms of 'working-class authoritarianism' and as 'primarily an apathetic working-class vote'. Other findings indicate the important role of party competition, with some noting how the Front tended to benefit in contests where it faced no opposition from Liberal candidates who might otherwise split the protest vote (Husbands 1975; Steed 1978). The observation that the Front polled particularly well in areas such as Bradford, Coventry, Leicester, parts of London's inner East End and Wolverhampton – all of which had a high concentration of early Black and Asian immigrants in Britain – led some to examine the relationship between ethnic composition and NF support. Above average levels of support for the NF in these areas was linked to higher immigrant populations, with the suggestion being that the NF benefited from a 'backlash' against the presence of 'non-whites' in local communities (Taylor, 1982: 30; also Taylor 1979a, 1979b). Actual or perceived ethnic competition occupied a central role in most explanations of NF support, with aggregate-level data suggesting 'that primarily economically marginal, culturally threatened white workers in heavily working-class districts felt attracted to the National Front' (Kitschelt, 1995: 255; also Ignazi, 2003: 183–4).

However, much of this research is weakened by a lack of data at the individual level. Owing to the electoral marginality of extreme-right parties in Britain and the small number of extreme-right voters identified in surveys, more sophisticated quantitative analysis has been lacking (see Kitschelt, 1995: 255–6). One attempt to shift the focus toward the individual level was the study by Harrop and colleagues (1980) who gathered a sample of 270 NF supporters by aggregating 22 vote intention surveys undertaken in the period October 1977–April 1978 (representing 0.7 per cent of the combined English sample).[5] The study revealed that the typical NF supporter was a young, employed and working-class male; over one-half of NF support (53 per cent) came from individuals under the age of 35 years old while over two-thirds (72 per cent) came from the working-class. Examining regional support for the NF, the study found that the party performed particularly strongly in Greater London and the West Midlands (areas which provided 48 per cent of NF support) but less well in districts in the North. In particular, NF support stemmed from skilled rather than semi- or unskilled workers, a finding interpreted as being 'consistent with those materially based explanations of NF support that emphasize the importance of the economic locations where competition between indigenous and immigrant populations for scarce and valuable resources is felt most acutely' (Harrop et al., 1980, p.276). In contrast to more privileged though also more insecure skilled workers, those at the bottom of the labour market have fewer resources to defend and thus appeared to feel less threatened by immigration and demographic change. It is worth noting, however, that other findings suggested that the NF appealed both to skilled and unskilled manual workers and that support for the extreme right in 1970s Britain had a more even age-distribution, with NF sympathy appearing stronger among those aged 25 years or under and those aged 46–55 years old (Husbands 1983).

Support for the British National Party

Following the demise of the NF the BNP has since emerged as the predominant representative of the extreme right in Britain. Whilst limited, existing aggregate-level studies provide some insight into the drivers of BNP support. As above, these studies indicate that it is primarily members of the working-class and individuals with a lower than average level of education who are more likely to turn out in elections for the extreme right. Focusing on the local elections in 2002 and 2003 Bowyer (2008) finds that the BNP performed strongest in economically deprived, urban areas and is most likely to field candidates and win votes in wards with relatively low average levels of education. Similarly, others find that at the level of wards the BNP recruits support primarily in deprived, urban areas and where there are higher proportions of skilled manual workers and individuals with no qualifications (JRRT 2005; Borisyuk et al. 2007). Examining wards where the BNP stood two or more candidates in local elections in 2003, John et al. (2006) also suggest that support stems from the lower middle-classes, in wards where there are higher numbers of individuals with no qualifications and higher numbers of residents aged between 45–69 years old (conversely, wards with higher numbers of young people appear less likely to support the party; see also JRRT 2005).

As already noted, the prominence of working-class and less well educated individuals is often linked to actual or perceived ethnic competition. As a result of their social status these groups are more likely to perceive themselves and the native in-group as under 'threat' from asylum-seekers, immigrants and minority ethnic groups. Existing studies of BNP voting patterns lend support to an explanation rooted in ethnic competition theories, though in particular with regard to Muslim communities and Islam. These findings reveal a positive relationship between the proportion of Pakistani and Bangladeshi residents and higher levels of support for the BNP, with the implication being that the extreme right performs strongest in areas where there are large numbers of Muslim residents. At local authority level John et al. (2006) find that BNP support is higher where there is a noticeable Asian population, though in particular Pakistani and Bangladeshi groups (meanwhile they find no relationship between the presence of Indian Asian groups and BNP support). As these authors suggest, given that support for the BNP appears more likely in areas with a large Muslim presence the party's adoption of anti-Islamic campaigns may be exerting a strong impact at the local level (see Chapter 8). Research by Bowyer (2008: 618) also reveals that at district level the BNP is more likely to contest elections and win votes where there is a large ethnic minority population, though in particular a large Pakistani and/or Bangladeshi community, leading to the conclusion that 'the BNP appeals to whites who are hostile to the emergence of racial and cultural diversity in their communities'. Interestingly, Bowyer also finds that at ward level ethnic diversity appears to reduce support for the BNP. In other words, while the party performs strongest in more ethnically diverse districts, 'its strength seems to be concentrated in wards where white residents are less likely to encounter members of ethnic minority groups than other whites in their districts; i.e. white enclaves within ethnically diverse cities' (Bowyer 2008: 617). Beyond voting, it is worth drawing attention to one qualitative study which similarly suggests that perceptions of ethnic competition and threat-though in particular linked to Islam and Muslim communities-feature prominently in the motivational accounts of BNP activists (Goodwin 2010). While there is a need for further research these findings should be seen within the context of studies elsewhere in Europe that similarly suggest a positive relationship between the proportion of individuals from Muslim countries and higher levels of support for the extreme right, a relationship that does not appear to hold with immigrants from non-Muslim countries (Coffé *et al.* 2007; also De Vos and Deurloo 1999).

Having provided a brief overview of existing research we now turn to examine extreme-right party voters in twenty-first-century Britain. While those existing studies above shed some light on the questions of who votes extreme right and what factors motivate this support, in our study we utilize data at the individual level which enables us to examine more closely the characteristics of these supporters and their concerns. Before presenting our findings in the next section we first discuss our data and methods.

Data and methods

One common difficulty presenting itself to researchers of extreme-right party support is that surveys often produce too few extreme right voters to permit reliable analysis. To overcome this difficulty we analyse aggregated omnibus data gathered in the period 2002–2006. Face-to-face interviews were conducted as part of the Ipsos MORI twice-monthly regular omnibus survey which is based on a nationally representative quota sample.[6] In total 190,882 adults (aged 15 years or over) were interviewed to ascertain their background characteristics, voting intention and views toward a range of social and political issues. From this sample emerged 1,001 respondents who stated either that they had voted for the BNP or modern day NF or that they would consider doing so, representing 0.5 per cent of the total sample.[7] While this sample does not allow us to probe more passive sympathizers discussed in Chapter 7, it does hold the advantage of capturing the more 'hardcore' supporters of the extreme right (i.e. individuals who are willing to openly express their support). As far as the authors are aware, this represents the largest sample of self-identified extreme right voters in Britain ever assembled and therefore provides a unique opportunity to examine this often neglected constituency.

Individual support for the extreme right: past and present

In Table 9.2 we compare the demographic distribution of contemporary extreme right supporters (i.e. 2002–2006) with the distribution of supporters of the earlier NF (i.e. 1977–78). We replicate the data presented by Harrop and colleagues (1980) in order to maximize comparability with their earlier study. Unfortunately

Table 9.2 Demographic comparison of BNP/NF supporters in 2002–2006 and NF supporters in 1977–1978

	% of adult population 1977–1978	*% of adult population 2002–2006*	*Change*	*% of NF support 1977–1978*	*% of BNP/NF support 2002–2006*	*Change*
Sex						
Male	48	47	−1	71	69	−2
Female	52	53	+1	29	31	+2
Age						
15–24 years	8	13	+5	37	11	−26
25–34 years	18	15	−3	16	14	−2
35–54 years	40	34	−6	29	39	+10
55 years +	34	38	+4	18	36	+18
Social class						
Higher non-manual (AB)	16	20	+4	6	11	+5
Lower non-manual (C1)	22	29	+7	22	19	−3
Skilled manual (C2)	35	21	−14	46	32	−14
Semi-/unskilled manual and residual (DE)	27	29	+2	26	38	+12
Region*						
East Anglia	4	11	+7	3	11	+8
East Midlands	7	8	+1	5	9	+4
Greater London	16	14	−2	25	6	−19
North	31	30	−1	15	41	+26
South East (ex. Greater London)	20	16	−4	17	11	−6
South West	9	11	+2	12	7	−5
West Midlands	12	10	−2	23	14	−9

(Continued)

Table 9.2 Cont'd

	% of adult population 1977–1978	% of adult population 2002–2006	Change	% of NF support 1977–1978	% of BNP/NF support 2002–2006	Change
Working status						
Full-time	47	38	−9	68	45	−23
Not-full-time	53	62	+9	32	55	+23
Property						
Owner/mortgage	55	70	+15	53	68	+15
Local-authority rented	34	21	−13	41	24	−17
Privately rented	9	8	−1	4	7	+3
Other	2	1	−1	2	1	−1
Social class by age by sex						
Male, 15–34, ABC1	7	9	+2	13	4	−9
Male, 15–34, C2DE	11	8	−3	25	17	−8
Male, 35 or more, ABC1	11	17	+6	9	13	+4
Male, 35 or more, C2DE	19	14	−5	24	36	+12
Female, 15–34, ABC1	7	8	+1	3	2	−1
Female, 15–34, C2DE	11	8	−3	11	7	−4
Female, 35 or more, ABC1	13	18	+5	3	6	+3
Female, 35 or more, C2DE	21	18	−3	11	16	+5

this earlier study did not examine some key variables, for example education and so we omit these from our initial comparison.

The most striking continuity between the two samples is a strong gender bias, with men making up around seven in ten of both groups of extreme right supporters. While this finding is consistent with the wider literature on extreme right support across Europe (see Mudde 2007, pp. 90–118) it also suggests that the BNP's concerted attempt to present a more moderate and family-friendly image has not increased its appeal among women. Yet while a male bias is often noted in studies of the extreme right an explanation for this gender gap remains under-developed (Kessler and Freeman 2005, p. 264). Some suggest that women have a lower level of political efficacy and may be discouraged from voting for parties such as the BNP as a result of their extremist image (Mudde 2007, p. 116; also Mayer 2002). An alternative explanation is found in the literature on racial prejudice and studies in the United States that report higher levels of hostility toward ethnic minorities among men (Kuklinski, Cobb and Gilens 1997; Johnson and Marini 1998). Research in Britain similarly reveals that while women, better educated individuals and those with high social status report less racial prejudice and anxiety over contact with minority ethnic groups, there remain significant pools of hostility to ethnic minorities among less qualified and young working-class men (Ford 2008).[8]

While there is continuity in respect to gender we also find evidence of a significant change in other aspects of the social distribution of extreme-right support between the two samples. In terms of age it is often suggested that younger voters are less attached to established mainstream political parties, are less secure in their labour market position and are therefore more likely to register support for challenger parties such as those on the extreme right wing. However, this is not the case in our British sample. Instead, we find that support for the extreme right in contemporary Britain is concentrated among older respondents, reversing the relationship identified in the earlier study by Harrop and colleagues. In their study, 37 per cent of NF supporters were under the age of 25 but only 11 per cent of supporters in our more recent sample were this young (below their share of the sample population). Meanwhile, the proportion of supporters aged 35–54 years old increases by 10 points (rising from 29 per cent to 39 per cent), while the proportion aged 55 or over doubles from 18 per cent to 36 per cent. This finding is consistent with those aggregate level studies discussed above, indicating that the BNP performs well in areas where there are larger numbers of middle-aged and older residents.

In terms of explaining this 'ageing' of the extreme right's support base we suggest that two factors may be at work. First, there is evidence of a generational shift in racial attitudes since the 1970s, with those citizens growing up after this period expressing much lower levels of racial prejudice and xenophobia (Ford 2008). Individuals socialized in more multicultural Britain are, on the whole, less likely to hold intolerant views and will therefore be less attracted to anti-immigrant and exclusionary campaigns. Second, while younger votes may be less inclined to support a party such as the BNP citizens socialized during the 1970s, a period that was characterized by intense political conflict over race and immigration, may have retained a greater level of concern with these issues and will therefore be more willing to lend support to parties espousing a tough line on these issues. This age cohort would now be middle-aged or older, which is precisely where we see the strongest contemporary extreme-right support.

In terms of social class the findings of Harrop *et al.* suggest that NF support was concentrated primarily among skilled manual workers. Like others, these scholars speculated that it was the skilled worker who was especially concerned about losing favourable positions in the labour market to incoming immigrants and minority ethnic groups. In our sample we find that support for the extreme right continues to be concentrated heavily among the working class. However, the strongest support now arrives from those at the bottom of the economic ladder, namely unskilled manual workers and the residual class of those who are dependent on state benefits. This growing economic marginality is also reflected in the sharp fall in the proportion of extreme-right supporters who are in full-time employment between the two samples. Though requiring further research, it appears that while skilled labourers might have worried over immigrant competition for jobs and promotion this more economically deprived and marginalized group may be more concerned over competition for state benefits, more resentful about their current socio-economic position and more willing to make ethnic minorities the scapegoat. Though the condition of local housing markets appears as an important driver of extreme-right support in research elsewhere (Bowyer 2008), in our study the distribution of support by housing tenure does not suggest that ethnic competition for social housing is driving up general support for the extreme right: supporters of the BNP and NF are no more likely than the general population to live in council housing.

Harrop *et al.* (1980) also argued that NF support was more socially differentiated in areas where the party was strong, suggesting that the NF was better able to mobilize an identifiable constituency in these regions. There is also evidence of this phenomenon in the contemporary sample. Support for the extreme right in Yorkshire and Humberside and the West Midlands, the two regions where support is strongest, is even more concentrated among the older age groups and the working classes. In both these regions we also see a concentration of extreme-right support among the skilled working classes that is not found in the other regions.

In addition, there has been a notable shift in the geographical distribution of extreme-right support. In the earlier study, support for the NF was concentrated primarily in London and the West Midlands, areas that both included historic strongholds for the extreme right. Yet in our more recent sample extreme right support has moved decisively northwards (there is also a higher share in the East Midlands), while there appear much lower shares of support in London and other regions in the South. The most obvious explanation for this shift toward the North concerns the extreme right's change of strategy. As discussed by Goodwin in Chapter 8, in recent years the BNP has switched its strategic focus away from traditional bastions of support in inner London toward Northern districts that have struggled with deindustrialization, the effects of socio-economic deprivation and, in more recent years, urban disturbances (though initially BNP Chairman Nick Griffin was resistant to this strategy, preferring instead to focus on appealing to rural constituencies).

If we break this region down further we see a particular concentration of support in Yorkshire and Humberside, which accounts for 20 per cent of extreme-right support but less than 10 per cent of the total population in our sample. There is some evidence that the BNP could be benefiting in this region from a successful exploitation of anti-Muslim sentiment following urban disturbances that occurred in Bradford, Burnley and Oldham in the summer of 2001. As highlighted in Figure 9.1, there is a relationship between extreme-right support and the Muslim share of the constituency population, suggesting that the presence of a large local Muslim population may well stimulate support for the BNP. However, this aggregate relationship is only indicative and is weaker or non-existent in other regions with large Muslim populations. While hostility to local Muslims is a

Figure 9.1 Constituency-level Muslim population shares and BNP support, Yorkshire and Humberside region.

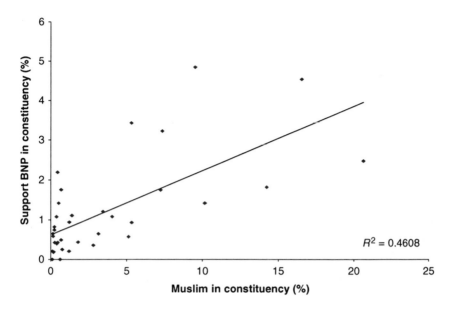

resource the BNP may seek to exploit, it is clearly not a universally effective recruitment tool (though see also Bowyer 2008).

Which of these factors are most significant in driving support for the extreme right? In Table 9.3 we present results from a logistic regression analysis, modelling extreme-right support in the 2002–2006 dataset. Logistic regression analysis is a statistical technique that enables us to clarify what aspects of voters' characteristics and backgrounds are most important in encouraging them to support the extreme right. The statistical model tells us how much each factor encourages extreme right support, while holding all other factors constant. Unfortunately, we have been unable to obtain the Harrop *et al.* data in order to conduct a similar analysis on previous NF support. The multivariate model also includes controls for the year the survey is conducted in order to control for the rising trend in extreme right support since 2002. This rising trend is reflected in the steadily increasing year dummy coefficients, although in 2005, the only election year in the sample, support levels are lower than in the other years, suggesting that some extreme right support may drift back to the main parties when a general election approaches.

The regression model confirms that support for the extreme right in twenty-first-century Britain is a male, working-class phenomenon, though in the multivariate model all three sections of the working-class support the extreme right at similar rates. Middle-aged respondents continue to be over-represented among supporters once controls are introduced, but respondents aged over 55 are not. This may provide some tentative evidence that the 35–55 age group, socialized during the

Table 9.3 Logistic regression analysis of extreme right support 2002–2006: individual level predictors

	Coefficient	Significance (p value)
Intercept	**−6.82**	0.000
Year (ref: 2002)	**0.008**	0.000
2003	**1.11**	0.000
2004	**1.25**	0.000
2005	**0.66**	0.000
2006	**1.55**	0.000
Sex		
Male	**1.03**	0.000
Age (ref: 15–24)		
25–34 years	0.23	0.08
35–54 years	**0.40**	0.000
55 years +	0.09	0.43
Class (ref: AB)		
Lower non-manual (C1)	0.12	0.32
Skilled manual (C2)	**0.74**	0.000
Semi- skilled manual (D)	**0.70**	0.000
Unskilled manual/residual (E)	**0.73**	0.000
HOUSING TENURE (ref: owner-occupier)		
Rent privately	−0.03	0.896
Rent from council	0.02	0.741
Region (ref: S. East)		
East Anglia	**0.34**	0.012
East Midlands	**0.32**	0.028
West Midlands	**0.63**	0.000
Greater London	−0.10	0.552
North West	0.23	0.089
North East	**0.38**	0.016
Yorkshire/Humber	**0.90**	0.000
South West	−0.17	0.284
Wales	**−0.93**	0.000
Scotland	**−1.74**	0.000
Education (ref: no quals)		
GCSE	−0.01	0.898
NVQ	**0.21**	0.049
A-level	−0.19	0.086
Degree	**−0.93**	0.000
Postgrad	**−1.35**	0.000
Chi-square	964.8	
Pseudo-R Square	0.079	
Log-likelihood (null)	−6,144	
Log-likelihood (model)	−5,662	
N	190,830	

1960s and 1970s, when political controversies over immigration and race were at their peak, have retained a greater propensity to support parties on the extreme right. The concentration of support in the English North and Midlands is also evident in the multivariate model. Extreme-right support is significantly higher in all the Northern and Midlands regions than in London and the South East even after controlling for the different social characteristics of voters in these different regions. Perhaps unsurprisingly support for the extreme right is very rare among those with a university education although other levels of education have no significant impact. The findings presented above provide important insight into the support base for the extreme right in modern Britain. In order to examine the drivers of this support more closely in the next section we shift our attention to a local case study.

Barking and Dagenham

The London borough of Barking and Dagenham provides a useful case study of the issues discussed above. In the local elections held in 2006 the BNP contested seven out of 17 local wards, winning at least one seat in each ward contested and overall gaining 12 seats on the local council. During the campaign BNP activists sought to embellish a sense of ethnic competition and threat among residents and were also careful to include references to a unique local 'East End' identity (Goodwin 2009). Shortly after the election, Ipsos-MORI undertook a survey in the local borough using quotas based on key demographic criteria. The fieldwork was carried out face-to-face in the period 19 August–18 October 2006.[9] While the number of respondents is small the survey provides valuable insight into the BNP's base of support, as well as the motivating factors that drove some residents to vote for the party.

In Table 9.4 we present a profile of BNP supporters in the local borough. Based on this data the BNP's support base closely resembles the characteristics of the general population in the area. However, a noticeable exception is social class: the BNP tends to draw relatively more support from skilled manual workers, supporting the assertion that BNP voters show greater social differentiation in areas where extreme-right parties have a strong presence than where their penetration is lower. BNP voters in Barking and Dagenham also appear significantly less likely than other voters to feel involved in their local community; respondents were twice as likely to say that they were involved in the local community either 'a great deal' or 'a fair amount' (33 per cent) than those who voted or would consider voting BNP (16 per cent).[10]

In terms of what drives BNP support half of residents who said they had voted BNP claimed to have done so 'as a protest' while fewer said they voted BNP because of 'support for its policies'. Clearly citizens might simultaneously protest against the political establishment while also making a rational choice for BNP policies. Yet in this case study our findings suggest that a particularly important factor was a sense of dissatisfaction among local residents with Labour. In the wider comparative literature it has been suggested that the failure of traditional

Table 9.4 Profile of BNP supporters in Barking and Dagenham, 2006

	BNP voters in BNP contested wards (122) %	All residents in BNP contested wards (411) %
Gender		
Male	45	46
Female	55	54
Age		
18–34	36	33
35–54	38	35
55+	26	31
Social grade		
AB	7	7
C1	14	25
C2	37	23
DE	43	44
Work status		
Working	47	47
Not working	53	53
Tenure		
Owner/occupier	55	51
Social rent	38	41
Private rent	4	6

Source: Ipsos-MORI, Aug–Oct 2006.

left-wing parties to respond effectively to the concerns of voters has created opportunities for extreme-right activists to capitalize on the 'politics of resentment' (Kessler and Freeman 2005: 265). In Barking and Dagenham, the politics of resentment appears to have been directed principally toward the local Labour Party grouping (49 per cent of BNP voters stated that it was a protest vote), though many also viewed their BNP vote as a protest against the government, Tony Blair or the Labour Party more generally (29 per cent). Indeed, it may be no coincidence in areas where the BNP has performed particularly strongly, such as Barking and Dagenham, Burnley, Sandwell and Stoke, local politics has historically been dominated by the Labour Party.

In Barking and Dagenham our findings indicate that voters also seem to have turned to the BNP in order to signal their objection to immigrants, asylum-seekers or ethnic minorities (22 per cent). This research points toward the dominance of immigration as a core issue of concern for BNP supporters. Yet importantly, and as highlighted in Figure 9.2, other 'local conflict' issues such as the allocation of council housing, crime, policing and jobs concerned BNP voters to a greater extent than other residents living in the area. This finding lends support to the view that the main initial drivers of BNP support derive not from an endorsement of right-wing extremist ideology but rather local issues and tensions over the allocation of resources.

Q *Which, if any, of these were important in helping you decide which party to vote for?*

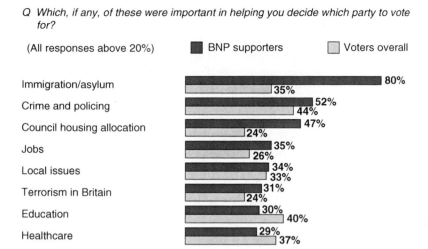

Figure 9.2 Key voting decision issues in Barking and Dagenham.

Source: Ipsos-MORI.

Base: All who voted/would have voted BNP (122); All who say they voted (620).

Our local case study suggests that the BNP's success in mobilizing support in the borough owed much to the party's own campaigning effort. In wards where BNP candidates stood, approximately three out of five residents (62 per cent) said they had received a BNP leaflet while nearly one in five (16 per cent) had been canvassed personally by a representative of the party. Though similar activity was reported for the Labour Party, Conservative Party activists were much less visible during the pre-election campaign, with less than one-third of residents receiving a leaflet (31 per cent) and only five per cent meeting a representative from the centre-right party. Therefore, BNP activists faced little competition from the only mainstream party with a reputation for tough immigration policies. If we look at BNP gains elsewhere, a weak or absent local Conservative Party similarly appears as an important contributory factor. In the borough of Burnley in Lancashire, in nine sets of local elections between 1992 and 2003 the Conservatives failed to field a full slate of candidates and in 2000, the point at which BNP activists began canvassing the borough, the Conservatives contested only one quarter of seats in local elections. Even when a full slate of Conservative candidates appeared in 2004 the majority were paper candidates and there was little in the way of serious grassroots campaigning. Perhaps unsurprisingly, some draw on these findings to argue that the electoral advance of the BNP must be set within the context of a more general decay of local democracy (Wilks-Heeg 2002).

Perhaps as a result of the BNP's intensive local campaigning, supporters of the Party in Barking and Dagenham appear to have felt that the party understood their concerns and was working in their interest. For example, two in five of BNP voters felt that the party 'understands the problems facing the area', is 'concerned about real people in need in the area', or 'looks after people like us'. To a certain extent these findings suggest that the BNP's community-based strategy resonates with some local residents. However, despite enjoying election success the BNP's image across the borough as a whole was not so positive, with findings lending support to the suggestion that the party lacks an image of respectability in the eyes of most voters (Chapter 8). Almost one-third of residents considered the BNP to be 'extreme' while one in five perceived the party as 'unpleasant'. Our findings also question the extent to which the BNP has been able to present itself as something more than merely a single-issue movement, even among its own supporters. Although BNP voters felt that the party had the best policies on immigration and asylum and race relations, less than half of all party supporters felt that it had the best policies on other issues, such as crime, healthcare, housing and jobs.

BNP success in areas such as Barking and Dagenham appears to rest on the quality of representation and service provision from the incumbent party (in this case) and in particular the management of local anxieties about immigration and diversity. These issues remain the BNP's core recruiting areas and if rising local concerns are neglected by the main parties then BNP support is likely to grow irrespective of the party's ability to deal with other issues.

Table 9.5 Perceptions of the BNP in Barking and Dagenham

	BNP supporters in Barking and Dagenham (122) %	Residents in Barking and Dagenham (1,006) %
Positive characteristics		
Understands problems facing the area	43	14
Concerned about the real people in need in the area	40	11
Looks after people like us	36	10
Has sensible policies	26	6
Represents all types of people	15	4
Keeps its promises	13	3
Professional	13	3
Moderate	8	3
Negative characteristics		
Extreme	14	30
Unpleasant	6	22
Will promise anything to win votes	14	18
Out of date	2	11
Out of touch with ordinary people	3	10
Corrupt	2	10
Divided	3	6

Source: Ipsos-MORI, Aug–Oct 2006.

Conclusion

In twenty-first-century Britain the organized electoral extreme right, as represented principally by the BNP, is enjoying increased support. Meanwhile, Nick Griffin's invitation onto 'Question Time' in October 2009 reflects the BNP's growing presence outside of the electoral arena. Clearly, it is important not to overstate this 'success'. In contrast to similar parties elsewhere in Europe the BNP has so far proven unable to enter the national legislature and internally there remain questions over the absence of strong and charismatic leadership, the party's weak financial resources and a tendency to internal conflict (see Chapter 8). Yet this support for the BNP does call for a re-examination of the party's social bases of support.

At the individual level we find that men, manual workers and those who are less well educated are more likely to self-identify with the contemporary extreme right. These groups are most inclined to make immigrants and minority ethnic groups the scapegoat for their adverse socio-economic condition and are therefore more likely to lend support to parties such as the BNP. Conversely, those with higher social status, women and higher levels of education are less inclined to vote, or consider voting, for the extreme right. We also compare this support base with earlier research on support for the 1970s NF. As noted in this earlier study (Harrop *et al.* 1980: 278), the typical picture of the modal NF voter was a young, urban and working-class male who was most likely located in parts of Greater London or the West Midlands. In our study, we similarly find a strong male bias in the support base for the extreme right though we also observe several significant changes. First, and possibly as a result of socialization effects, it appears that the extreme right in twenty-first-century Britain recruits more support among older age groups. Second, the extreme right now recruits more support from those at the bottom of the economic ladder, mainly unskilled workers and the residual class of those who are dependent on state benefits. Third, we observe variation in the geographic spread of extreme right support, though most noticeably a decisive shift toward the North.

As indicated in our study of BNP support in Barking and Dagenham, the core drivers of support for the party at the local level centre on the quality of local representative democracy and the way in which locally orientated anxieties over increased ethno-cultural diversity and resource allocation are managed. Much depends therefore on the question of whether mainstream parties are able to counter the decay of grassroots local democracy in some boroughs and also how local authorities allocate limited resources in a manner that is perceived to be transparent and 'fair'.

Notes

1 T. Lecomber (2005) 'General election 2005', *Identity*, Issue 55 (June): 9.
2 N. Griffin (2005) 'On "nationalist" unity', *Identity*, Issue 55 (June): 5.
3 Though two local candidates standing on behalf of an NF breakaway party, the National Party (NP), were elected in Blackburn in 1976.

4   It is important to note that in the comparative literature on extreme right or radical right-wing support there is some variation, for example the finding that in some countries support stems more from the mid-school stratum (Evans 2005; Arzheimer and Carter 2006; Rydgren 2008) and evidence that support for these parties, in respect to age, is not restricted to younger cohorts. As noted by Evans (2005), while the probability of voting for radical right-wing parties is seen to be higher for younger voters, there are examples to the contrary, for example the mobilization of older cohorts in support of Jean-Marie Le Pen in the 2002 French Presidential elections or the prevalence of older voters among supporters of the Swiss Democrats in 2003.

5   The authors asked NOP Market Research to cumulate 22 studies of voting intentions conducted between October 6 1977 and April 5 1978 as part of its regular random (weekly) omnibus surveys. Each of the surveys was a national probability sample of the adult British population conducted in a total of 120 constituencies, with one cluster drawn per constituency per week. Interlocking weights by age, sex and region were applied to each survey. A supporter of the NF was defined as anyone in England who mentioned the NF or the National Party (a breakaway group from the NF) when asked the following question; 'How would you vote if there were a General Election tomorrow?' or subsequently, 'Which party are you most inclined to support?'

6   The survey uses nationally representative quota samples. There are 210 sampling points, each consisting of a census ward or ward-sized area of approximately 3,500–508,000 households. Each sampling point is carefully selected to ensure that the sample universe is representative at regional level on a large number of demographic and other criteria. There is a maximum, constituencies included are also representative in terms of their collective general election voting. Within each sampling point, an interviewer is set a quota of ten interviews, with a different quota for each sampling point based on its census profile – quotas are set on gender, age, housing tenure and work status (full time workers versus others). This chapter builds on research undertaken at the Young Foundation; see Ali, R., Buonfino., A., Goodwin, M.J. and Bailey, G. (2005) *Drivers of Far Right Support*, London: Young Foundation.

7   Respondents were asked, 'How would you vote if there were a general election tomorrow?' and then shown a card listing 'Conservative', 'Labour', 'Liberal Democrat' and 'other'. All those who replied that they were undecided or who refused to answer were then asked a second question: 'Which party are you most inclined to support?' Voting intention for each party combines those who expressed support at either the first or second question. Self-identified supporters of the extreme right were those respondents whose verbatim answer recorded support for 'British National Party', 'BNP', 'National Front', 'NF' or any obvious variant of those.

8   Interestingly, though voter support for the extreme right in Britain is concentrated more heavily among men one qualitative study finds that women often occupy important positions inside the BNP (Goodwin 2010), a finding which similarly appears in the wider European literature (see for example Mudde, 2007: 97–111).

9   All data presented here are weighted. Weights were calculated according to the known population profile of Barking and Dagenham.

10 Respondents were asked: 'Overall, how involved do you feel in the local community? (By "local community" I mean all the different people who live in this area)'. Possible responses were 'a great deal', 'a fair amount', 'not very much', 'not at all' and 'don't know'.

References

Arzheimer, K. and Carter, E. (2006) 'Political opportunity structures and right-wing extremist party success', *European Journal of Political Research*, 45: 419–43.

Betz, H.-G. (1994) *Radical Right-Wing Populism in Western Europe*, New York: St Martin's Press.

Borisyuk, G., Rallings, C., Thrasher, M. and Kolk, H. van der (2007) 'Voter support for minor parties: Assessing the social and political context of voting at the 2004 European elections in Greater London', Party Politics 13(6), pp. 669–693.

Bowyer, B. (2008) 'Local context and extreme right support in England: the British National Party in the 2002 and 2003 local elections', *Electoral Studies*, 27: 611–20.

Coffé, H., Heyndels, B. and Vermeir, J. (2007) 'Fertile grounds for extreme right-wing parties: explaining the Vlaams Blok's electoral success', *Electoral Studies*, 26: 142–55.

Copsey, N. (2008) *Contemporary British Fascism: The British National Party and the Quest for Legitimacy*, Basingstoke: Palgrave Macmillan.

De Vos, S. and Deurloo, R. (1999) 'Right extremist votes and the presence of foreigners: an analysis of the 1994 elections in Amsterdam', *Tijdschrift voor Economische en Sociale Geografie*, 90: 129–41.

Eatwell, R. (2004) 'The extreme right in Britain: the long road to 'modernization', in R. Eatwell and C. Mudde (eds) *Western Democracies and the New Extreme Right Challenge*, pp. 62–79, London: Routledge.

Evans, J.A.J. (2005) 'The dynamics of social change in radical right-wing populist party support', *Comparative European Politics*, 3: 76–101.

Ford, R. (2008) 'Is racial prejudice declining in Britain', *British Journal of Sociology*, 59(4): 609–35.

Goodwin, M.J. (2010) 'Backlash in the "hood": exploring support for the British National Party at the local level', in A. Mammone, E. Godin and B. Jenkins (eds) *Mapping the Far Right in Contemporary Europe: Local, National, Comparative, Transnational*, Berghahn Books (forthcoming).

—— (2010) *The New British Fascism: Rise of the BNP*, London and New York: Routledge.

Harrop, M., England, J. and Husbands, C.T. (1980) 'The bases of National Front support', *Political Studies*, 18, 271–83.

Husbands, C.T. (1975) 'The NF: A response to crisis', *New Society*, 15 May: 403–5.

—— (1983) *Racial Exclusionism and the City*, London: George Allen and Unwin.

Ignazi, P. (2003) *Extreme Right Parties in Western Europe*, Oxford: Oxford University Press.

John, P., Margetts, H., Rowland, D. and Weir, S. (2006) *The BNP: The Roots of its Appeal*, University of Essex: Democratic Audit.

Johnson, M. and Marini, M. (1998) 'Bridging the racial divide in the United States: the effect of gender', *Social Psychology Quarterly*, 61(3): 247–58.

JRRT (2005) *The Far Right in London: A Challenge for Local Democracy?*, York: Joseph Rowntree Reform Trust.

Kessler, A.E. and Freeman, G.P. (2005) 'Support for extreme right-wing parties in Western Europe: Individual attributes, political attitudes and national context', *Comparative European Politics*, 3: 261–88.

Kitschelt, H. (in collaboration with McGann, A.) (1995) *The Radical Right in Western Europe: A Comparative Analysis*, Ann Arbor, MI: University of Michigan Press.

Kuklinski, J., Cobb, M. and Gilens, M. (1997) 'Racial attitudes and the "new south"', *Journal of Politics*, 59(2): 323–49.

Lubbers, M., Gijsberts, M. and Scheepers, P. (2002) 'Extreme right-wing voting in Western Europe', *European Journal of Political Research*, 41, 345–78.

Mayer, N. (2002) *Ces Français qui votent Le Pen*, Paris: Flammarion.

Mudde, C. (2007) *Populist Radical Right Parties in Europe*, Cambridge: Cambridge University Press.

Rhodes, J. (2006) 'Far right breakthrough: the support for the BNP in Burnley', PhD Dissertation, University of Manchester.

Rydgren, J. (2008) 'Immigration sceptics, xenophobes or racists? Radical right-wing voting in six West European countries', *European Journal of Political Research*, 47: 737–65.

Särlvik, B. and Crewe, I. (1983) *Decade of Dealignment: the Conservative Victory of 1979 and Electoral Trends in the 1980s*, Cambridge: Cambridge University Press.

Steed, M. (1978) 'The National Front vote', *Parliamentary Affairs*, 31: 282–93.

Studlar, D. (1978), 'Policy voting in Britain: the coloured immigration issue in the 1964, 1996 and 1970 General Elections', *American Political Science Review*, 72(1), 46–64.

Taylor, S. (1982) *The National Front in English Politics*, London: Macmillan.

Taylor, S. (1979a) 'The incidence of coloured populations and support for the National Front', *British Journal of Political Science*, 9, 250–5.

Taylor, S. (1979b) 'The National Front: Anatomy of a Political Movement', in R. Miles and A. Phizacklea (eds) *Racism and Political Action*, pp. 124–46, London: Routledge and Kegan Paul.

Van der Brug, W. (2003) 'How the LPF fuelled discontent: empirical tests of explanations of LPF support', *Acta Politica*, 38(1): 89–106.

Whiteley, P. (1979) 'The National Front vote in the 1977 GLC Elections: an aggregative data analysis', *British Journal of Political Science*, 9, 370–80.

Wilks-Heeg, S. (2008) 'The canary in the coalmine? Explaining the emergence of the British National Party in English local politics', *Parliamentary Affairs*, 62(3): 377–98.

10 Responses to the extreme right in Britain

Roger Eatwell

Introduction

Concerns about the Muslim community and the threat from violent Islamists have led to a variety of responses from the British government. Following the 2001 northern riots, which involved both Muslims and young whites, policy mainly focused on 'community cohesion' as recommended in official reports by Ted Cantle and others. However, the 2005 London bombings led to high priority being accorded to the Preventing Violent Extremism (PVE) programme to counter home-grown terrorists, a policy which critics claim has reinforced negative stereotypes of Muslims and furthered Muslim alienation (see Chapter 6). Indeed, there is now an emerging body of research focused on the question of how public policymakers should respond to Islamism and other issues within the Muslim community (Saggar 2009).

Public policy with regard to the extreme right has been very different. A first difference concerns the fact that the terrorist threat has largely been seen in terms of 'lone wolves', such as David Copeland, who planted three bombs in 1999 aimed at ethnic minorities and gays, killing three people. Similarly Martin Gilleard and Neil Lewington, who were convicted of bomb making with the intention of fomenting race war in 2008 and 2009 respectively, acted alone. Copeland had been active in the BNP and Gilleard was a member of more extreme right-wing groups such as the National Front (NF), British People's Party (BPP) and White Nationalist Party (WNP), but there is no evidence that any of these have seriously planned concerted and sustained action. Moreover, extensive Internet propaganda preaching 'leaderless resistance' has not led to a repeat of the 1995 Oklahoma City mass killings, though recently the Domestic Extremist Unit of the police has taken the extreme-right threat more seriously and during 2009 there emerged growing evidence of plans to bomb targets such as mosques. Policy concerns have, therefore, until very recently focused more on random racial attacks, most notoriously the unsolved murder of black teenager Stephen Lawrence, which led an official enquiry to deem the Metropolitan Police to be 'institutionally racist' (Macpherson 1999).

A second difference stems from the fact that prior to the onset of major recession in 2008, and especially the scandals which afflicted many MPs in 2009, the vast majority of British people were not politically alienated. Although a handful of academics have argued that strands in British public opinion are far from inimical to extreme right ideology (see especially Eatwell 2000), the post-2001 rise of the BNP in areas such as Burnley has largely been seen in terms of short-term localized protest voting, which will decline as grievances diminish and/or the incompetence of BNP councillors and leadership becomes clear. Even the BNP's 'success' in returning two MEPs in the 2009 elections must be seen in the context of the party winning only 6 per cent of national vote, in spite of a very low turnout and widespread political disaffection. Indeed, in May 2009 opinion polls indicated that views about MPs' motives were the most negative ever, with a remarkable 80 per cent of respondents saying that they blamed not just MPs for recent expenses' scandals but the parliamentary system itself![1] Thus until very recently little serious discussion has taken place about the need to counter the BNP by seeking to reconnect voters with the political mainstream, especially part of the working class (for a sign of change in relation to deprived white communities see National Community Forum 2009).

Nevertheless, it is important to examine responses to the rise of the extreme right in Britain. These responses raise an important qualification to the three previous chapters, which suggest the possibility of the BNP achieving a major electoral breakthrough in the near future. This analysis is based on both demand-side factors, such as hostility to new immigration, and supply-side factors, especially the 'modernization' of the party under Griffin (see especially Chapter 9). However, the demand side cannot be separated from the policies of government and parties. For example, public concern with immigration can stem from major party policies as well as direct experiential factors. Indeed, some scholars have argued that perceptions of threat among West European citizens have been heavily affected, if not primarily shaped, by mainstream actors such as political parties, government, political elites and bureaucrats, as well as by the actions and discourse of extreme right-wing agitators (for example Messina 2007). Moreover, analysis of the supply side involves more than a consideration of the 'modernized' BNP's own propaganda. Other parties, the media and civil society groups are all part of the battle for legitimacy and support. Surprisingly, while aspects of these have been studied, there has been no holistic attempt to consider responses to the British extreme right.

Put in more theoretical terms, at the comparative European level, socio-economic 'grievance' models that focus on specific trends such as immigration or unemployment have been relatively poor predictors of extreme-right party success. A similar point could be made about studies based on related attitudes. A major alternative approach argues that 'political opportunity structure' models have more explanatory power (for example Koopmans *et al.* 2005). However, the latter tend to place excessive emphasis on the macro role of factors such as state institutions and the behaviour of mainstream parties while downplaying or ignoring other actors, especially the national media. They also downplay meso-level factors, such as the local press or community-based extreme-right organization and propaganda (Eatwell 2003). The last point is important, as the pattern of BNP voting shows notable variation across localities that appear to have similar socio-economic traits: for example, why did the BNP make a major breakthrough in Burnley after 2001, but not in similar industrially declining towns? A full analysis of the electoral potential of the BNP would also require careful consideration of the micro dimension, namely individual motivation. While the BNP undoubtedly attracts voters who hold racist views, it is important to examine the rise of what might be termed the 'pessimistariat' – namely a group of mainly male working-class voters who are extremely pessimistic about the future and place little or no faith in mainstream parties and institutions. Polls indicate that this pessimistariat constituted an important foundation of the BNP vote in 2009.[2]

However, fully developing such a three-dimensional Macro-Meso-Micro (MMM) approach is not the main focus of what follows. Rather, the main emphasis will be on broadly analysing the main forms of responses to the extreme right, especially since the turn of the new millennium. These responses, which have both helped and harmed the BNP electorally, are divided into four sections based on the nature of the actors: public policy; the major parties; the media; and civil society including self-styled 'anti-fascist' groups.

In the Conclusion, these responses are regrouped into three types: high profile responses involving direct reference to the BNP; low profile ones where the attempt to counter the party is more indirect; and no profile, where both the BNP and the issues which have helped nurture it are largely ignored. The main concluding point is that there needs to be much greater emphasis on the first two approaches. Silence, or simply tagging the BNP as 'fascist', are likely to increasingly fail as prophylactics given that the BNP's policies echo the concerns and fears of a notable minority of the electorate (see Chapters 7 and 8).

Public policy responses

In recent years the British government has sought to exclude individual foreigners likely to incite racial or religious hatred. For example, in May 2009 the Home Secretary issued a list of those who had been barred from Britain in the previous months. Most were Islamists, but two skinhead murderers, a neo-Nazi and former Ku Klux Klan (KKK) Grand Wizard were also banned from entry. So too was the Dutch parliamentarian and leader of the Freedom Party, Geert Wilders, who had received a private invitation to show his anti-Muslim film, *Fitna*, in the House of Lords – though he was later allowed entry after a Tribunal judged that it was more important to allow free speech than to take restrictive action based on speculation that his visit might foment serious social discord.

While there have been periodic calls to ban the BNP, British constitutional practice in this sphere has more in common with the American First Amendment, which enshrines freedom of speech (subject to Time, Place and Manner considerations) than with the postwar German 'defensive democracy' model. Moreover, there are two specific factors why banning the BNP has not been a serious option for the government. First, where extreme-right parties in Western Europe have a realistic hope of electoral success levels of racially motivated violence appear to have been limited (though problems in gathering and comparing statistics mean this hypothesis has been contested). Activists are drawn into conventional political activity, and the leadership seeks to court respectability. For example, Griffin specifically referred in *BNP News* to the 'sickening wave of racist violence' at the time of the attacks on Romanians in Northern Ireland during 2009.[3] More importantly, in terms of explaining policy, as the case of the Vlaams Blok (VB) in Belgium during 2004 shows, banning a party can simply result in the organization adopting a new name. In this case, it re-emerged as the Vlaams Belang with only minor changes in its programme (for international comparison on the impact of bans see Bale [2007] and Minkenberg [2006]). Similarly, when the independent but statutory Equalities and Human Rights Commission (EHRC) brought a court hearing against the BNP in late 2009 over its whites-only membership policy, the result was a plan to change the constitution rather than proscription.

However, there have been more limited forms of proscription in the public sector. For example, the Association of Chief Constables and Police Officers issued a ban on BNP membership in 2004 as it was held to be in conflict with the force's duty to promote race equality. Likewise, during 2009 the Department for Children, Schools and Families said it was considering banning teachers in England from joining the BNP. Another area where such a ban has been considered is the National Health Service, in which there are many ethnic minority and immigrant workers. The trade union UNISON's Health Care Service Group conference has passed a motion arguing that there was no place for BNP members in nursing. However, the magazine *Nursing Times* on 22 April 2009 reported that it had 'received a large number of responses from nurses and former nurses to the motion, claiming it was at odds with free speech', a reflection of the strength of the liberal tradition in Britain.

There have also been notable curbs on discourse stemming from race relations legislation since the 1960s. Some have argued this could be used even more extensively. For example, the anti-fascist Searchlight organization called in 2008 for prosecution of the BNP for its widely circulated *Racism Cuts Both Ways* booklet, which claimed that there was an epidemic of attacks on whites. There have also been calls for changes in the Public Order Act, which requires demonstrating an intention to 'stir up racial hatred' or a likelihood that such tension would created. This can be very difficult to prove. The offence also only applies to acts that take place or are witnessed in public. This means that it does not cover leaflets which are, say, distributed via letter boxes. It also does not offer protection against the publication of inaccurate or false information, such as in *Racism Cuts both Ways*.

However, an attempt to convict Griffin and a leading member of the BNP on charges of stirring up racial hatred failed in 2006. The defendants countered that the issues of immigration and Islam were of legitimate public concern, and that their statements were fair and accurate. Such prosecutions in the future, therefore, need careful weighing of both the likelihood of success and of the publicity that accompanies such trials. The BNP would certainly use such trials to argue that the state was seeking to suppress free speech, an argument likely to further anti-mainstream alienation, fuel the 'outsider' status of the BNP and possibly even encourage violence.

An alternative institutionalist school of thought focuses on possible changes to the electoral system. The BNP won both its regional seats in the 2009 European elections with under 10 per cent of the vote, while it has won seats with under 30 per cent in local elections. It has been argued that using the single transferable vote (STV) system in European elections and alternative vote in single-member local elections would make it much more difficult for the BNP to win seats (for example Electoral Reform Society 2004). Some have also called for the introduction of compulsory voting, partly because the BNP can benefit when potential mainstream party voters do not turn out to vote.[4] There are good general reasons for considering electoral reform. However, while the governing parties have in the past toyed with major electoral change when faring badly in polls, they have quickly forgotten when their fortunes improve. Moreover, there are dangers in making changes to second order elections, which could again be portrayed as specifically aimed at the BNP, furthering a sense of victimhood.

Besides, banning the BNP or seeking to curb it through the law will not necessarily remove the sentiments that lead people to vote for the party. Although the post-2001 'community cohesion' policy was largely aimed at ethnic minorities, especially Muslims, it also encompassed an element of seeking to lessen alienation and prejudice among the white population. However, because the BNP was initially seen as a localized and passing phenomenon, policy responses were not directly targeted at its threat. Indeed, in some areas there was widespread denial among officials and other community leaders of the potential for the BNP.

A major aspect of the community cohesion policy was a move away from the multiculturalism which had constituted the policy framework for decades prior to 2001, in the belief that this had encouraged separation and lack of inter-communal understanding. However, the new policy combined a mixture of continuing to recognize ethnic minority structures, especially through dealings with Muslim communal leaders to help combat terrorism (see Part 1, especially Chapters 5 and 6), while seeking to find an overarching set of acts and values which could constitute the basis of a new shared 'Britishness'. Critics of the former policy have argued that this has led to cooperation with some who are hostile to liberal British values and who support violence elsewhere (Maher and Frampton 2009). Critics of the latter policies have seen them as at best unlikely to have 'any purchase among a diverse sophisticated population' (Preston 2007: 158), and at worst as a form of 'integrationist racism' likely to increase antagonism to ethnic minorities by setting up an unattainably broad goal (Kundnani 2007; McGhee 2009).

This emphasis on Britishness has been part of a wider 'New' Labour tendency to focus on cultural change rather than traditional social democratic concerns such as poverty and unemployment, which remained nationally low until the onset of depression after 2007. However, there seems little doubt that relative poverty has been a factor which has helped the extreme right. All four official reports following the 2001 riots placed the issue of deprivation, together with communal segregation, as a core factor (for example, Burnley Task Force 2001). Certainly most of the white youths involved in the violence came from poorer areas. Nevertheless, although extreme right groups played a role in fomenting these troubles (Lowles 2001), there has not developed in Britain the localized sub-cultures found in parts of former East Germany, where extreme-right youths have established *Angsträume* (spaces of fear for minorities). This in part explains the lack of emphasis in Britain compared to Germany and some Scandinavia countries on the task of rehabilitating extremist youths (on such programmes see Bjørgo and Horgan [2009]).

However, this does not mean that the police and intelligence services have not been interested in alienated whites who might turn to terrorism. During the 1990s, MI5 placed at least one agent in the National Front (NF) and its splinter groups, and it seems clear that Combat 18 (C18) was penetrated too. Although the main focus since 9/11 has been on Muslim terrorism, there has undoubtedly been monitoring of the extreme-right potential. Indeed, over the summer of 2009 a leading member of the London Metropolitan Police's counter-terrorism command (SO15), Shaun Sawyer, told a meeting of the Muslim Safety Forum that there was a high risk of a 'spectacular' bombing. Although it is difficult to assess the general effect of such surveillance, it has almost certainly been an important factor in limiting extreme-right violence. Whether this will remain the case given the demands of heavy surveillance on Islamists and general impact of economic depression remains another matter.

Turning to BNP voting, two towns with among the lowest skills base in Britain – Barking and Stoke – have been relative strongholds in recent years. For example, at the time of the BNP breakthrough, six Stoke wards were in the 10 per cent most deprived in the country and a further 10 wards in the next 10 per cent. Some regeneration funds have been targeted at such areas, but in general there has been an unwillingness on the part of government to use large-scale resources. This has been accompanied by an emphasis on local responses, in part a reflection of an uncritical acceptance of 'communitarian' critiques of 'Old' Labour statism and social capital theory belief that bringing communities more together would necessarily produce harmony (Flint and Robinson 2008).

New immigration has also been a source of tension in some areas. After 1997 the Labour government accepted that parts of the British economy needed immigrant labour both to cover skill shortages (for instance in the NHS) and to provide cheap labour (such as in crop-picking areas like Boston). Additionally, Britain witnessed a growth in the number of asylum seekers, peaking in 2002 at just over 100,000 requests. This contributed to the fact that 7.5 per cent of Britain's 2001 population had been born overseas, compared to 5.7 in 1991. Government policy sought to disperse these new immigrants, which caused some alarm in areas where immigration had not been an issue, though settlement mainly reinforced existing patterns.

Predictably, BNP propaganda very much focused on these new arrivals and stoking a sense of 'threat' among white citizens. For example, the June 2001 issue of its journal *The Voice of Freedom* claimed that 'every single "asylum-seeker" will be getting far bigger handouts' than millions of British pensioners and unemployed, and the nearly one-in-five British children who live below the poverty line. Such claims have been especially effective in areas where the BNP had sufficient organization to help disseminate or reinforce local stories about favourable treatment of ethnic minorities. A good example is Burnley, where the party organized a campaign of letters to the *Burnley Express*, without stating that they came from the BNP (Smith 2004). Partly as a result of this type of propaganda, many local white residents grossly over-estimated both the number of immigrants living in the town and the public support that they were receiving.

However, a report published in 2006 showed a significant reduction in Burnley residents' fears about ethnic minorities, and an accompanying awareness of the nature of the different communities which made up the town (Burnley Action Partnership 2006). One policy response to the BNP's breakthrough was the issuing of a Council code of conduct in 2002 which required members to promote equality by not discriminating unlawfully: the three BNP councillors elected that year all signed up. Another response was a campaign, led by the Community Cohesion Officer, Mike Waite, to counter misleading propaganda (see also Waite [2009] on wider policy issues). This included a decision that, in cases where BNP representatives presented inaccurate arguments, officers could publicly criticize the party where the issue was one of fact.

This type of 'myth-busting' increasingly became a core policy in other areas where there were ethnic tensions. The importance of myth busting has been stressed in several official reports (for example, Local Government Association 2006; National Community Forum 2009). However, this approach is based on a liberal-rationalist view of public opinion, which holds that if only people knew the 'truth', they would hold different values. An approach informed more by cognitive dissonance theory would hold that such information is likely to be fitted into existing prejudices. Thus stating that the primarily Muslim Daneshouse ward in Burnley is one of the poorest in the country can be countered by asking 'do we not have many of our own poor?'; noting that a particular group of asylum seekers are fleeing appalling persecution can be countered by asking 'is Britain not already over-full?' Such rhetorical devices are an important means of constructing a self-image of reasonableness rather than racism.

A further problem for myth busting is that there can be more than an element of truth in 'myths'. For example, in 2007 the Local Government Association (LGA) argued that: 'Extra funding should be given to areas that experience rapid population change ... Analysis indicates that the number of migrants in many areas has been significantly underestimated'.[5] A House of Commons Committee in 2008 endorsed the view that sudden influxes of immigrants could cause both major pressures on public services such as housing and education and heighten local tensions (including with existing ethnic minorities). Some idea of the size of the problem can be gauged from the fact that the LGA called for a £250 million contingency fund to be made available to councils facing such pressures. Such tensions appear to have been a major factor in the BNP's rise in Barking and

Dagenham, areas that experienced rapid demographic change and where the party's anti-Muslim propaganda had little local resonance other than through a diffuse fear of terrorism.

In April 2006 Margaret Hodge, the MP for Barking and Minister of State at the Department for Work and Pensions, commented that eight out of 10 white, working-class voters in her constituency might be tempted to vote BNP in the forthcoming local elections, arguing that the government needed to promote very strongly the benefits of multi-racial society as many constituents felt no one was listening to concerns (after the BNP's vote leapt forward in the subsequent elections, it sent a bouquet of roses to her). In another controversial speech the following year, Hodge argued that housing should be allocated more on entitlement than need, which tended to favour new arrivals and push indigenous people down waiting lists.

After the BNP won two seats in the 2009 European elections, new policies were announced to allocate housing more on the basis of entitlement and to engage in a new building programme. This 'British homes for British people' policy was clearly aimed at appeasing the 1.6 million households on council waiting lists, mainly in former Labour heartlands. There was also an attempt to show that immigrants received a relatively low percentage of social housing, though a report from Civitas that challenged the basis of this claim gave the BNP another opportunity to argue that PC bodies like the EHRC 'had been caught out lying again'.[6]

Major parties' responses

The point about housing illustrates the impossibility of distinguishing neatly between public policy and party political responses in a system characterized by single party national government. It also illustrates how the impact of the BNP increasingly needs considering in terms of its impact on policy and other parties.

At the time he became Prime Minister, Gordon Brown clearly realized that 'New' Labour's links with the working class were weakening, a point which had been made for some time by critics within the Labour Party like John Cruddas, the MP for Dagenham. Although the BNP was perceived as a serious threat in only a small number of localities, in September 2007 Brown pledged to find 'British jobs for every British worker', launch a crackdown on migrant workers, and toughen the points system for immigrants including English-language tests. As the recession deepened during 2008, these themes initially receded. The focus turned more to Brown's past track record as a successful Chancellor of the Exchequer, which made him a 'safe pair of hands'. The crisis in some ways also helped to re-establish 'Old' Labour credentials, with big government intervention in areas such as the banking system. However, by the autumn of 2008 Labour was again falling in polls and there were further attempts to shore up working-class support.

In October 2008 the *BNP News* even claimed that: 'Immigration Minister Phil Woolas, has brazenly lifted policy from the BNP manifesto and called upon

British employers to give priority in jobs to Britons and to make it a priority to retrain and "up-skill" British workers.'[7] In February 2009, against a background of wildcat strikes over the employment of Italian and Portuguese labourers at an oil refinery, Woolas returned to the 'British jobs for British workers' theme. He stated that he was considering tightening still further the points immigration system, though the main intention in this case was to help the ever-growing number of skilled young unemployed rather than the working class.

Further signs of concern can be seen when, in January 2009 Hazel Blears, the Secretary of State for Communities and Local Government (CLG), spoke about poorer people having 'acute fears' about immigration. Following considerable publicity about her expenses, a *Sunday Express* poll on 24 May indicated she had good cause to be concerned about retaining her Salford seat, which contained notable pockets of relatively poor working class areas, as it gave the BNP 38 per cent of the vote per cent compared to Labour's 19 per cent (though the small poll sample almost certainly exaggerated BNP support). Harriet Harman, the Deputy Labour Leader, spoke in May 2009 about the danger of a low turnout in the European elections, which she saw as likely to help the BNP. Previously the Labour leadership rarely referred to the BNP at the national level.

The last point has been less true at the local level, where there has been an increasing desire to prevent the BNP winning any form of representation and thus increasing its claims to be a 'normal' party. This has not only involved campaigns specifically targeting the BNP, often linked to trade unions, but has even encompassed accepting that other parties might be best placed to defeat the BNP. During 2009 in Barnsley, once a Labour stronghold in which 15,000 men were employed in the pits there as recently as the early 1980s, some Labour councillors even urged disgruntled voters to vote Tory or Liberal rather than BNP. The fact that the BNP went on to win 16.7 per cent of the vote there, one of its best performances nationally, underlines both the threat to Labour and the alienation from mainstream politics felt by many voters.

In the past, Labour has also lost votes to the Conservatives over race-related issues. Especially after Enoch Powell's notorious 1968 'river of blood' speech, which predicted racial violence, the Conservatives gained issue ownership of being tough on immigration. While the link was weakened when Powell left the Party in 1974 over his opposition to joining the European Union (EU), by 1978 Margaret Thatcher in particular had again associated the party with a 'hard' line on immigration. Most analyses of the Conservative victory in 1979 stress the important role played by economic factors, but fears about immigration and even race war figured prominently in many voters' minds and helped weaken the appeal of the National Front (Studlar 1985). There is further evidence that immigration was also a factor in the late swing away from Labour to the Conservatives in the 1992 general election, though in this case tabloid newspapers such as the *Sun* played the more important role (Thomas 2005).

In the 2001 and 2005 general elections the Conservatives similarly played the immigration card, though in the latter case the tabloid media once more played a prominent part in setting the agenda. However, polls show that in these elections voters cared more about issues such as the economy and services. Moreover, the Conservatives were beginning to lose their ownership of the immigration issue. This began in the 1990s, partly as a result of Prime Minister John Major's hostility to using the 'race' issue. By 2005, the Conservatives not only faced the challenge of the growing BNP, but also UKIP which had taken 16 per cent of the vote in the 2004 European elections, with 40 per cent of this coming from 2001 Tory voters. Although UKIP's main campaign themes were hostility to the EU and mainstream parties, in some areas it undoubtedly benefited from anti-immigrant sentiment. For instance, its highest vote in 2004 was in Boston where migrants working on farms and in associated packaging industries had caused tensions (Geddes and Tonge 2005; Kavanagh and Butler 2005).

The emphasis on immigration in 2001 and 2005 has led some critics to argue that the Conservatives have been seeking to rehabilitate Powell and his tradition (for example Bourne 2008). However, the Conservatives have been increasingly unwilling to tolerate racists and those with extreme-right links in their ranks, a policy that resulted in the expulsion of Griffin's father in 2001. Moreover, after 2005 new Conservative leader David Cameron has steered the party away from immigration as a major theme (despite himself playing a key role in the design of the Conservatives' 2005 manifesto). As well as personal antipathy to the use of such themes, the 2005 Conservative campaign helped shore up its vote against the UKIP incursion, but lost liberal and ethnic minority voters to Labour and the Liberal Democrats. Although Cameron, like the Labour leadership, has largely eschewed direct reference to the BNP, recently there have been signs of change. For example, in May 2009 he specifically stated that: 'If you vote for the BNP you are voting for a bunch of fascists.'[8]

This reflected wider Conservative strategy. Thus James Forsyth wrote in the Conservative-supporting weekly, *The Spectator*, on 15 May 2009 that: 'The strategy of trying to deal with the BNP by denying them the oxygen of publicity is out of date … we need to take the BNP on, to make sure that people know that a vote for the BNP isn't a protest against political sleaze or the establishment but a vote for racism and thuggery'. A further sign of changing strategies can be found in the ConservativeHome blog of Tim Montgomerie and James Bethell, who in 2009 started a 'Nothing British about the BNP' campaign in an attempt to create a serious centre-right alternative to the centrist and especially left dominated groups and websites that have taken on the BNP[9] (on civil society responses see below).

Last but by no means least in the context of Conservative responses, in May 2009 former Thatcherite minister Norman Tebbit urged people to boycott major parties as a result of the sleaze and general disillusionment. Although he made it clear that he was not endorsing the BNP, his widely publicized comments were seen by the media as effectively supporting UKIP.

Media responses

In the run-up to the 2009 European elections, UKIP benefited from significant direct national press coverage, often stressing that it was set to win a major share of the vote. For example, the *Daily Mail* on 17 May noted that in the week following the exposure of sleaze regarding MPs' expenses, the Labour vote had slumped by six points while UKIP's had risen seven, leaving the parties neck and neck at 17 per cent, with the BNP stuck on 5 per cent.

After these elections, Griffin claimed that there had been the 'most staggering anti-BNP campaign ever in the media'.[10] The belief that extensive media bias exists against the party has been a long-standing one within the BNP. In the late 1990s, the party had published a pamphlet on the issue, linking it to claims that the media were dominated by Jews (BNP n.d./1997?). Shortly afterwards, the party set up a Media Monitoring Unit headed by Dr Stuart Russell (aka Phil Edwards). He has recently stated that: 'Similarly with journalists, public figures, teachers and academics – only those who appear to go with the politically correct (PC) agenda keep their jobs'.[11]

Until recently the national media have mainly tried to starve the BNP of publicity, though at times sections have been downright hostile. After it won its first local council seat in Millwall, the Labour-supporting *Daily Mirror*, on 18 September 1993, greeted the victory with the headline: 'SIEG HEIL ... and Now He's a British Councillor'. After the BNP's wider set of breakthroughs in 2001 the Conservative-supporting *Daily Express* ran a headline on 2 May 2002 calling voters in local elections to 'VOTE THESE NAZIS OUT'. In the run-up to the 2009 European elections, several tabloids openly attacked the BNP. For example, the *Daily Mail*'s front page headline on 21 May warned of a 'FASCIST ON THE PALACE LAWN' after it had been reported that Greater London Authority BNP representative, Richard Barnbrook, would take Griffin to a Queen's garden party. At the same time, the *Daily Mirror* published an exposé showing that Griffin and other BNP leaders had earlier met a KKK leader, who was banned from Britain earlier in 2009.[12]

A veritable barrage of press flak was aimed at Griffin on 23 October 2009, the day following his breakthrough appearance on the BBC television's flagship current affairs programme, *Question Time*. For example, the *Sun*'s main headline ran 'WHEN AUNTIE MET NAZI'; the *Daily Mail*'s front page proclaimed 'BIGOT AT BAY'; and the *Daily Express*'s headline stated that Griffin was 'A DISGRACE TO HUMANITY'. All contained extensive further attacks on inside pages, including a *Sun* article entitled ' A DEDICATED SWALLOWER OF FASCISM'.

Unlike the press, the broadcast media have a statutory obligation to be 'balanced', though this requirement has not prevented exposures of BNP extremism. For example, in July 2004 the BBC programme *The Secret Agent* depicted BNP activists admitting hostility towards Muslims and showing the violent face of the party. Although it is difficult to measure media effects, a study of Burnley at this time revealed that this programme seems to have detered some from voting BNP or at least 'provoked sufficient doubt to put their support for the party into question' (Rhodes 2009: 150ff.). However, after the 2009 European elections there were signs that the broadcast media were willing to give the BNP more air-time.

This happened most controversially when Griffin appeared on *Question Time*. Critics of this decision argued that 'balance' did not require giving a platform to a racist party which rejected democracy, even if it had won 1 million votes earlier in the year. Many senior BBC managers thought it did, though there were clearly divisions over the decision to invite Griffin and some saw it as a chance to expose him rather than give him a platform. During the programme, Griffin was faced by both a hostile panel and audience, and he subsequently complained to the BBC about its 'lynch mob' nature, which included a change of format to focus on the BNP and especially its leader rather than broad issues in the news.[13]

Previously Griffin had proved to be an articulate speaker when given limited opportunities on programmes such as the BBC's *Newsnight*, but in this case he appeared nervous and struggled, especially with questions about his extremist past. This was used by those who supported his appearance as evidence that putting the BNP under the media spotlight would reveal both its true nature and weak leadership. Some also argued that Griffin, who had never exerted a strong 'coterie' charisma over a BNP which continued to be riven by factionalism, had struggled to appease the BNP hard core whilst seeking to expand the party's base. Certainly Griffin does not exude the wider 'centripetal' charismatic appeal which helps to broaden extreme right support by presenting a multi-faceted appeal, especially to those not normally interested in party politics. Nor does he have the personal-image skills which made leaders such as Jean-Marie Le Pen and Jörg Haider attractive to media 'gate-keepers' as their parties began to gather support (Eatwell 2005).

Nevertheless, the 'lynching' almost certainly reinforced support among the BNP's core constituency, as it could be seen as part of a wider Establishment conspiracy against the BNP. *Question Time* on 22 October 2009, which attracted a record audience, probably also helped to spread awareness of BNP policies which have a resonance with a wider audience, especially concerning immigration, and underlined the evasions of Labour especially in this area. Certainly polls taken immediately afterwards showed that potential BNP support had if anything grown to at least 20 per cent, and the BNP claimed record numbers of applications to become a member.

This evidence was used by critics of the BBC to argue that it is important to starve extremism of the oxygen of publicity, clearly worried that this appearance marked the beginning of a wider set of invitations to the BNP. However, in the British case leader personality and direct media coverage of the extreme right have so far been been far less important in the rise of the extreme right than the way mass circulation tabloid press have helped to set an agenda which has in some ways favoured these parties, especially the BNP in recent years. As well as a strong dose of Euroscepticism in papers such as the *Sun*, common themes have included the threat from immigration and more specifically from Islam.

Immigration featured prominently as an issue after numbers began to rise again in the late 1990s. Two examples from one paper in 2009 serve to illustrate the nature and frequency of such reporting. The *Daily Express*'s main headline on 27 March proclaimed 'A MILLION MIGRANTS POUR INTO BRITAIN'. On 24 April its main headline stated 'BRITAIN HERE WE COME', accompanied by a picture of Afghans, Kurds and others at Calais allegedly waiting to 'flood' into Britain and holding a banner saying 'We want our human rights!' Inside were details of a telephone poll for readers to comment on 'Should Britain close its borders to immigrants', a highly inaccurate straw poll of opinion.

The threat from Islam has been another major theme since 2001, with considerable emphasis on terrorism, and more diffusely on cultural issues that seek to demonstrate irreconcilable difference. For instance, the *Daily Mail*'s main headline on 29 June 2009 claimed that 'BRITAIN HAS 85 SHARIA COURTS', which the paper's editorial claimed 'emphasise separateness and division.' Some reporting is based on highly misleading or erroneous information. For example, the main headline of the *Daily Express* on 2 November 2005 proclaimed that 'CHRISTMAS IS BANNED: IT OFFENDS MUSLIMS'. This referred to the use of the term 'Winter' rather than 'Christmas' lights by a low level official in Lambeth, a council that stated that it had no intention of banning the Christmas celebration including the traditional tree outside the town hall.

Such reporting has led some critics to talk of media 'Islamophobia' (Amali *et al.* 2007; Moore *et al.* 2008). Indeed, a MI5 briefing note has argued that this has been a factor in the alienation and radicalization of British Muslims.[14] However, the European Union Monitoring Commission specifically praised the British press in the aftermath of the 2005 bombings for 'balanced and objective' reporting[15] and the media have also shown restraint at other times, for example not reproducing the Danish cartoons that offended Muslims in 2006. In relation to the last issue it could be countered that at the heart of a liberal democracy is what Dutch Muslim apostate MP Ayaan Hirsi has called the 'right to offend'. Nevertheless, research shows that when such freedoms are used to attack Muslims and other ethnic minorities they increase intolerance (Van Donselaar and Rodrigues 2008), and there seems little doubt that the media in general have played an important role in disseminating negative stereotypes.

Media coverage of the BNP and related issues also needs understanding in a local context. The Burnley Task Force Report (2001: Appendix 7a) concluded that local media coverage could well have contributed to tensions, highlighting allegedly favourable treatment of minorities as a particular concern. The local media in some areas at this time set other agendas that favoured the extreme right. For example, prior to the 2001 disturbances the *Oldham Chronicle* had reported an allegedly high level of Asian attacks on whites and claimed there were local 'no go' areas. In some cases the local media furthered a sense of pessimism. For instance, columnist Barry Ayrton wrote in the *Burnley Express* on 2 March 2001 that: 'Those who think living in Burnley has all the attraction of a des res downwind of Sellafield – or a large cardboard box with a welcome mat outside in Albania – received some good news this week – life expectancy in Burnley is low, so they won't have to put up with it for (too) long'. In Dagenham, the council even set up its own paper believing that the local press unduly focused on negative stories about the authority.

As the BNP grew, in some localities the press began to treat it as a normal party. For example, in Broxbourne the *Mercury* not only reported that the BNP would contest all seats in the 2008 local elections, but ran its own straw poll which misleadingly indicated that the BNP would win 54 per cent of the vote. Other local papers adopted a policy of seeking to minimize coverage of the BNP, even silence, clearly holding that almost any publicity helped the party. For example, in the run up to the 2004 European elections the *Brighton Argus* ignored the BNP whenever possible. Although the local press tend to eschew editorializing about political parties, some have taken a strong anti-BNP line. On 20 November 2002, the day before polling in a Blackburn local by-election, the *Lancashire Evening Telegraph* ran a front page picture of Tony Blair with the headline plea: 'DON'T LET THEM IN – BLAIR'. A more sustained campaign was run by the *Manchester Evening News* during the 2009 European elections.

However, the fact that the BNP went on to win the Blackburn seat in 2002 with 32 per cent of the vote in a four-cornered race illustrates the dangers of assuming the media necessarily have great power. And while the fact that in 2009 Griffin won a seat for the BNP in the North West region does not prove that the *Manchester Evening News* campaign had little effect; it is interesting to note that the BNP subsequently claimed that its letters column has been full to the brim with readers' letters angrily blaming the paper for the party's breakthrough.[16]

Civil society responses

Although not directly aimed at the BNP, a variety of groups in recent years have run anti-racist campaigns. For example, the professional Football Association (FA) has run a 'Kick Racism out of Football' scheme, including high profile endorsements from leading players. Some have criticized the occasional star involvement in such programmes as tokenism, pointing more to the need for regular grass roots activity of the type run by the Watford Football Club Community Sports and Education Trust to break down prejudice, an award winning Institute for Community Cohesion (iCoCo) programme.[17] However, it is important to note that the Kick Racism out of Football campaign has been picked up in the chart-topping FIFA football game used on home game consoles. This has disseminated the message broadly among the primarily young players of such games, though whether this has more impact upon those who are prejudiced than myth busting is again open to debate.

In recent years, many trade unions have also sought to counter both racism and the BNP more directly at the grass roots level. For example, after relatively high votes in Oldham after 2001, a TUC-backed Oldham Coalition was launched, which won local endorsements from both the council and local media, and local activists claim its activities were important in halting the further rise of the BNP. Other ways in which unions have sought to resist include proposing bans on BNP members both in their own organizations and the public sector. For example, the *Independent* on 20 November 2008 reported the National Union of Schoolmasters-Union of Women Teachers (NASUWT) General Secretary, Chris Yeates, as saying: 'Those who declare their affiliation to the BNP should not be allowed to work in the teaching profession or in public services'.

Like the unions, Christian churches in Britain have lower memberships and almost certainly less influence than they did 50 years ago. However, these churches have also become more concerned with combating racism in recent years. Although the Bishop of Rochester has blamed the rise of extremism on the loss of Christian values, a theme picked up disingenuously by the BNP, the Archbishop of Canterbury has spoken of accepting parts of Sharia law and during May 2009 both he and the Archbishop of York urged people not to vote BNP. At the same time, there was significant church mobilization in some localities, especially in the North West, against the BNP. This was also true within parts of the Muslim community, for example the Central Lancashire mosques, although many Muslims remain largely disconnected from the political process. Far more active was the Jewish community, with the Board of Deputies running a 'Your Voice Or Theirs' campaign, which sought to encourage voting for anyone other than the BNP, and which supplied material to churches, mosques and other non-Jewish interested organizations.[18]

There has been a long tradition of responses from self-styled 'anti-fascist' groups, which have often had strong links with the extreme left, dating back to the 1930s. The NF's failure to make an electoral breakthrough in the 1970s is often portrayed as stemming from the activities of groups like the Anti-Nazi League (ANL), which fought the NF through a mix of street confrontation, demonstrations, pop concerts and celebrity endorsements (Renton 2001; see also Copsey 2000). However, this underestimates some factors such as the way in which the media excluded and even damned the NF, and the fact that some leading Conservatives pitched for the racist vote in the run-in to the 1979 general election, not to mention the continual factionalism within the NF which prevented the party from presenting a unified front.

During the 1970s these groups increasingly attracted ethnic minority support, but as extreme-right activity declined in the 1980s anti-fascist groups faded, though in some localities ethnic minority groups began to spring up with a wider set of concerns including lobbying for government resources (which later was to be a source of white resentment). However, the BNP victory in Millwall and the violent activities of the overtly-Nazi C18 led to a revival of wider anti-fascist activity during the 1990s. This included the re-establishment of the ANL, alongside groups such as Anti-Fascist Action (AFA) which had been formed in the 1980s, partly to engage in ideological struggle in working-class areas, which it saw as the main recruiting grounds for 'fascism'.

These organizations adopted, to varying degrees, an overt policy of street confrontation and violent opposition to fascism. During 2001, there were signs that this was leading to a spiral of violence in some areas. For example, the NF reported a confrontation in Pudsey on 8 September in the words: 'Four Arse Fuckers Federation aggressors ... were beaten back ... They have threatened they will now be visiting people at their houses. This is a mistake and we will repay in kind and that's a promise!'[19] (anti-fascist groups are typically portrayed by the extreme right as riddled with gays: hence this name for AFA, or 'ANAL' for the ANL).

However, as the BNP turned more towards 'community politics' some anti-fascists sought to do the same. For instance, Red Action, arguably the most militant section within AFA, disbanded and formed the Independent Working Class Association. More importantly, in 2003–2004 a new group emerged called Unite against Fascism (UAF). Although this included the ANL, it had endorsements from leading parties and trade unions. Ken Livingstone, former Labour MP and Mayor of London, became its high profile chair. It has organized several large protests against the BNP, including outside the House of Commons when the party's two new MEPs sought to hold a press conference in 2009.

There has always been a tendency towards sectarianism among anti-fascist groups, and in 2005 Searchlight disaffiliated from the UAF. One issue was the need to move on from traditional anti-fascist campaigns. As the magazine *Searchlight* noted in its September 2008 issue, seeking to tag the BNP as 'fascist' had some effect where the party was not established but this was 'far less effective in areas where the BNP is well established'. *Searchlight* argued that the time had come to accept that the BNP exploited real issues, and there was a need both to work in these communities to help solve the issues and to point to the failings of the BNP's remedies.

Running up to the 2009 European elections, Searchlight's Hope Not Hate campaign was given extensive coverage by the *Daily Mirror* and further support by large unions such as UNISON and GMB. Among its activities was the distribution of 3.4 million newspapers and leaflets, 1.6 million in the North West alone, seeking to counter BNP propaganda. The campaign's website included personality endorsements from soap opera and football stars. More innovatively, and similar to the centre-right campaign against the BNP that has directed much of its efforts toward an online strategy, Searchlight employed the Blue State Digital organization, which had helped Barack Obama's presidential campaign, to set up an extensive email list to exchange information, encourage local participation and raise funds.

However, the precise impact of these various campaigns remains unclear. For example there was a widespread campaign in 2009 simply to get people to turn out to vote for anyone other than the BNP, but the turnout dropped from 37.6 per cent in 2004 to 34 per cent. Perhaps it would have been even lower given the disillusionment with the mainstream parties, but questions need to be posed about aspects of the anti-fascist campaign. In spite of discussion of the need to counter the BNP's policies on specific issues, there remained a tendency to engage in high profile rallies and old forms of name calling. A good example of the latter is a YouTube video issued by Searchlight in May 2009 which superimposed a Nick Griffin 'talking head' onto a Nazi body at the 1934 Nuremberg Rally.

There are also signs that some anti-fascists still prefer confrontation to counter-argument. For example, *The Times* on 13 June 2009 reported the Joint Secretary of the UAF, Weyman Bennett as saying that 'The BNP should be physically confronted'. The leadership of the UAF does not advocate street violence, but more ominous was the May Day 2009 Antifa statement that claimed: 'The BNP were smashed off the streets by militant antifascists in the past, but now they are crawling back … It is time to stand and fight … By any means possible'.[20] Thus the possibility for the growth of 'cumulative extremism' (Eatwell 2006; see also the Introduction) does not simply involve confrontation between the extreme right and ethnic minorities.

Conclusion

Any attempt to understand the recent performance of the 'modernized' BNP, especially the failure of the party to achieve anything like the potential which opinion poll evidence indicates that it possesses (see Chapters 7–9), requires an examination of responses to the extreme right. These can be grouped within into three broad types: high profile, low profile and no profile.

High profile responses include activities such as direct attacks on the nature and policies of the BNP by political and religious leaders or the media at the national or local level. Low profile responses do not mention the BNP directly, but operate through policies such as council myth busting or liaison with the editors of local newspapers to try to ensure that reporting does not set an agenda which helps the extreme right. The no profile response has sometimes stemmed from factors such as council officers being in denial that there is a local problem of racism, but it can also reflect a strategic decision. High profile responses risk giving the BNP publicity and even low profile responses can lead to increased alienation towards a PC 'Establishment', who are seen as, at best distant from the problems of day-to-day life, and at worst as downright liars. The no profile response holds that the BNP will fade away as a significant electoral force, not least because of its *un*-modernized nature. This points to facts such as continuing BNP local links with violence, and the low quality of most of its councillors and leadership.

However, the no profile response glosses over the way in which the media, anti-fascists and others have helped to delegitimize the BNP. It also neglects the fact that while some BNP councillors have been characterized by poor attendance and an inability to engage in constructive policy debate, they have tended in places such as Stoke to become engaged in community rather than council chamber politics. As well as building grass roots support, this implicitly rejects the consensual bargaining model that lies at the heart of liberal democratic politics in favour of a more populist style aimed especially at alienated sections of the electorate.

There has undoubtedly been a variety of recent low profile attempts to appease such voters. For example, the Housing Minister, John Healey, specifically stated that the changes in housing allocation over the summer of 2009 were designed to tackle the 'myth' that the allocation system was unfair to indigenous whites. However, the plans seem inadequate to solve the problem given the large number of people who were on waiting lists at the time. More generally, there remains an unwillingness to talk about the fact that Britain is one of the most unequal and socially immobile of the wealthy Western democracies. The response also seems inadequate given that the onset of recession is likely for some time to worsen the position of the poorest and increase the size of the pessimistariat.

There appear to be strong grounds for thinking that higher profile policies are now needed. For example, there needs to be a more open discussion of the gains, and problems, which stem from immigration linked to a critique of the BNP's semi-autarchic economic policies. There is also a need for a more strategic approach especially in the field of public policy, which would coordinate national and local responses more. In many cases these will necessarily involve a low profile approach, as direct attacks on the BNP are not possible in the work of local government unless the issue is one of fact. For example, in Burnley the Good Relations Programme has set up workshops and discussions seeking to explain why areas are targeted for regeneration, involving all parties including the BNP.

Whatever the future brings for the BNP electorally, there is no doubt that it represents views which are similar to those of a notable minority of British people, even a majority on issues such as concerns about the impact of new immigration and population growth. It is important, therefore, to engage with these views more directly, not only to counter the BNP but more generally to reinvigorate Britain's liberal democratic culture.

Acknowledgement

I am grateful to a variety of people for interview-based information and opinion. I would especially like to thank: Community Relations Officer Mike Waite in Burnley; Councillor and Cabinet member Shaun Carroll in Dagenham; and Craig Fowlie for sharing his knowledge of the anti-fascist movement.

Notes

1 Ipsos-MORI – http://www.ipsos-mori.com/researchpublications/researcharchive/poll.aspx?oItemId=2349 (accessed 10 June 2009).
2 http://www.channel4.com/news/media/2009/06/day08/yougovpoll_080609.pdf (accessed 12 June 2009).
3 *BNP News*, 19 June 2009 – http://bnp.org.uk/20http://bnp.org.uk/2009/06/bnp-leader-reiterates-position-on-belfast-gypsy-incident/09/06/bnp-leader-reiterates-position-on-belfast-gypsy-incident/ (accessed 22 June 2009).
4 For example, Fabian Society, 'Kellner on the BNP' – http://www.fabians.org.uk/debates/democracy/kellner-on-the-bnp-dont-do-something-sit-there (accessed 6 July 2009).
5 http://www.lga.gov.uk/lga/core/page.do?pageId=41570 (accessed 15 January 2008).
6 *BNP News*, 21 July 2009 – http://bnp.org.uk/2009/07/social-housing-trevor-phillips-and-the-ehrc-caught-out-lying-again/ (accessed 22 July 2009).
7 *BNP News*, 21 October 2008 – http://www.bnp.org.uk/2008/10/the-bnp-is-already-changing-government-immigration-policy/ (accessed 21 October 2008).
8 *Daily Telegraph*, 27 May 2009 – http://www.telegraph.co.uk/news/newstopics/mps-expenses/5395358/David-Cameron-attacks-fascist-BNP.html (accessed 27 May 2009).
9 http://www.nothingbritish.com/
10 *BNP News*, 5 June 2009 – http://bnp.org.uk/2009/06/bnp-wins-first-ever-county-council-seats-as-chairman-cautions-against-over-optimism/ (accessed 5 June 2009). See also *BNP News*, 30 June 2009 – http://bnp.org.uk/2009/06/the-mass-media-is-our-main-enemy-cllr-paul-golding-tells-crawley-bnp/ (accessed 2 July 2009).

11 Comments made to the author 28 November 2008.
12 http://www.mirror.co.uk/news/top-stories/2009/05/06/exposed-when-bnp-met-the-kkk-115875-21335664/ (accessed 10 July 2009).
13 *BNP News* 23 October 2009, http://bnp.org.uk/2009/10lynch-mob-question-time-becomes-biggest-recruitment-night-ever-for-bnp (accessed 23 October 2009).
14 *Guardian*, 20 August 2008 – http://www.guardian.co.uk/uk/2008/aug/20/uksecurity.terrorism (accessed 21 August 2008).
15 http://fra.europa.eu/fra/material/pub/London/London-Bomb-attacks-EN.pdf (accessed 10 March 2008).
16 *BNP News*, 16 June 2009 – http://bnp.org.uk/2009/06/victory-for-the-bnp-humiliation-for-the-manchester-evening-news/ (accessed 16 June 2009).
17 http://www.bridgingcultures.org.uk/Results/VoluntarySectorOver1m/WatfordFc (accessed 7 July 2009).
18 http://www.fight-racism.co.uk/index.php (accessed 22 July 2009).
19 NF website – http://www.natfront.org.uk (accessed 30 November 2001).
20 http://www.antifa.org.uk/nopasaran.htm (accessed 18 May 2009).

Bibliography

Amali, S.R., Marandai, S., Ahmed, S.T., Kara, S. and Merali A. (2007) *The British Media and Muslim Representation: The Ideology of Demonization*, London: Islamic Human Rights Commission.

Bale, T. (2007) 'Are bans on political parties bound to turn out badly? A comparative investigation of three 'intolerant' democracies: Turkey, Spain and Belgium', *Comparative European Politics*, 5(2): 141–57.

Bjørgo, T. and Horgan, J. (eds) (2009) *Leaving Terrorism Behind: Individual and Collective Disengagement*, Abingdon: Routledge.

BNP (n.d./1997?) *Who Are the Mind-benders?*, Welling: BNP.

Bourne, J. (2008) 'The beatification of Enoch Powell', *Race and Class*, 49(4): 82–7.

Burnley Action Partnership (2006) *Burnley 2006. The Real Story*, Burnley: Burnley Social and Community Cohesion Group.

Burnley Task Force (2001) *Burnley Speaks, Who Listens?*, Burnley: Burnley Task Force.

Copsey, N. (2000) *Anti-fascism in Britain*, Basingstoke: Palgrave Macmillan.

Eatwell, R. (2000) 'The extreme right and British exceptionalism: the primacy of politics', in P. Hainsworth (ed.) *The Politics of the Extreme Right*, London: Pinter.

—— (2003) 'Ten theories of the extreme right', in P. Merkl and L. Weinberg (eds) *The Revival of the Extreme Right*, London: Frank Cass.

—— (2005) 'Charisma and the rise of the contemporary extreme right', in J. Rydgren (ed.) *Movements of Exclusion: Radical Right-wing Populism in the Western World*, New York: Nova Science.

—— (2006) 'Community cohesion and cumulative extremism in contemporary Britain', *Political Quarterly*, 77(2): 204–16.

Electoral Reform Society (2004) *Burnley and the BNP and the Case for Electoral Reform*, London: Electoral Reform Society.

Flint, J. and Robinson, D. (2008) *Community Cohesion in Crisis?*, Oxford: Polity.

Geddes, A. and Tonge, J. (eds) (2005) *Britain Decides: The UK General Election 2005*, Basingstoke: Palgrave Macmillan.

Kavanagh, D. and Butler, D. (2005) *The British General Election of 2005*, Basingstoke: Palgrave Macmillan.

Koopmans, R., Statham, P., Giugni, M. and Passy, F. (2005) *Contested Citizenship. Immigration and Cultural Diversity in Europe*, Minneapolis, MN: University of Minnesota Press.

Kundnani, A. (2007) *The End of Tolerance: Racism in 21st Century Britain*, London: Pluto.

Local Government Association (2006) *Leading Cohesive Communities*, London: LGA Publications.

Lowles, N. (2001) *White Riot. The Rise and Fall of Combat 18*, Burnley: Milo Books.

Macpherson, Sir William (1999) *The Stephen Lawrence Inquiry*, London: The Stationery Office.

Maher, S. and Frampton, M. (2009) *Choosing Our Friends Wisely. Criteria for Engagement with Muslim Groups*, London: Policy Exchange.

McGhee, D. (2009) 'The paths to citizenship: a critical examination of immigration policy in Britain since 2001', *Patterns of Prejudice*, 43(1): 41–64.

Messina, A. (2007) *The Logics and Politics of Post-WWII Migration to Western Europe*, Cambridge: Cambridge University Press.

Minkenberg, M. (2006) 'Repression and reaction: militant democracy and the radical right in Germany and France', *Patterns of Prejudice*, 40(1): 25–44.

Moore, K., Mason, P. and Lewis, J. (2008) *Images of Islam in the UK. The Representation of British Muslims in the National Print Media 2000–2008*, Cardiff: Cardiff School of Journalism, Media and Cultural Studies.

National Community Forum (2009) *Sources of Resentment, and Perceptions of Ethnic Minorities Among Poor White People*, London: DCLG.

Preston, P. (2007) 'Freedom from "Britain": a comment on recent elite-sponsored political cultural identities', *British Journal of Politics and International Relations*, 9(1): 158–64.

Renton, D. (2001) *This Rough Game: Fascism and Anti-fascism*, Stroud: Sutton Publishers.

Rhodes, R. (2009) 'The Banal National Party: the routine nature of legitimacy', *Patterns of Prejudice*, 43(2): 142–60.

Saggar, S. (2009) *Pariah Politics: Understanding Western Radical Islamism and What Should Be Done*, Oxford: Oxford University Press.

Smith, S. (2004) *How It Was Done: The Rise of Burnley BNP*, Burnley: Cliviger Press.

Studlar, D.T. (1985) 'Waiting for the catastrophe? Race and the political agenda in Britain', *Patterns of Prejudice*, 19(1): 3–15.

Thomas, J. (2005) *Popular Newspapers, the Labour Party and British Politics*, London: Routledge.

Van Donselaar, J. and Rodrigues, P.R. (2008) *Monitor racisme & extremisme*, Amsterdam: Anne Frank Stichting. English language web version available at: http://www.annefrank.org/upload/downloads/Mon8-UK-Ch1.pdf (accessed 23 April 2009).

Waite, M. (2009) *Combining Diversity with Common Citizenship*, York: Joseph Rowntree Charitable Trust.

Conclusion

Roger Eatwell and Matthew J. Goodwin

In this conclusion we draw together observations made in the Introduction, summarize key findings of individual studies and highlight the implications these hold, both in terms of future research and policy. In the Introduction, we put forward two main observations about the study of the 'new extremism' in twenty-first-century Britain. First, we made the case for adopting a more holistic approach to the challenges this poses. In its various forms, organized extremism is one of the major challenges facing national government and local authorities. While studies of these phenomena provide important insights they typically treat different forms of extremism in isolation, whether in respect to Islamism (Saggar 2009) or the extreme right (Mudde 2007). We have argued that a broader, more holistic perspective provides additional insights into both the causes and responses required to such threats. Clearly, there are limits to what can be achieved by comparing across different social and political movements (especially in a single volume!). Moreover, it may well be that this more holistic approach is particularly suited for work at the micro-level, for example comparative research on individual recruitment into extremist Islamist movements and right-wing extremist groups, or alternatively more meso-level research that examines the effects of extreme-right party campaigning on nearby Muslim communities. In contrast, it may be more difficult to adapt this holistic lens to questions that lie at a higher level. That said, implicit in our emphasis on the need for a more holistic approach is the belief that the respective literatures on right-wing and Islamist extremism can learn from each other.

Second, we made the case for 'closing the gap' between, on one side, theory and research and, on the other, policy and practice. In recent years a number of factors have combined to produce an upsurge of interest in extremist movements, their social bases of support and the more immediate question of how best to respond to the extremist challenge. As noted at various points throughout this book, there have been heated and often highly politicized debates over the dynamics of issues such as the integration of the Muslim community in Britain and its relationship to Islamist terrorism; the causes of rising electoral support for the extreme right; the future impact of a deep economic recession on intergroup relations generally; and a more specific concern over the 'abandonment' of the 'white working class'. However, much of this debate has remained detached from the underlying evidence base. As a result, examples of best practice or policy recommendations often owe more to anecdotal evidence and speculation than to rigorous empirical research.

As noted in the Introduction, this book does not seek to cover all forms of contemporary extremism in Britain, nor provide a full assessment of the wider impact of organized extremism in areas such as civil rights, levels of racially motivated violence, social cohesion, or rates of political participation among minority ethnic groups.[1] The task of examining the impact of extremist Islamism or the extreme-right BNP on these factors, and at the level of local communities or individuals warrants a series of studies in its own right. Moreover, as reflected in recent acts perpetrated by animal-rights' extremists and renegade Irish Republican groups, the extremist challenge facing modern Britain is multifaceted in nature and is by no means confined solely to the manifestations that are the focus of this book. However, these alternative forms do not currently pose a serious threat to the liberal democratic order. Instead, Parts I and II focus on two major forms of extremism which, in differing ways, do pose such a threat, namely Islamism and the organized and electorally resurgent extreme right-wing (noting in passing the growing threat from extreme-right terrorism by 'lone wolves').

In seeking to cast light on the causes and consequences of the extremist challenge, one main contribution of this book has been to present new (and timely) empirical evidence, thereby adding considerable value to the existing research base. Much of this evidence calls into question some of the assumptions inherent in current debates over the dynamics of extremism. In turn, these chapters question some of the conventional wisdom concerning what constitutes an 'effective' response. For example, much of the attention to date in terms of tackling the extremist challenge has focused on preventing Islamist extremism while downplaying or ignoring outright the challenge posed by organized right-wing extremism. Yet analysis of opinion and survey data that is presented in Chapter 7 tells a different story, suggesting that the core components of extreme-right ideology enjoy a level of public support that far outstrips existing levels of extreme-right voting. Indeed more recent polls that followed the appearance of Nick Griffin on *Question Time* in October 2009 suggested that around one-fifth of voters would consider voting BNP and that more than half of respondents agreed that the party 'had a point' in wishing to 'speak up for the interests of the indigeneous white British people', indicating that the level of potential support for the extreme right has remained relatively constant since the 1970s. Given that the recent economic difficulties are likely to exacerbate conflict and tensions over scarce resources (i.e. jobs, housing, etc.), the political climate appears especially favourable to parties that campaign on nativist and anti-immigrant themes. As discussed below, there is a clear need to examine more closely the issues and grievances, especially in working-class communities, that typically provide the bedrock of BNP support. It is also commonplace to draw parallels between support for the modern day BNP and the 1970s National Front (NF). Yet research presented in Chapter 9 highlights the changing nature of support for the contemporary extreme right, in turn pointing toward the need to re-evaluate the way in which different actors (i.e. mainstream parties, anti-fascist organizers, media, etc.) respond to this challenge (Chapter 10).

The major overarching point which we wish to make by way of conclusion is that the judgements presented in these chapters need testing by further research. Islamism and extreme right-wing extremism are elusive topics to research objectively. Moreover, although a considerable body of new evidence is deployed in this collection, much empirical work remains to be done. In the remainder of this Conclusion, therefore, we not only set out some key points made about the new extremism in Britain, but also delineate linked areas which we feel especially warrant the attention of researchers and policymakers. Reflecting observations made in the Introduction about a more holistic approach, the first four highlighted here relate to both the threat from Islamism and the extreme right.

Holistic future research agendas

The first need for further work concerns the impact of economic recession, especially as socio-economic 'demand-side' factors have in general not been a major focus of this collection. Muslims are the poorest large ethnic minority group in Britain. Will the recession hit this community even harder, leading to growing resentment against British society? Will the British government pay serious attention to alleviating the 'grinding poverty' that afflicts many Muslim areas, such as Daneshouse in Burnley, which was a centre of the northern rioting in 2001 (Burnley Task Force 2001: 7)? If government retrenchment, or wider political concerns, make this difficult or impossible then Muslim resentment could be deepened. Conversely, would providing such support further antagonize members of the white working-class community who, the evidence suggests, perceive themselves as being in competition for public resources? As discussed in Chapter 9, support for the BNP is strongest in economically deprived, urban areas and stems primarily from male working-class voters who are concerned with both socio-economic and wider identity-based issues. Indeed, the BNP undertook a concerted attempt to appeal to precisely this group, most notably in the run up to the European elections in June 2009 when the party adopted the slogan 'British Jobs for British Workers'.

The second broad area that requires further research concerns identity. After 2001, the 'community cohesion' agenda was seen by some to prioritize ethnic over class divisions, and local over national action. But is it necessary to bring local communities more together to build cohesion and understanding? Jewish communities are often highly segregated geographically, but Jews have for many decades been an integrated and socio-economically successful minority. There remain fundamental questions over the extent to which different ethnic and cultural groups do and should interact with one another. While social contact between different ethnic groups has generally become more frequent as a result of demographic change, recent evidence suggests that BNP support stems from areas that lack such contact, i.e. 'white enclaves' in which residents have little or no substantive social interaction with members of other ethnic groups

(Bowyer 2008). Such findings introduce important questions over the capacity of national, but particularly local government, to bring together different (and sometimes transient) ethnic groups around a set of core values and understandings.

Jonathan Sachs, the Chief Rabbi, has argued that Jewish immigrants over the years have adapted not only to British cultural icons such as Shakespeare, but have also imbued his patriotic fervour (*The Times*, 1 October 2005). This seems to point to a need to develop a new form of Britishness, which can also appeal to a disoriented white working class. Certainly political leaders such as Gordon Brown have recently spoken of developing a new sense of British shared identity (though this is in part aimed at Scottish separatism). However, the precise content of this identity remains unclear, especially as English and then British historic identity was partly built on demonizing the threat from the 'Other' – in chronological order, France, Spain, Germany and later the Soviet Union (with the Islamic demon lurking in the background especially via popular images of the Crusades). Moreover, the power of elite-driven rhetoric and symbolism, like the new citizenship ceremonies, to condition opinion in what has become a highly diverse and pluralistic contemporary Britain is highly debatable. Clearly considerable further thought needs to be given to both the content and possibilities of such a culturalist approach.

A third need concerns the dearth of in-depth local studies. Why, for example, has the BNP become a major force electorally in areas such as Barking and Stoke, whereas it has made much less impact on some neighbouring areas that have relatively similar socio-economic characteristics? This variability points to the importance of supply-side factors, such as the specific nature of the BNP's 'community politics'. A full analysis also requires analysing supply-side factors that are largely outside the control of the BNP, such as local media, including small-scale papers like the *Royton Rag* in Oldham, another centre of 2001 rioting. In the context of Islamism, there is a need for more research of the type depicted by Githens-Mazer, Spalek and Lambert, and Lowndes and Thorpe in their chapters above. We need to know more about how to achieve good relations between the police and Muslim communities, about how to achieve the local community trust upon which much successful policing is based, plus the role of local context in the implementation of PVE initiatives. We need to know more about the relative power of transnational propaganda, such as Internet-based material that depicts the repression of Muslims in areas such as Palestine by Israel, compared to localized 'charismatic' recruiters to the terrorist cause (see also Githens-Mazer 2008). In research terms, this points to the need for more innovative studies, particularly those at the micro-level.

A fourth need is for more international comparison. For example, a worrying trend in some of the poorer areas of Germany is the attempt by extreme-right *Kameradschaften* to infiltrate autonomous youth groups in search of recruits. Where a significant local base is achieved, they seek to create 'free spaces' in which minorities and opposition are eliminated (Bundesamt für Verfassungsschutz 2008). Could such a trend emerge in areas of Britain that become particularly hard-hit by depression, especially if the BNP fails to become a significant electoral force? Or is this development linked to specifically East German conditions, especially a pervasive authoritarian and holistic culture among parents brought up under a communist regime, and a more general lack of democratic role models in some localities? More comparative research may also cast much needed light on the *impact* of extreme-right parties once they assume positions of power, whether at the local, national or European level. Though some research has focused on the impact of these parties on immigration policy (for an overview see Mudde, 2007: 277–92), much less attention is directed toward the impact on local communities. For example, is there a relationship between extreme-right party campaigning or elected representation and levels of racial prejudice, anti-immigrant hostility or racially motivated violence?

Turning to Islam, the Dutch Intelligence and Security Service has recently begun to talk about 'neo-radicalism' – a non-violent creed that preaches the case for the establishment of Islamized enclaves, physical areas in which practices such as Sharia law prevail and separation disrupts attempts to build bridges (AIVD 2007). For example, Khalil el-Moumni, imam of al-Nasr Mosque in Rotterdam, has described homosexuality as a contagious disease and described Western civilization as lacking in morals. Have such views been encouraged by the Dutch tradition of accepting multiculturalism rather than the French historic emphasis on assimilationism (Kepel 2008)? Or is the trend a much newer one, in part a response to moves away from Dutch multiculturalism in the new millennium? Given similar developments in British conceptions of citizenship since 2001 (though compare Meer and Modood 2009), can Britain avoid the growth of radical separatism, especially among younger generations? Or is the key point the fact that liberal democracies are in some ways responding to these broad new challenges with a form of illiberal sectarianism (Levey and Modood 2009)? Turning to a more normative framework, is there not an urgent need to build links with not just the Muslim community but more generally with a civil society which has become increasingly divorced from democracy, especially its classic liberal mode of participation – the political party?

Islamism in Britain

Part I of this book sets out the case that the Muslim community in Britain is far less alienated from British society than is normally assumed and argues that, although there have been some problems with counter-extremism policy, important progress is being made. As is made clear in the two chapters that focus on the role of policing, the Muslim community has been offended by heavy-handed policing, which on occasion has led to arrests though no terrorism charges have been subsequently brought. But notable successes include, as Gregory notes, greater intelligence coordination and halting plots for major attacks. The chapter by Spalek and Lambert reveals the way in which, despite the difficult climate, pioneering work which aims to build more trusting relationships between police and Muslim communities is feasible. Other apparent steps forward include the PVE programme which has sought 'local solutions to local problems', especially by engaging a variety of groups within the Muslim community, a policy studied in three local case studies by Lowndes and Thorpe in Chapter 6. At the same time, however, these studies also draw attention to the potential risk of such local innovation being constrained by policy, practice and pronouncements at the national level. In respect to policing, attempts at engagement and partnership faced significant difficulties in the wider socio-political environment; in respect to PVE initiatives, local innovation may well be jeopardized by enforcing a 'top-down' approach to policy, and by adhering to crude distinctions between, on the one hand, risk reduction strategies and, on the other, community capacity building.

There have been other developments from within the Muslim community that point towards growing levels of political and social integration and participation. There has been a growth of groups like the Muslim Public Affairs Committee UK (MPACUK), which has sought to mobilize Muslims to use their 'voice' within the British system on a wide range of policies. This has often been accompanied by criticism of imams, who are seen as distant from the concerns of the young, especially women. Elders within the community are often criticized for similar reasons. Thus its email newsletter sent out on 11 November 2008 claimed that 'Islamic leadership is in a rut ... Too many mosques act as vote gatekeepers for Zionist MP after Zionist MP' – a clear reference to links with MPs like former Foreign Secretary, Jack Straw, in Blackburn. However, while MPACUK rejects the use of violence in Britain, it supports terrorism in the context of Israel. For example, on 26 December 2008 it sent out on its email list the claim that 'any Muslim who fights and dies against Israel ... is a martyr and will be granted paradise'.

This highlights the need for further work on the nature of both radical and extreme forms of Islam in Britain and beyond. The former does not endorse violence within Britain, but it can support it elsewhere. Moreover, such radicals may help condition a climate of tacit support for violence within Britain, especially as criticism of British policy over Israel and the wars in Iraq and Afghanistan frequently accompany the call for an independent Palestine. This is an important point as terrorists historically have included only a minute proportion of the community they claim to defend, but they rely on forms of wider support that can range from providing safe houses through to an unwillingness to supply relevant information to the intelligence services. It has been argued, for example, that while much of the attention to date has focused narrowly on preventing violent plots from crystallizing, there is good reason to be concerned about the attitudes and values among those *surrounding* the men of violence. Seen from this perspective, 'policy interventions that fail to tackle tacit supporters will hold very little prospect of long-term success' (Saggar 2009: 267).

There is also a need to look more carefully at trends within Islamic thought and Muslim attitudes to democracy more generally. As noted by Sobolewska in Chapter 1, much speculation abounds over the role of religion and levels of alienation within British Muslim communities. It appears that many in contemporary Britain subscribe to the belief that there is a broad swathe of alienated Muslim youths who are putty in the hands of extreme and violent

Muslim clerics. Yet this chapter offers important new evidence which challenges the belief that the majority of British Muslims are alienated, hold anti-democratic views and lack a sense of belonging to Britain. Rather, drawing on quantitative data Sobolewska suggests that religious identity does not appear as a replacement for British citizenship, finding that Muslims show high rates of trust, have a stronger sense of belonging to Britain than other minority religious groups and generally appear well-integrated into the political arena. In this respect, Sobolewska suggests that the current debate is losing sight of the problem by 'hunting the ghost' of a supposedly larger circle of 'tacit' supporters of terrorism.

However, her claim that there is 'agreement among Islamic scholars' that their religion is not incompatible with Western democracy is debatable. Although this is the case among many scholars, there have been exceptions – such as the early prophet of the 'clash of civilizations', Bernard Lewis (Lewis 1993; cf. Bonney 2008). Moreover, the real issue is about reifying traditions: reading the Koran will not reveal if Islam and democracy are compatible any more than reading the Bible will tell whether Christianity and democracy are compatible. In practice, each is interpreted in particular contexts. Thus in the 'real' world there are forms of Islamic democracy in, for example Indonesia. But there appears to be much more of a problem in the Arab world, where progressive thought in recent decades has largely been eclipsed by more extreme and radical forms (Ajami 1999).

This raises the issue of the role of imams in Britain, given that many come from abroad and some are Wahhabis with links with Saudi Arabia, where mosques have been accused of recruiting terrorists (for example, *Sunday Times*, 4 November 2007). In Britain, a small number of imams, like Abu Hamza, have clearly been linked with preaching jihad and recruiting terrorists. We need to know more about whether such examples have been replaced by a more extensive form of radicalism. A Channel 4 *Dispatches* television programme broadcast on 1 September 2008 showed preachers calling for Muslims to lead separate lives and for adulterers, homosexuals and Muslim apostates to be killed. The same programme showed that in some mosques extremist DVDs were also on sale.[2] This clearly underlines the importance of questions touched upon by Bleich in his chapter above concerning the selection and training of imams. It also raises the issue of possible prosecution and whether British government funds should be withheld from activities linked to the open espousal of such views. Under the current PVE programme this is certainly not the case. For example, the Conservative think tank, the Policy Exchange, has argued that West Midlands Police tolerated a radical preacher because it believed he had access to potential terrorists, who posed a greater direct threat (Maher and Frampton 2009).

Within Britain, the physical separation of Muslim communities is typically explained by fears of white racist attack, by poverty, and by past local authority housing policy. For example, at the end of the 1990s only 2 per cent of Bradford's council housing was in the hands of Asians, while in Oldham the authority allocated inferior blocks of housing to Asians (Flint and Robinson 2008, *passim*; Kundnani 2007: 43). However, Patrick Sokhdeo, a controversial convert to Christianity, has written that in 1980 the Islamic Council of Europe stated that a fundamental rule was never to integrate. Rather, Muslims should congregate and become a majority in an area with halal food shops, Islamic schools, etc. (*Sunday Telegraph*, 19 February 2006). Some academic sources have also noted similar sentiments, though far more work needs to be undertaken to assess whether this is anything more than a marginal trend. For example, it has been argued that while most Muslims in the 2001 Bradford riots were not inspired by religion (some even expressed contempt for mosques), many young men involved 'have developed a "purist", separatist version of islam that they use to promote antagonism towards non-Muslim individuals, groups and society' (Macey 2007: 164–5).

A factor which appears to have heightened some Muslims' sense of separation concerns the government's post-9/11 support for the US 'war on terror', including the role of British troops in the invasions and occupations of Afghanistan and Iraq. There also appears to have been growing resentment about the way in which government statements and especially media coverage of issues relating to Islam reinforce a deeper-rooted Islamophobia (Ameli *et al.* 2007; Moore *et al.* 2008). In 2007, an Islamic Human Rights Commission (IHRC) study showed that 63.4 per cent of British Muslims felt media portrayal to be Islamophobic; a further 15.5 per cent felt it to be racist and 9.4 per cent thought it as 'covertly destructive'.[3] The tendency in parts of the British media to present Islam as 'the problem', or to portray Muslim communities as pariahs in wider society, is a problem identified by several contributors to this book. As noted by Githens-Mazer in his study of recruitment to radical violent *takfiri* Islamism (RVTI), many interviewees revealed how Islam has acquired a street credibility, or a 'coolness' precisely because of its stark contrast to the experiences and expectation of white 'middle England'. Likewise, Bleich draws attention to the difficult task that faces policymakers: while they must demonstrate that 'the state' is capable of disrupting terrorist networks and promoting national cohesion, they must simultaneously demonstrate to Muslim communities that they can be full citizens and not simply national pariahs. The Institute for Race Relations' (IRR) Director, A. Sivanandan, has even claimed that 'the war on terror, following on from 9/11 and 7/7, has created a populist anti-Muslim, anti-asylum culture, based on the politics of fear' (Sivanandan 2007: vii).

There is no doubt that some mass circulation papers have set agendas which have made not just terrorism but Islam a major issue (Chapter 10). For example, on 11 March 2009 the *Sun*'s main headline was 'HATE FOR HEROES. MUSLIMS IN VILE DEMO'; the accompanying article referred to protests about a celebratory march by the Royal Anglian Regiment which had just returned from a tour of duty in Iraq. Although only a small number of Muslims were involved in the protest, in spite of attempts to create a mass demonstration in Luton which has a sizeable Muslim population, the *Daily Express* returned to the attack on 13 March 2009 with a large front-cover picture of the marching soldiers and a headline that stated: 'OUR HEROES: Britain's Answer to the Preachers of Hate'.

However, while such coverage can be seen as part of a wider discourse that portrays extremism as common within the Muslim community, there is a narrow line between stoking prejudice and raising legitimate issues. For example, on 2 May 2003 the *Daily Mail*'s front page was dominated by a picture of Abu Hamza, complete with iron claw hand, and the headline 'HOOKED BY THE SHEIK OF HATE'. Given that the British government had tolerated for so long the presence of a small number in 'Londonistan' who clearly supported terrorism, it could be argued that questioning such policy was in the public interest (a common explanation of this apparent lacuna is that it helped intelligence services monitor extremist groups, whereas driving them underground would make the task more difficult). There is also a tendency in studies of media Islamophobia to focus on the most provocative coverage, while ignoring more balanced reporting. For example, the European Centre on Racism and Xenophobia praised the British press in the aftermath of the 2005 London bombings for balanced and objective reporting.[4] Studies of Islamophobia in the media also tend to focus on content analysis rather than effects. Indeed, there is a general need to know more about issues such as the media's impact on Muslims' opinions – with the emphasis on the plural, as there are notable differences within the Muslim community based on past origins, age, gender and other factors.

The electoral extreme right in Britain

Part II of this collection focuses on the extreme right and, in so doing, adopts an integrated approach by examining: (1) levels of public support for positions and policies associated with the extreme right; (2) the changing strategy of the extreme right in an attempt to mobilize support; (3) actual supporters of the extreme right; and (4) responses, especially to the BNP. This section of the book provides important new evidence which indicates that there is significant electoral potential for the extreme right in contemporary Britain. Nor is this potential confined to second-order elections in a small number of localities, as is commonly assumed. As Goodwin makes clear in Chapter 8, while the threat from the terrorist right should not be ignored, one of the most significant changes to have occurred on the British extreme-right scene in recent years has been the attempt to 'modernize' the BNP.

Under the leadership of Nick Griffin, the party has sought to publicly distance itself from its fascist roots while redirecting its electoral strategy toward community-based activism – a crucial development in an era that has seen a general decay in the quality of local representative politics and a decline of the major parties' links with civil society. In some localities, especially former Labour Party strongholds, there is no question that the BNP has emerged as an important political force, mobilizing a significant grassroots presence and taking advantage of lacklustre campaigning and organizational decay which often characterize the mainstream parties. As Ford shows in his chapter, the BNP's electoral potential becomes especially clear when poll evidence about opinion on crime, immigration and terrorism are analysed. Many who currently do not vote BNP hold very similar views to its core policies on these issues.

However, as the chapters in Part II also make clear, the BNP remains a minor party in most areas. So why has it been so unsuccessful given the apparently fertile soil in which to till? And has the situation changed sufficiently to support the argument that it has the potential for major gains? The onset of recession undoubtedly offers new opportunities for the extreme right as, especially should it deepen further, a likely result is the reinforcement of hostility to mainstream politicians, who have already been mired in sleaze allegations, especially during a spate of revelations during 2009 which led to headlines such as the *Daily Express*'s front page claim on 13 October that: 'MPS GET AWAY WITH MURDER'. Nevertheless, a broad trend of declining party identification has been visible for some time without the BNP benefiting outside a few localities.

A reasonable hypothesis to explain this failure is that the extreme right in Britain continues to suffer from a 'spoiled identity'. As highlighted by Goodwin, although the BNP has pursued a strategy of 'modernization', there are clear signs that the party has not fully abandoned crude biological racism and anti-Semitism, ideological components that are associated with the much less successful 'old' extreme right (Chapter 8). The fact that Griffin, during his October 2009 BBC *Question Time* appearance, sought to defend his links with David Duke by arguing that he belonged to a non-violent part of the Ku Klux Klan, illustrates this inability to realize that old agendas, and associates, damage the party. Indeed in the aftermath of the programme many voters remained unconvinced over the extent to which the BNP had truly 'modernized', as suggested by Goodwin. For example, one poll by YouGov revealed that two-thirds of voters would not consider voting BNP 'under any circumstances'. Partly related to this, the BNP shares a long-standing British extreme-right tendency to schism over both ideological and personal issues, which periodically wracks the organization. Nevertheless, there is clearly a need for research to ascertain whether the BNP has thrown off its image as the party of loutish thugs and hardcore Nazis. This requires examining three dimensions.

First, more work needs to be undertaken on the more active followers of the extreme right. One new study that draws on evidence from qualitative interviews with activists in the BNP indicates that they are far from the stereotypical beer-swilling youth, or blockheaded 'authoritarian personality' (Goodwin 2010). Similarly, another study of extreme right activists in contemporary Europe generally concluded that they appeared as 'perfectly normal people, socially integrated, connected in one way or another to mainstream groups and ideas' (Klandermans and Mayer 2006: 269). Much like their European counterparts, these BNP activists did not consider themselves extreme right and disassociated themselves strongly from earlier movements such as the National Front (NF). Rather than adhering to militant neo-Nazism, conspiratorial anti-Semitism or a belief in the need for a strong and all-embracing charismatic leader, a common reason given for the decision to become involved is a sense of injustice over the allocation of local resources and a sense of betrayal by the political 'mainstream', though in particular the Labour Party. The list of 12,000 BNP members' names that was leaked in 2008 further indicates that many activists appear to come from respectable backgrounds. However, the list also includes people with email addresses including '18' or '88', a common code from the first and eighth letter of the alphabet – AH or HH, namely Adolf Hitler and Heil Hitler. While it is difficult to pick up the genuine hard core in academic interview-based studies and wider surveys, there is little doubt that a violent extreme-right fringe remains in Britain.

The second dimension concerns a need for up-to-date focus group and poll evidence about whether voters perceive the BNP still to be extreme. There have been several academic studies of how the BNP has sought to rebrand itself, but we know far less about precisely what impact this has had on perceptions of the party. Findings presented in Chapter 9 indicate that a third of BNP voters in Barking and Dagenham still saw it as 'extreme', which may even have attracted some protest voters. But it is not clear whether other BNP supporters saw the party as legitimate, perhaps influenced by a well-publicized comment shortly before the 2006 elections when the local Labour MP, Margaret Hodge stated that many local voters were tempted to vote BNP as no one was listening to their concerns about asylum seekers, unemployment, etc.

Third, there needs to be more work done on responses to the BNP. As Eatwell shows, the dominant response by groups such as the mainstream parties and media to the BNP so far has largely been one of silence, though at times the party has been clearly tagged as extreme and/or fascist (Chapter 10). Even national newspapers which have featured immigration-related issues prominently are wary of any form of direct endorsement of the BNP (not least as the purpose of some of them appears to have been to help the Conservatives electorally and/or to encourage the Conservatives to give these issues a high priority). Even normally apolitical local papers often tag the BNP with pejorative epithets, such as the editorial of the *Oldham Chronicle* on 8 June 2001 on the BNP's electoral leap forward in the area, which was headed 'EXTREMISM AND APATHY ARE WINNERS'. Exactly what impact this tagging has is another matter, as there is growing evidence that simple labelling is far less effective than in the past – especially once the BNP has begun to gain a foothold in localities and seeks to show it really is the voice of a neglected working class.

The last point highlights the need for a more dynamic and probing analysis of the changing British white working class, a particularly important task against the backdrop of serious economic recession. Even before the recent onset of depression, in some areas there was a clear sense of bleak prospects. For example, the borough of Burnley in Lancashire, which was already suffering from notable deindustrialization and low wages, lost 30 per cent of its jobs in the manufacturing industry between 1997 and 2001. The recent downturn is likely to sharpen local tensions around the allocation of limited resources (i.e. jobs and housing) which, as discussed in Chapter 9, have been a key driver of support for the BNP in some local districts. Whereas in the 1960s the working class was romanticized as a mix of old community (*Coronation Street*) and bright young men (The Beatles), popular images of the working class today focus more on the 'chav' and the workshy (Waite 2009). There is an element of corresponding reality, with part of the white working class appearing to have become more isolated and despondent.

Although there is evidence of an overall decline in levels of racial prejudice in Britain, particularly among those citizens who grew up after mass immigration began in the late 1940s and 1950s, some findings suggest that there remain significant 'pools of hostility' to minority ethnic groups among less qualified, young working-class men (Ford 2008). Some have drawn particular attention to the way in which this hostility has been directed toward Asian minorities who appear more culturally distinct (Modood 2005). As discussed in Chapter 9, there is worrying evidence that points toward a positive relationship between the presence of a large Muslim population and higher levels of support for the BNP (though in some strongholds, such as Barking, this does not appear to have been the case). While underscoring the need to look more closely at this interplay, such findings indicate that perceptions of ethnic competition and a 'threatened' native in-group stem not solely from concerns over socio-economic resources but also cultural factors, thus raising difficult and highly sensitive issues for those in national and local government who are involved in formulating a policy response.

While the BNP may fan the flames, the party often exploits genuine concerns about deprivation and other local issues typically linked to immigration. In some areas, these have included white people feeling ' "intimidated" by groups of Asian youths' (Phillips *et al.* 2008: 93). For example, tensions had been heightened in Oldham prior to the riots in 2001 by misleading reports about attacks on non-whites, including a pensioner war hero. While early gains in Oldham by the BNP were not sustained, in areas such as Barking and Dagenham, Burnley and Stoke-on-Trent, there are signs of an emerging base of support that is based on concerns about local issues such as pressure on social housing, which is largely immune to anti-fascist labelling. Indeed, in Barking and Dagenham the BNP has grown in spite of extensive anti-fascist activity there and local newspaper coverage which is critical of the party. For instance, the (London) *Evening Standard* on 13 April 2006 included an article by BBC television correspondent Andrew Gilligan headlined 'BNP'S DIRTY TRICKS IN THE SCRAMBLE FOR VOTES'.

Since the official reports on the 2001 riots, considerable emphasis has been placed on local 'myth busting' about issues such as immigrants and ethnic minorities receiving unfair amounts of resources (National Community Forum 2009). Some local qualitative research indicates that this sense of unfairness is an important driver of BNP support (Rhodes 2006). However, insufficient work has been done on the effects of myth-busting campaigns. Cognitive dissonance theory indicates that uncomfortable 'facts' are filtered out if they do not correspond with pre-existing views. Moreover, there is a strong element of truth in some of the 'myths' that most concern BNP voters. For example the Local Government Association asked during 2007–8 for an additional £250 million of funding to help areas that were receiving large numbers of new immigrants and asylum seekers, who after the 1990s were spread out more around Britain rather than concentrated in London. This put pressure on local services such as health, housing and schools in some areas. And jobs which might have gone to British people have been taken by recent immigrants, for example since EU expansion in 2004, which brought in many young and high-quality workers from countries like Poland (there are signs that this phenomenon has peaked, though economic meltdown in some East European EU members could lead to new inflows).

As Eatwell notes in Chapter 10, in spite of the labour market benefits that have come from immigration, the Labour government since 1997 has been remarkably reluctant to defend in public its relatively open border policy. Indeed, in a 2007 speech to the Trade Union Congress Gordon Brown talked of 'British jobs for British workers', a slogan which came back to haunt him in 2009 when it appeared on the placards of demonstrators protesting against contractors in Britain who only employed foreign workers. During the 2001 and especially the 2005 general elections, the Conservatives went on the attack over immigration, but they appear to have won few votes on the issue while losing potential support to the centre. Since the choice of a new leader in 2005, immigration has hardly featured in Conservative campaigns. Although the Conservatives promise to cut the number of new immigrants, it is hard not to conclude that they have largely lost the issue ownership of immigration which they achieved during the 1960s. If this is the case, the potential for the BNP seems even greater – although as the 2009 European elections demonstrate, in some ways the BNP competes with the UK Independence Party (UKIP). While more work needs to be done on this, polls indicate that far fewer voters hold hostile views towards UKIP, and it thus may in the longer run serve as a notable alternative for potential BNP coverts.

Cumulative extremism?

One key theme linking the last two sections concerns the fact that long-standing structural inequalities, reinforced by rising unemployment against a background of recession, are affecting both the white working class and poor members of ethnic minorities. In this respect, the argument that policymakers should strive to counter the development of a 'Muslim underclass' (Saggar 2009: 280) echoes concerns about poor whites. Indeed, Herman Ouseley, a former Chair of the Commission for Racial Equality, has written in relation to deprivation generally that 'it it is getting more crowded on the lower decks' (*Guardian*, 23 February 2009). However, there is no simple relationship between poverty and extremism: the poor can be apathetic whilst the educated can become radicalized.

In this final section of the Conclusion the focus turns, therefore, to the highlighting of a political rather than structural dynamic as there is potential relationship between Islamism and the extreme right, which seems inconceivable between other forms of extremism in Britain, such as animal rights. As noted in the Introduction, this is an important reason why these two forms of extremism form the basis of this book, as 'cumulative extremism' is more threatening to the liberal democratic order than attacks from lone wolf extreme right-wingers or even al-Qaeda-inspired spectacular bombings.

The 2001 riots in northern towns showed the potential for a spiral of violence. As pointed out above, in the case of Bradford, young Muslims were not motivated largely by Islamism. Rather they reacted to long-running grievances centred on socio-economic matters and policing, and especially to incursion and provocation by the extreme right. Although the BNP sought to distance itself from street violence in 2001, there is little doubt that local activists were involved.

Others involved included racist football coteries and remnants of the NF, who planned a provocative march in Bradford. This was banned in accordance with the Public Order Act 1986, but the NF's website later added that small groups of 'activists dispersed themselves around the city'.[5] Yet others involved included hard core violent extremists linked to Combat 18 who sought to provoke a wider escalation of race war (Lowles 2003).

The BNP banned membership of C18 following a bitter dispute in the 1990s, which weakened the party after its initial electoral breakthrough in Millwall. Especially since Griffin has been leader, there has been a more general attempt to distance the party from violence. For example, Griffin has encouraged rank and file activists to compare pictures of skinheads and the BNP founder John Tyndall in Nazi regalia to pictures of recently elected BNP councillors, stating; 'That is how much the BNP has changed. That is the new face of our party. That is our future. The rest is history.'[6] In 2009, Griffin 'completely proscribed' BNP members from participating in the provocative activities of the English Defence League (EDL), although the latter shared the BNP's focus on Muslim immigration and terrorism, adding that it was an intelligence services' 'honey trap'.

Claims of impending civil war and apocalypticism are common in right-wing extremist groups, encouraged by American websites such as Stormfront, which have been particularly obsessed with the survival of the white race since the election of President Obama.[7] Major recession too has fanned the fears both of the collapse of the American way of life and of poor ethnic minority violence. The potential for these frames to mobilize acts outside of the electoral arena was aptly revealed in July 2007 when a former BNP candidate was convicted of stockpiling chemical explosives. As stated by the judge, Robert Cottage expressed his belief that '"the evils of uncontrolled immigration" would lead to civil war which would be imminent and inevitable'.[8] While there has so far been no repeat of the murderous David Copeland bombing in 1999, a belief in an impending and inevitable interethnic conflict appears to be relatively widespread among BNP activists as well as in party literature. Several other extreme right wingers have been arrested in recent years in connection with plotting violence and there is growing concern about such activities in the Muslim community.[9]

The violent extreme right currently does not have the organization capable of mounting any form of sustained attacks. Indeed, there appears to be a one-man-and-his-dog side to some of these 'movements', while others are more a coterie of 'Hollywood Nazis' whose self-publicizing activities endear them to journalists looking for rent-a-quote interviews. Nevertheless, the risk must not be minimized as individuals acting separately could undertake more than one attack in a short period, especially as studies of rioting sometimes point to the importance of copycat activities (on the 1981 riots see Scarman 1981, especially p. 111). Moreover, a major bombing by extreme right wingers which provoked some form of violent Muslim response (or vice-versa) could lead to a further spiral of violence.

Certainly there are radical Muslims who warn, in the words of a MPACUK *Newsletter* on 16 July 2009, that 'Muslims must never fall into the kind of complacency that led to the genocide in the former Yugoslavia'. Interestingly, such parallels with Yugoslavia have been an important aspect of the armoury of Islamists recruiting young terrorists in Britain (Hussain 2007). Groups like MPACUK have also sought to use anti-semitic prejudice to stoke tensions. For example, its email circular on 30 September 2009 claimed that 'Muslim hatred among the Jewish community within Britain is well known' and claimed that 'it is widely suspected that Jewish Zionists even attended the fascist marches of the EDL'.

Another possible cause of escalating street violence stems from the changing relationship between the extreme right and militant anti-fascist groups. From the 1970s, groups such as the Anti-Nazi League (ANL) were willing to use open confrontation, and members were present at Bradford during the riots confronting racists as well as the police (who, reflecting the extreme left connections of many of these groups, were also seen as the enemy).[10] However, following these events anti-fascist street activity declined, reflecting the BNP's move away from street politics and the further dwindling of support for groups like the NF. As the BNP now concentrated on community politics, it was argued that anti-fascist groups should do the same. Some of the fringe groups sought to contest elections, with even poorer results than the BNP (though there was an element of anti-fascist organization in George Galloway's Respect Party, whose leader won back his Labour seat aided by Muslim votes in the 2005 general election).

There appear to be signs among the militants that they desire more confrontation. For example, Antifa's website states that the BNP 'have done their utmost to hide their fascist politics beneath a thin veneer of respectability' and that 'destroying the BNP is our current priority'. It adds that 'We utilise a wide range of tactics and believe it is important to confront fascism physically as well as ideologically.'[11] Two factors seem likely to trigger a more violent response. The first will be if the BNP wins significant electoral support in the near future. The second, especially if it fails to make the hoped for major political breakthrough, will be if it reverts to a more confrontational 'street-style' of politics. A recent proposed Liverpool rally shows that even when the prospects for progress seem good, there remain important elements in the BNP who think a combination of factors, such as the parliamentary electoral system and mainstream party and media opposition, doom the party to never achieving power via the ballot box.

However, while many challenges remain there is room for optimism. As demonstrated by the chapters in this book, important work is being undertaken in isolating potential extremists. In part, this builds on experience from the struggles in Northern Ireland, but innovative new work is being undertaken both in the security field and in integrating more fully the vast majority of Muslims into British society. Also, while some trends discussed above give obvious cause for concern, there are more positive ways of analysing the situation. For example, while support for positions associated with the extreme right appears greater than is often assumed, the vast majority of the British electorate still appear unwilling to lend their support to a party such as the BNP. Furthermore, evidence presented above suggests that the support base for the extreme right in

Britain is ageing, indicating that in general a more tolerant youth is simply not interested in supporting movements on the extremist fringe (though a racist fringe remains).

This point can be seen simply by considering football. Although racist coteries around clubs have not fully been eliminated and some forms of institutional racism remain (for instance the dearth of non-white team managers), we live in a far different world from the 1970s when England could turn out an all-white team, or the 1980s when black star John Barnes was greeted by his club's fans throwing banana skins onto the pitch while making monkey sounds! The face of the crowd is beginning to change too, with teams such as Arsenal no longer supported by a sea of purely white faces. Squad-loads of young fans play football games on their Xboxes and Playstations which feature the slogan 'Let's Kick Racism out of Football', and they are the future. There is no evidence how many of these players are Muslim, but we can only hope that they take the advice of Maha on a chat line when he commented in 2009: 'I am not a fan of football but as I see its the only sport that can gather all peoples regardless their other interests so how do you find this game?'[12] Football is currently not perceived by most Muslims as part of their culture, but identity is not destiny.

Note

1 Indeed, as observed in one survey of the European extreme right, the question of what impact these parties exert on various institutions, policies and environments is one of the least examined subfields of research (Mudde 2007).
2 Available online: http://www.channel4.com/news/articles/dispatches/undercover+mosque+the+return/2436087 (accessed 30 September 2008).
3 Available online: http://www.ihrc.org.uk/show.php?id=2493 (accessed 21 April 2007).
4 Available online: http://fra.europa.eu/fra/material/pub/London/London-Bomb-attacks EN.pdf (accessed 10 March 2008).
5 http://www.natfront.org.uk (accessed 30 November 2001).
6 N. Griffin (2002) 'Moving forward for good', *Identity*, Issue 21 (June): 4–5.
7 http://www.stormfront.org/
8 'Ex-BNP man jailed over chemicals', BBC 31 July 2007, available at: http://news.bbc.co.uk (accessed 15 March 2009).
9 For example, Muslim Public Affairs Committee UK, 'A Home-Grown UK Terrorist', 1 July 2009, available at: http://www.mpacuk.org/content/view/5812/102/ (accessed 2 July 2009).
10 See for example online: www.socialistworker.co.uk/1757/IX.HTM (accessed 13 December 2001).
11 Available at: http://www.antifa.org.uk/foundstat.htm (accessed 17 March 2009).
12 Available at: http://www.islamonline.net/LiveDialogue/English/Browse.asp?hGuestID=LayrZP (accessed 17 March 2009).

References

AIVD (2007) *The radical dawa in transition. The rise of Islamic neoradicalism in the Netherlands*, Hague: General Intelligence and Security Service in the Netherlands.
Ajami, F. (1999) *Dream Palace of the Arabs: A Generation's Odyssey*, Vintage: New York.

Ameli, S.R., Marandai, S., Ahmed, S.T., Kara, S. and Merali A. (2007) *The British Media and Muslim Representation: The Ideology of Demonisation*, London: Islamic Human Rights Commission.

Bowyer, B. (2008) 'Local context and extreme right support in England: the British National Party in the 2002 and 2003 local elections', *Electoral Studies*, 27(X): 611–20.

Bonney, R. (2008) *False Prophets: The 'Clash of Civilizations' and the Global War on Terror*, Oxford: Peter Lang.

Bundesamt für Verfassungsschutz (2008) *Verfassungsschutzgegen Rechextremismus*, Cologne: BfV.

Burnley Task Force (2001) *Burnley Speaks, Who Listens?*, Burnley: Burnley Task Force.

Eatwell, R. (2006) 'Community cohesion and cumulative extremism in contemporary Britain', *Political Quarterly*, 77(2): 204–16.

Flint, J. and Robinson, D. (2008) *Community Cohesion in Crisis?*, Oxford: Polity.

Ford, R. (2008) 'Is racial prejudice declining in Britain', *British Journal of Sociology*, 59(4): 609–36.

General Intelligence and Security Service (2007) *The Radical Dawa in Transition. The Rise of Islamic Neoradicalism in the Netherlands*, The Hague: AIVD.

Githens-Mazer, J. (2008) 'Islamic radicalisation among north Africans in Britain', *British Journal of Politics and International Relations*, 10(4): 550–70.

Goodwin, M.J. (2010) *The New British Fascism: Rise of the British National Party*, London: Routledge.

Hussain, E. (2007) *The Islamist*, London: Penguin Books.

Kepel, G. (2008) *Beyond Terror and Martyrdom*, Boston, MA: Harvard University Press.

Klandermans, B. and Mayer, N. (eds) (2006) *Extreme Right Activists in Europe: Through the Magnifying Glass*, London: Routledge.

Kundnani, A. (2007) *The End of Tolerance*, London: Pluto.

Levey, G.B. and Modood, T. (eds) (2009) *Secularism, Religion and Multicultural Citizenship*, Cambridge: Cambridge University Press.

Lewis, B. (1993) *Islam and the West*. Oxford: Oxford University Press.

Lowles, N. (2003) *White Riot: The Rise and Fall of Combat 18*, London: Milo Books.

Macey, M. (2007) 'Islamic political radicalism in Britain: Muslim men in Bradford', in T. Abbas (ed.) *Islamic Political Radicalism. A European Perspective*, Edinburgh: Edinburgh University Press.

Maher, S and Frampton, M. (2009) *Choosing Our Friends Wisely. Criteria for Engagement with Muslim Groups*, London: Policy Exchange.

Meer, S. and Modood, T. (2009) 'The multicultural state we're in: Muslims, "Multiculture" and the "Civic Re-balancing" of British multiculturalism', *Political Studies*, 57(3): 473-497.

Modood, T. (2005) *Multicultural Politics: Racism, Ethnicity and Muslims in Britain*, Edinburgh: Edinburgh University Press.

Moore, K., Mason, P. and Lewis, J. (2008) *Images of Islam in the UK. The Representation of British Muslims in the National Print News Media 2000–2008*, Cardiff: Cardiff School of Journalism, Media and Cultural Studies. Available at: http://www.cardiff.ac.uk/jomec/resources/08channel4-dispatches.pdf (accessed 25 November 2008).

Mudde, C. (2007) *Populist Radical Right Parties in Europe*, Cambridge: Cambridge University Press.

National Community Forum (2009) *Sources of Resentment, and Perceptions of Ethnic Minorities among Poor White People in England*, London: DCLG.

Phillips, D., Simpson, L. and Ahmed, S. (1998) 'Shifting geographies of minority ethnic settlement: remaking communities in Oldham and Rochdale', in J. Flint and D. Robertson (eds) *Community Cohesion in Crisis?*, Bristol: the Policy Press.

Rhodes, J. (2006) 'Far right breakthrough: the support for the BNP in Burnley', PhD dissertation, University of Manchester.

Saggar, S. (2009) *Pariah Politics. Understanding Western Radical Islamism and What Should Be Done*, Oxford: Oxford University Press.

Scarman Inquiry (1981) *The Brixton Disorders 10–12 April 1981. Report of an Inquiry by the Rt. Hon. Lord Scarman*, Cmnd 8427, London: HMSO.

Sivanandan, A. (2007) 'Foreword', in A. Kundnai (ed.) *The End of Tolerance*, London: Pluto.

Waite, M. (2009) *Combining Diversity with Common Citizenship*, York: Joseph Rowntree Charitable Trust.

Index